Contemporary Discourse of Halal and Islamic Entrepreneurship

Lukman Raimi · Salisu Monsuru Adekunle ·
Muhammad Salman Shabbir
Editors

Contemporary Discourse of Halal and Islamic Entrepreneurship

Trends and Future Opportunities

Springer

Editors
Lukman Raimi
School of Business and Economics
Universiti Brunei Darussalam
Bandar Seri Begawan, Brunei Darussalam

Salisu Monsuru Adekunle
Faculty of Technical and Vocational
Sultan Idris Education University
Tanjong Malim, Perak, Malaysia

Muhammad Salman Shabbir
School of Business
Universiti Brunei Darussalam
Bandar Seri Begawan, Brunei Darussalam

ISBN 978-981-99-6426-0   ISBN 978-981-99-6427-7 (eBook)
https://doi.org/10.1007/978-981-99-6427-7

This Springer imprint is published by the registered company Springer Nature Singapore Pte Ltd.
The registered company address is: 152 Beach Road, #21-01/04 Gateway East, Singapore 189721, Singapore

Foreword

As the General Manager of the Yanbu Branch of Taibah University and Dean of the College of Business Administration, I am honoured to present the foreword for this insightful and timely book, "An Overview of Halal Entrepreneurship in the Islamic Economy: Contemporary Trends and Future Opportunities" by Lukman Raimi, Salisu Monsuru Adekunle, and Muhammad Salman Shabbir.

In the rapidly evolving global economy, the significance of the Islamic economy and Halal entrepreneurship cannot be overstated. This book serves as an invaluable resource for academics, Islamic finance specialists, Halal supporters, and business model advisors. It provides a comprehensive exploration of the concepts of Halal entrepreneurship, which are fast becoming the bedrock of economies in Muslim countries. The authors have meticulously examined the growth of the Halal Industry, highlighting the increasing global demand for Halal products and services. They have underscored the potential of this sector, which is projected to grow exponentially with the anticipated increase in the Muslim population. This book not only provides intellectual nourishment but also covers a wide range of topics including Halal production and consumption, business ethics, impact investing in Islamic entrepreneurship, and the guiding principles of Shari'ah in business model innovation.

What sets this book apart is its focus on the intersection of traditional Islamic principles and modern disruptive technologies. The authors delve into the use of digital ventures, fintech, the Internet of Things (IoT), 3D printing, cloud computing, automation, robotics, artificial intelligence, data analytics, digital platforms, and blockchain technologies in the context of the Halal industry. This fusion of tradition and innovation is a testament to the adaptability and resilience of the Islamic economy. The book also addresses the Sustainable Development Goals (SDGs), halalization, cultures, social entrepreneurship, sustainability issues, and the emergence of Islamic fintech in both Muslim-majority and non-Muslim countries. It provides a comprehensive overview of the interface between Halal Entrepreneurship and Science Technology, Engineering, and Mathematics (STEM).

In my capacity as an academic leader, I appreciate the book's potential as a resource for universities, Islamic training academies, and centres. It provides the necessary theoretical, theological, professional, and intellectual resources to address the challenges of financial exclusion, social inequality, social exclusion, and Riba, Maysir, and Gharar. The authors' vision to popularize Halal entrepreneurship models as complementary alternative models for business development, wealth creation, job creation, responsible production, and sustainable consumption is commendable.

In conclusion, this book is a significant contribution to the field of Halal entrepreneurship. It is a must-read for Islamic entrepreneurs, social entrepreneurs, technology entrepreneurs, industry experts, and policymakers. It will undoubtedly create greater awareness of Halal entrepreneurship as ultra-religious sustainable models to boost entrepreneurial activity and economic growth in the global economy.

Dr. Abdussalam Aljadani
FCEnt
Dean, College of Business
Administration and General Manager
Taibah University
Yanbu Branch
Kingdom of Saudi Arabia

Introduction: An Overview of Halal Entrepreneurship in the Islamic Economy: Contemporary Trends and Future Opportunities

Preamble

In the rapidly evolving global economy, an edited book on 'Halal entrepreneurship in Islamic Economy' is an invaluable resource for Halal academics, Islamic finance specialists, Halal supporters and Halal business model advisors. The concepts of halal entrepreneurship in the Islamic economy have advanced in different parts of the world and both are fast becoming the bedrock of the economies of Muslim countries. For instance, 1.9 billion Muslims (knowingly or unknowingly) spent USD 2 trillion on food, pharmaceutical, cosmetics, fashion, travel, media, and recreation sectors in 2021, leading to 8.9% year-over-year growth. The trend is projected by analysts to grow further because the Muslim population is expected to grow up to 3 billion by 2060, covering 30% of the global population (Malaysia Digital Economy Corporation, 2022). Moreover, with the growing awareness of halal concepts among 2.18 billion Muslims, the value of the global halal industry is estimated at around US$2.3 trillion, coupled with increased global demand for halal products, services, and user-based technologies (Azam & Abdullah, 2020).

Aside from intellectual nourishment, the edited book also covers halal production and consumption, business ethics and impact investing in Islamic entrepreneurship, Shari'ah principles guiding business model innovation, and the use of disruptive technologies such as digital ventures, fintech and the Internet of Things (IoT), three-dimensional (3D) printing, cloud computing, automation, robotics and artificial intelligence, data analytics, digital platforms and blockchain technologies. Blockchain, among others (Salaheldeen et al., 2021; Salaheldeen, 2022). Other hot topics raised by the contributors include Sustainable Development Goals (SDGs), halalization, cultures, social entrepreneurship, sustainability issues and the emergence of Islamic fintech in Muslim-majority and non-Muslim countries, including the interface between Halal Entrepreneurship and Science Technology, Engineering and Mathematics (STEM).

To meet the growing needs of universities, Islamic training academies and centres, this edited book would provide the necessary theoretical, theological, professional, and intellectual resources to address the challenges of financial exclusion, social inequality, social exclusion and Riba, Maysir and Gharar to master Muslims in all communities and countries. Therefore, this book seeks to popularize halal entrepreneurship models as complementary alternative models for business development, wealth creation, job creation, responsible production and sustainable consumption, and capitalists for the achievement of sustainable development goals. In this context, the growing number of Islamic entrepreneurs, social entrepreneurs, technology entrepreneurs, industry experts and policymakers also make this book worthwhile as it will create greater awareness of Halal entrepreneurship as ultra-religious sustainable models to boost entrepreneurial activity and economic growth in the global economy.

Overview of Book Chapters

The book consists of 17 chapters, professionally discussed, and carefully arranged to provide a wide range of knowledge seekers with essential knowledge about Halal entrepreneurship, including enriching academic and professional curricula for teaching Halal entrepreneurship in the Islamic economy.

While Islamic faith-based entrepreneurship models such as halal entrepreneurship, Islamic digital economy and Islamic business ethics are accepted and adopted, they have not been adequately discussed and researched. To fill this essential gap, Chapter "Historical, Theological, and Theoretical Underpinnings of Islamic and Halal Entrepreneurship" provides an overview of the historical, theological, and theoretical underpinnings of Islamic and Halal entrepreneurship to improve understanding and acceptance of the developmental ideals of these two concepts, including far-reaching suggestions on the misconceptions identified about the Islamic and Halal entrepreneurship on a global scale.

In the fields of natural and social sciences, conceptual definitions of phenomena are important for better understanding, measurement, and improvement. Albert Einstein had long advised: If you can't explain it simply, you don't understand it well enough (Scaramuzza & Rabbone, 2021). In parallel with the foregoing, Chapter "Understanding Islamic and Halal Entrepreneurship from the Maqasidul Shari'ah Perspective" discusses the definitions of Islamic entrepreneurship, and Halal entrepreneurship in the context of the Maqasidus Shari'ah perspective to enhance the understanding of professionals, researchers, and practitioners in the converging Islamic economy. The article concludes with valuable suggestions on how to maintain the links between the three concepts in the face of scandals in the emerging Islamic economy. Three theoretical implications emerged from this chapter.

In a highly competitive world with numerous hidden opportunities, emerging entrepreneurs and established entrepreneurs are expected to be vigilant, smart, and visible by discovering new environmental opportunities that many cannot see or by creating new opportunities that are not currently available, to become long-term competitive advantage and profitability (Raimi, 2015). To empower readers' ability to discover and create new opportunities, Chapter "Opportunities for Entrepreneurs in the Attainment of Sustainable Development Goals (SDGs) Through Halal Entrepreneurship" examines opportunities for Halal entrepreneurs to accelerate the achievement of the Sustainable Development Goals (SDGs) by 2030. The focus is on the development of environmentally friendly products and services and the introduction of climate-friendly technologies, as well as ethical investments and the promotion of responsible production and consumption, which are in line with the provisions of Sharia on which Halal entrepreneurship is based. Finally, recommendations are made to encourage halal entrepreneurs to ensure their products and services are environmentally friendly and to disclose ESG activities in their annual reports.

Halal entrepreneurship, like contemporary entrepreneurship, emphasizes legal and regulatory issues, as ignorance of the law does not excuse anyone (Lao, 2019). To provide guidance on complying with international and national rules and requirements, Chapter "Strengthen the Sustainability of Halal Entrepreneurs Through International Consumer Rights Laws" examines the legal and regulatory issues, with a focus on how the sustainability of Halal entrepreneurs can be strengthened through international consumer rights laws that protect the interests of Muslims and non-Muslims alike. It highlights the fact that industry players urgently need to develop new laws to protect Halal consumer rights and establish mechanisms to harmonize existing standards based on the provisions of the Qur'an and Hadith.

Chapter "Institutionalization of Halal Entrepreneurship for a Sustainable Economy", like the previous chapter, explains the need to institutionalize halal entrepreneurship for a sustainable economy in the face of unethical practices and fraudulent activities in the supply chains of manufactured products and services around the world. Unethical practices in the supply chain pose a threat to the planet (environment), people (social) and profit (economic), referred to as the triple bottom line of the 3Ps. In summary, all Halal entrepreneurship actors are required to be aware of Allah (taqwa) and refrain from unethical practices and fraudulent activities.

Several good startups die within five years of their inception for lack of resources and skills that incubators can provide. To reduce the failure rate in Halal companies, Chapter "Development of Halal Entrepreneurship Framework Through Business Incubator Service for Sustainability Using PRISMA" examines the development of a Halal entrepreneurship framework by a sustainability incubator service using the PRISMA systematic review protocol. The results showed that halal entrepreneurship plays a crucial role in fostering innovation, job creation, societal well-being, and global economic growth. It concludes that the Viable Systems Model (VSM) is useful for the Halal sector to adapt to its environment, serve the interests of stakeholders and uphold Islamic ideals.

In the Red Ocean business landscape, strong business models have become an important tool for value creation, value delivery and value capture (Zhao et al., 2020). To capitalize on this understanding, Chapter "Designing Sustainable Business Models for Islamic Entrepreneurship" explains the process of developing sustainable business models for Islamic entrepreneurship to counteract the high failure rate of Muslim companies caused by the lack of such models in the halal industry. The failure rate of Muslim companies is higher than usual as many of them find it difficult to remain profitable while upholding Islamic ideals. To keep up with trends, the chapter emphasizes the need for a shift towards sustainable business models that are in line with Islamic values by undertaking an in-depth analysis of the common causes of these failures.

Digitisation has changed the way business is done globally and Halal entrepreneurship must seize the tremendous opportunities it presents on both the supply and demand sides of the industry. Chapter "Halal Entrepreneurship in Islamic Digital Economy from a Cultural Perspective" discusses the relationship between halal entrepreneurship and the Islamic digital economy from a cultural perspective. The former refers to an alternative way of incorporating and running a business in accordance with Sharia principles to provide halal products and services, while the latter refers to all Sharia-compliant economic activities in the regulated digital space. The alliance of both concepts is expected to have a positive impact on the production of halal products and services, sales and marketing, internationalization, market visibility, the ability to reach broader customer segments, as well as better access to fintech and outreach to al-Falah will affect (double prosperity) and economic growth.

Everything in the world is built on an ecosystem. Indeed, the emergence and evolution of ecosystems in the corporate landscape have produced a coherent circular value proposition (de Vasconcelos Gomes et al., 2023). For halal entrepreneurship to survive, a circular and integrated ecosystem is required. Chapter "Nexus of Halal Entrepreneurship and Islamic Finance for the Creation of a Strong Halal Ecosystem", therefore, provides a solid awareness of the connection between Halal entrepreneurship and Islamic finance to create a strong Halal ecosystem. Halal entrepreneurship and Islamic finance are interdependent and symbiotic. Awareness of the Halal ecosystem creates a better understanding of the contribution of both Halal entrepreneurship and Islamic finance to the Halal ecosystem and provides a basis for further research. The chapter emphasizes that to create a strong halal ecosystem, halal entrepreneurship must be fully strengthened through Islamic finance integration.

Halal has evolved into a marketing brand that has also opened the door to Halal food fraud and counterfeit products in the Halal industry. Therefore, there is a need for Halal standardization and certification (Abd Rashid et al., 2023). To shed light on the Halal certification process, Chapter "Halalisation: Challenges and Opportunities in Halal Food and Beverages Industry for Halalpreneurs" examines the concept of Halalization, challenges and opportunities in the Halal food and beverage industry for Halal entrepreneurs. The issue of halalization is a priority issue to ensure the legitimacy and certification of various lifestyle products such as food, beverage, fashion, tourism, cosmetics, fashion, and pharmaceuticals. The chapter emphasized that the existence of Halal certification will offer different sectors and economic operators legally guaranteed added value in the sale and production of their products.

Halal entrepreneurship is based on Halal (Permissible) and Toyyib (Healthy), which are inseparable and integrated. Chapter "Influence of Religious and Health Factors on the Halal Cosmetics Industry" analyzes the influence of religious and health factors on the halal cosmetics industry. Analyzing religious influence is crucial as the Halal cosmetics industry has seen exponential growth in recent years due to the increasing demand for Halal products. Halal cosmetics must conform to Islamic principles, including the ban on alcohol and animal ingredients in the manufacturing process, competitive prices, and ethical standards. The chapter shows that religion and health are two important factors influencing the purchase and development of halal cosmetics.

Building on the previously discussed strengths of digitalization, Chapter "Halal Digital Entrepreneurship and Disruptive Technologies from the Lenses of *Maqasid al-Shari'ah*" examines halal digital entrepreneurship and disruptive technologies from the perspective of Maqasid-al-Shariah. Digital entrepreneurship has become a popular field as the introduction of disruptive technologies opens new opportunities for startups.

Halal tourism differs from traditional tourism as the former is based on the adoption of Islamic teachings and principles in all aspects of tourism activities. Chapter "Innovative Opportunities for Halal Entrepreneurs in the Tourism Sector" discusses in detail the innovative opportunities for Halal entrepreneurs in the tourism sector due to the increasing demand for Halal products and general services, mainly due to the spread of the Islamic worldview, the rising purchasing power of the Islamic community and the fast-growing Muslim tourism sector is on the attributed to the industry in the west.

Moreover, Chapter "Reshaping the Mindset of Halal Entrepreneurs Toward Sustainable Business: The Case of Indonesia" discusses the agenda to transform the mindset of halal entrepreneurs towards sustainable business (cases from Indonesia). The chapter provides information and reference for stakeholders focused on Islamic economics, Islamic finance, and environmental sustainability. The novelty of this chapter of the book is related to the relationship between sustainable economic activity and the concept of Islamic economics.

Chapter "The 21st Century Innovative Marketing Strategies for Halal Entrepreneurs in the Various Segments of the Halal Industry" offers valuable insights into the innovative marketing strategies of the 21st century for Halal entrepreneurs in the different segments of the Halal industry. The chapter noted that effective innovative marketing strategies for halal entrepreneurs include digital marketing, social media marketing, and influencer marketing, among others. The chapter recommends that Halal entrepreneurs consider local culture and trends when implementing marketing strategies.

Green entrepreneurship touches all aspects of human lifestyle due to existential threats from environmental abuse, climate change and other industrial externalities (Chandel, 2022). Therefore, Chapter "Green Marketing as an Ethical Practice for Halal Entrepreneurs for a Sustainable Ecosystem" discusses green marketing as an ethical practice for halal entrepreneurs for a sustainable ecosystem as new global concerns about environmental issues arise. The chapter posits that all Halal business models should be geared towards green marketing since respect for the well-being of society and the environment is paramount in Islamic business. The integration of Islamic values with green imperatives is transforming entrepreneurs in the halal sector through certain characteristics that justify the use of the terms halalpreneurs and halalpreneurship.

Finally, like the previous chapter, Chapter "Halal Entrepreneurship and Its Impact on Sustainable Economy: Opportunities and Challenges" examines the impact of halal entrepreneurship on a sustainable economy. The discussion extends to the opportunities and challenges of the growth trend in the global economy due to the increasing demand from Muslim consumers for Halal products and services. This chapter provided recommendations for policymakers and entrepreneurs to support the development of halal entrepreneurship and promote a sustainable economy.

In summary, all 17 chapters of the book emphasize the need for Islamic theorists, researchers, professionals, and policymakers to improve knowledge and awareness about halal entrepreneurship to increase the growth of halal markets, which include food, tourism, and fashion, as well as medical areas. If all the innovative ideas, models and insights contained in this book are implemented, the pace of Islamic economic development will accelerate enormously for the benefit of all.

Lukman Raimi
Salisu Monsuru Adekunle
Muhammad Salman Shabbir

References

Abd Rashid, N. R., Ahmad, A. N., Dahlal, N. M., & Abdullah, M. A. (2023). Applying Ethical Climate Theory in Whistleblowing Intentions Study Among Employees in Halal Food Companies: A Protocol. *Halalpshere, 3*(1), 47–54.

Abdullah, M. A., & Azam, M. S. E. (2020). Halal entrepreneurship from Maqasid-al-Sharia'h perspective: inseparable concept for Halalpreneurs. *Food Research, 4*(1), 34–42.

Chandel, T. A. (2022). Green Entrepreneurship and Sustainable Development. In *International Perspectives on Value Creation and Sustainability Through Social Entrepreneurship* (pp. 173–208). IGI Global.

de Vasconcelos Gomes, L. A., de Faria, A. M., Braz, A. C., de Mello, A. M., Borini, F. M., & Ometto, A. R. (2023). Circular ecosystem management: Orchestrating ecosystem value proposition and configuration. *International Journal of Production Economics, 256*, 108725.

Lao, C. V. (2019). Ignorance of the law excuses no one. *Likhaan: The Journal of Contemporary Philippine Literature, 13*.

Malaysia Digital Economy Corporation (2022). Islamic Digital Economy (IDE): Driving Investments Through Islamic Digital Economy. https://mydigitalinvestment.gov.my/islamic-digital-economy

Salaheldeen, M. (2022). Opportunities for Halal Entrepreneurs in the Islamic digital economy: future and trends from a cultural entrepreneurship perspective. In *Cultural Entrepreneurship: New Societal Trends* (pp. 95–107). Singapore: Springer Nature Singapore.

Salaheldeen, M., Battour, M., Nazri, M. A., & Bustamam, U. S. A. (2021). Prospects for achieving the sustainable development goals 2030 through a proposed halal entrepreneurship success index (HESI). In *SHS Web of Conferences* (Vol. 124, p. 08001). EDP Sciences.

Scaramuzza, A., & Rabbone, I. (2021). If you can't explain it simply, you don't understand it well enough (Albert Einstein): the role of postgraduate schools in the careers of young pediatric endocrinologists. *Minerva Pediatrics*, *73*(6), 471–473.

Zhao, Y., Von Delft, S., Morgan-Thomas, A., & Buck, T. (2020). The evolution of platform business models: Exploring competitive battles in the world of platforms. *Long Range Planning*, *53*(4), 101892.

Contents

Editors and Contributors

About the Editors

Dr. Lukman Raimi is an Assistant Professor, Program Coordinator in the Entrepreneurship Major and Chair of the Learning and Development Committee at Universiti Brunei Darussalam, Brunei. He was also formerly the Graduate Program Coordinator at the School of Business & Entrepreneurship and Director of the Center for Entrepreneurship at the American University of Nigeria. His research interests include business-oriented entrepreneurship, social entrepreneurship, halal entrepreneurship, and innovation management among others. He is currently Associate Editor of the Journal of Business and Economic Analysis, Universiti Brunei Darussalam, Brunei; Associate Editor, GUSAU Journal of Entrepreneurship Development, Federal University Gusau, Nigeria; Member, Editorial Board, Indonesian Journal of Sustainability Accounting & Management Indonesia; Member, Editorial Advisory Board, Emerald Emerging Markets Case Studies, UK; Member, Editorial Advisory Board, Journal of Developmental Entrepreneurship USA; Member, Editorial Board, African Journal of Innovation and Entrepreneurship, UK; and Member of the Editorial Board, International Journal of Circular Economy and Waste Management, IGI Global Publisher, USA.

Dr. Salisu Monsuru Adekunle is a Senior Lecturer at the Faculty of Technical and Vocational Education, Sultan Idris Education University, Malaysia. He is a Senior Fellow of the Halal Professional and Executive Consultant of Halal Compliance and Food Safety (HaCFoS). His research interests include soil fertility, plant nutrient management, Halal Industrial Management, Food Safety and Sustainability. He is the Editor-in-Chief of the Journal Sustainable Agriculture Food & Environment-SAFE, Member, Editorial Board, AgroTech-Food Science, Technology and Environment, Malaysia and Member, Editorial Board, Journal of Underutilized Legume (JUL), Nigeria, and a reviewer for several journals indexed in Scopus and Web of Science (WoS). He has developed Halal training modules and he has served as a facilitator for several Halal training and workshops, including Halal Product Recall and Halal Assurance System (HAS). His publications are indexed in Scopus, WoS, and Google Scholar.

Dr. Muhammad Salman Shabbir is an Assistant Professor of Entrepreneurship at Universiti Brunei Darussalam. His research interests include entrepreneurship, green entrepreneurship, and entrepreneurial skills. He obtained his Ph.D. in Entrepreneurship from the University Utara Malaysia. He has served as a Postdoctoral Fellow at University Utara Malaysia and Universiti Sains Malaysia. He has also worked as a Management Director and Assistant Professor at various institutions. He has published over 60 journal articles and conference proceedings in reputable journals. He is a member of several professional organizations and serves as a Guest Editor for a journal.

Contributors

Ibrahim Adeniyi Abdur-Rauf Department of Shariah, Universiti Sultan Zainal Abidin, Kuala Terengganu, Terengganu, Malaysia

Erry Yulian Adesta Universitas Indo Global Mandiri (UIGM), Palembang, Indonesia

Saheed Afolabi Ashafa Department of Religions, Osun State University, Osun State, Osogbo, Nigeria

Md Siddique E Azam International Institute for Halal Research and Training (INHART), Kuala Lumpur, IIUM, Malaysia

Siti Nur Azizah Universitas Muhammadiyah Purwokerto, Purwokerto, Indonesia

Nurudeen Babatunde Bamiro Department of Language, Arts and Social Science Education, Faculty of Education, Lagos State University, Lagos, Nigeria; Department of Economics, Faculty of Management and Economics, Universiti Pendidikan Sultan Idris (UPSI), Perak, Malaysia

Kamarudeen Babatunde Bello Department of Business Administration, Modibbo Adama University, Yola, Nigeria

Shukurat M. Bello Department of Business Administration and Entrepreneurship, Dangote Business School, Bayero University Kano, Kano, Nigeria

Amal A. M. Elgharbawy International Institute for Halal Research and Training (INHART), International Islamic University Malaysia, Kuala Lumpur, Malaysia

Nabila Huda Ibrahim University of Malaya, Kuala Lumpur, Malaysia

Mohammad Mominul Islam UBD School of Business and Economics, Universiti Brunei Darussalam, Jalan Tungku Link, BE, Brunei

Betania Kartika International Institute for Halal Research and Training (INHART), Kuala Lumpur, IIUM, Malaysia

Mariam Kotachi School of Business, Shenandoah University, Winchester, VA, USA

Tijani Usman Moyosore Lagos State University, Lagos, Nigeria

Muazu Hassan Muazu Department of Business Administration and Entrepreneurship, Dangote Business School, Bayero University Kano, Kano, Nigeria

Basit Adekunle Nasiru Department of Language, Arts and Social Science Education, Faculty of Education, Lagos State University, Lagos, Nigeria

Lucky Nugroho Universitas Mercu Buana, Jakarta, Indonesia

Saheed Adebowale Nurein American University of Nigeria, Yola, Nigeria

Basirat Olaide Raimi School of Social Entrepreneurship, Roxbourg Institute of Social Entrepreneurship, La Sarraz, Switzerland

Lukman Raimi Department of Business Administration, Universiti Brunei Darussalam, Gadong, Bandar Seri Begawan, Brunei

Monsuru Adekunle Salisu Faculty of Technical and Vocational, Sultan Idris Education University, Tanjung Malim, Perak, Malaysia

Rafiu K. Showole International Institute for Halal Research and Training (INHART), International Islamic University (IIUM), Kuala Lumpur, Malaysia

Effa Ratna Sjahrir Exemplar Synergy Consultancy, Kuala Lumpur, Malaysia

Naelati Tubastuvi Faculty of Economics and Business, Universitas Muhammadiyah Purwokerto Jalan KH. Ahmad Dahlan Dukuhwaluh, Purwokerto, Indonesia

Umar Habibu Umar Department of Accounting and Finance, Universiti Brunei Darussalam, Darussalam, Brunei

Yan Aldo Wiliantoro Faculty of Economics and Business, Universitas Muhammadiyah Purwokerto Jalan KH. Ahmad Dahlan Dukuhwaluh, Purwokerto, Indonesia; Litera, Business School, Purwokerto, Indonesia

Avicenna Yuhan Universitas Indo Global Mandiri (UIGM), Palembang, Indonesia

Zainizam Bin Zakariya Department of Economics, Faculty of Management and Economics, Universiti Pendidikan Sultan Idris (UPSI), Perak, Malaysia

Historical, Theological, and Theoretical Underpinnings of Islamic and Halal Entrepreneurship

Lukman Raimi, Ibrahim Adeniyi Abdur-Rauf, and Saheed Afolabi Ashafa

Abstract In the global business landscape, the concepts of Islamic and Halal entrepreneurship are often misunderstood and misrepresented. This chapter aims to expand knowledge on Islamic entrepreneurship by discussing its historical, theological, and theoretical foundations. By doing so, we hope to improve understanding and acceptance of the developmental ideals behind these two concepts. To answer our research questions, we have critically reviewed scientific papers and systematically analyzed the collected data using a critical literature review (CLR). Drawing insights from 69 articles, we provide detailed explanations of the conceptual definitions of Islamic and Halal entrepreneurship. Additionally, we delve into the historical, theological, and theoretical foundations of these concepts. Furthermore, we identify and address four misconceptions that both Muslims and non-Muslims have about Islamic and Halal entrepreneurship as new ultra-religious concepts in the global business landscape. Finally, the chapter concludes with far-reaching suggestions on how to address these misconceptions on a global scale.

Keywords Halal entrepreneurship · History · Islamic entrepreneurship · Theology · Theory

L. Raimi (✉)
Department of Business Administration, Universiti Brunei Darussalam, Bandar Seri Begawan, Brunei
e-mail: luq_man2001@yahoo.com

I. A. Abdur-Rauf
Department of Shariah, Universiti Sultan Zainal Abidin, Kuala Terengganu, Terengganu, Malaysia

S. A. Ashafa
Department of Religions, Osun State University, Osun State, Osogbo, Nigeria

L. Raimi et al. (eds.), *Contemporary Discourse of Halal and Islamic Entrepreneurship*,
https://doi.org/10.1007/978-981-99-6427-7_1

1 Introduction

In the global business landscape, entrepreneurship has attracted increasing attention in research, policy, and business circles. Traditional entrepreneurship can be roughly divided into two categories: Schumpeterian entrepreneurship and non-Schumpeterian entrepreneurship. While Schumpeterian entrepreneurship is characterized by risk-taking behavior aimed at radical innovation and high corporate growth, non-Schumpeterian entrepreneurship is characterized by risk-avoiding behavior aimed at imitation and low corporate growth (Dilli et al., 2018). Other more common typologies of entrepreneurship are social entrepreneurship, commercial entrepreneurship, emerging/transitional entrepreneurship, women's entrepreneurship, medical entrepreneurship, and digital entrepreneurship (Herman, 2022; Raimi et al., 2023; Raimi, Dodo & Sule, 2022). Regardless of its variants, entrepreneurship finds relevance across cultures, contexts, and countries due to its transformative nature. Undoubtedly, entrepreneurship has promoted and supported economic progress and prosperity in both developed and developing countries. Some of the outcomes of entrepreneurship include job creation, wealth creation, and innovations that bring tremendous benefits to society (Hitt et al., 2011).

Recently, new variants of entrepreneurship called Islamic and Halal entrepreneurship have emerged. Islamic entrepreneurship refers to starting and managing a business according to Islamic ethics, principles, and values. Its meaning extends to conducting business activities in accordance with the Islamic teachings of fairness, justice, honesty, and compassion (Harizan & Mustafa, 2020). Halal entrepreneurship refers to the practice of establishing and operating businesses and engaging in economic activities that are permitted under Sharia law (Abdullah & Azam, 2020a, 2020b, 2020c) and conform to the principles of ethics, social responsibility, and sustainability.

More importantly, the emergence of Islamic and Halal entrepreneurship has been accompanied by the growth of the Islamic finance industry, which reached US$2.2 trillion in assets in 2016 and is expected to reach US$3.8 trillion in 2022 (Denham, 2019). The connection between Islamic finance and Islamic and Halal entrepreneurship can be described as an input–output process. The former serves as an input to mobilize investment funds, while the latter serves as an output to produce goods and services that meet people's needs. The World Economic Forum (2017) noted that the revitalization of entrepreneurship in Islamic finance has the prospect of addressing the United Nations SDGs, as Islamic financial institutions are better positioned to provide better brokerage for small and medium-sized enterprises (SMEs), and infrastructure investments become possible.

As mentioned above, Islamic and Halal entrepreneurship have emerged as ultra-religious entrepreneurship typologies catering to Muslim communities and people with a penchant for Islamic ethical products, services, fashion, cosmetics, health, tourism, and financial solutions (Amir & Abdukic, 2021). Compared to several other sectors, Halal business, which symbolizes the global Islamic economy, is one of the fastest-growing sectors in the world (Salaheldeen et al., 2022). The global halal business caters to 1.8 billion Muslims with an estimated annual spend of US$2.2 trillion (Akram, 2022). Halal entrepreneurs in the food, beverage, cosmetics, clothing, and fashion sectors, as well as other essential services, are the main contributors to the global halal business, hence they are often referred to as halalpreneurs (Abdullah & Azam, 2020a, 2020b, 2020c; Akram, 2022).

Although both concepts have their roots in Islam and Islamic laws, they are not attempts to Islamize or force Islamic thoughts on diverse global populations but merely alternative models for deepening responsible production and consumption in the quickly changing world of multiple economic systems following Shariah principles (Hassan, 2016; Madi, 2014). The Shariah principles are derived from the Quran and Hadith, the two primary sources of Islamic laws that guide socioeconomic issues at personal and group levels, otherwise called Fiqh al-Mu'āmalāt (Ismail & Arshad, 2009; Yusuf & Raimi, 2021).

One of the proactive ways for marginalized Muslims and ethical Muslim entrepreneurs to overcome social inequality and social exclusion caused by Riba, Maysir, and Gharar is to embrace Islamic business ethics to balance the link between economic opportunities and economic outcomes (A'la Mawdudi, 2013).

We contribute to the existing knowledge in two ways. First, we expand practical knowledge of Islamic and Halal entrepreneurship, which is still in its infancy among Islamic finance professionals, Halal consultants, academic researchers, and students who have ambitions to enter these two fields. Second, we correct inaccurate views of Muslims and non-Muslims on these two religious concepts. In retrospect, Zarabozo (2007; p. 5) explained that the negative views and misrepresentations of Islam are not just a matter of personal religious beliefs. The impact goes far beyond that, affecting world security and politics. Most pernicious, however, is that Islam is misunderstood and constantly portrayed as the source of evil. As a result, many people are prevented from understanding the beauty and priceless truths that Islam and its ideals offer mankind. In these troubled times, it is very important to turn to God for guidance.

In the absence of a simplified article that refutes the grossly misunderstood concept of Islamic and Halal entrepreneurship, this chapter aims to enhance the body of knowledge by discussing the historical, theological, and theoretical foundations of Islamic and Halal entrepreneurship. The goal is to promote understanding and the adoption of these deeply religious ideals. This chapter specifically addresses the following three questions:

- Research question 1: What are the conceptual definitions of Islamic and Halal entrepreneurship?
- Research question 2: What are the historical, theological, and theoretical foundations of Islamic and Halal entrepreneurship?
- Research question 3: What are the misconceptions about Islamic and Halal entrepreneurship on a global scale?

We ask the research questions mentioned above because their answers would guide readers, entrepreneurs, and other stakeholders in better conceptualizing, embracing, and disseminating the ideals of ultra-religious entrepreneurship for mutually beneficial purposes in the rapidly changing global business landscape. Overall, a better understanding of Islamic and Halal entrepreneurship would help academics, researchers, practitioners, consultants, and policymakers improve the growth of Islamic start-ups and small and medium-sized enterprises (SMEs) by enhancing social and financial inclusion, and by accelerating the achievement of the 17 Sustainable Development Goals (SDG3). The chapter is divided into five sections. Section 1 provides the introductory background, Sect. 2 covers the methodology, Sect. 3 focuses on the conceptual definitions of Islamic and Halal entrepreneurship, Sect. 4 explores the historical, theological, and theoretical foundations of Islamic and Halal entrepreneurship, and Sect. 5 describes the plethora of challenges facing Islamic and Halal entrepreneurship on a global scale. Finally, Sect. 5 concludes with a summary of the discussion and recommendations aimed at strengthening the growth of Islamic and Halal entrepreneurship worldwide.

2 Methods and Analysis Review

This chapter employs a qualitative research method and an interpretive research paradigm. We used the desk research technique, in which academic papers were reviewed to find answers to the research questions. To fill existing knowledge gaps, we critically reviewed scholarly works to uncover the historical, theological, and theoretical underpinnings of Islamic and Halal entrepreneurship following the methods of Yusuf and Raimi (2021). This is useful in providing clarity about the understanding, adoption, and dissemination of the goals of these ultra-religious ideals. The collected data were systematically nalysed using a critical literature review (CLR). Operationally, the CLR is a systematic analysis and evaluation of multiple articles and texts on a given topic that, if objectively evaluated and nalysed using appropriate language, would yield new insights, more facts, richer insights, and a deeper understanding (Saunders & Rojon, 2011; Saunders et al., 2012). To ensure a degree of objectivity in the selection of academic papers, a search of academic databases for publications on Islamic and Halal entrepreneurship yielded over 130 academic articles and working papers from different parts of the world. The authors used the purposive sampling technique and systematically selected and reviewed 69 articles and texts that are appropriate and relevant to the topics studied, according to the purposive sampling rationale of Raimi et al. (2023).

3 Critical Literature Review

3.1 Conceptual Issues

In this chapter, it is necessary to provide an explanation of Islam, Halal, and Entrepreneurship as the underlying concepts. Islam is a comprehensive religion with well-defined beliefs, rituals, and precepts that encompass all aspects of life and offer guidance on rituals, worship, and worldly activities (Muneeza & Mustapha, 2021; Yusuf & Raimi, 2021). Additionally, Islam is recognized as a monotheistic religion that governs and covers every facet of life, including individual, social, material, moral, ethical, legal, cultural, political, economic, and global aspects (Choudhury, 2008). The Qur'an and the Hadith are the primary and widely accepted sources of Islam. The Qur'an is the sacred book revealed by Allah to the Prophet Muhammad (peace and blessings of Allaah be upon him), while the Hadith consists of the Prophet's own words and guidance (Zarabozo, 2007). The principles of Islam are eternal and aim to achieve global peace, human progress, economic growth, and sustainable development. Specifically, the United Nations' seventeen (17) Sustainable Development Goals (SDGs) align with the five (5) thematic goals of Islamic law, known as Maqasid al-Shariah, which include the preservation of religion, life, intellect, offspring, and wealth (Yusuf & Raimi, 2021). Therefore, it is not surprising to witness the emergence of Islamic and Halal entrepreneurship.

The term "halal," when used in Islamic jurisprudence, means lawful or permitted, and its opposite is "haram," meaning unlawful and forbidden. The deeper meaning of halal is a code of conduct or divine law that governs all aspects of the religious and secular life of Muslims. When used in relation to socio-economic and political aspects, halal refers to business activities and transactions conducted in a manner considered permissible in Islam (Johan & Hussain, 2019; Mohamed et al., 2008). Similarly, the term halal, used in relation to consumption, refers to food, beverages, financial services, tourism, and other consumer goods that meet the standards of Islamic law in terms of legality, purity, hygiene, and safety (Johan & Hussain, 2019). Halal has become a significant issue in the rapidly changing business landscape as Muslim consumers worldwide become more informed and knowledgeable about their religion. As a result, they are more aware, selective, and discerning about the types of products and services they consume or use (Temizhan et al., 2000). Muslims around the world are concerned about the legality of what they eat, drink, and do. This renewed consciousness has given rise to the emergence of halal entrepreneurship and the halal industry. Some spin-off words related to halal include halalpreneur, halalpreneurship, halal goods, halal services, halal industry, halal logo, halal certification, and halalization (Gauthier, 2021; Salaheldeen et al., 2022).

Entrepreneurship refers to the discovery and creation of opportunities by individuals and groups who are vigilant, shrewd, and alert to the external environment (Yu, 2001). Stevenson (2000) clearly defines entrepreneurship as the pursuit of opportunities beyond resources controlled by people (entrepreneurs) and organizations (corporate entrepreneurs). Opportunity is the hallmark of entrepreneurship. The concept of opportunity in the definition of entrepreneurship reinvents itself in four ways: (a) pioneering a truly innovative product; (b) developing a new business model; (c) creating a better or cheaper version of an existing product; and (d) targeting an existing product to new customer groups (Eisenmann, 2013). By developing new business models, entrepreneurship greatly improves the quality of life by creating new technologies and cutting-edge services that make life easier, increase productivity, provide more entertainment, improve healthcare systems, and enhance communication between people and nations through disruptive technologies (Bozeman et al., 2013).

In the fields of Islamic economics and management, the concept of entrepreneurship shares many similarities with the conventional understanding but is not identical in terms of its conceptual framework. This section of the chapter offers a conceptual explanation of entrepreneurship from an Islamic perspective. Prominent scholars in this field, Kayed and Hassan (2013), define Islamic entrepreneurship as the approach to establishing, managing, and expanding businesses and other economic activities within the context of an Islamic economy and society. Similarly, Hoque et al. (2014) define Islamic entrepreneurship as the process of initiating a business to produce goods or provide services that are halal in order to generate reasonable profits. Although Islamic entrepreneurship may appear similar to conventional entrepreneurship, a closer analysis of their fundamental philosophies reveals that while conventional entrepreneurship aims for profit maximization (in the case of commercial enterprises) and maximization of social welfare (in the case of social enterprises), Islamic entrepreneurship has a distinct focus aligned with Islamic principles.

In contrast to conventional entrepreneurship, the goal of Islamic entrepreneurship is double success (al-falah), which entails prosperity in two dimensions. The first domain is economic prosperity, profitability, and maximizing social well-being in worldly life. The second domain is the attainment of success in the afterlife by addressing the socio-economic and environmental problems faced by people and communities through entrepreneurial activities (Abdullahi & Ramli, 2019). Comparatively, Halal entrepreneurship refers to the practice of establishing and operating businesses and engaging in economic activities that are permitted under Sharia law (Abdullah & Azam, 2020a, 2020b, 2020c) and conform to the principles of ethics, social responsibility, and sustainability. However, the application of Halal entrepreneurship includes companies that provide Halal products and services, such as Halal food and drink, Islamic fashion, or financial services that comply with Sharia Law on Finance, Fashion, and General Business (Mohsin et al., 2016).

Islamic and Halal entrepreneurship Muslim entrepreneurs, as actors in their business ventures, are by Islamic ethics and regard commercial success as an act worship to gain Allah's (Machmud & idayat, 202). Furthermore, the nature of entrepreneurial activities, opportunity recognition, innovation, risk-taking, resource management, ethics, and social responsibility (ESR), and sound decision in conventional entrepreneurship are similar to those of Islamic and halal entrepreneurship in several respects (Ramdani et al., 2017). Muslim entrepreneurs are encouraged to be resourceful, creative, proactive, and competitive like conventional entrepreneurs by following ethical standards set by Islamic laws (Javaid, 2022).

Furthermore, Ramdani et al. (2017) examined the identical actions, duties, and goals of Muslim entrepreneurs in the Islamic economy in their research. Additionally, Islamic entrepreneurship and entrepreneurship have been coined to refute the notion that Islam is inherently opposed to modernization and development (Kayed & Hassan, 2010, 2013). Similarly, Islamic entrepreneurship has been justified as a term defining entrepreneurship in Islam (Ratten et al., 2017a, 2017b). The term "halalpreneurship" was coined to describe halal-oriented entrepreneurship and understand the motivation of small and medium-sized enterprises (SMEs) to become halalpreneurs (Soltanian et al., 2016). Entrepreneurs in the halal grocery business have commonly been defined, used, and researched (Rahman & Mohamed, 2011). However, the term "Halalpreneurship" has yet to be defined and operationalized. Therefore, the biggest gap in halal business practice and research is the lack of a globally agreed definition and proper understanding of halalpreneurship (Soltanian et al., 2016). Based on the above, a halalpreneur refers to a Muslim who conducts an entrepreneurial business in the global halal market with the aim of providing only halal products and services while adhering to Shari'ah-compliant business practices (Abdullah & Azam, 2020a, 2020b, 2020c). To offer halal products and services, a halalpreneur must apply for a halal certificate for the specific product or service. Likewise, all Halal criteria are designed in accordance with Maqasid-al-Shariah (Abdullah & Azam, 2020a, 2020b, 2020c).

A review of the current market positions of the various sectors within the halal industry will assist Islamic entrepreneurs and Halalpreneurs in recognizing the business potential within the global halal market. The halal food and beverage sector is the largest segment of the halal industry, second only to Islamic banking, and is followed by modest fashion, media and leisure, Muslim-friendly tourism, halal medicine, and halal cosmetics (Ajaib & Altunişik, 2022; Hassan et al., 2021; Suhartanto et al., 2020).

3.2 *Historical Underpinning of Islamic and Halal Entrepreneurship*

Entrepreneurship has a long history that can be traced back to the pre-Islamic era within Arab civilization. The Qur'an references the Quraysh tribe, who engaged in caravan trading, journeying to Yemen in winter and Syria in summer to ensure the economic prosperity and social well-being of their community, protecting them from hunger and fear (Qur'an 106:1–4). However, despite the presence of entrepreneurship, the ancient Arab civilization faced challenges due to the lack of proper spirituality, morals, knowledge, and a progressive worldview. It was with the arrival and teachings of Prophet Muhammad (peace be upon him) that entrepreneurship underwent a transformation, bringing about significant changes in its purpose, ethics, and implementation.

> The Qur'an reminds us: "He it is Who sent among the unlettered ones a Messenger from among themselves, reciting to them His verses, purifying them, and teaching them the Book and the Hikmah (wisdom)." (The Qur'an 64:2–3).

Machmud and Hidayat (2020) stated that prior to his appointment as the Prophet, Muhammad (peace be upon him) worked with Khadijah bin Khuwaylid as an intrapreneur, learning valuable qualities of Islamic entrepreneurship such as honesty, a strong work ethic, and keeping promises. These ethical qualities earned him the titles Al-Amin (The Trustworthy) and As-Siddiq (The Honest). The history of Prophet Muhammad's commitment to business-oriented entrepreneurship began when he started managing his uncle Abu Talib's business. Later, he was hired as a professional to run Khadijah's business (Razak et al., 2022). Furthermore, when entrusted with political leadership, he transformed the state of Medina al-Munawwarah (Madinah the City of Light) into an inclusive society where Muslims, Christians, and Jews coexisted under the Constitution of Madinah. Funding is inherently tied to entrepreneurship as the former cannot exist without the latter. Some of the Islamic forms of finance that support Islamic entrepreneurship, as pioneered by the Prophet Muhammad (peace be upon him), include:

i. Wakalah refers to custodianship, where people entrusted their money with the Prophet, Al-Amin.
ii. Shirkah is a partnership model based on profit-and-loss sharing (PLS).
iii. Al-Qard Al-Hasan is a benevolent loan that is enjoined by Allah on rich Muslims.
iv. Salam is a forward contract and sales method that is prevalent among farmers and traders.
v. Sarf involves the exchange of money, such as gold for gold and silver for silver, within the same sitting. vi. Ijarah is the leasing of tools and grains.
vi. Zakat, Sadaqat, and Waqf are diverse social security nets in Islam.
vii. Trans-regional trade occurs in trade caravans from Makkah to Syria and vice versa (Hassan, Kayed & Oseni, 2013).

After the era of the Prophet (peace be upon him), early Muslims established their presence in various parts of the world through long-distance trade and entrepreneurship. Some claim that Islam and its ethics were spread by swords and conquests, as the West believes (Rahman, 1980). However, Kuran (2010) discovered that the spread of Islam in the early seventh century CE, like the development of other major religions, required entrepreneurial acts of immense ingenuity. Moreover, Prange (2018) confirmed that during the Middle Ages, one of the most significant transmissions was the spread of Islam along the monsoon coasts of Asia by Muslim merchants who established communities in all the thriving port cities of the Indian Ocean. Islamic beliefs and practices became widespread and encountered diverse societies on a scale comparable only to the initial expansion of the caliphate in the seventh century. He emphatically stated that the movement of Muslim traders along the maritime trade routes was not based on military conquest, political hegemony, or imperial schemes. The spread of Muslim communities in monsoon Asia between the twelfth and sixteenth centuries coincided with the development of Muslim trade networks. The main actors in this expansion of the medieval Muslim world were not sultans, soldiers, or scholars, but ordinary merchants whose main aim was to make a profit. The personality traits and ethical standards of Muslim traders and missionaries were the unique selling points that led Africans, Asians, and other people to embrace Islam (Ahmed & Yasmeen, 2020; Risso, 2018).

3.3 Theological Underpinning of Islamic and Halal Entrepreneurship

The socioeconomic aspirations of conscious Muslims are shaped and linked to religiosity (Wilson & Ayad, 2021). Furthermore, religion determines an individual's core values and beliefs and shapes their attitudes, behaviors, decisions, and entrepreneurial actions (Khurana et al., 2021; Ramadani et al., 2017). Because Islam covers all facets of life, it provides guidance in rituals, worship, and worldly activities (Muneeza & Mustapha, 2021). It is therefore not surprising that Islamic teachings encourage their followers to become active and innovative business owners and entrepreneurs (Kayed & Hassan, 2010). The theological underpinning of Islamic and Halal entrepreneurship is rooted in Maqasid al-Shariah. The term Maqasid al-Shari'ah means the goals of Shari'ah (Islamic law). Maqasid al-Shariah is used by Islamic jurists to analyze and evaluate bioethical issues to determine their compatibility and relevance to the principles of Islamic law (Yusuf & Raimi, 2021). The analysis of issues based on Maqasid al-Shariah is essentially based on three aspects: intention, method, and output/final goal, while the assessment of issues based on Maqasid al-Shariah is based on human interest hierarchy, inclusivity, and the degree of certainty (Ibrahim et al., 2019).

In the contemporary discourse, Duderija (2014) notes that Maqāṣid al-Sharīʿah also includes concepts such as (a) public interests (al masaliḥ al-ammah), (b) interests (al-masaliḥ al-murs), (c) juridical preference (istiḥsān), (d) presumption of continuity (istiḥsāb), and (e) avoidance of mischief (al-mafsadah). The five Maqāṣid al-Sharīʿah include safeguarding religion (Hifzul Deen), safeguarding souls (Hifzul Nafs), safeguarding intellect (Hifzul Aqeel), safeguarding offspring/lineage (Hifzul Nasl), and safeguarding wealth (Hifzul Mal). The application of the five Maqāṣid al-Sharīʿah to economics and entrepreneurship is discussed below.

i. Preservation of religion: All economic agents (governments, individuals, corporations) engaged in entrepreneurship are believed to exist to protect the sanctity of belief in God, as the lack of access to economic opportunities and employment can lead to poverty and disbelief.
ii. Preservation of life: Economic actors are expected to work together in economic activities and entrepreneurship to sustain the lives of poverty-stricken communities and individuals at the bottom of the social pyramid through Islam's mission of social justice.

iii. Preservation of intellect: All economic agents engaged in entrepreneurship, investment, and other economic activities are expected to support and protect intellectual integrity, intellectual property, research results, intellectual rigor, and sound science.
iv. Preservation of progeny: In the face of moral decadence, all economic actors must find new ways to protect their lineage and safeguard future generations through principled business relationships, ethical entrepreneurship, and noble business ethics, in order to prepare new generations who are resilient and disciplined to achieve socio-economic, environmental, and political development goals.
v. Preservation of wealth: All economic actors exist to preserve wealth and promote economic and financial activity through ethical institutional governance for long-term socio-economic benefits (Yusuf & Raimi, 2021)

Apart from the five aims of Islamic law discussed above, Ismail and Arshad (2009) have stated that in Islamic economics there are five principles that entrepreneurs and managers must consider for the benefit of society. These principles are:

(a) The principle of right and wrong: The Islamic economic system fundamentally distinguishes between what is permitted (halal) and what is forbidden (haram).

(b) The principle of use: People are obligated to make full use of the gifts bestowed on them by God within the limits of what is lawful (halal) and what is not lawful (haram) prescribed by Allah.

(c) The principle of moderation: Islam unequivocally discourages its followers from going beyond the limits set by Allah, emphasizing moderation and avoidance of extremism.

(d) The principle of economic liberty: Everyone is granted the freedom to be responsible in the world and to reward good deeds and punish bad deeds in the hereafter.

(e) The principle of justice: The Islamic principle of justice operates in production, distribution, consumption, exchange, and other aspects of economic life.

3.4 *Theoretical Underpinning of Islamic and Halal Entrepreneurship*

Three theories explain the emergence of Islamic and Halal entrepreneurship in modern times: the Maududian Affirmative Islamic Revivalism Theory, the Faith-Based Model (FBM), and the Theory of Islamic Revivalism. These theories provide insight into why these two ultra-religious forms of entrepreneurship have become widespread, particularly among Muslims, and have gained global recognition. According to the Maududian theory of affirmative Islamic revivalism, Muslims are motivated to revive their religion by avoiding undesirable and unethical socio-economic issues in society through a better understanding of the Qur'an, Sunna, and Islamic provisions (Ali, 2012; Yusuf & Raimi, 2021). Applied to Islamic and

Halal entrepreneurship, this theory suggests that Muslim entrepreneurs adopt a more ethical approach in their business practices, investments, and commercial transactions due to their enhanced knowledge of Islam and Islamic laws. On the other hand, the Faith-Based Model (FBM) is an ethical framework that explains how Islamic business models (such as Murabaha, Musharakah, and Ijarah) and Islamic social security (such as CSR, Sadaqat, Waqf, and Zakat) function in contemporary society to promote economic empowerment and address issues like illiteracy, poverty, and unemployment faced by marginalized individuals (Raimi et al., 2014; Raimi, Bello & Mobolaji, 2010). When applied to Islamic and Halal entrepreneurship, this theory suggests that Muslim entrepreneurs incorporate Islamic business models and social security measures into their ventures and business development to achieve the dual objectives of Al-Falah (success). As sole proprietors and entrepreneurs, they bear both economic and social responsibilities.

Finally, the theory of Islamic revivalism states that the socio-economic challenges and frustrations brought about by modernism have forced Muslims to reconsider the liberal conception of religion in avour of an Islamic lifestyle rooted in religious orthodoxy. The proponents of revivalism view Islam as a viable solution to poverty and other socioeconomic disadvantages faced by Muslims (Carvalho, 2009; Yusuf & Raimi, 2021). When applied to Islamic and Halal entrepreneurship, the theory simply explains that Muslim entrepreneurs embrace religious-ethical entrepreneurship, such as Islamic banking, the halal food and beverage business, fashion, media and leisure, Muslim-friendly tourism, halal medicines, and halal cosmetics, due to better awareness and rethinking of liberal thoughts about religion (Ajaib & Altunişik, 2022; Suhartanto et al., 2020; Yusuf & Raimi, 2021).

4 Misconceptions About Islamic and Halal Entrepreneurship

There are several misconceptions and myths about Islamic and Halal entrepreneurship. Firstly, many Muslims and non-Muslims perceive Islam only as a ritual, leading them to consider intrusion into socio-economic activities as extremism. This misinformed notion stems from a poor understanding of Islam. However, Islam actually offers its followers genuine opportunities to venture into different types of businesses while maintaining a balance between making business profits and pursuing spiritual rewards. The combination of economic and spiritual success in Islamic business ethics helps Muslim entrepreneurs avoid deviations from generally accepted business ethics and spirituality (Oukil, 2013). While the Western system uses material incentives to motivate individuals to engage in entrepreneurial activities, Islam mainly relies on moral incentives without neglecting the material incentive (Kayed & Hassan, 2010).

Secondly, Islamic entrepreneurship and halal entrepreneurship are not attempts to Islamize non-Muslims or impose Islamic thought on them. These ideals can be pursued not only in Muslim-majority countries but also in other contexts. Additionally, the products and services offered in these entrepreneurial endeavors do not necessarily have to be solely focused on the Muslim market (Gumusay, 2015). Islamic economics encompasses two belief-based concepts, namely, Islamic banking and Islamic finance, which provide alternative models within the ever-evolving landscape of plural economic systems. The accusation of Islamization arises due to the adherence of Islamic and halal entrepreneurship to Sharia principles derived from the Quran and Hadith. It should be noted that because these models are rooted in Islam, they must be guided by the two primary sources of Islamic law. The aspect of Islamic law that governs socio-economic affairs at the individual and collective levels is known as Fiqhu al-Mu'āmalāt. To ensure inclusivity, Islamic and halal entrepreneurship is subject to conventional laws and regulations enforced by governments and relevant agencies responsible for entrepreneurship and industry.

Thirdly, Islamic entrepreneurship is distrusted by some Muslims and criticized as a call to capitalism, particularly the excessive material acquisitions warned against in the Quran. The right attitude in Islam is modesty and balance. The Quran states: "Seek by means of the wealth that Allah has granted you the Abode of the Hereafter but forget not your share in this world and do good as Allah has been good to you and do not strive to create mischief in the land, for Allah loves not those who create mischief" (The Quran 28:77). According to Mahmud and Hoque (2015), Islamic entrepreneurship is a social duty that involves making basic products such as food, clothing, and shelter available to the buying public. Ideally, it is a collective duty of Muslims (Fardul Kifaya), but if it is not fulfilled, it becomes an individual duty (Fardul Ayn) for those who are able. In Muslim communities, it is imperative that individuals with entrepreneurial knowledge, skills, and abilities engage in entrepreneurship to produce and provide essential goods, services, and business solutions that meet people's needs. The Islamic jurists of the Shafi'i school of thought, such as Imam Ahmad bin Hanbal, Abu Hamid al-Ghazali, and Abu al-Farj Ibn al-Jawzi, agree that entrepreneurial activity must be perceived and treated as a social responsibility since life without taking on the responsibility of entrepreneurship is pointless (Abdul Hamid & Che, 2011; Mahmud & Hoque, 2015).

Fourthly, Islam is often perceived as a religion that hinders business development and entrepreneurship, with Muslim theorists only adopting Western and secular approaches and values that are compatible with Islam (Pistrui & Fahed-Sreih, 2010). However, this view is riddled with misinformation. Islam actually grants people free will and freedom to meet their needs using the resources that God provides on earth, based on Shariah principles (Shaheen & Polbitsyn, 2021). Therefore, it could be argued that Islamic entrepreneurship, Islamic finance, and halal entrepreneurship are religious models that aim to demystify the widespread misconception in the public sphere that Islam is a regressive religion that resists economic development (Ratten, Rammal, & Ramadani, 2017a, 2017b).

5 Conclusion, Implications, and Suggestions

The chapter is dedicated to discussing the historical, theological, and theoretical foundations of Islamic and Halal entrepreneurship in order to facilitate the understanding, acceptance, and dissemination of these deeply religious ideals. In the Critical Literature Review (CLR), we provide detailed explanations of the conceptual definitions of Islamic and Halal entrepreneurship. Additionally, we analyze the historical, theological, and theoretical foundations of Islamic and Halal entrepreneurship. Furthermore, we identify and report four misconceptions that Muslims and non-Muslims have about Islamic and Halal entrepreneurship as new religious concepts in the global business landscape. Finally, we make far-reaching suggestions regarding the identified misconceptions about Islamic and Halal entrepreneurship on a global scale.

This chapter presents three theoretical implications. Firstly, discussing the historical, theological, and theoretical underpinnings of Islamic and Halal entrepreneurship provides researchers and practitioners with a well-informed understanding of these religious and Sharia-compliant ideals. Secondly, providing evidence-based information to dispel misconceptions about Islamic and Halal entrepreneurship would strengthen the adoption and spread of this religious entrepreneurship among both well-informed Muslims and non-Muslims. Thirdly, linking Islamic and Halal entrepreneurship to three belief-based theories gives researchers a foundation and opportunity to base their research on any of these theories.

For the future, we suggest the following recommendations to address the misconceptions about Islamic and Halal entrepreneurship.

i. There is a need for more conceptual, theoretical, and empirical studies on Islamic and halal entrepreneurship to dispel misconceptions and misunderstandings about these alternative entrepreneurship models.
ii. Islamic universities, Islamic research centers, Islamic banks, and financial institutions, as enablers and strategic partners of Islamic and halal entrepreneurship, need to organize awareness programs and seminars for entrepreneurs and the general public on the prospects of these alternative entrepreneurial models for Muslims and Muslim communities, as the benefits cannot be overlooked.
iii. The public needs to be educated through the media, radio, newspapers, and schools that Islamic and halal entrepreneurship are religious models that only promote ethical entrepreneurship and socio-economic development based on Shari'ah principles. They pose no threats to non-Muslims.

References

Abdul Hamid, S., & Che, Z. S. (2011). Reconstructing entrepreneur's development based on al-Qur'an and al-hadith. *International Journal of Business and Social Science, 2*(9), 110–116.

Abdullah, M. A., & Azam, M. S. (2020a). Halal entrepreneurship from Maqasidal-Sharia'h perspective: Inseparable concept for Halalpreneurs. *Food Research., 4*(1), 34–42.

Abdullah, A., Abdullah, S., & Ramli, A. J. (2019). Entrepreneurship according to the hadeeth. *International Journal of Business and Management, 3*(4), 01–05.

Abdullah, M. A., & Azam, M. S. E. (2020). Halal entrepreneurship: concept and business opportunities. Entrepreneurship—Contemporary Issues, (Ed) Mladen Turuk, IntechOpen, https://doi.org/10.5772/intechopen.93657

Abdullah, M. A., & Azam, M. S. E. (2020c). Halal entrepreneurship from Maqasid-al-Sharia'h perspective: Inseparable concept for Halalpreneurs. *Food Research, 4*(1), 34–42.

Ahmed, T. S., & Yasmeen, B. N. (2020). A historical background of Muslim communities in Chennai-a study. *International Journal of Research in Social Sciences, 10*(1), 140–146.

Ajaib, N., Altunişik, R. (2022). Emerging Modest Fashion Industry: What Plays a Greater Role in Modest Dressing, Religion or Culture? Implications for Strategic Marketing. In: Alserhan, B. A., Ramadani, V., Zeqiri, J., Dana, LP. (eds.) Strategic Islamic Marketing. *Contributions to Management Science. Springer, Cham.* https://doi.org/10.1007/978-3-030-98160-0_16

Akram, H. W. (2022). Global halal business: A sectoral analysis. *International Journal of Business and Globalisation, 30*(1), 111–130.

A'la Mawdudi, S. A. (2013). *First principles of Islamic economics.* Kube Publishing Ltd.

Ali, J. A. (2012). *Islamic revivalism encounters the modern world: A Study of the Tabligh Jamaʿat.* Sterling Publishers.

Amir, H., & Abdukic, A. (2021). The spiritual nature based on ethics in the halal entrepreneurial industry. *Turkish Online Journal of Qualitative Inquiry, 12*(10), 6212–6236.

Bozeman, B., Fay, D., & Slade, C. P. (2013). Research collaboration in universities and academic entrepreneurship: The state-of-the-art. *The Journal of Technology Transfer, 38*(1), 1–67.

Carvalho, J. (2009) A theory of the islamic revival. Discussion Paper, Number 424, Department of Economics, University of Oxford. Available: http://tuvalu.santafe.edu/~bowles/TheoryIslamicRevival.pdf

Choudhury, M. A. (2008). Global ethics in the light of islamic political economy. *International Journal of Arab Culture, Management and Sustainable Development, 1*(1), 65–81.

Denham, K. (2019) Islamic finance 101: Debunking the common myths. City A.M. Limited. https://www.cityam.com/islamic-finance-101-debunking-the-common-myths/

Dilli, S., Elert, N., & Herrmann, A. M. (2018). Varieties of entrepreneurship: Exploring the institutional foundations of different entrepreneurship types through 'Varieties-of-Capitalism' arguments. *Small Business Economics, 51*, 293–320.

Duderija, A. (2014). Contemporary muslim reformist thought and maqāṣid cum maṣlaḥa approaches to islamic law: an introduction. In *Maqāṣid al-Sharīʿa and Contemporary Reformist Muslim Thought* (pp. 1–11). Palgrave Macmillan, New York

Eisenmann, T. R. (2013). Entrepreneurship: A working definition. *Harvard Business Review, 10*, 2013.

Gauthier, F. (2021). The halalisation of Islam. *Sociology of Islam, 9*(2), 131–151.

Gümüsay, A. A. (2015). Entrepreneurship from an Islamic perspective. *Journal of Business Ethics, 130*, 199–208.

Harizan, S. H. M., & Mustafa, M. S. (2020). Islamic entrepreneurship: analysis of research trend. *Islamiyyat, 42*(2), 71–84.

Hassan, A. (2016). Islamic ethical responsibilities for business and sustainable development. *Humanomics, 32*(1), 80–94.

Hassan, M. K., Kayed, R. N. & Oseni, U.A. (2013) Introduction to Islamic Banking and Finance: Principles and Practice. Pearson Education Limited, England

Hassan, M. K., Rabbani, M. R., & Chebab, D. (2021). Integrating Islamic finance and Halal industry: Current landscape and future-forward. *International Journal of Islamic Marketing and Branding, 6*(1), 60–78.

Herman, E. (2022). The interplay between digital entrepreneurship and sustainable development in the context of the EU digital economy: A multivariate analysis. *Mathematics, 10*(10), 1682. https://doi.org/10.3390/math10101682

Hitt, M. A., Ireland, R. D., Sirmon, D. G., & Trahms, C. A. (2011). Strategic entrepreneurship: Creating value for individuals, organizations, and society. *Academy of Management Perspectives, 25*(2), 57–75.

Hoque, N., Mamun, A., & Mamun, A. M. A. (2014). Dynamics and traits of entrepreneurship: An Islamic approach. *World Journal of Entrepreneurship, Management and Sustainable Development, 10*(2), 128–142.

Ibrahim, A. H., Rahman, N. N. A., Saifuddeen, S. M., & Baharuddin, M. (2019). Maqasid al-shariah based islamic bioethics: a comprehensive approach. *Journal of Bioethical Inquiry, 16*(3), 333–345.

Ismail, A. G., & Arshad, N. C. (2009). Islamic Economic System: From Principles to Microeconomics and Macroeconomics Fields. In *International Conference on Islamic Economics, Banking and Finance* (pp. 1–16).

Javaid, O. (2022). An Islamic vision and approach for entrepreneurship: Developing through a multi-stage comparative analysis of systems, ideologies and code of ethics. *International Journal of Ethics and Systems, 38*(1), 125–146.

Johan, Z. J., & Hussain, M. Z. (2019). What do bankers think about Halal financial services? *Journal of Emerging Economies & Islamic Research, 7*(2), 1–14.

Karahalil, E. (2020). Principles of halal-compliant fermentations: Microbial alternatives for the halal food industry. *Trends in Food Science & Technology*. https://doi.org/10.1016/j.tifs.2020.01.031

Kayed, R. N., & Hassan, M. K. (2010). Islamic entrepreneurship: A case study of Saudi Arabia. *Journal of Developmental Entrepreneurship, 15*(04), 379–413.

Kayed, R. N., & Hassan, M. K. (2013). *Islamic entrepreneurship*. Routledge.

Khurana, I., Ghura, A. S., & Dutta, D. K. (2021). The influence of religion on the humane orientation of entrepreneurs. *Journal of Small Business Management, 59*(3), 417–442.

Kuran, T. (2010). The scale of entrepreneurship in Middle Eastern history: Inhibitive roles of Islamic institutions. *The Invention of Enterprise: Entrepreneurship from Ancient Mesopotamia to Modern Times*, 62–87.

Machmud, A., & Hidayat, Y. M. (2020). Characteristics of Islamic entrepreneurship and the business success of SMEs in Indonesia. *Journal of Entrepreneurship Education, 23*(2), 1–16.

Madi, O. (2014). From Islamic radicalism to Islamic capitalism: The promises and predicaments of Turkish-Islamic entrepreneurship in a capitalist system (the case of IGIAD). *Middle Eastern Studies, 50*(1), 144–161.

Mahmud, T. B., & Hoque, S. (2015). Entrepreneurship: A Culture Embedded in The Religion of Islam. *European Journal of Business and Management, 7*(16), 12–26.

Mohamed, Z., Rezai, G., Shamsudin, M. N., & Chiew, E. F. C. (2008). Halal logo and consumers' confidence: What are the important factors. *Economic and Technology Management Review, 3*(1), 37–45.

Mohsin, A., Ramli, N., & Alkhulayfi, B. A. (2016). Halal tourism: Emerging opportunities. *Tourism Management Perspectives, 19*, 137–143.

Muneeza, A., & Mustapha, Z. (2021). Halal certification process for fisheries products in Maldives. *Journal of Islamic Marketing, 12*(2), 451–466. https://doi.org/10.1108/JIMA-02-2019-0035

Oukil, M. S. (2013). Entrepreneurship and entrepreneurs in an Islamic context. *Journal of Islamic and Human Advanced Research, 3*(3), 111–131.

Pistrui, D., & Fahed-Sreih, J. (2010). Islam, entrepreneurship and business values in the Middle East. *International Journal of Entrepreneurship and Innovation Management, 12*(1), 107–118.

Prange, S. R. (2018). *Monsoon Islam: Trade and faith on the medieval Malabar Coast*. Cambridge University Press.

Prayag, G. (2020). Halal tourism: Looking into the future through the past. *Tourism Recreation Research, 45*(4), 557–559.

Rahman, F. (1980). Islam: Legacy and Contemporary Challenge. *Islamic Studies, 19*(4), 235–246.

Raimi, L., Bello, M. A., Mobolaji, H. I. (2010). Faith-based and Business System Models: A Policy Response to the Millennium Development Goals (MDGS) in Nigeria. *Humanomics*, 26(2), 124–138. Emerald Publishing UK

Raimi, L., Dodo, F., & Sule, R. (2022). Comparative discourse of social enterprises in the developed and developing countries using theory of change framework: a qualitative analysis. In Social Entrepreneurs (Vol. 18, pp. 29–54). Emerald Publishing Limited.

Raimi, L., Panait, M., Gigauri, I., & Apostu, S. A. (2023). Thematic review of motivational factors, types of uncertainty, and entrepreneurship strategies of transitional entrepreneurship among ethnic minorities, immigrants, and women entrepreneurs. *Journal of Risk and Financial Management, 16*(2), 83. https://doi.org/10.3390/jrfm16020083

Raimi, L., Patel, A., & Adelopo, I. (2014). Corporate social responsibility, Waqf System and Zakat System as Faith-Based model for poverty reduction. *World Journal of Entrepreneurship, Management and Sustainable Development, 10*(3), 228–242.

Ramadani, V., Dana, L. P., Gërguri-Rashiti, S., & Ratten, V. (2017). An introduction to entrepreneurship and management in an Islamic context. *Entrepreneurship and Management in an Islamic Context* (pp. 1–5). Springer.

Ramadani, V. (2021). Islamic entrepreneurship. In *World Encyclopedia of Entrepreneurship* (pp. 457–470). Edward Elgar Publishing.

Ratten, V., Ramadani, V., Dana, L. P., & Gërguri-Rashiti, S. (2017). Islamic entrepreneurship and management: Future research directions. *Entrepreneurship and management in an Islamic context*, 227–242.

Ratten, V., Rammal, H., & Ramadani, V. (2017). Islamic finance: An entrepreneurial management perspective. *Entrepreneurship and Management in an Islamic Context*, 119–132.

Razak, T. M. T. A., Hairi, N. A., Rahman, N. A. A., Shamsuddin, Z., Bin Jaafar, A. B., Rahim, H., & Haron, M. S. (2022). The concept of islamic entrepreneurship in forming influential personality: a personal analysis of the prophet saw. *International Journal of Early Childhood Special Education, 14*(3), 3097–3103.

Risso, P. A. (2018). Merchants and faith: Muslim commerce and culture in the Indian Ocean. Routledge.

Salaheldeen, M., Battour, M., Nazri, M. A., Bustamam, U. S. A., & Hashim, A. J. C. M. (2022). The perception of success in the halal market: developing a halal entrepreneurship success scale. Journal of Islamic Marketing, *14*(3) 799–825. https://doi.org/10.1108/JIMA-10-2021-0341

Saunders M, Lewis P, Thornhill A (eds.) (2012). Research methods for business students. Pearson Education Limited, Harlow

Saunders, M. N., & Rojon, C. (2011). On the attributes of a critical literature review. *Coaching: An International Journal of Theory, Research and Practice*, *4*(2), 156–162.

Shaheen, N., & Polbitsyn, S. N. (2021). The Specifics of Entrepreneurships in Islamic Countries. *Стратегии развития социальных общностей, институтов и территорий.—Т. 1.—Екатеринбург, 1*, 125–129

Soltanian, M., Zailani, S., Iranmanesh, M., & Aziz, A. A. (2016). Motivations of SME entrepreneurs to become halalpreneurs. *Journal of Science and Technology Policy Management, 7*(2), 173–189. https://doi.org/10.1108/JSTPM-07-2015-0023

Stevenson, H. H. (2000). Why entrepreneurship has won. Coleman White Paper, USASBE Plenary Address, February 16–19

Suhartanto, Dwi, et al. (2020). Does religiosity matter for customer loyalty? Evidence from halal cosmetics. *Journal of Islamic Marketing* 12.8: 1521–1534

Temizhan, A., Tandogan, I., Donderici, O., & Demirbas,. (2000). The effects of Ramadan fasting on blood lipid levels. *American Journal of Medicine, 109*, 341–342.

The Qur'an, English Translation and notes by Sahih International, Jeddah, Kingdom of Saudi Arabia. https://muslimcouncil.org.hk/wp-content/uploads/2019/01/Quran-English.pdf

Wilson, J. A. J., & Ayad, N. I. A. (2022). Religiosity and Egyptian Muslim millennials' views on offensive advertising. *Journal of Islamic Marketing, 13*(12), 2759–2777. https://doi.org/10.1108/JIMA-05-2021-0171

World Economic Forum (2017). Islamic finance could be the answer to Africa's growth problems. https://www.weforum.org/agenda/2017/10/islamic-finance-could-be-the-answer-to-africas-growth-problems/

Yu, T. F. L. (2001). Entrepreneurial alertness and discovery. *The Review of Austrian Economics, 14*, 47–63.

Yusuf, T. O., & Raimi, L. (2021). How compatible are SDGs with divine principles? A critical literature review (CLR). *Islamic Wealth and the SDGs: Global Strategies for Socio-economic Impact*, 3–27

Zarabozo, J. A. D. M. (2007). *What is Islam*? Under-Secretariat of Publications and Research, Ministry of Islamic Affairs, Endowments, Da'wah, and Guidance. http://www.sabbora.com/wp-content/uploads/2016/06/What-is-Islam-14x21-Final.pdf

[illegible]

Understanding Islamic and Halal Entrepreneurship from the Maqasidul Shari'ah Perspective

Ibrahim Adeniyi Abdur-Rauf and Lukman Raimi

Abstract There have been paradigm shifts in entrepreneurship models in the global business landscape, including the Muslim world. However, the paradigm shifts that have given rise to Islamic and Halal entrepreneurship as deeply religious models have not been addressed in a manner that can be easily understood by both Muslims and non-Muslims. In this chapter, we aim to discuss Islamic and Halal entrepreneurship within the context of the Maqasidul Shari'ah perspective in order to enhance the understanding of these concepts among professionals, researchers, and practitioners in the converging Islamic economy. We have conducted a critical review of scientific papers to seek answers to our research questions. The collected data were systematically analyzed using a critical literature review (CLR) approach. Drawing insights from 54 articles that were critically reviewed, we have provided detailed explanations of the definitions of Islam, Halal, Islamic Entrepreneurship, Halal Entrepreneurship, and Maqasidul Shari'ah. Additionally, we have established strong connections between Islamic entrepreneurship and Halal entrepreneurship, as well as the Maqasidul Shari'ah perspective. Finally, we have made suggestions on how to maintain the interrelationships among these three concepts in light of the misconceptions that have occurred in the emerging Islamic economy. This chapter yields three theoretical implications.

Keywords Halal entrepreneurship · Islamic entrepreneurship · Maqasidul Shari'ah

I. A. Abdur-Rauf (✉)
Department of Shariah, Universiti Sultan Zainal Abidin, Kuala Terengganu, Terengganu, Malaysia
e-mail: abdurraufadeniyi@gmail.com

L. Raimi
Department of Business Administration, Universiti Brunei Darussalam, Gadong, Brunei

L. Raimi et al. (eds.), *Contemporary Discourse of Halal and Islamic Entrepreneurship*,
https://doi.org/10.1007/978-981-99-6427-7_2

1 Introduction

There have been paradigm shifts in entrepreneurship models in the global business landscape, including within the Muslim world. However, these paradigm shifts, which have given rise to Islamic and Halal entrepreneurship, have had a significant impact on marketing, services, retail, finance, investment, banking, and insurance in Muslim communities (Liizzah et al., 2023; Maksum & Kamaludin, 2023). The new ultra-religious models of entrepreneurship offer Muslim entrepreneurs and ethical communities a fresh approach to conducting business in full compliance with Maqasidul Shari'ah, also known as the fundamental principles of Islamic law (Soltanian et al., 2016; Janssen & Bacq, 2017). Conventional entrepreneurship is founded on the belief that entrepreneurs are the pillars of the market economy, established with the objective of maximizing profits by adding value, creating jobs, and providing multiple benefits to consumers (Janssen & Bacq, 2017). In contrast, both Islamic entrepreneurship and Halal entrepreneurship generate value, create jobs, and offer numerous benefits to consumers. However, the goal of Muslim entrepreneurs and Halalpreneurs is the realization of Al-Falah, a religious-economic concept that signifies double prosperity, not only in this world but also in the hereafter (Rafiki & Wahab, 2013; Suselo, 2018). The Islamic perspective of success has also been described in four dimensions: Islamic success, economic success, social success, and ecological success (Salaheldeen et al., 2023).

Islamic and Halal entrepreneurship both share roots with Islam and Halal concepts. Halal, in Islamic law, strictly means lawful, acceptable, or free from legally binding restrictions. However, the meaning of Halal has been enriched and expanded to become a branding platform where entrepreneurs can expand their ventures (Salindal, 2019). Moreover, the terms Halal entrepreneurship and Islamic entrepreneurship (or Halal-oriented entrepreneurship) can be used interchangeably (Ramadani et al., 2015; Soltanian et al., 2016). Although, Islamic entrepreneurship arguably underpins halal entrepreneurship, as the latter involves the process of entrepreneurs establishing and running businesses according to Islamic principles in all sectors, including the halal industry (Ratten et al., 2017). The idea of entrepreneurship is therefore not new to Islam and Muslims, as evidenced by the Prophet (peace and blessings be upon him) and his followers who practiced it as a respectable profession.

To distinguish Halal entrepreneurship from conventional entrepreneurship, which does not differentiate between halal and non-halal activities, Islamic economists and theorists have introduced the terms "Islamic entrepreneurship" and "halal entrepreneurship". Muslim entrepreneurs and Halalpreneurs operate in various critical sectors of the global economy, including the rapidly expanding halal sector, which encompasses the entire Islamic economy. The key stakeholders in the global halal market include Muslim halal entrepreneurs, corporate halal-certified companies, regulators, halal professionals, and halal consumers/enthusiasts. Furthermore, while Halal originally held purely religious significance, it has now become a branding construct that enables business owners who adhere to the Halal philosophy to expand their businesses while adhering to Islamic ethics (Salindal, 2019).

In clear terms, Islamic entrepreneurship is based on three pillars: the entrepreneurial pillar, the socio-economic/ethical pillar, and the spiritual-religious pillar (Ramadani et al., 2015).

Meanwhile, conventional entrepreneurship differs from Islamic entrepreneurship as explained earlier (Sallam, 2013). The variant of conventional entrepreneurship that closely resembles Islamic entrepreneurship is social entrepreneurship. However, from a Western perspective, social entrepreneurship is primarily considered as a form of entrepreneurship with dual objectives: a combination of economic and social impact goals. Nevertheless, since this perspective lacks religious influence, it can be argued that it does not align with religious principles (Mulyaningsih & Ramadani, 2017).

Furthermore, Islamic entrepreneurship and Halal entrepreneurship are carried out in compliance with the Maqasidul Shari'ah, which clearly refers to the higher goals of Shari'ah rules. These goals aim to improve the regular functioning of society by promoting the common good (maslahah) and social and economic justice (Yusuf & Raimi, 2021). Islamic and Halal entrepreneurship, being related to Maqasidul Shari'ah, actively avoid engaging in activities that have the potential to harm people, the environment, and society as a whole (Hunter, 2014). Both forms of entrepreneurship represent innovative business models with a social focus, similar to social entrepreneurship. However, they surpass social entrepreneurship as they are based on the two primary sources of Islamic law, the Qur'an and As-Sunnah (Abd Muin et al., 2019).

We make two contributions to the existing body of knowledge in this emerging field. First, we expand practical knowledge about Islamic and Halal entrepreneurship, which is still in its early stages. Second, we correct misconceptions held by both Muslims and non-Muslims about these two deeply religious concepts. Therefore, this chapter aims to advance Islamic and Halal entrepreneurship by discussing them in the context of the Maqasidul Shari'ah perspective. Currently, non-Muslim entrepreneurs in the halal industry must have a clear understanding and accurate perception of the halal concept. This understanding will help create a halal business environment and improve compliance with Halal standards among participants and key players in the industry. It will also encourage the investment of resources in Halal research and development, positioning Singapore as a leader in the Halal market (Mohamad et al., 2015). This chapter contributes significantly to Islamic entrepreneurship theory and the practice of the halal industry, specifically addressing the following Thematic Research Questions (RQs):

Research question 1: What are the bases of Islamic and Halal entrepreneurship in the existing literature?

Research question 2: In what ways are Islamic and Halal entrepreneurship related to the Maqasidul Shari'ah perspective?

The research questions mentioned above would assist readers, researchers, entrepreneurs, and other stakeholders in comprehending, adopting, and promoting these highly religious ideals of entrepreneurship to achieve more effective outcomes for all stakeholders in the rapidly advancing global economy. Ultimately, a deeper understanding of Islamic and Halal entrepreneurship from the perspective of Maqasidul Shari'ah would enhance the growth of Islamic start-ups and small and medium-sized enterprises (SMEs) operated by Muslim entrepreneurs and Halal-preneurs. There are six sections in this chapter. Section 1 provides the introductory background to the discourse. Section 2 encompasses the methodology. Section 3 focuses on the Critical Literature Review (CLR), specifically emphasizing conceptual definitions of Islam, Halal, Islamic, and Halal entrepreneurship. Section 4 delves into the concept of Maqasidul Shari'ah, its applications, and its relationship to Islamic and Halal entrepreneurship. Finally, Sect. 5 concludes with a summary of the discussion, implications, and limitations.

2 Methodology

To achieve the aforementioned objectives, a qualitative research methodology was employed for developing this chapter. In order to address the research questions, we conducted a critical review of academic papers to define Islamic and Halal entrepreneurship, as well as their connections to Maqasidul Shari'ah, following the methods outlined by Yusuf and Raimi (2021) and Abdullah and Azam (2020a, 2020b). We gathered non-numerical data from 54 articles and texts, which were systematically analyzed through a critical literature review (CLR). Furthermore, we critically analyzed current articles and texts pertaining to the Halal industry and the global Islamic economy. The term CLR refers to a systematic analysis and evaluation of multiple articles and texts on a given topic, which, when objectively assessed and analyzed using appropriate language, can contribute to new knowledge, additional facts, and a more comprehensive understanding (Saunders & Rojon, 2011; Saunders et al., 2012). To ensure a certain level of objectivity in the application of purposive sampling when selecting academic papers from the academic Google database, we followed the inclusion criteria of recency, relevance and reliability of articles outlined by Raimi et al. (2023).

3 Critical Literature Review

This section critically discusses the conceptual definitions of Islam, Halal, Islamic, and Halal entrepreneurship.

3.1 Defining Islam and Halal

Both Islam and Halal underpin these discourses. Islam is a monotheistic religion practiced by over 1.8 billion people worldwide, making it the second-largest religion in the world (Shukri, 2022). As a religion, its theological foundation is based on the belief in one God (Allah) and the Prophethood of Muhammad, while its core principles or pillars are summarized in the Five Pillars of Islam, namely: The Regular Creed (Shahada), daily prayer (Salat), offerings (Zakat), fasting (Sawm), and pilgrimage to Mecca (Hajj) based on the consensus of Muslim and non-Muslim scholars (Abu-Raiya, 2015; Cornell, 2007; Kettell, 2011; Meidina & Mokan, 2023). Beyond rituals, the teachings of Islam include socioeconomic, regulatory, and moral issues such as respect for all human beings, peaceful coexistence, diversity, family values, social justice, and the pursuit of knowledge for the advancement of human civilization (Albrithen, 2023; Nakissa, 2023), without excluding art and aesthetics, education, medicine, culture, literature, science, technology, and business (Mohamed, 2023; Weick et al., 2023; Yusuf & Raimi, 2021). This explains why Islam is called a comprehensive religion.

The term "halal" literally means an activity or something that is permitted or lawful in Islamic law (Yusuf & Raimi, 2021). The conceptualization of halal is one of the most important concepts in contemporary Islamic economic research (Baran, 2021). Its meaning extends and applies to all aspects of human behavior, whether social, personal, economic, cultural, or political. Furthermore, Islam bases its conception of entrepreneurship on three interrelated pillars: the entrepreneurial, the religio-spiritual, and ultimately the socio-economic/ethical (Salindal, 2019). However, halal entrepreneurship refers to a concept in which halal is viewed as an entrepreneurial approach to creatively using opportunities to achieve social justice and economic rewards on an equal footing (Faizal et al., 2013). Halal used to be considered solely a religious matter but has now evolved into a marketing tool for business owners wishing to market their products internationally (Kayed & Hassan, 2010). In other words, Islam warmly welcomes all Muslims to be entrepreneurs in their lives by outlining the guidelines that all Muslims should adhere to, which are extracted from the Quran and Hadith (Karia & Asaari, 2016). One of the fastest-growing markets is the global halal market and the halal food business. Malaysia has been a leader in the halal sector since 1974 (Ramadani et al., 2015).

The emergence of Islamic and Halal entrepreneurship as alternative models is timely because the halal industry is estimated to be worth trillions of dollars annually. The products and services of the Halal industry are increasingly accepted by non-Muslims, creating opportunities for producing countries. The industry focuses on bringing a better quality of life to the world, and Halal products are recognized worldwide as the benchmark for safety and quality assurance (Mohamad et al., 2015). Malaysia is arguably the first nation in the world to adopt halal food indicators, ahead of the United Arab Emirates and Australia, where halal entrepreneurship has significantly increased (Khalek, 2018).

3.2 Understanding Islamic Entrepreneurship

Entrepreneurship, whether Islamic or non-Islamic, refers to the discovery and creation of opportunities by individuals and groups who are alert, wise, and attentive to the external environment (Yu, 2001). The understanding of entrepreneurship includes the pursuit of opportunities beyond the resources controlled by the entrepreneur (Stevenson, 2000). In comparison, Islamic entrepreneurship is defined as the perspective on how businesses and other economic activities are created, managed, and grown in the context of an Islamic economy and society (Kayed & Hassan, 2013). Correspondingly, Hoque et al. (2014) define Islamic entrepreneurship as the process of starting a business to produce goods or provide services that are halal to make reasonable profits, while conducting business activities in accordance with Islamic teachings, principles of social responsibility, religious business ethics, and moral values. It is not a business model limited to Muslim entrepreneurs but is open to non-Muslims and all ethical enthusiasts who share the values of Islamic entrepreneurship. Indeed, many non-Muslim entrepreneurs in different parts of the world have adopted Islamic principles in their businesses and have seen the benefits that come with this approach. The tenets of Islamic entrepreneurship include the concept of tawhid (the oneness of God), the concept of zakat (charitable donation), the concept of justice and fairness, and the concept of risk sharing.

Islamic entrepreneurship may initially appear similar to conventional entrepreneurship, but a closer examination reveals a fundamental difference in their underlying philosophies. Conventional entrepreneurship aims to maximize profit for business enterprises or maximize social welfare for social enterprises. On the other hand, Islamic entrepreneurship seeks a double success, known as "al-falah," which encompasses prosperity in two dimensions. The first dimension involves economic prosperity, profitability, and the maximization of social well-being in worldly life. The second dimension focuses on attaining success in the afterlife by addressing socio-economic and environmental issues through entrepreneurial activities (Abdullahi & Ramli, 2019). In essence, Islamic entrepreneurship represents a comprehensive approach to business that integrates the rights of God and the rights of humanity, all while pursuing economic gain in business ventures.

3.3 Understanding Halal Entrepreneurship

In both Muslim and non-Muslim economies, entrepreneurship plays a crucial role in human existence (Petrevska et al., 2023). However, in Islam, entrepreneurship is viewed as being intimately connected to the religion, and it follows a distinct business model called halalpreneurship (Wilson, 2014). The infusion of Islamic values brings about a transformation in both the entrepreneurial process itself and the individuals involved, leading to the emergence of terms such as halalpreneurs and halalpreneurship (Abdullah & Azam, 2020a, 2020b). Moreover, from an Islamic standpoint, entrepreneurship can be described as a social process that extends across various domains of activity beyond just the economic sphere (Tok & Kaminski, 2018).

Besides, Halalpreneurship is a concept in Islam that encompasses entrepreneurship within the framework of Shari'ah, including Aqeedah, Fiqh, and Akhlaq. It emphasizes man's role as Khalifa to help the world develop and prosper, and entrepreneurship should contribute to the well-being and prosperity of society, the Ummah, and humanity. The term Halalpreneurs, on the other hand, refers to Muslim entrepreneurs who manufacture goods and services that comply with Islamic laws known as Maqasidul Shari'ah. Even non-Muslim entrepreneurs can be considered Halalpreneurs if they follow Shari'ah Laws in their products and services for the benefit of the Ummah (Muslim community) and humanity. This is permissible based on the concept of maslahah or public interest (Abdullah & Azam, 2020a, 2020b). Halalpreneurship differs from conventional entrepreneurship in terms of what is produced, how it is produced, for whom it is produced, drivers and perceptions of business success, the manner of stakeholder management, fear of God, and other ethical standards (Abdullah & Azam, 2020a, 2020b).

4 Concept of Maqasidul Shari'ah and Applications

From the perspective of Islamic jurisprudence, the concept of Maqasidul Shari'ah refers to the fundamental goals of Islamic law. Similarly, Ibn Ashur (2006) explained that the Arabic word Maqasid (plural maqsad) denotes goals or purposes, and when it refers to Shari'ah, i.e., Maqasidul Shari'ah, it specifically refers to the goals and purposes of Shari'ah. The term Maqasidul Shari'ah is derived from two Arabic words: Maqasid, which means intentions or goals, and Shari'ah, which refers to Islamic law (Bahri, 2020). The principles of Maqasidul Shari'ah are based on the belief that the objective of Islamic law is to promote the well-being of people and protect their five rights (Yusuf & Raimi, 2021). These principles are derived from the Qur'an and Sunna and are utilized to interpret and apply Islamic law in all aspects of Muslim social, economic, and political life, with the aim of benefiting all members of society.

Auda (2022) noted that the application of Maqasidul Shari'ah extends to various areas of Islamic law, including family law, criminal law, business ethics, and financial law. In family law, the principle of Maqasidul Shari'ah is applied to ensure the protection of women's and children's rights and to promote the stability of the family unit. In criminal law, the principle of Maqasidul Shari'ah is utilized to promote justice and safeguard the rights of the accused. In business ethics and financial law, the principle of Maqasidul Shari'ah ensures that economic transactions are conducted fairly, transparently, and free from haram practices such as gambling, usury, exploitation, extortion, and procedural injustice (Amin, 2021; Auda, 2022; Bahri, 2020).

Historically, however, Hamid-Al-Ghazali (d. 1111) was the first scholar credited with expressing the concept of Maqasidul Shari'ah in his discourse. He asserted that Maslaha was God's ultimate purpose in revealing divine law and that his aim was the preservation of five fundamental aspects of human well-being: religion, life, intellect, lineage, and property (Opwis, 2007). Although the human need model and the notion of Maqasid in Islam date back to 1399 CE in 1946 (Khan & Ghifari, 1992). Connecting Maqasidul Shari'ah with entrepreneurship (Islamic and Halal entrepreneurship) obligates the need for Muslim entrepreneurs to act by making money while adhering to Islamic rules, serving the buying public in order to understand the aims and purposes of Shari'ah, which includes five basic areas necessary for peaceful life according to the Qur'an and Sunnah.

There is a consensus among scholars that there are five key areas that must be present for mankind to live peacefully in this world in accordance with the Quran and Sunnah (Yusuf & Raimi, 2021). Overall, the general and specific applications of Maqasidul Shari'ah by Muslim entrepreneurs and halalpreneurs are based on the views of several scholars (Bahri, 2020; Amin, 2021; Abdullah & Azam, 2020a, 2020b; Yusuf & Raimi, 2021; Auda, 2022), covering the five areas discussed below.

a. **Protection of Religion**: In general, Muslim leaders must be able to uphold and respect the rights of all religions that existed before Islam, not just Islam, allowing them to freely practice their rituals. They should also consider their demands and ensure the proper management of their financial resources. The Qur'an warns: "Let there be no compulsion in religion, for the truth stands out clearly from falsehood. So whoever renounces false gods and believes in Allah has certainly grasped the firmest, unfailing handhold. And Allah is All-Hearing, All-Knowing" (Q2:256). This principle is aimed at creating an inclusive environment. However, Muslim entrepreneurs also have a responsibility to protect the sanctity of belief in God while engaging in entrepreneurship, as a lack of access to economic opportunities and employment can lead to poverty and disbelief.
b. **Protection of Life**: In general, Islam forbids the termination of life except for justifiable reasons determined by the courts. This also extends to abstaining from the consumption or production of dangerous goods and products that can lead to killing, murder, or loss of life. Furthermore, it is essential to avoid causing harm to others, as Allah has prohibited it. In cases of unjust killings, the successor of the victim has the authority to seek justice, but it is crucial to exercise restraint and not excessively take lives. In fact, the law supports this notion. Allah warns against the killing of children out of fear of poverty, emphasizing that He provides for both them and their parents. Thus, killing them is a grave sin (Q17:31). Muslim entrepreneurs, as economic actors, are expected to collaborate in economic activities and entrepreneurship to sustain the lives of impoverished communities and individuals at the bottom of the social hierarchy, in line with Islam's mission of social justice.
c. **Protection of lineage and future offspring**: In general, Islam strongly advises people to get married and forbids any sexual relations before marriage. This principle applies to promoting sustainable development, specifically by fostering a development process that caters to the present generation without causing harm to future generations. Allah counsels: "Do not kill your children for fear of poverty. We provide for them and for you. Surely killing them is a heinous sin" (Q17:31). Additionally, the story of Zachariah serves as a reminder. He

called upon his Lord, saying: "My Lord! Do not leave me alone [childless] when You are the best of inheritors" (Q21:89). These verses emphasize the importance of Muslim entrepreneurs designing business models that protect the human lineage and future generations through principled business relationships, ethical entrepreneurship, and noble business ethics. This is crucial in preparing new generations to be resilient and disciplined in their pursuit of socio-economic, environmental, and political development goals.

d. **Protection of Intellect or Faculty of Reason**: Islam prohibits the consumption of substances such as alcohol and intoxicants that can harm the brain and impair intellectual abilities. Allah warns, "Many are the Jinns and men we have made for Hell: They have hearts wherewith they understand not, eyes wherewith they see not, and ears wherewith they hear not. They are like cattle, nay more misguided: for they are heedless (of warning)" (Q7: 179). This prohibition also extends to trading in illicit substances and heinous products. When applied to Islamic and Halal entrepreneurship, this principle emphasizes that Muslim entrepreneurs involved in business activities should uphold intellectual integrity, protect intellectual property, prioritize research outcomes, maintain intellectual rigor, and support sound science. These actions contribute to sustainable development, human development, and the safeguarding of intellectual capabilities.
e. **Protection of Material Wealth**: Islam encourages people to pursue the creation, utilization, and preservation of wealth in ethical and lawful manners. For this reason, certain unfair business practices, such as usury (riba), are prohibited in Islam. Allah warns: "And take provisions with you, but indeed, the best provision is the consciousness of Allah" (Quran 2:197). "And do not approach the orphan's property except in the best manner until he reaches maturity. And give full measure and weight in justice" (Quran 6:152). "And those who, when they spend, do so not excessively or sparingly but are moderate in between" (Quran 25:67). Those who steal someone else's property are also subject to severe punishment. Specifically, this principle explains that Muslim entrepreneurs exist to preserve prosperity and promote economic and financial activity through ethical institutional leadership for long-term socioeconomic benefits.

4.1 Islamic Entrepreneurship and Maqasidul Shari'ah

The relationship between Islamic entrepreneurship and Maqasidul Shari'ah is based on the principles of Islamic law, which govern the economic activities of Muslim entrepreneurs. Muslims who practice Islamic entrepreneurship are obligated to uphold five human rights, namely: the preservation of faith, human life, intellect, posterity, and property. In other words, Muslim entrepreneurs are expected to conduct their business in accordance with the five principles of Maqasidul Shari'ah.

In practice, the relationship between Islamic entrepreneurship and Maqasidul Shari'ah has several implications. First, Muslim entrepreneurs are expected to conduct their business in an ethical and socially responsible manner. Therefore, they must avoid engaging in activities that are harmful to society, such as making or selling products that are forbidden in Islam, such as alcohol or pork. Second, Muslim entrepreneurs are expected to be transparent and honest in their dealings and avoid fraud, deception, or any unfair practices. Third, Muslim entrepreneurs encourage the creation of wealth and the allocation of resources in a way that is fair and just and benefits society. Consequently, they are expected to create employment opportunities, invest in social welfare projects, and contribute to the development of the communities in which they operate. Overall, the relationship between Islamic entrepreneurship and Maqasidul Shari'ah is best described as mutual reinforcement and self-regulation in conformity with Islamic principles.

4.2 *Halal Entrepreneurship and Maqasidul Shari'ah*

Halal Entrepreneurship and Maqasidul Shari'ah are closely related principles in Islamic finance, ethical investing, and Halal standards/compliance. Maqasidul Shari'ah refers to the aims and purposes of Islamic law, while Halal entrepreneurship refers to the application of Islamic law in business practices, aligning with Islamic values. The primary objective of Maqasidul Shari'ah is to promote societal well-being, which is achieved through the implementation of Halal principles in business practices. Halal entrepreneurship, therefore, follows the principles of Maqasidul Shari'ah to ensure businesses operate in accordance with Islamic law and values. The application of Halal entrepreneurship in business practices has several implications. Firstly, it requires entrepreneurs in various fields to adhere to a set of Halal guidelines and principles derived from Islamic law. Secondly, Halalpreneurs must utilize the principles of Maqasidul Shari'ah to guide their business decisions, ensuring that their operations benefit society and uphold the fundamental rights of individuals. In summary, Halal Entrepreneurship and Maqasidul Shari'ah are interconnected. By adhering to Islamic ethical principles regarding Halal standards, procedures, reports, and disclosures, Halal entrepreneurship aligns with Maqasidul Shari'ah.

5 Conclusion, Implications, and Limitations

The chapter discusses Islamic and Halal entrepreneurship in the context of the Maqasidul Shari'ah perspective, aiming to enhance the understanding of these concepts among professionals, researchers, and practitioners in the growing Islamic economy. At the end of the Critical Literature Review (CLR), detailed explanations are provided for the conceptual definitions of Islam, Halal, Islamic Entrepreneurship, Halal Entrepreneurship, and Maqasidul Shari'ah. Additionally, solid relationships are established between Islamic and Halal entrepreneurship and the Maqasidul Shari'ah perspective. Finally, suggestions are made on how to maintain the relationship between Islamic and Halal entrepreneurship and Maqasidul Shari'ah in light of misconceptions in the emerging Islamic economy. Three theoretical implications emerge from this chapter.

In practice, the links between Islamic entrepreneurship, Halal entrepreneurship, and Maqasidul Shari'ah have five implications. Firstly, Muslim entrepreneurs are expected to conduct their business in an ethical and socially responsible manner. Therefore, Muslim entrepreneurs must avoid engaging in activities that are harmful to society, such as manufacturing or selling counterfeit products and articles forbidden in Islam, such as alcohol or pork. Secondly, Muslim entrepreneurs are expected to be transparent and honest in their dealings, avoiding fraud, deception, or unfair practices that have rocked conventional entrepreneurship. Thirdly, Muslim entrepreneurs are expected to pursue wealth creation and resource allocation in a manner that is fair and just and benefits society. Consequently, they are expected to create employment opportunities, invest in social welfare projects, and contribute to the development of the communities in which they operate. Fourthly, the Halalpreneurs engaged in various fields of entrepreneurship are expected to adhere to a set of Halal guidelines and principles derived from Islamic law, especially Islamic business ethics. Lastly, the principles of Maqasidul Shari'ah must be used by Halalpreneurs to guide their business decisions and ensure the business operates in a way that benefits society and promotes the five rights of the people.

Commendable as the findings of this chapter are, they represent a preliminary examination of Islamic and Halal entrepreneurship in the context of the Maqasidul Shari'ah perspective, based on a limited body of scholarly work. Given the generic context of the chapter's contribution, a more specific field investigation is imperative for future studies. Therefore, the insightful findings of the current study must be empirically verified. In this context, the options of a survey, interview, ethnography, focus groups, and case studies are proposed to validate some of the insights expressed in this chapter.

References

Abd Muin, M. A., Abdullah, S., & Che Omar, A. (2019). The fiqh method in Islamic social entrepreneurship: an introduction. In *Islamic Development Management* (pp. 225–238). Springer.

Abdullah, M. A., & Azam, M. S. E. (2020a). Halal entrepreneurship from Maqasidul Shari'ah perspective: Inseparable concept for Halalpreneurs. *Food Research, 4*(1), 34–42.

Abdullah, M. A., & Azam, M. S. E. (2020b). Halal entrepreneurship: concept and business opportunities. In *Entrepreneurship*. IntechOpen.

Abu-Raiya, H. (2015). Working with religious Muslim clients: A dynamic, Qura'nic-based model of psychotherapy. *Spirituality in Clinical Practice, 2*(2), 120.

Albrithen, A. (2023). The Islamic basis of social work in the modern world. *International Journal of Social Work Values and Ethics, 171.*

Ali, A. Y. (2001). *English translation of the Holy Quran.* Lushena Books.

Ali, M. A., Kabil, M., Alayan, R., Magda, R., & Dávid, L. D. (2021). Entrepreneurship ecosystem performance in Egypt: An empirical study based on the global entrepreneurship index (Gei). *Sustainability, 13*(13), 7171.

Almari, J. (2014). *Social entrepreneurship in practice: The multifaceted nature of social entrepreneurship and the role of the state within an Islamic context*. University of Oulu.
Amin, H. (2021). *Lectures in Islamic banking*. Universiti Malaysia Sabah Press.
Auda, J. (2022). *Maqasidul Shari'ah as Philosophy of Islamic Law*. Occasional papers series 14. International Institute of Islamic Thought (IIIT), Washington.
Bahri, S. (2020). The construction of indonesian political Fiqh: Maqasidul Shari'ah perspective and Ahmad Ar-Raisuni's thoughts. *Jurnal Justicia Islamica, 17*(1), 35–52.
Baran, T. (2021). A literature review and classification of the studies on 'halal' in Islamic business journals (2010–2018). *Journal of Islamic Marketing, 12*(5), 1012–1024. https://doi.org/10.1108/JIMA-10-2019-0206
Cornell, V. J. (2007). *Voices of Islam*. Greenwood Publishing Group.
Faizal, P. R. M., Ridhwan, A. A. M., & Kalsom, A. W. (2013). The entrepreneur's characteristic from al-Quran and al-Hadis. *International Journal of Trade, Economics and Finance, 4*(4), 191.
Hamid, S. A., & Sa'ari, C. Z. (2011). Reconstructing entrepreneur's development based on al-Qur'an and al-Hadith. *International Journal of Business and Social Science, 2*(19).
Hart, M., Bonner, K., Prashar, N., Ri, A., Levie, J., & Mwaura, S. (2020). *Global entrepreneurship monitor: United Kingdom 2019 monitoring report*.
Hervainé Szabó, G. (2020). Stakeholder capitalism and the EFQM Model 2020 for Corporate Management. POLGÁRI SZEMLE: GAZDASÁGI ÉS TÁRSADALMI FOLYÓIRAT, 16(Spec.), 368–384.
Hunter, M. (2014). Entrepreneurship as a means to create Islamic economy. *Economics, Management, and Financial Markets, 9*(1), 75–100.
Ibn Ashur, M. A. T. (2006). *Ibn Ashur treatise on Maqasidul Shari'ah*. The Other Press.
Janssen, F., & Bacq, S. (2017). The entrepreneur, wealth creator and growth seeker: myth or reality? *Projectics/Proyéctica/Projectique*, (3), 51–68.
Karia, N., & Asaari, M. H. A. H. (2016). Halal business and sustainability: Strategies, resources and capabilities of halal third-party logistics (3PLs). *Progress in Industrial Ecology, an International Journal, 10*(2–3), 286–300.
Kayed, R. N., & Hassan, M. K. (2010). Islamic entrepreneurship: A case study of Saudi Arabia. *Journal of Developmental Entrepreneurship, 15*(04), 379–413.
Kedah, Z., Adamu, I. M., Kadir, M. A. B. A., & Anwar, M. A. (2015). Effects of business Jihad on entrepreneurs' ethical behaviour and corporate social responsibility: A qualitative study. *International Journal of Business and Globalisation, 15*(3), 425–442.
Kettell, B. (2011). *Introduction to Islamic banking and finance* (Vol. 551). Wiley.
Khalek, A. A. (2018). Entrepreneurship and the halal wave in Malaysia. In *Global entrepreneurship and new venture creation in the sharing economy* (pp. 191–205). IGI Global.
Khan, M. F., & Ghifari, N. M. (1992). Shatibi's objectives of Shari'ah and some implications for consumer theory. *Readings in Islamic Economic Thought: Selected Readings, 176*, 202.
Liizzah, I., Priyono, A. A., & Masitah, D. (2023). Islamic views and calls to invest according to the Al-Qur'an Surah Al-Hashr Verse 18. *Dirasah: International Journal of Islamic Studies, 1*(1), 18–26.
Maksum, A., & Kamaludin, F. S. (2023). Innovation using Islamic values as sustainable competitive advantage: Case study on Muslim clothing MSMEs. *International Journal of Advanced Research in Economics and Finance (IJAREF), 5*(1), 189–201.
Meidina, A. R., & Mokan, Z. A. M. (2023). Shifting meaning: Islamic philanthropy according to the view of Muhammadiyah. *Journal of Islamic Economics and Philanthropy, 6*(1), 29–40.
Menger, C. (1990). *Carl Menger and his legacy in economics* (Vol. 22). Duke University Press.
Mohamed, E. S. H. (2023). Aesthetics of Islamic architecture and its application to printed hotel furnishing fabrics. *International Design Journal, 13*(2), 151–160.
Mohamad, A. A., Baharuddin, A. S., & Ruskam, A. (2015). Halal industry in Singapore: A case study of nutraceutical products. *Sains Humanika, 4*(2), 35–40.
Mulyaningsih, H. D., & Ramadani, V. (2017). Social entrepreneurship in an Islamic context. In *Entrepreneurship and management in an Islamic context* (pp. 143–158). Springer.

Nakissa, A. (2023). Comparing moralities in the abrahamic and indic religions using cognitive science: Kindness, peace, and love versus justice, violence, and hate. *Religions, 14*(2), 203.
Opwis, F. (2007). Islamic law and legal change: The concept of Maslaha in classical and contemporary Islamic legal theory. *Shari'ah: Islamic law in the contemporary context* (pp. 62–82).
Petrevska Nechkoska, R., Angeloska Dichovska, M., Angeleski, M., Koltovska Nechoska, D., & Bogdanoska Jovanovska, M. (2023). MultiCREATION: Multi-stakeholder problem-driven approach: entrepreneurship and social entrepreneurship. *Facilitation in complexity: from creation to co-creation, from dreaming to co-dreaming, from evolution to co-evolution* (pp. 205–235). Springer International Publishing.
Rafiki, A., & Wahab, K. A. (2013). Influences of Islamic practices on small firm performance: A study in North Sumatera, Indonesia. *Islamic Management and Business, 5*(11), 64–82.
Raimi, L., Panait, M., Gigauri, I., & Apostu, S. A. (2023). Thematic review of motivational factors, types of uncertainty, and entrepreneurship strategies of transitional entrepreneurship among ethnic minorities, immigrants, and women entrepreneurs. *Journal of Risk and Financial Management, 16*(2), 83. https://doi.org/10.3390/jrfm16020083
Ramadani, V., Dana, L. P., Ratten, V., & Tahiri, S. (2015). The context of Islamic entrepreneurship and business: Concept, principles and perspectives. *International Journal of Business and Globalisation, 15*(3), 244–261.
Ratten, V., Ramadani, V., Dana, L. P., & Gerguri-Rashiti, S. (2017). Islamic entrepreneurship and management: Culture, religion and society. *Entrepreneurship and management in an Islamic context* (pp. 7–17).
Salaheldeen, M., Battour, M., Nazri, M. A., Ahmad Bustamam, U. S., & Hashim, A. J. C. M. (2023). The perception of success in the halal market: Developing a halal entrepreneurship success scale. *Journal of Islamic Marketing, 14*(3), 799–825. https://doi.org/10.1108/JIMA-10-2021-0341
Salindal, N. A. (2019). Halal certification compliance and its effects on companies' innovative and market performance. *Journal of Islamic Marketing, 10*(2), 589–605.
Sallam, A. A. E. A. (2013). Where is Saudi Arabian society heading? *Contemporary Readings in Law and Social Justice, 5*(2), 141.
Saunders, M. N., & Rojon, C. (2011). On the attributes of a critical literature review. *Coaching: An International Journal of Theory, Research and Practice, 4*(2), 156–162.
Saunders, M., Lewis, P., & Thornhill, A. (eds.). (2012). *Research methods for business students*. Pearson Education Limited, Harlow.
Shukri, A. S. M. (2022). Expository outlines of Islamic Daᶜwah: An overview on its objectives, sources and those called to Islam (Madᶜu). *Al-Itqan: Journal Of Islamic Sciences And Comparative Studies, 6*(1), 5–30.
Soltanian, M., Zailani, S., Iranmanesh, M., & Aziz, A. A. (2016). Motivations of SME entrepreneurs to become halalpreneurs. *Journal of Science and Technology Policy Management, 7*(2), 173–189. https://doi.org/10.1108/JSTPM-07-2015-0023
Stevenson, H. H. (2000). Why entrepreneurship has won. *Coleman White Paper, 2*(4), 483.
Suselo, D. (2018). Business and religiosity: Review of business ethics Mayangkara group. *Jurnal Pendidikan Ekonomi Dan Bisnis (JPEB), 6*(2), 82–92.
Tok, M. E., & Kaminski, J. (2018). *Islam, entrepreneurship, and embeddedness*. https://doi.org/10.1002/tie.21970
Weick, C. W., Aamir, N., & Reichart, J. (2023). The ethnobotanical evolution of the Mediterranean Cypress (Cupressus sempervirens). *Economic Botany*, 1–19.
Wilson, J. A. (2014). The halal phenomenon: An extension or a new paradigm? *Social Business, 4*(3), 255–271.
Yu, T. F. L. (2001). Entrepreneurial alertness and discovery. *The Review of Austrian Economics, 14*, 47–63.
Yusuf, T. O., & Raimi, L. (2021). How compatible are SDGs with divine principles? A critical literature review (CLR). *Islamic Wealth and the SDGs: Global Strategies for Socio-economic Impact*, 3–27.

Zuboff, S. (2019). *The age of surveillance capitalism: The fight for a human future at the new frontier of power: Barack Obama's books of 2019*. Profile Books.

Opportunities for Entrepreneurs in the Attainment of Sustainable Development Goals (SDGs) Through Halal Entrepreneurship

Umar Habibu Umar

Abstract This paper explores the opportunities for halal entrepreneurs to fast-track the achievement of sustainable development goals (SDGs) by 2030. It is purely based on the literature review by using published papers and other online documents from reliable sources. The study shows that developing green products and services, adopting climate-friendly technologies, making ethical investments and promoting responsible production and consumption align with the provisions of Shariá upon which *halal* entrepreneurship is based. Besides, it reveals that investing in environmental, social and governance (ESG) activities by halal entrepreneurs is also consistent with Islamic law, which can potentially contribute to the sustainability of halal businesses, preservation of the environment and welfare of current and future generations. Consequently, supporting the achievement of the SDGs and investing in ESG projects strictly in accordance with Shari'a might offer opportunities for halal entrepreneurs to satisfy the needs of their various stakeholders (such as customers, employees, shareholders/investors, government and regulatory bodies, society, creditors, etc.), which will likely sustain the operations of halal businesses in both Islamic and non-Islamic countries. Finally, the chapter recommends essential ways of improving the role of halal businesses in achieving SGDs and stimulating halal entrepreneurs to ensure their products and services are green and disclose ESG activities in the annual reports.

Keywords *Halal* · *Halal* entrepreneurship · *Halal* entrepreneurs · Sustainable development goals (SDGs) · Environmental · Social and governance (ESG) · ESG report

---

U. H. Umar (✉)
Department of Accounting and Finance, Universiti Brunei Darussalam, Darussalam, Brunei
e-mail: 20h8931@ubd.edu.bn

L. Raimi et al. (eds.), *Contemporary Discourse of Halal and Islamic Entrepreneurship*,
https://doi.org/10.1007/978-981-99-6427-7_3

1 Introduction

Halal has gained popularity across all sectors of the global economy, including food and beverage products, finance and lifestyle (Qomaro, 2019). It incorporates sustainable development, a global issue affecting all facets of human existence, which include the economic, environmental and social dimensions (Azam et al., 2019). The *halal* industry constitutes an integral part of Islamic economic activities, which strongly supports the attainment of sustainable development goals (SDGs) (Trimulato et al., 2022). The industry is considered crucial to the future development of Muslims worldwide (Qoyum & Fauziyyah, 2019). It has become the fastest-growing sector of the global economy at 20% annually (Azam & Abdullah, 2020; Azam et al., 2019). The growth is strongly supported by the increasing number of consumers (Ramli et al., 2022). This happened because *halal* products and services are now patronized by Muslims and non-Muslims around the globe due to their cleanness, harmlessness, authenticity, quality and legality. Besides, Azam and Abdullah (2020) state that several nations dominated by non-Muslims have also realized the potential of *halal* businesses. They added that the top 10 nations in the Global Islamic Economy Indicator (GIEI) score for various *halal* industries include Brazil, Australia, New Zealand, Italy, India and Germany. Also, non-Muslim majority nations like Japan, Australia, Thailand, New Zealand and others produce *halal* tourism products (Qomaro, 2019).

Moreover, a study by Azam and Abdullah (2020) revealed three reasons for the growth of the global *halal* market. First, the growth of the Muslim population by 1.8% per annum. The global Muslim population is expected to reach 2.2 billion by 2030 (Zailani et al., 2017). The population is growing at a greater rate, indicating a continuous increase in the demand and consumption of *halal* products (Salleh & Harun, 2022). Second, improvement in economic activities indicates an increase in Muslim consumers' ability to purchase. Third, *halal* market expansion to non-Muslim countries. Accordingly, the global *halal* market is projected to be worth US$2.3 trillion, with an estimated annual value of U$560 billion (Azam & Abdullah, 2020). Besides, the *halal* market has extended beyond the boundaries of the food industry to include cosmetics and pharmaceuticals, toiletries and medical devices, as well as elements of the service sector like logistics, marketing, print and electronic media, packaging, branding and financing, among others (Azam & Abdullah, 2020; Busari & Sitiris, 2021).

Halal products benefit existing and future generations as the safety of animals, employees and the environment are all considered in the production and consumption processes (Busari & Sitiris, 2021). This implies that the sustainable development goals (SDGs) program could be accomplished through the *halal* businesses as an important component of Islam (Busari & Sitiris, 2021; Trimulato et al., 2022). SDGs consist of 17 goals that should be attained by both developing and developed countries (Salaheldeen et al., 2021). The SDGs' goal of attaining and maintaining progress for humanity is similar to that of the *maqasid Shariá* (Khan, 2019). Besides, SDGs address numerous issues connected to *maqasid al-sharia* or *Sharia* objectives (Busari & Sitiris, 2021). *Maqasid al-sharia* aims to protect and preserve society regarding religious, mental, intellectual, descent and property conservation (Haqqoni et al., 2020).

Moreover, entrepreneurship is an essential issue that can lead to high performance and sustainability of *halal* businesses toward attaining SDGs. Entrepreneurship simply means making imaginative utilization of resources to substantially influence market performance (Abdullah & Azam, 2020). The idea of entrepreneurship is not new to Islam, as Prophet Muhammad (peace be upon him) and his companions engaged in it as a respectable occupation (Abdullah & Azam, 2020). Besides, the *halal* entrepreneurship success scale (HESS) has four interconnected components: religious, economic, social and environmental (Salaheldeen et al., 2021). It can potentially be a game-changing force, providing the framework for realizing the SDGs and accelerating economic growth based on sustainable development principles (Salaheldeen et al., 2019). A study by Salaheldeen et al. (2021) indicates that *halal* entrepreneurship can potentially contribute to attaining SDGs because its goals align substantially with those of SDGs. Hence, *halal* entrepreneurship proliferates across all industries (Salaheldeen et al., 2021). Besides, *halal* (lawful) and *haram* (prohibited) are two Islamic trade concepts that contribute to attaining the environmental, social and governance (ESG) initiatives (Hidayat et al., 2021). The significance of ESG and halal practices emphasizes the necessity of coordination between the two tasks (Ramli et al., 2022). Also, ESG has crucial elements that assist in actualizing sustainability (Miskam & Abdullah, 2021). This signifies that ESG can play a critical role in sustaining the operation of halal companies.

Against the above backdrop, this paper explores the opportunities for entrepreneurs to achieve SDGs through *halal* entrepreneurship. It consists of five sections. Followed by this introduction, Sect. 2 explains the concept of *halal* entrepreneurship. Section 3 discusses sustainable development goals (SDGs), covering issues on green products and services, ethical investments, climate-friendly technologies and responsible production and consumption. Section 4 shows the need to adopt ESG practices in halal entrepreneurship. Finally, Sect. 5 concludes the paper.

2 *Halal* Entrepreneurship

The concept of *halal* entrepreneurship consists of two different terms, "halal" and "entrepreneurship." For a better understanding of the concept, it is better to understand the two terms separately before explaining their meaning jointly. The term "halal" derives from an Arabic word that implies in accordance with Islamic law, "permissible" or "lawful," which means everything that is permitted by Islamic law and beneficial to people (Azam et al., 2019). The idea of "halal," which is no longer limited to food exclusively, has given the *halal* industry a new potential growth segment in the global economy (Azam & Abdullah, 2020). It is attributed to Muslim and non-Muslim consumers, though it primarily targets the former (Azam et al., 2019). Besides, the idea of *halal* is attributed to Muslim and non-Muslim consumers, though it primarily targets the former (Azam et al., 2019). Hence, halal has become a universal concept (Baharuddin et al., 2015).

Moreover, sometimes the concept of "halal" is connected with the concept of "tayyiban," which signifies great (Azam et al., 2019; Hashim & Sulaiman, 2022). The term also connotes "good" for people (Azam et al., 2019). Tayyiban promotes the cleanliness and purity of food production and ensures ethical behavior and intentions throughout the production process, which are anchored in the fundamental tenets of Islamic teaching (Idris et al., 2022). Islamically speaking, *halal and tayyiban* stand for quality, cleanliness and safety, which should be incorporated into the creation of products (Hashim & Sulaiman, 2022). They have the potential to contribute to achieving SDGs and safeguarding the environment (Busari & Sitiris, 2021). Besides, the two terms "halal" and "tayyiban" can be jointly used as "halalan tayyiban," which entails every component that is of high quality, healthy and safe for consumption (Hashim & Sulaiman, 2022). *Halalan tayyiban* also entails all the activities that ensure fairness and justice in trading, which assist producers and improve sustainability (Idris et al., 2022). It also promotes an environmentally and friendly attitude that respects the natural world and works to preserve and care for the environment (Idris et al., 2022).

The word "entrepreneurship" comes from the French word "entreprendre," which means "to embrace" or "to accomplish something" (Abdullah & Azam, 2020). Entrepreneurship is a creative endeavor that depends on the capacity to create and establish something out of almost nothing (Abdullah & Azam, 2020). From a business perspective, entrepreneurs can attain the aim of human prosperity and they ensure that their business activities are *halal* (Qoyum & Fauziyyah, 2019).

The term "halal entrepreneurship" or "halalpreneurship" has recently been used by Islamic economic researchers to describe and distinguish entrepreneurs in the *halal* market from their conventional counterparts (Abdullah & Azam, 2020). These terms describe how Islamic values transform entrepreneurs in the *halal* market (Abdullah & Azam, 2020). *Halal* entrepreneurs are more inclined to find chances for sustainable development (Salaheldeen et al., 2019). Similarly, *halal* entrepreneurs' religious background inspires them to contribute constructively to their society and environmental development (Salaheldeen et al., 2021). *Halalan tayyibah* provides a path for small entrepreneurs to generate income (Busari & Sitiris, 2021). Moreover, *halal* entrepreneurship has the potential to be a sustainability driver since it offers the foundation for achieving and delivering the SDGs while fostering sustainable economic growth (Salaheldeen et al., 2021). Specifically, the *halal* industry can prospectively contribute to the attainment of the core issues of the SDGs, such as economic, health, social and environmental (Busari & Sitiris, 2021).

3 Sustainable Development Goals (SDGs)

SDGs advance the uncompleted tasks of the Millennium Development Goals (MDGs) and go much beyond (Ahmed et al., 2015). SDGs provide a unified plan for the present and future peace and prosperity of humanity to be attained by all the members of the

United Nations by 2030 (Salaheldeen et al., 2021). They are introduced to balance the social, economic and environmental issues (Pratiwi et al., 2022). In specific, the following are the 17 goals of the United Nations: SDG-1 "no poverty," SDG-2 "zero hunger," SDG-3 "good health and well-being," SDG-4 "quality education," SDG-5 "gender equality," SDG-6 "clean water and sanitation," SDG-7 "affordable and clean energy," SDG-8 "decent work and economic growth," SDG-9 "industry, innovation and infrastructure," SDG-10 "reduced inequalities," SDG-11 "sustainable cities and communities," SDG-12 "responsible consumption and production," SDG-13 "climate action," SDG-14 "life below water," SDG-15 "life on land," SDG-16 "peace, justice and strong institutions" and SDG-17 "partnership for the goals" (United Nations, 2020). According to Hashim and Sulaiman (2022), most of these 17 goals align with the objectives of *maqasid al-shariá*. Similarly, the development of the *halal* business can play a part in achieving a number of SDGs (Trimulato et al., 2022).

Summarily, the goals consist of three key components: economic growth, social inclusion and environmental conservation (Hidayat et al., 2021). SDGs center on actions that will reduce poverty, provide prosperity and safeguard all elements of the planet (Busari & Sitiris, 2021). Similarly, SDGs are anticipated to address concerns on a global scale, such as eradicating poverty and hunger, improving health and educational activities, constructing sustainable cities, battling climate change and preserving oceans and forests (Qomaro, 2019). These could be attained through effective *halal* entrepreneurship.

From an Islamic perspective, Islamic finance is anticipated to play a crucial role in accomplishing the SDGs (Khan, 2019). Islamic finance is an integral part of *halal* market, which can provide Shariá-compliant funds to non-financial *halal* businesses. Ahmed et al. (2015) pointed out five avenues for Islamic finance to assist in achieving the SDGs: infrastructure funding, social and environmental initiatives, financial stability, financial inclusion and decreasing vulnerability. Besides, the SDGs for each sector of the Islamic economy are published in the Islamic Economy Report 2018/2019, which sees them as a key factor in the development of the global Islamic economy (Haqqoni et al., 2020). Also, Islamic Economics and its constituents are crucial to accomplishing SDGs in order to generate wealth and reduce poverty (Trimulato et al., 2022).

3.1 Green Products and Services

In a complete *halal* ecosystem, the transition to a net-zero economy is unquestionably essential and aims to achieve a net-zero economy by 2050 with a view to striking a balance between greenhouse gas production and its removal from the environment (Ramli et al., 2022). Therefore, the net-zero economy is attainable through the *halal* green. The *halal*-green concept enhances goodwill relationships between people and the environment and promotes the relationship between people and the creator, which is integrated into the process of developing *halal* products and plays a vital role in attaining the SDGs agenda and Shariá objectives (Hashim & Sulaiman, 2022). Besides, companies with strong ESG scores are more likely to receive funding from green investment funds and socially responsible investors (Al Ansari & Alanzarouti, 2020).

Moreover, finance plays an essential role in providing green products and services. The concept of sustainable/green finance has become an issue of concern in the global finance industry. The terms "sustainable finance" and "green finance" have risen in prominence over the last decade in mainstream financial discourse (Liu & Lai, 2021). Sustainable finance or green finance refers to financial instruments whose proceeds are used to fund projects and initiatives for sustainable development, enhance environmental outcomes and promote green economic transformation for attaining low-carbon and climate-resilient pathways (Liu & Lai, 2021). According to Busari and Sitiris (2021), five SDGs are centered on attaining a sustainable and green environment: SDG-6 (water & sanitation), SDG-7 (affordable & clean energy), SDG-9 (industrial innovation & infrastructure), SDG-11 (sustainable cities & communities) and SD-13 (climate action). Recent efforts to transition to a greener and more inclusive economy offer opportunities for achieving the SDGs of the 2030 agenda for sustainable development (Hashim & Sulaiman, 2022).

3.2 *Ethical Investments*

Generally, ethics consist of beliefs, norms and values established by a person or groups of individuals. The words "ethical investments" and "socially responsible investments" are used synonymously (Anas & Mounira, 2009). Ethical investment/investing is otherwise known as "green investing," "faith investing," and "socially responsible investing" (DeLorenzo, 2001). Cowton (1994) describes ethical investing as employing ethical and social standards in selecting and managing investment portfolios. It is based on the philosophical, religious, or moral beliefs of individuals or collective investors who disregard some of their total investments in industries that they deem to be at odds with their beliefs (Anas & Mounira, 2009). Also, ethical investment regards the attributes of potential investments together with anticipated risks and returns as well as improves and safeguards the reputation of corporations and fosters trust (Hussein, 2004). According to proponents of ethical investment, appraising possible investment opportunities based on both financial and ethical criteria benefits society and the economy at large (Hussein & Omran, 2005). Besides, a firm that implements and adheres to a sound corporate responsibility policy has a greater opportunity to avert any environmental and social problems that might culminate in reputation damage, increased production costs, production loss, increased security costs and higher insurance premiums (Hussein, 2004).

Religion plays a significant role in establishing beliefs, norms and values that influence the personability and behaviors of people, including some elements of investment decision-making (Anas & Mounira, 2009). Ethical investing has roots in some religious institutions that attempt to avoid the sin industries, such as gambling and tobacco products (Murninghan, 1992). From an Islamic point of view, ethical investments are based on the teachings of the Shariá (Islamic law). Islamic investing entails low debt, which is non-financial and consciously social-ethical (Hussein & Omran, 2005). Islamic investing, like other contemporary forms of ethical investing such as green, faith-based or socially responsible investments, focuses on low-debt, non-financial and social-ethical investment vehicles in order to produce low volatility returns and value improvement opportunities (DeLorenzo, 2001).

Moreover, *Shariá*-compliant investments are founded based on the prohibition of *riba* (interest), *maisir* (gambling) and *gharar* (uncertainty) as well as the use of a negative screening method when dealing with tobacco, alcohol, weapons and other non-*halal* products and services (Miskam & Abdullah, 2021). Therefore, ethical investment from a religious point of view can lead to negative screening as many investments are often disregarded because they are seen as "sinful" activities, such as those involved in the manufacturing of alcohol, cigarettes, nuclear energy, or gambling (Anas & Mounira, 2009). Besides, Islamic investors have a variety of options when building a financial portfolio, such as interest-free bank deposits, investments in Islamic unit trusts and investment firms, private placements in Muslim-owned enterprises and investments in conventional institutions and corporations that agree to use financing from Islamic investors in a *halal* manner (Wilson, 1997). Hence, based on the teachings of Islam, *halal* entrepreneurs are prohibited from businesses that involve interest, gambling, excessive risks and pornography. They must not also engage in buying and selling products that are not allowed to consume by Islam, such as alcohol, pork and tobacco, among others.

A key issue to stress more from the above is that *halal* entrepreneurs are totally prohibited from financing their businesses with interest-based funds. There are many Shariá-compliant contracts, modes or sources of finance that could be utilized by *halal* entrepreneurs to undertake their businesses effectively in order to attain sustainable development. This study considers the following:

1. *Musharakah* (venture capital): In simple terms, *musharakah* or *shirkah* is a type of partnership or joint venture in which two or more people agree to pool their resources, whether in the form of money or kind, in order to share the profits and losses. Umar (2019) described it as an equity comprising a minimum of two persons, not necessarily including an Islamic bank, who contribute capital either in cash or kind or both to undertake a business that complies with the Shariá. In this case, *halal* entrepreneurs contribute capital and participate in managing *halal* business activities. There is also a special form of partnership called *shirkat al-milk ghayr ikhtiyari* (compulsory partnership), which enables heirs of deceased Muslims to be directly admitted into the inherited business as partners by allocating the business equity among them (Umar & Kurawa, 2019; Umar et al., 2020; Umar & Haron, 2021). In this case, the death of a *halal* business owner can enable his/her heirs to be admitted to the business as partners.
2. *Mudharabah* (profit sharing contract): The concept of *mudharabah*, which stipulates that one party supplies capital and the other provides labor, skills and work only, is what distinguishes it from *musharakah* principles (Billah, 2019). The

one who gives the capital is known as *rab-ul-maal or sahib ul mal*, while the person who provides the entrepreneurship skills to manage the business is known as *mudharib*. Specifically, one party provides capital to a *halal* entrepreneur who uses his/her skills to effectively and efficiently manage the business. In this case, the entrepreneur shares only profit with the capital provider. Therefore, the capital provider bears the entire loss unless the entrepreneur is found guilty of breaching the agreements of *mudharabah*. Besides, Umar and Haron (2021) state that heirs who inherit wealth can use *mudharabah* by giving their wealth to an entrepreneur who has the necessary skills and knowledge to undertake business on their behalf. Also, heirs can entrust their inherited wealth to *halal* entrepreneurs in order to undertake *halal* businesses and maximize it as required by the Shariá. In this contract, the *halal* entrepreneur contributes no capital to the business but shares profit with the capital provider based on the agreed sharing ratio.

3. *Murabaha* (cost-plus financing): *Murabaha* is the practice of selling items or commodities for the amount the seller paid, plus a markup on the price, which must be disclosed to the buyer (Billah, 2019). Here, an individual or a financial institution can purchase materials or any other assets or pay for services needed by the entrepreneur and charge a specified percentage of the amount spent as a profit. Specifically, a *halal* entrepreneur can enter into a *murabaha* contract with an Islamic bank or an individual who will purchase the items or materials needed to successfully run the *halal* business at a pre-determined profit rate.
4. *Ijarah* (Lease): *Ijarah* is a contract between one party, the lessor, who buys an asset for another person, known as the lessee, for a rental payment over a certain fixed period. This Islamic contract can be categorized into two: *ijarah wa iqtina* (where the lessee agrees to buy the property at the end of the contract period) and *Ijarah al-Muntahia bittamlik* (where the lessee is not going to purchase the property leased (Billah, 2019). Using this contract, *halal* entrepreneurs can acquire machines from Islamic banks or individuals.
5. *Qard al-hasan* (benevolent loan): This is an interest-free loan given to an entrepreneur without anything in return other than to pay back the actual amount collected as a loan at the end of the agreed period of time. Government and non-governmental organizations (NGOs) can use this mode of finance to support small and medium *halal* enterprises toward economic and sustainable development. This source can enable *halal* entrepreneurs to obtain funds necessary to run their *halal* businesses.
6. *Zakat* (Islamic tax): Islam requires wealthy Muslims to provide 2.5% of their wealth to the poor and needy members of society to alleviate poverty (Umar & Abubakar, 2021). This implies that *zakat* provides funds that could be utilized to finance poverty alleviation programs and socio-economic development. Umar et al. (2022a) argue that *zakat* can effectively eradicate poverty when it is integrated with Islamic microfinance and *waqf* (Islamic endowment). In this case, *zakat* collections could support micro and small *halal* entrepreneurs facing financial challenges.
7. Corporate social responsibility (CSR): Through CSR, firms spend a lot to assist the members of society. A study by Umar et al. (2022b) revealed that Islamic

banks provide financial support to micro and small enterprises in order to eradicate poverty through their CSR activities. Accordingly, *halal* entrepreneurs could be supported through CSR initiatives, particularly by Islamic banks and other Shariá-compliant firms.

3.3 Climate-Friendly Technologies

Addressing climate change has become one of the key issues in the twenty-first century (Brown & Sovacool, 2011). It could be addressed by applying green and commercially viable technologies that could reduce greenhouse gas (GHG) emissions. Green technology enables the environment and other natural resources to be preserved and utilized for the benefit of the existing generation without threatening the benefits that future generations will enjoy. The four goals of commercially accessible GHG reduction technologies are lowering emissions from energy end-use and infrastructure, decreasing emissions from energy supply, absorbing and sequestering CO_2 and reducing emissions of non-CO_2 GHGs (Brown & Sovacool, 2011). RECAM (2023) provides 10 key contemporary environmentally-friendly green technologies that can be used to minimize carbon emissions to the barest minimum as follows: emission treatments, waste to energy, recycling and waste management, biofuels, wastewater treatments, solar energy, wave and tidal energy, eco vehicles, smart buildings and vertical gardens and farms. The costs of climate-friendly technologies need to be affordable to enable businesses to operate in such a way as to emit little or no GHG.

Moreover, the idea of *halalan tayyiban* (clean and pure) encompasses social justice, animal rights, environmental pro-green products and using environmentally conscious packaging consisting of parts that are safe, non-toxic and recyclable in order to minimize the negative environmental consequences of product usage (Fakhira et al., 2022). *Halal* green product development should also prioritize environmental sustainability through the effective use of renewable energy sources, eco-friendly raw materials and waste management (Hashim & Sulaiman, 2022). Accordingly, *halal* entrepreneurs should adopt viable environmentally-friendly technologies to reduce the amount of wastage and pollution to the lowest level and enable materials to be recycled and reutilized whenever possible. Besides, environmentally better products may enable firms to differentiate their products and improve customer loyalty (Hussein, 2004). Also, environmentally conscious companies are less likely to face environmental penalties and legal actions (Hussein & Omran, 2005). Many verses of the Noble Qurán teach against environmental damage and forbid waste, which is all aligned with sustainability practices (Salleh & Harun, 2022).

3.4 Responsible Production and Consumption

Halal entrepreneurs are required to avoid in totality the production and distribution of forbidden products in Islam. This is because the primary goal of *halal* food and products, especially food manufacturing and processing, is to safeguard Muslim customers from consuming and using non-*halal* items that might harm their lives (Ibrahim et al., 2010). Therefore, Islamic law limits consumption, such as refraining from drinking alcohol, eating meat from dead animals, meat produced by suffocating animals, etc. (Mohsin et al., 2016).

The wholesomeness notion of *halal* encompasses the Shariá requirements and the sustainability concept of cleanliness, sanitation and safety element, which makes halal food easily acceptable to customers who care about food safety and healthy lifestyles (Baharuddin et al., 2015). Similarly, the *halal* industry has the ability and natural wholesomeness to support a sustainable environment by improving sanitation, cleanliness and safety, which increases customer acceptance of *halal* products, particularly in Muslim-majority countries (Busari & Sitiris, 2021). Therefore, *halalan tayyiban* products are safe, non-toxic and harm-free (Hashim & Sulaiman, 2022). Consequently, the quality and safety of halal products make them attractive to non-Muslims (Jaafar et al., 2021).

Moreover, Islam strongly encourages sustainability practices and in the Quran as Allah calls on Muslims to preserve the environment and refrain from wasting resources (Salleh & Harun, 2022). Hence, *halal* products are required not to be contaminated with *haram* and hazardous products (Jaafar et al., 2021). This could be achieved when every step of the process, from manufacturing to distribution, complies with Islamic law (Jaafar et al., 2021). Unfortunately, the current food production, distribution and consumption practices have a substantial negative influence on the environment, depleting natural resources and causing ecosystems to deteriorate (Idris et al., 2022). This indicates the need to take measures by policymakers and regulators to ensure production and consumption are responsible by complying with policies and regulations that ensure the products and services are halal, healthy, clean, safe, non-harmful and non-toxic for the welfare of consumers and the environmental protection.

4 Adopting ESG Practices in Halal Entrepreneurship

During the last decade, customers, employees, public organizations and regulatory bodies have all increased their focus on companies' performance with regard to environmental, social and governance (ESG) (Khan, 2019). ESG entails three components of non-financial attributes, environmental, social and governance that are useful in measuring the sustainability and ethical impact of an investment in a firm (Sairally, 2015). It is crucial because businesses that strive for good ESG performance can reap a number of financial gains (Al Ansari & Alanzarouti, 2020). ESG covers various topics about business operations concerning ESG issues to encourage sustainable business practices (Miskam & Abdullah, 2021). ESG investing is a kind of "sustainable investing," which is an umbrella for investments that entail pursuing favorable returns while taking into account the long-term effects that business practices have on society, the environment and the success of the firm itself (Al Ansari & Alanzarouti, 2020).

Adopting or investing in ESG by firms has a lot of benefits. Many investors now consider social, ethical and environmental issues critical when making investment decisions (Barom, 2019). Companies with high ESG investments gain the confidence and support of stakeholders based on the instrumental viewpoint (Zheng et al., 2023). Besides, the Bursa Malaysia Sustainability Reporting Guidelines provide several benefits of integrating sustainability into firm operations, such as better risk management, encouraging innovations, attracting new customers, maintenance of a business license, accessing more capital, increase in productivity, cost savings and enhancement of firm value and reputation (Ramli et al., 2022).

Moreover, ESG practices are not only required to be implemented by large corporate entities but also SMEs. Research by the OECD on ESG activities in Asian SMEs published in 2021 raised concern about the fact that SMEs account for 97–99% of all enterprises in the ASEAN area and are also largely to blame for industrial pollution since they are subject to fewer regulations than big corporations (Allen, 2023). Hence, SMEs must participate in ESG more deeply by utilizing the alternatives, support and help of diverse stakeholders, including international institutions (Hu & Kee, 2022).

It is worth noting that implementing ESG could be beneficial to SMEs too. ESG provides SMEs with a competitive edge, which helps them to comprehend risks better, streamline processes and enhance profitability (Chan, 2022; Shalhoob & Hussainey, 2023). Consequently, in many developed and developing countries, SMEs have started adopting ESG practices. According to the Catalysts of Sustainability report by DBS Bank, the biggest bank in Southeast Asia, 8 out of 10 (83%) SMEs claimed to have developed ESG strategies, but only 37% have a clear roadmap outlining how to attain the goals of ESG (Allen, 2023). Therefore, a lot needs to be done to stimulate SMEs to enhance their ESG practices.

From an Islamic point of view, the ESG concept and Shariá requirements have several things in common, like conserving the environment, fostering economic development and promoting sound governance in the financial sector (Ma'ruf et al., 2021). Islam gives environmental and societal considerations a lot of weight (Mustafida & Fauziah, 2021). Promoting social values is one of the common goals of both Shari'a-compliant firms and ESG investing (Miskam & Abdullah, 2021). Generally speaking, Shari'a criteria and ESG ideas aim to improve moral behavior in undertaking business activities (Ma'ruf et al., 2021). A strong justification for paying attention to ESG issues is clearly provided by the *halal* industry's development and the net-zero economy's significance (Ramli et al., 2022). Firms in the halal industry are expected to adopt ESG policies that adhere to the provision of Shariá (Ramli et al., 2022). In fact, the global trends point to more synergy between the investment strategies of Islamic funds and ESG, as asset managers, investors and regulators increasingly acknowledge ESG principles and the SDGs (Miskam & Abdullah, 2021). Besides, many Islamic banks have been encouraging sustainability through their funding and efforts for years, putting them forefront in terms of ESG (Al Ansari & Alanzarouti, 2020). Empirically, Paltrinieri et al. (2020) established a positive association between the new Islamic Finance Development Indicator (IFDI) and ESG scores. Also, infusing ESG factors into Shariá investment (including halal entrepreneurship) aligns with the core Shariá requirements that advance equality, social justice and financial inclusion (Miskam & Abdullah, 2021). Hence, businesses are developing several sustainable investing opportunities offered to clients worldwide as investors place increasing weight on ESG performance (Kalia & Aggarwal, 2023).

From a financial reporting perspective, firms should invest in ESG activities and disclose them in their annual reports. Recently, ESG investing has attracted the substantial attention of local and foreign investors (Mohammad & Wasiuzzaman, 2021). Hence, stakeholders and fund managers believe that companies that disclose significant amounts of ESG information are expected to perform better, generate greater returns and reduce firm-specific risks (Shaikh, 2022). The growing demand from investors for non-financial information from firms has led to the development of a number of sustainability accounting frameworks to improve the standardization of ESG reporting (Ramli et al., 2022). Similarly, Saudi Exchange released ESG reporting guidelines that are relevant to all firms of different sizes (large and SMEs) with the view to improving ESG practices in Saudi Arabia. (PR Newswire, 2023). Firms are invigorated to apply sustainable practices by providing sustainability information in their annual reports (Salleh & Harun, 2022). Hence, halal businesses are expected to invest in ESG activities and disclose ESG information in their annual reports to reap the benefits mentioned above.

5 Conclusion

This paper underscores the opportunities for halal entrepreneurs toward fast-tracking the attainment of SDGs by 2030. The chapter shows that in line with the provisions of Shariá, halal entrepreneurs can develop green products and services, adopt climate-friendly technologies, make ethical investments and promote responsible production and consumption. These are believed to play a vital in achieving various SDGs. Besides, it shows that investing in ESG by halal entrepreneurs is consistent with Islamic law, which can potentially contribute to the sustainability of halal businesses, the environment and the welfare of current and future generations. Thus, promoting the attainment of the SDGs and investment in ESG initiatives in strict compliance with the Shari'a could provide opportunities for halal entrepreneurs to satisfy the needs of their various stakeholders (like customers, employees, shareholders/investors, government and regulatory bodies, society, creditors, etc.) which are expected to sustain the operations of halal businesses in both Muslim and non-Muslim dominated countries.

In view of the above, this study offers three essential suggestions. First, as halal entrepreneurship becomes a universal issue, halal entrepreneurs need to be educated on the benefits of providing green products and services toward attaining SDGs from both Islamic views. Second, there is a need to provide policies and regulations that could stimulate halal entrepreneurs to provide green products and services and viably adopt climate-friendly technologies. Third, halal businesses should be encouraged to disclose adequate information regarding ESG activities in their annual reports to convince their stakeholders of their commitment to ESG practices. These could be actualized when regulatory agencies publish guidelines for adopting and reporting ESG practices in countries that are hubs for halal businesses. Also, developing global guidelines for reporting ESG activities adoptable by large and small firms could greatly help to harmonize and converge ESG disclosure in the annual reports.

References

Abdullah, M. A., & Azam, M. S. E. (2020). Halal entrepreneurship: concept and business opportunities. In *Entrepreneurship*. IntechOpen.

Ahmed, H., Mohieldin, M., Verbeek, J., & Aboulmagd, F. (2015). *On the sustainable development goals and the role of Islamic finance*. (World Bank Policy Research Working Paper No.7266).

Ahmed, M. J., & Akbaba, A. (2018). The potential of halal tourism in Ethiopia: Opportunities, challenges and prospects. *International Journal of Contemporary Tourism Research, 2*(1), 13–22.

Al Ansari, R., & Alanzarouti, F. (2020). ESG and Islamic finance: An ethical bridge built on shared values. *Journal of Islamic Financial Studies, 6*(1), 5–11.

Allen, A. (2023). How can SMEs implement and measure ESG strategies ?*Procurement, Supply chain, Sustainability*. Retrieved from https://www.cips.org/supply-management/news/2023/march/how-can-smes-implement-and-measure-esg-strategies/

Anas, E. L. M. E. L. K. I., & Mounira, B. A. (2009). Ethical investment and the social responsibilities of the Islamic banks. *International Business Research, 2*(2), 123–130.

Azam, M. S. E., & Abdullah, M. A. (2020). Global halal industry: Realities and opportunities. *International Journal of Islamic Business Ethics, 5*(1), 47–59.

Azam, M. S. E., Abdullah, M. A., & Razak, D. A. (2019). Halal tourism: Definition, justification, and scopes towards sustainable development. *International Journal of Business, Economics and Law, 18*(3), 23–31.

Baharuddin, K., Kassim, N. A., Nordin, S. K., & Buyong, S. Z. (2015). Understanding the halal concept and the importance of information on halal food business needed by potential Malaysian entrepreneurs. *International Journal of Academic Research in Business and Social Sciences, 5*(2), 170–180.

Barom, M. N. (2019). Understanding socially responsible investing and its implications for Islamic investment industry. *Journal of Emerging Economies and Islamic Research, 7*(1), 1–13.

Belsey, C. (2006). Poststructuralism. In S. Malpas & P. Wake (Eds.), *The Routledge companion to critical theory* (pp. 51–61). Routledge.

Billah, M. M. (2019). *Halal* Investment in Sustainable Development Goals. In M. M. Billah (Ed), *Modern Islamic Investment Management*. Palgrave Macmillan, Cham (pp. 167–181). https://doi.org/10.1007/978-3-030-17628-0_12

Brown, M. A., & Sovacool, B. K. (2011). Barriers to the diffusion of climate-friendly technologies. *International Journal of Technology Transfer and Commercialisation, 10*(1), 43–62.

Busari, S. A., & Sitiris, M. (2021). Standardisation of halal industry towards sustainable development goals (SDGs)(Penyeragaman industri halal ke arah matlamat pembangunan yang mampan (SDGs)). *Journal of Islam in Asia, 18*(1), 163–198.

Chan, W. (2022). *The importance of ESG for SMEs*. Retrieved from https://www.business.hsbc.com/en-gb/insights/sustainability/the-importance-of-esg-for-smes

Charles, A., Darné, O., & Pop, A. (2015). Risk and ethical investment: Empirical evidence from Dow Jones Islamic indexes. *Research in International Business and Finance, 35*, 33–56.

Cowton, C. J. (1994). The development of ethical investment products. In Andreas R. Prindl & B. Prodhan (Eds.), *Ethical Conflicts in Finance*. Blackwell Finance, pp. 213–232.

DeLorenzo, Y. T. (2000). Shariah supervision of Islamic mutual funds. In *4th Annual Harvard Forum on Islamic Finance* (Vol. 3, No. 6). Harvard University Cambridge, MA.

Fakhira, K., Mismiwati, Africano, F., Riduwansah, & Riski, O. (2022). The effect of green product, halal label and safi cosmetic brand image on purchase decisions moderated by word of mouth in the Muslim community of palembang city. *Journal of Business Studies and Management Review, 5*(2), 266-274.

Haqqoni, N. S., Aprilia, F. P., & Maulina, I. N. (2020). Awareness level of halal food products and healthy lifestyles for realizing SDGs (comparative study before and when covid-19). *Airlangga International Journal of Islamic Economics and Finance, 3*(2), 111–130.

Hashim, N., & Sulaiman, N. S. (2022). A case study of halal green concept integration in halal product development. *Journal of Halal Service Research, 3*(2), 56–67.

Hidayat, S. E., Izharivan, Y., & Sari, C. A. (2021). Islamic finance and sustainable economy: A new model of islamic financial ecosystem. In M. K. Hassan, M. Saraç, & A. Khan (Eds.), *Islamic Finance and Sustainable Development: A Sustainable Economic Framework for Muslim and Non-Muslim Countries* (pp. 265–284). Springer International Publishing.

Hu, M. K., & Kee, D. M. H. (2022). Global institutions and ESG integration to accelerate SME development and sustainability. In N. Baporikar (Ed.), *Handbook of Research on Global Institutional Roles for Inclusive Development* (pp. 139–156). IGI Global. https://doi.org/10.4018/978-1-6684-2448-3

Hussein, K. (2004). Ethical investment: Empirical evidence from FTSE Islamic index. *Islamic Economic Studies, 12*(1), 22–40.

Hussein, K., & Omran, M. (2005). Ethical investment revisited: Evidence from Dow Jones Islamic indexes. *The Journal of Investing, 14*(3), 105–126.

Ibrahim, O., Samsi, S. Z. M., & Ahmad, M. F. (2010). Halal business corporate social responsibility. In *International University Social Responsibility Conference and Exhibition 2010 (IUSRCE 2010 & 2nd USRIC 2010), PWTC, Kuala Lumpur.*

Idris, R., Musa, F., & Sumardi, H. (2022). Halal-tayyiban and sustainable development goals: A SWOT analysis. *International Journal of Asian Business and Information Management, 13*(2), 1–16. https://doi.org/10.4018/IJABIM.20220701.oa9

Jaafar, H. S., Abd Aziz, M. L., Ahmad, M. R., & Faisol, N. (2021). Creating innovation in achieving sustainability: Halal-friendly sustainable port. *Sustainability, 13*(23), 13339.

Kalia, D., & Aggarwal, D. (2023). Examining impact of ESG score on financial performance of healthcare companies. *Journal of Global Responsibility, 14*(1), 155–176.

Khan, T. (2019). Reforming Islamic finance for achieving sustainable development goals. *Journal of King Abdulaziz University: Islamic Economics, 32*(1), 3–21. https://doi.org/10.4197/Islec.32-1.1

Liu, F. H., & Lai, K. P. (2021). Ecologies of green finance: Green sukuk and development of green Islamic finance in Malaysia. *Environment and Planning a: Economy and Space, 53*(8), 1896–1914.

Ma'ruf, A., Mahomed, Z., & Mohamad, S. (2021). Sustainable finance and a Sharī'analysis of environmental, social and governance (ESG) criteria. In M. K. Hassan, M. Saraç & A. Khan (Eds.), *Islamic Finance and Sustainable Development: A Sustainable Economic Framework for Muslim and Non-Muslim Countries*, (pp. 193–217). Springer International Publishing.

Miskam, S., & Abdullah, M. (2021). Integrating environmental, social and governance (ESG) into Shariah-compliant fund investment portfolios: legal and regulatory initiatives in Malaysia. In *International Conference on Syariah and Law 2021 (ICONSYAL 2021).*

Mohammad, W. M. W., & Wasiuzzaman, S. (2021). Environmental, Social and Governance (ESG) disclosure, competitive advantage and performance of firms in Malaysia. *Cleaner Environmental Systems, 2*, 100015. https://doi.org/10.1016/j.cesys.2021.100015

Mohsin, A., Ramli, N., & Alkhulayfi, B. A. (2016). Halal tourism: Emerging opportunities. *Tourism Management Perspectives, 19*, 137–143.

Murninghan, M. (1992). Corporations and social responsibilities: a historical perspective. In P. D. Kinder, S. D. Lydenberg, & A. L. Domini (Eds.), *The Social Investment Almanac*, New York: Henry Holt and Company.

Mustafida, R., & Fauziah, N. N. (2021). Implementing ESG concept in Sharia stock screening process. *Hasanuddin Economics and Business Review, 5*(1), 1–7.

Paltrinieri, A., Dreassi, A., Migliavacca, M., & Piserà, S. (2020). Islamic finance development and banking ESG scores: Evidence from a cross-country analysis. *Research in International Business and Finance, 51*, 101100.

PR Newswire. (2023). *Saudi Exchange issues ESG disclosure guidelines for listed companies.* Retrieved 2 April, 2023, from https://www.prnewswire.com/news-releases/saudi-exchange-issues-esg-disclosure-guidelines-for-listed-companies-301410935.html

Pratiwi, L. F. L., Millaty, M., & Dewi, M. P. (2022). Development strategy for palm sugar product attribute: A competitive product to achieving sustainable development goals (SDGs). In *IOP Conference Series: Earth and Environmental Science* (Vol. 1018, No. 1, p. 012001). IOP Publishing.

Qomaro, G. W. (2019). Pesantren as halal tourism co-branding: Halal industry for sustainable development goals. *Maqdis: Jurnal Kajian Ekonomi Islam, 4*(1), 11–22.

Qoyum, A., & Fauziyyah, N. E. (2019). The halal aspect and islamic financing among micro, small, and medium enterprises (MSMEs) in Yogyakarta: Does berkah matter? *Journal of Islamic Monetary Economics and Finance, 5*(1), 215–236.

Ramli, N. M., Kam, A. N. S., Jamil, N. N. B., & Harun, H. (2022). Could ESG and halal practices be converged? Preliminary evidence based on integrated reporting and sustainability reporting of a halal-certified company. *Journal of Fatwa Management and Research, 27*(4), 16–32.

RECAM. (2023). 10 examples of green technology. Retrieved 10 April, 2023, from https://tecamgroup.com/10-examples-of-green-technology/

Sairally, B. S. (2015). Integrating environmental, social and governance (ESG) factors in Islamic finance: Towards the realisation of maqāṣid al-sharīʿah. *ISRA International Journal of Islamic Finance, 7*(2), 145–154.

Salaheldeen, M., Battour, M., & Nazri, M. A. (2019). Halal entrepreneurship and its role in sustainable development goals 2030 (SDGs). In *International Conference on Dakwah and Islamic Management (IC-DAIM 2019) Malaysia* (pp. 1–12).

Salaheldeen, M., Battour, M., Nazri, M. A., & Bustamam, U. S. A. (2021). Prospects for achieving the sustainable development goals 2030 through a proposed halal entrepreneurship success index (HESI). In *SHS Web of Conferences* (Vol. 124, p. 1–8). EDP Sciences.

Salleh, M. M., & Harun, E. H. (2022). Halal food supply chain (HFSC) and sustainability concept. *Journal of Islamic, 7*(49), 26–34.

Shaikh, I. (2022). Environmental, social, and governance (ESG) practice and firm performance: An international evidence. *Journal of Business Economics and Management, 23*(1), 218–237.

Shalhoob, H., & Hussainey, K. (2023). Environmental, social and governance (ESG) disclosure and the small and medium enterprises (SMEs) sustainability performance. *Sustainability, 15*(1), 200.

Talaei, A., Ahadi, M. S., & Maghsoudy, S. (2014). Climate friendly technology transfer in the energy sector: A case study of Iran. *Energy Policy, 64*, 349–363.

Trimulato, T., Syarifuddin, S., & Lorenza, P. (2022). The role Halal industry to support sustainable development goals (SDGs). *Annual Conference on Islamic Economy and Law, 1*(2), 205–217.

Umar, U. H., & Abubakar, M. (2021). Maximizing zakat revenues in the COVID-19 period. *International Journal of Zakat, 6*(2), 63–74.
Umar, U. H., & Haron, M. H. (2021). The Islamic need for investing inherited wealth and accounting treatments. *The Journal of Muamalat and Islamic Finance Research, 18*(1), 1–13. https://doi.org/10.33102/jmifr.v18i1.323
Umar, U. H., Kademi, T. T., & Haron, M. H. (2020). Integrating WqÄ f and Business: Ensuring business sustainability for the welfare of heirs and non-heirs. *International Journal of Economics, Management and Accounting, 28*(1), 191–213.
Umar, U. H. (2019). A basic comprehensive accounting package for mushārakah: consolidation of islamic and conventional practices. In E. Ghazal, D. Mutum, M. Rashid, & J. Ahmed (Eds.), *Management of Sharīʿah Compliant Businesses. Management for Professionals*, (pp. 85–93). Springer, Cham.
Umar, U. H., & Kurawa, J. M. (2019). Business succession from an Islamic accounting perspective. *ISRA International Journal of Islamic Finance, 11*(2), 267–281. https://doi.org/10.1108/IJIF-06-2018-0059
Umar, U. H., Baita, A. J., Haron, M. H. B., & Kabiru, S. H. (2022a). The potential of Islamic social finance to alleviate poverty in the era of COVID-19: The moderating effect of ethical orientation. *International Journal of Islamic and Middle Eastern Finance and Management, 15*(2), 255–270. https://doi.org/10.1108/IMEFM-07-2020-0371
Umar, U. H., Besar, M. H. A., & Abduh, M. (2022b). Compatibility of the CSR practices of Islamic banks with the United Nations SDGs amidst COVID-19: A documentary evidence. *International Journal of Ethics and Systems*. https://doi.org/10.1108/IJOES-12-2021-0221
United Nations. (2020). Sustainable development goals guidelines for the use of the SDG logo including the colour wheel and 17 icons. Retrieved 16 April, 2021 from https://sdgs.un.org/
Wilson, R. (1997). Islamic finance and ethical investment. *International Journal of Social Economics, 24*(11), 1325–1342. https://doi.org/10.1108/03068299710193624
Zailani, S., Iranmanesh, M., Aziz, A. A., & Kanapathy, K. (2017). Halal logistics opportunities and challenges. *Journal of Islamic Marketing, 8*(1), 127–139. https://doi.org/10.1108/JIMA-04-2015-0028
Zheng, Z., Li, J., Ren, X., & Guo, J. M. (2023). Does corporate ESG create value? New evidence from M&As in China. *Pacific-Basin Finance Journal, 77*, 101916.

Strengthen the Sustainability of Halal Entrepreneurs Through International Consumer Rights Laws

Kamarudeen Babatunde Bello

Abstract The global halal industry continues to experience growth and acceptance by Muslims and non-Muslims alike. This has created opportunities for expanded buyer–seller relationships. In such situations, potential for conflicts also increases, which may arise from dissatisfaction emanating from the non-observance of customer rights. To this end, this chapter provides an exposition on the growth of halal entrepreneurship, along with the fundamental consumer rights as contained in the United Nations Guidelines for Consumer Protection (UNGCP). The chapter further discusses the need for halal entrepreneurs to imbibe the UNGCP guidelines as a means towards strengthening relationship with customers so as to strengthen the industry further. In line with existing literature, the chapter notes the fact that prescriptions contained in the Qur'an and the Hadiths have provided sufficient laws to cater for protection of halal consumer rights; hence, no need for new laws to protect halal consumer rights. Rather, industry players should set up mechanisms to harmonize existing standard set by countries based on the provisions of the Qur'an and Hadith.

Keywords Halal entrepreneurs · Entrepreneurship · Consumer rights laws · Sharia

1 Introduction

Entrepreneurship is globally acknowledged as a major driver of economic growth and development (Azim, 2011; Hassan, 2022; Naude, 2010). It is a concept that has gained high regards, not only as a major contributor in eradication of poverty (Azam & Abdallah, 2021) but also for employment generation and improved living conditions through provision of innovative goods and services (Azam & Abdallah, 2021; Ratten et al., 2017; Schumpeter, 1934). The ubiquitous nature of the entrepreneurship concept has made it a topic of discourse in several facets of human lives, such that contemporary literature is replete with various branches (aspects) of entrepreneurship such as youth entrepreneurship, women entrepreneurship, social

K. B. Bello (✉)
Department of Business Administration, Modibbo Adama University, Yola, Nigeria
e-mail: kbbello@mau.edu.ng

L. Raimi et al. (eds.), *Contemporary Discourse of Halal and Islamic Entrepreneurship*,
https://doi.org/10.1007/978-981-99-6427-7_4

entrepreneurship, disability entrepreneurship, and religious entrepreneurship. These aspects of entrepreneurship have jointly and individually enhanced the growth of the entrepreneurial concept, while also creating opportunities for distinct group of persons to gain a livelihood and make meaningful contributions to the general well-being of societies across the world (Abdullah et al., 2021; Glancey & McQuaid, 2000; Ratten et al., 2017).

From the aspect of religious, entrepreneurship comes the concept of Islamic entrepreneurship, which has been described as a unique form of religious entrepreneurship; because it centers on individuals who choose to pursue entrepreneurship, not just for economic and social gains, but to also seek favors of Allah (Abdullah et al., 2021; Machmud & Hidayat, 2020); through keeping faith to their deep religious injunctions of honesty, equality, and fair trading with all, irrespective of differences in religion (Hoque et al., 2014; Ratten et al., 2017). Observance of these injunctions requires that concerned entrepreneurs pay attention to, and differentiate between that which is halal (permitted) and that which is forbidden (haram) in all dealings. Generally, Muslims strive to incorporate their religious beliefs into their activities (Ratten et al., 2017), and thus, strive to pursue halal in order to achieve the promised earthly and eternal rewards with the same vigor that they strive to avoid haram so as to avoid the associated stern punishment in the world and the hereafter (Wiryani et al., 2018).

The quest for piety through honesty, equality, and fair trade has made it incumbent upon Muslim entrepreneurs to incorporate halal into their business activities. This underscores the growing popularity of the halal entrepreneurship concept, which is defined in this chapter to mean processes for conducting business activities strictly under the guidance of Sharia. Individuals or groups pursuing this kind of entrepreneurship are referred to as 'Halal Entrepreneurs'. It is however important to stress the fact despite being deeply rooted in the Sharia Law, the halal entrepreneur concept is not exclusive to Muslims, as it accommodates non-Muslims who find the practice attractive and are willing to abide by the Sharia codes (Azam & Abdallah, 2021).

Pursuance of religious commandments for equality and fair trade in dealings with all and sundry is likened to the requirements for ethics and social responsibility in the secular business world (Chowdhury, 2008). The general requirement for social responsibility entails that business considers the interests of all of its stakeholders—owners, workers, customers, suppliers, financiers, community, larger society and entire ummah in the case of Islamic entrepreneurship (Azam & Abdallah, 2021). Among all the stakeholder groups, the customers have been given a pride of place in terms of expectations of companies' ethical and responsible behavior, albeit without prejudice to all the other groups. The customer is considered a veritable representation of all stakeholder groups, as encapsulated in the notion of generalized customer proposed by Daub & Ergenzinger (2005). To this end, issues bothering on protection of customer rights in relation to business have received global attention, with the United Nations going as much as advancing guidelines for the protection of consumer rights, which every business is expected to comply. It is important to point out that evidences from contemporary literature tend to indicate that there is still lots of rooms for improvement in terms of observance and protection of customer rights by businesses.

With the above background, given the growing popularity of halal entrepreneurship, coupled with the unique requirements for the protection of the halal rights of halal conscious (not just Muslim) consumers; this chapter presents an exposition on the imperative for halal entrepreneurship to operate within the ambit of the guidelines for the United Nations Consumer Protection (UNGCP). The chapter places particular emphasis on the halal food segment, which has obviously received the most attention of all halal entrepreneurship sectors.

2 Literature Review/Conceptual Clarifications

The discourse in this chapter centers on the means to strengthen halal entrepreneurs through international consumer rights laws. To get a better grasp of the discourse, few core concepts need to be effectively clarified. These clarifications are presented in the subsequent subsections.

2.1 *Entrepreneurship*

The term entrepreneurship is generally believed to have evolved from the French verb 'entreprendre', which connotes 'to undertake/begin' (Davis, 2013); or 'to accomplish/embrace' (Azam & Abdallah, 2021). In terms of modern application, there has been multiplicity of definitions for the concept of entrepreneurship, with all expanding on the original French verb. Key components of entrepreneurship common to most definitions include the possession of essential skills, capacity to innovate, willingness to assume risk, and capacity to spot opportunities and mobilize resources to tap same (Azam & Abdallah, 2021; Ratten et al., 2017; Ronstadt, 1984; Schumpeter, 1934; Stevenson & Jarillo, 1990). Individuals who possess these characteristics and put them into action to create goods and services or other benefits with the hope of reaping some returns are referred to entrepreneurs.

Nonetheless, it is equally important to note that definition of entrepreneurship is not restricted to persons who start, own and operate businesses only. It generally extends to individuals who may be currently employed in a firm, but who develop new business ideas for their employers either or through a combination of new products, new business outlets or new processes (Bosma et al., 2010). However, due to the peculiarity of the subject matter of this chapter, and for the sake of clarity, discussion on entrepreneurs(hip) will reference only individuals who seize entrepreneurial opportunities to start and run businesses by themselves.

2.2 The 'Halal' Concept

The halal concept has its origin in the Arabic language; and it gained prominence over 1400 years ago (Dahlan & Sani, 2016), through Allah's command in the Holy Qur'an, that believers should consume only that which is permitted/lawful and pure/clean (Azam & Abdallah, 2021; Azam & Abdallah, 2021; Dahlan & Sani, 2016). Hence, the often-referred twin concepts of 'Halal and Toyyib' as explicitly captured in Qur'an (16:114):

> Then eat from what Allah has provided for you (which is) lawful and good; and be grateful for the favor of Allah, if it is (indeed) Him that you worship.

On its own, 'halal' refers to that which is permissible, allowed or lawful, and for which there is/are attached rewards for persons who observed it—even if spiritual. Similarly, the twin concept 'Toyyib' refers to that which is pure, clean, quality, safe, or wholesome (Dahlan & Sani, 2016). Halal and Toyyib have very strong bases in Islamic Sharia and are considered important by Muslims, who generally have strong desire to incorporate religious beliefs into daily activities (Ratten et al., 2017). Although the halal concept is mostly popularized in the food industry, Muslims are enjoined to observe it in all spheres of their lives as is currently being witnessed in other aspects such as cosmetics, pharmaceuticals, financing, supply-chain, tourism, and all other activities/engagements with fellow beings.

The meaning of halal in Muslim lives can be further understood when contrasted with its opposite 'haram', which refers that anything that is prohibited or forbidden, and for which punishment is prescribed. This fact is buttressed by the Qur'anic verse:

> Prohibited to you are dead animals, blood, the flesh of swine, and that which has been dedicated to other than Allah, and [those animals] killed by strangling or by a violent blow or by a head-long fall or by the goring of horns, and those from which a wild animal has eaten, except what you [are able to] slaughter [before its death], and those which are sacrificed on stone altars, and [prohibited is] that you seek decision through divining arrows. That is grave disobedience. (Quran, 5:3)

Similarly, Hadith of the Holy Prophet further emphasizes the grave punishment prescribed for persons who engaged in consumption of haram products or engaged in any form of haram activities:

> That flesh will not enter Paradise which has grown from Haram, and all that flesh which has grown from Haram, the fire (of hell) is more worthy of it. (Ahmed, Darimi, Baihaqi).

To this end, understanding of the concepts of halal and haram presents a sound basis for understanding the importance that Muslims attach to obeying the divine injunctions as a means to not only seeking Allah's bounties but to also avoid His wrath and punishment.

2.3 Halal Entrepreneurship

Halal entrepreneurship can be defined as the commitment to producing only good and services that meets the halal standard, and to conduct business activities under strict Sharia-compliance. It entails the recognition of the inherent opportunities in the halal industry, mobilizing of resources to tap into these opportunities, and to provide goods, services and other benefits, seeking not just economic benefits, but also the spiritual benefits that are granted solely by Allah. Engaging in this form of entrepreneurship qualifies individuals to be described as halal entrepreneurs, not minding whether such an individual is a Muslim or adherents of other faiths (Azam & Abdallah, 2021; Ratten et al., 2017).

Although, the growth of the halal entrepreneurship concept can be considered as relatively new, the practice of entrepreneurship is acclaimed to be as old as the origin of the religion of Islam itself. Azam & Abdallah (2021) highlight the fact that the noble Prophet Mohammed and his companions engaged in some form of entrepreneurship or the other. However, it is observed that the term 'entrepreneur' had not been used to address persons engaged in such activities during the seventh century; thus, the term could not have gained popularity at that time (Davis, 2013). To buttress the importance of entrepreneurship in Islam, the noble Prophet is reported to given expressed encouragement for entrepreneurial activities as against acts of begging or indolence, when he admonished:

> It is better for anyone of you to take a rope and cut the wood (from the forest) and carry it over his back and sell it [as a means of earning a living] rather than to ask a person for something and that person may give him or not. (S. Bukhari Vol. 2, Book 24, Number 549).

This prophetic injunction, apart from condemning the act of begging, gives credence to the pursuance of entrepreneurial opportunities in any environment or situation one may find himself/herself. Furthermore, the injunction also underscores the importance of eating from toils of one's hands.

2.4 Consumer Rights Laws

Contemporary literature credits President J. F Kennedy of the United States as the first to codify the consumer rights in the consumer bill of rights presented on 15 March 1962. President Kennedy's initial declaration included four basic rights of the consumers, which he proclaimed must be protected in all situations involving buyer–seller relations (Gok et al., 2013). These first set of rights mentioned by Kennedy are the consumer's rights (1) to safety, (2) right to information, (3) to choose, and (4) to be heard. These basic rights attained popularity through the years, up to 1985, when they were formally espoused by the United Nations General Assembly (Gok et al., 2013), with addition of four new rights, namely, the right to satisfaction of basic needs, the right to redress, the right to consumer education and the right to a healthy environment (Gok et al., 2013; Henry, 2010); thus, extending the number of consumer rights to eight, that have formed the basis for the United Nations Guidelines for Consumer Protection (UNGCP). These rights were subsequently declared by the UNGA as the fundamental consumer rights, and all member nations were advised to adopt and domesticate them. The eight fundamental rights are highlighted below.

i. Right to Basic Needs: consumers' rights to all goods and services necessary for existence. These include food, clothing, shelter, healthcare, education, and sanitation.
ii. Right to Safety: protection of consumers against the production, distribution, and sales of goods and services that have real or potential hazard to health and life.
iii. Right to Information: consumers' rights to relevant, complete, truthful, and timely information to enhance consumer choices, especially with regards to product labeling and advertising.
iv. Right to Choice: consumers' rights to make choices freely, among goods and services of suitable quality and competitive prices; and to prevent consumers' exposure to all forms of untoward business behavior such as monopoly, planned obsolesces, product hoarding, and profiteering.
v. Right to Representation: guarantees consumers' rights to voice out and express their opinions and interests, even in the formulation and execution of government policies that have direct or indirect effects on consumers.
vi. Right to Redress: guarantees consumers' rights to receive compensation in the event of proven misconduct such as deception, faulty goods, or substandard services from business.
vii. Right to Consumer Education: ensures consumers' rights to avail themselves with opportunity to acquire relevant knowledge and necessary skills to facilitate right choices under any circumstances.
viii. Right to Healthy Environment: guarantees consumers' rights to safe habitat, free of danger and threats; and promotes dignity and general well-being.

These rights have been adopted by most countries, and also adapted to specific industries and situations involving buyer–seller relations; and have also been the focus of academic researches across the globe. Hence, the literature has documented specific rights for different buyer–seller situations, like consumer banking rights, patients' rights in healthcare services, passengers' rights in air travels, to mention a few. Hence, consideration of consumer rights in the halal industry is considered a worthy venture.

3 Situating Consumer Halal Rights Within the UNGCP

Given the growing popularity of the halal industry across the globe, it is imperative that halal entrepreneurs strengthen their relationship with the customer by adopting the consumer rights laws as stipulated in the UNGCP. As noted by Ab-Halim & Mohd Salleh (2020), existing legal statutes and provisions of the Qur'an and Hadith have made implied as well as direct provisions for consumer halal rights, efforts are required to connect the rights to those stipulated in the UNGCP as a way to enhance the halal consumers' satisfaction, while also strengthening the sustainability of the halal industry. Thus, as is the practice in most contemporary literature focusing on consumer rights laws and protection, the codified rights in the UNGCP form the bedrock for situating the halal consumer rights.

While noting the fact that halal consumer rights cover all aspects of buyer–seller relations in the halal industry, the current study places emphasis on the halal food segment. This position is informed by the need for clarity, and the fact that the segment has gained popularity over the years. This is evidenced by the increasing awareness on the need for halal certification by companies, and the growing consciousness of the halal logo by consumers at the point of making product choices and patronage. As pointed out by several scholars, the halal food industry has gained prominence over the years and has been embraced even by non-Muslims. Thus, the industry represents a veritable market for willing and committed entrepreneurs (Azam & Abdallah, 2021; Ratten et al., 2017).

To further emphasize the importance of laws for protecting halal consumer rights in the halal food sector, researchers have pointed to the growing popularity of the halal industry, to the extent that it is valued at over $2.3 trillion annually (Dahlan & Sani, 2016; Thomson Reuters, 2018). With the ever-growing population of Muslims globally, coupled with the increasing acceptance of halal products even among the non-Muslim community, there is no doubt that the sector will continue to present opportunities for Halal entrepreneurs to carve a niche that helps in satisfying their aspirations of reaping economic, social and spiritual benefits, as well as solve societal problems. Achieving these goals, however, depends on the ability of the halal entrepreneurs to leverage on the provisions of the UNGCP in ensuring customer rights protection and eventual satisfaction. The interlinking of the halal consumer rights with the UNGCP (Fig. 1) is presented in Table 1.

4 Conclusion and Suggestions

This chapter discusses the need to strengthen the sustainability of Halal Entrepreneurs through International Consumer Rights laws. It is an acknowledged fact that disputes are inevitable in buyer–seller relationships. This fact informed the evolution of consumer rights laws that have gained international prominence through the adoption by the United Nations General Assembly. The literature has provided evidences of domestication of these guidelines in several industries; hence, the need to achieve same in the halal industry, and particularly in the food segment.

The literature has also provided evidences to the fact that existing legal provisions and injunctions from the Qur'an and the Hadiths have provided sufficient laws to cater for protection of halal consumer rights. Although it is equally noted that the diversities in standards and accrediting bodies across different countries have created some form of difficulties in implementing uniform halal regulations across the globe.

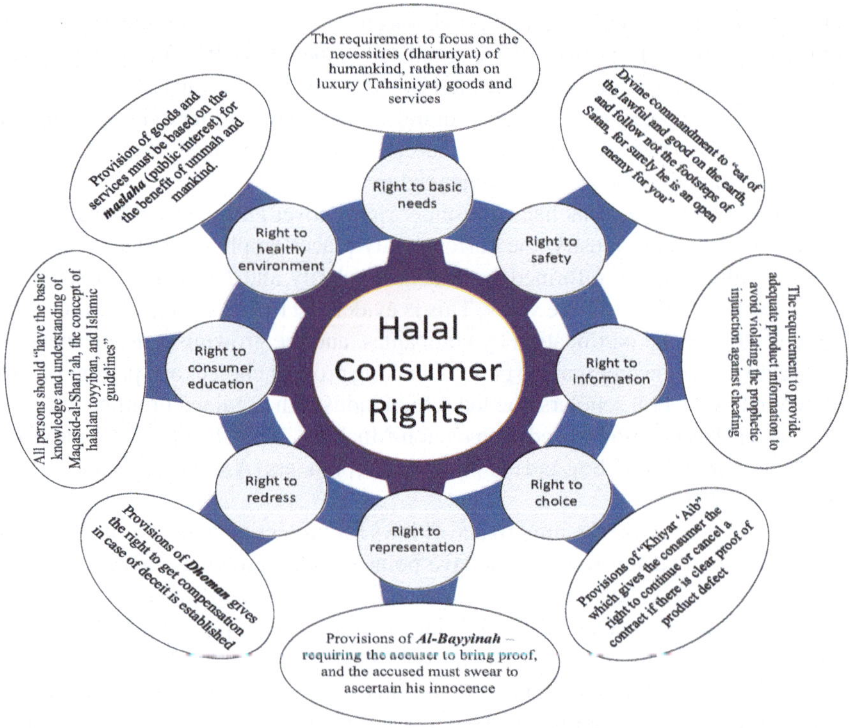

Fig. 1 Linking halal consumer rights to the UNGCP. *Source* Author's configuration based on the literature

However, the fact that all laws relating to halal consumer rights have same origin (i.e., from the Qur'an and Hadith) signifies the possibilities of achieving harmony in global halal consumer rights protection.

Achieving this harmony is largely dependent on concerted efforts of all parties such as the government, NGOs, religious elites and scholars, manufacturers, traders, suppliers, consumer associations, and the individual consumers. Specifically, entrepreneurs and consumers need to familiarize themselves with the relevant prescriptions regarding the Maqasid-al-Sharia and the Islamic guidelines relating to halal and haram. This will help in bridging the gaps in understanding between the two parties, thereby reducing the potentialities for conflict. On the part of the government, efforts are required towards ensuring strict observance of halal certification requirements and monitoring of compliance, with effective sanctions for violators. The NGOs and consumer associations will do well to provide support for the government in the area of monitoring and compliance; while also providing support to consumers in the form of consumer education and empowerment, especially to those consumers at the bottom of the pyramid. As for the religious elites and scholars, they would be required to tap into their fountain of knowledge, through research, to explore the commonalities in the Qur'an and Hadith (as major sources of

Table 1 Linking halal consumer rights to the UNGCP

SN	Consumer right	Description	Link with halal consumer rights
1	Right to basic needs	Consumers' rights to all products/services necessary for existence. These include food, clothing, shelter, healthcare, education, and sanitation	Halal entrepreneurs should focus on the necessities (dharuriyat) of humankind, rather than on luxury (Tahsiniyat) goods and services (Azam & Abdallah, 2021)
2	Right to safety	Protection of consumers against the production, distribution and sales of goods and services that have real or potential hazard to health and life	The commandment to "eat of the lawful and good on the earth, and follow not the footsteps of Satan, for surely he is an open enemy for you" (Qur'an, 2:168)
3	Right to information	Consumers' rights to relevant, complete, truthful and timely information to enhance consumer choices, especially with regards to product labeling and advertising	The requirement for Halal Entrepreneurs to provide adequate product information to avoid violating the prophetic injunction "He who cheats does not belong to us" (Muslim)
4	Right to choice	Consumers' rights to make choices freely, among goods and services of suitable quality and competitive prices; and to prevent consumers' exposure to all forms of untoward business behavior such as monopoly, planned obsolesces, product hoarding, and profiteering	Provisions of 'Khiyar Aib' which gives the consumer the right to continue or cancel a contract if there is clear proof of product defect (Ab-Halim & Mohd Salleh, 2020)
5	Right to representation	Guarantees consumers' rights to voice out and express their opinions and interests, even in the formulation and execution of government policies that have direct or indirect effects on consumers	Provisions of ***Al-Bayyinah,*** i.e., the accuser brings proof, and the accused must swear to that (Ab-Halim & Mohd Salleh, 2020)
6	Right to redress	Guarantees consumers' rights to receive compensation in the event of proven misconduct such as deception, faulty goods or substandard services from business	Provisions of ***Dhoman*** gives the right to get compensation in case of deceit (Ab-Halim & Mohd Salleh, 2020)

(continued)

Table 1 (continued)

SN	Consumer right	Description	Link with halal consumer rights
7	Right to consumer education	Ensures consumers' rights to avail themselves with opportunity acquire relevant knowledge and necessary skills to facilitate right choices under any circumstances	The requirement that Halal entrepreneurs and customers should "have the basic knowledge and understanding of Maqasid-al-Shari'ah, the concept of halalan toyyiban, and Islamic guidelines" (Azam & Abdallah, 2021)
8	Right to healthy environment	Guarantees consumers' rights to safe habitat, free of danger and threats; and which promotes dignity and general well-being	Provision of goods and services must be based on the ***maslaha*** (public interest) for the benefit of ummah and mankind (Azam & Abdallah, 2021)

halal guides) to harmonize the provisions of diverse halal standards across different climes, and seek possibilities for implementing uniform halal regulations that meet international standards similar to the UNGCP.

References

Abdullah, A. M., & Azam, S. E, Md. (2021). Halal entrepreneurship: Concept and business opportunities. In M. Turuk (ed.), *Entrepreneurship—contemporary issues.* IntechOpen. https://doi.org/10.5777/intechopen.93657

Ab-Halim, M. A., & Mohd Salleh, M. M. (2020). Consumer rights in halal products: a study based on legal and Syariah perspectives. *Food Research, 4*(Suppl. 1), 281–290

Azam, S. E., & Abdullah, A. M. (2021). Halal standards globally: A comparative study of unities and diversities among the most popular halal standards globally. *Halalsphere, 1*(1), 11–31.

Azim, M. T. (2011). *Entrepreneurship development in Bangladesh* (1st ed.). UGC.

Bosma, N., Wennekers, S., & Stam, F. (2010). Intrapreneurship—an international study, scales research reports H201005. *EIM Business and Policy Research*

Chowdhury, A. J. M. N. (2008). Towards an Islamic model of entrepreneurship. In M. Loqman (Ed.), *Management Islamic perspective* (pp. 6–19). BIIT.

Dahlan, H. A., & Sani, N. A. (2016) "Halal Laws": From conception to current challenges. In Proceedings of the Persiswa law conference 2016. Persloc

Daub, C.-H., & Ergenzinger, R. (2005). Enabling sustainable management through a new multidisciplinary concept of customer satisfaction. *European Journal of Marketing, 39*(9/10), 998–1012.

Davis, M. K. (2013). Entrepreneurship: An Islamic perspective. *International Journal of Entrepreneurship and Small Business, 20*(1), 63–69.

Glancey, K. S., & McQuaid, R. W. (2000). *Entrepreneurial economics.* Palgrave.

Gok, G., Ozen, U., & Yoruk, E. (2013). Knowledge and attidutes of university students on consumer rights. *Procedia—Social and Behavioral Sciences, 106*, 1656–1668.

Hassan, Y. (2022). A decade of research on Muslim entrepreneurship. *Journal of Islamic Marketing, 13*(6), pp. 1288–1311

Henry, P. C. (2010). How mainstream consumers think about consumer rights and responsibilities. *Journal of Consumer Research, 37*(4), 670–687.

Hoque, N., Mamun, A., & Mamun, A. M. A. (2014). Dynamic and traits of entrepreneurship: An Islamic approach. *World Journal of Entrepreneurship Management and Sustainable Development, 10*(2), 128–142.

Machmud, A., & Hidayat, Y.M. (2020). Characteristics of Islamic entrepreneurship and the business success of SMEs in Indonesia. *Journal of Entrepreneurship Education, 23*(2).

Naude, W. (2010). Entrepreneurship, developing countries, and development economics: New approaches and insights. *Small Business Economics, 34*(1), 1.

Ratten, V., Ramadani, V., Dana, L. P., & Gerguri-Rashiti, S. (2017). Islamic entrepreneurship and management: Culture, religion and society. In *Entrepreneurship and management in an Islamic context* (pp. 7–17). Springer.

Reuters, T. (2018). State of the global Islamic economy report 2018/19.

Ronstadt, R. (1984). *Entrepreneurship: text, cases and notes*. Lord.

Schumpeter, J. A. (1934). *The theory of economic development*. Harvard University Press.

Stevenson, H. H., & Jarillo, J. C. (1990). A paradigm of entrepreneurship: Entrepreneurial management. *Strategic Management Journal, 11*(5), 17–27.

Wiryani, F., Najih, M., & Haris, A. (2018). An analysis of legal protection of halal and thoyib food consumers in court judgments. *IOP Conference Series Earth and Environmental Science, 175*(1), 012195. https://doi.org/10.1088/1755-1315/175/1/012195

Institutionalization of Halal Entrepreneurship for a Sustainable Economy

Mohammad Mominul Islam

Abstract This chapter explicates the imperatives of institutionalizing halal entrepreneurship for a sustainable Islamic economy in the face of unethical practices and fraudulent activities in the supply chains of products across the globe. Imperatively, the planet, people, and profit (3Ps) can shape a sustainable Islamic economy. Halal entrepreneurs can galvanize the Islamic sustainability model, resulting from the triple bottom lines of the 3Ps. The institutionalization of Halal entrepreneurship and sustainability relies on how the concerned stakeholders actively perform their roles. For instance, halal entrepreneurs, supply chain members, Islamic scholars, and policymakers can collaboratively institutionalize halal entrepreneurship. Again, halal entrepreneurs must consider halal certification as a spiritual, legal, and profit-making tool for halal entrepreneurship. The government and other legislative authorities must ensure that the halal certification management process is user-friendly, rigorous, and authentic. Besides, Islamic scholars can galvanize sustainable halal certification by using prescriptive Islamic principles to set sustainable halal standards to support the certification. Based on the halal certification, upstream stakeholders must form a sustainable supply chain to lubricate halal entrepreneurship. All the agents of halal entrepreneurship must be conscious of Allah (*Taqwa*) to refrain from unethical practices and fraudulent activities.

Keywords Halal entrepreneurship · Halal marketing mix · Sustainable economic development · Halal supply chain

1 Introduction

The Institutional Theory (IT) entails coercive, normative, and mimetic pressures for institutional change (DiMaggio & Powell, 2000). The coercive view from the government (Fikru, 2014), the normative aspect from industry (Tarí et al., 2014), and

M. M. Islam (✉)
UBD School of Business and Economics, Universiti Brunei Darussalam, Jalan Tungku Link, BE 1410, Brunei
e-mail: 21h8961@ubd.edu.bn

L. Raimi et al. (eds.), *Contemporary Discourse of Halal and Islamic Entrepreneurship*,
https://doi.org/10.1007/978-981-99-6427-7_5

the mimetic dimension from competitors collectively embed isomorphic pressures (Mariotti et al., 2014). Particularly, IT with Islamic principles can navigate halal business (Islam et al., 2023).

The institutionalization process in traditional management entertains pressure from homogenous groups. They include coercive, normative, and mimic pressures from the policymakers, industry, and producers. The government forces the industry to accept any change, the industry amends the new trend, and producers imitate the change process for traditional institutionalization.

Institutionalization refers to the process of aligning homogeneous forces for a change. The homogeneous actors in a change process must work as the stakeholders for the same end. The stakeholders may include policymakers, legislative authorities, and upstream and downstream members. The government is primarily responsible for bonding with the other stakeholders to attain the goal of institutionalization.

However, the typical institutional process does not incorporate spiritual guidelines, which is crucial in Islamic entrepreneurship for a sustainable economy. Sustainability and entrepreneurship from an Islamic perspective differ from the traditional one. Further, traditional entrepreneurship strives to maximize profit in a capitalistic economy. Typical entrepreneurs do not consider permissible or forbidden notions that halal entrepreneurs accept as the rules of thumb. Again, sustainability encompasses economy, ecology, and ethics in a traditional economy, while a sustainable Islamic economy must center on *Shariah* (Islamic) guidelines to ensure people's welfare.

2 Literature Review

2.1 Halal Entrepreneurship

Halal means what is allowed in Islamic Shariah, mentioned in the Noble Quran chapter 2, verse 168 (Islam, 2022a). Halal translates into Muslims' beliefs, daily living, moral conduct (Wilson & Liu, 2010), and regular consumption (Hashim & Mat Hashim, 2013). Halal businesses are exchanges of halal products to earn profit compliant with Islamic principles. Islamic principles have documented several halal businesses, including *salam* (buying and selling advance) and *musharraka* (partnership based on profit-loss and capital sharing). Also, *mudaraba* (partnership followed by labor, capital, and profit where the capital owner bears the financial loss, and another partner does not take financial loss except labor and time) and *ijarah* (leasing) are other forms of businesses followed by halal principles (Islam, 2022b).

Entrepreneurship is a way to create employment to resolve unemployment or improve the economic state (Chigunta, 2017). Entrepreneurship influences entrepreneurial intentions and vice versa (Anwar et al., 2021). Under the Islamic prescription, halal entrepreneurship might include five crucial issues: the right motivation, halal business ideas, human resource management, finance, and marketing (Islam, 2022c).

Intention or mindset is crucial for halal entrepreneurship. Materialistic end like profit-making is not the goal; instead, Allah's satisfaction is the prime objective of halal entrepreneurs. Then, profit is the reward of entrepreneurship and a halal means of sustaining worldly life. Also, profit is the extrinsic motivation resulting from sustainable business ideas, human resource management, finance, and marketing functions.

2.2 Institutionalization of Halal Entrepreneurship

Halal entrepreneurs, supply chain members, Islamic scholars, and policymakers can collaboratively institutionalize halal entrepreneurship. Policymakers like the government and other legislative authorities must create a level playing ground to sustain halal businesses. They can contribute to creating a sustainable halal certification management process to formalize halal entrepreneurship. Islamic scholars can galvanize the sustainable halal certification by using prescriptive Islamic principles to set sustainable halal standards to support the certification. Based on the halal certification, upstream stakeholders must form a sustainable supply chain to lubricate halal entrepreneurship. Importantly, halal entrepreneurs can create a source of sustainable halal competitive advantage to last halal entrepreneurship.

3 Methodology

A qualitative approach has been followed to showcase the institutionalization of halal entrepreneurship. Halal principles of the Noble Quran were the main focus to strengthen the theatrical lenses of halal business. Selected Quranic verses and authentic hadiths or prophetic traditions, the prescriptive and spiritual guidelines, have helped to conceptualize the economic sustainability model. Further, how halal competitive advantages and supply chain can be attained has been prioritized. Halal certification and standards governed by Islamic principles were the crucial elements of the thematic analysis. The institutionalization of halal entrepreneurship was the main consideration of the thematic analysis via qualitative data analysis software ATLAS.ti.

4 Findings

4.1 Sustainable Economy for Halal Entrepreneurship

People, the planet, and profit can be the lenses for a sustainable Islamic economy. People are the center of the planet's creation (The Noble Quran, 2: 29). Importantly, Allah has maintained balance in earth's creation, and people must be cautious about maintaining the balance (The Noble Quran, 55: 7–8). By maintaining a balance on the planet, people will deal in halal business for profit, not causing injustice to others or being unjustified by others (The Noble Quran, 2: 275–279). Hence, in a sustainable Islamic economy, people must justifiably manage the planet for profit (Fig. 1).

4.1.1 Planet

Allah created the world as a living place in 6 days (The Noble Quran, 7: 54). Allah made people (The Noble Quran, 3: 55) the best creation (The Noble Quran, 98: 7) and subjected other creations to the people (The Noble Quran, 2: 29). In creating the planet, Allah maintained a balanced state and forbade people to violate the balance (The Noble Quran, 55: 8). When people occur imbalance, natural disasters come into the world (The Noble Quran, 41: 30). Hence, ecological balance on the planet is crucial for sustainability.

4.1.2 People

Allah created people only to worship Him (The Noble Quran, 51: 56). Allah's worship covers people's deeds between life and death (The Noble Quran, 2: 162).

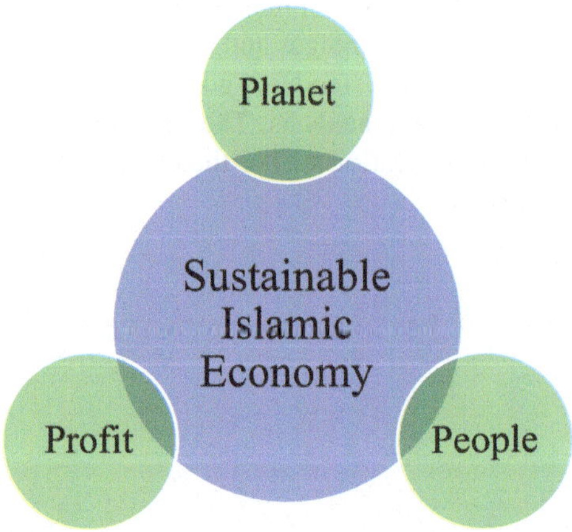

Fig. 1 Sustainable Islamic economy (Original)

From an entrepreneurship perspective, individual people may have different identities: producers, policymakers, suppliers, and retailers. The individuals must play their roles according to Allah's commandments which is monotheism. As such, monotheism (*Towhid*) is the basis for uniting all stakeholders in Islamic business or entrepreneurship.

4.1.3 Profit

Allah has made business halal (The Noble Quran, 2: 275) that may generate profit or loss. The stakeholders must pursue halal entrepreneurship for profit and share the portion justifiably so that nobody becomes the victim of injustice (The Noble Quran, 4: 29; 2: 279). So, an equitable profit must contribute to shaping Islamic sustainability.

The profit formula might look like downsizing costs and enhancing benefits. As interest (usury) is prohibited (The Noble Quran, 3: 130), entrepreneurs must not introduce interest. Interest-based entrepreneurship does not sustain (The Noble Quran, 2: 276). Again, entrepreneurship without interest-based capital will result in a low cost of production, which is the key to increasing profit. Further, Allah has prohibited wastage and abuses of resources (The Noble Quran, 17: 27) and guided us to optimally use resources (The Noble Quran, 17: 29). Consequently, profit will result from the value-added halal products guarding interest and cost.

The planet, people, and profit (3Ps) can shape a sustainable Islamic economy. Islamic entrepreneurship can galvanize the sustainability model, which is the product of the triple bottom lines of the 3Ps. The institutionalization of Islamic entrepreneurship and sustainability relies on how the concerned stakeholders actively perform their roles.

4.2 Sustainable Halal Competitive Advantage (SHCA)

Seven of the marketing Ps can help shape competitive advantage for entrepreneurship. They include people, product, price, promotion, place, process, and physical evidence. As process and physical evidence are associated with *tayiib*, five of the halal marketing principles mainly can devise a sustainable halal competitive advantage (SHCA). Proper blending of halal marketing mixes will yield a strategic position for the halal firm in the halal economy.

4.2.1 Halal Product

Figure 2 conceptualizes the five halal marketing Ps to result in competitive advantages. Halal products are the primary variable for sustainable advantage. Allah has ordered Muslims and others to consume *halal* and *tayyib* (The Noble Quran, 2:

Fig. 2 Conceptualizing halal sustainable competitive advantage (Original)

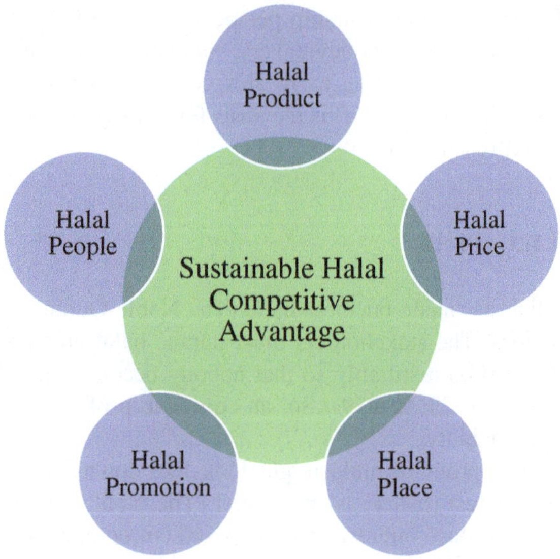

168,172). Even the Quran instructs the great messengers of Allah to consume *halal* and *tayyib* (The Noble Quran, 23: 51). Hence, the boundary of halal products is more comprehensive, and the halal industry is expanding every year. Research shows that Muslims and non-Muslims prefer halal products, resulting in increasing halal product demand. So, the halal products market will be sustainable, and marketers will get a competitive advantage over non-halal products.

4.2.2 Halal Price

Halal price means pricing halal products without *riba* or interest. Interest increases product prices many folds, which further causes consumers inconvenience and reduces consumers' value. Alternatively, consumers' value will increase if their costs decrease, which only interest-free pricing can gift. Allah has forbidden interest in a business in any form or amount (The Noble Quran 2: 275, 276; 3: 130).

4.2.3 Halal Promotion

Halal promotion means advertising halal products following Islamic principles to increase sales and profit. In halal advertising, message, model, and media are crucial. The halal products' promotion should be authentic (The Noble Quran, 33: 70), free from falsehood and exaggeration (The Noble Quran, 2: 42), and effective (The Noble Quran, 2: 83). So, halal entrepreneurs must design advertisement messages about products according to The Quranic guidelines.

Halal entrepreneurs must select advertising models (actors) considering the Nobel Quran guidelines that forbade displaying the man or woman's private parts (The Noble Quran, 24: 30, 31; 33: 59). Avoiding prohibited models that show their private organs and promote sexuality and pollute Islamic culture will save advertisement cost. Modest and cost-saving halal product-focused advertisements will be another source for producers' sustainable competitive advantage.

4.2.4 Halal Place

Halal entrepreneurs need to ensure that halal products reach convenient places for consumers. Further, the networking of all the chains must be halal integrated. Also, halal entrepreneurs must source raw materials, produce finished products, and channel the product to the consumers' hands in a halal way. The combination of all channels of distribution process the halal products to ultimate consumers is a halal place in Islamic marketing. The Noble Quran has outlined the process by saying it is *tayyib* (The Noble Quran, 2: 275). Such halal distribution can make a sustainable advantage for halal entrepreneurs.

4.2.5 Halal People

Individuals who abide by halal principles are halal people who can form a base of halal human resource management. They will sustain an advantage in the other 4 Ps, or the entire marketing process will be questionable. For instance, halal certification and supply chain fraud may question halal products. Allah will make individual Muslims accountable on the Day of Judgment for business, and this belief (*Imaan*) will result in halal integrity. Being aware of Allah, believers can grow such trustworthiness to be halal, integral, and respected here and hereafter (The Noble Quran, 49: 13).

Besides trustworthiness, acquiring reliability, knowledge, and physical fitness help develop halal human resources (The Noble Quran, 28: 26; 12: 55). Managing people under Quranic guidelines will result in Islamic people. These people will leverage the other 4 Ps in halal marketing management to create and sustain a competitive advantage.

Since Islam is the code of halal entrepreneurship, competitive advantage can result from Islamic resources like the halal product, price, place, promotion, and people, known as the Islamic five Ps. These five Ps are unique that non-halal entrepreneurship cannot readily be able to copy or replicate. Therefore, halal entrepreneurs can enjoy SHCA over the competition by cementing the Islamic principles in setting a vision, mission, objective, and strategy. Halal entrepreneurs can only compete with traditional entrepreneurs if they attain SHCA as a strategic tool. Resultantly, SHCA only can foster the institutionalization of halal entrepreneurship for a sustainable economy.

4.3 Sustainable Halal Supply Chain (SHSC)

A sustainable halal supply chain is a precondition for halal entrepreneurship in a sustainable economy. Research shows that a lack of halal inputs impedes halal businesses (Khan et al., 2022; Soon et al., 2017; Talib, 2021; Zailani et al., 2017). Therefore, the institutionalization of halal entrepreneurship is only possible with SHSC.

The application of halal principles into Supply Chain Management (SCM) is Halal Supply Chain Management (HSCM) that outlines the functioning of producing and shipping products to consumers' hands. Management needs to ensure halal integrity along the supply chain, certification, and protocol of halal integrity assurance, including halal committee, supervision, and appointment of the halal compliance officer (Mohamed et al., 2020). Halal certification is the backbone of HSCM (Hassan & Sengupta, 2019; Khan et al., 2019).

Halal, *tayyib*, environment, stakeholder, product flow, efficiency, value creation, and firm-to-fork approach are the constructs for HSCM (Khan et al., 2018). Strategic supplier, customer relationship, and information sharing are the essential functions to be sustained in line with price, quality, delivery dependability, and time-to-market product innovation for HSCM (Hashim et al., 2020). Notably, technological adaptation, halal integrity, the consciousness of the halal stakeholders, halal logistics, and Islamic principles are the components of a sustainable halal supply chain to institutionalize halal entrepreneurship.

4.3.1 Islamic Principles in HSCM

Halal managerial principles (Islam, 2019) and halal marketing doctrine (Islam, 2018; Islam & Reza, 2021) can help halal entrepreneurs sustain halal entrepreneurship (HE). For a successful HE, the *halal* and *tayyib* process is critical. So, HSCM primarily needs to prioritize the *halal* and *tayyib* phenomena for the sustainability of HSC (Khan et al., 2022). Further, halal is subject; *tayyib* is a process that facilitates halal, while *khabith* must be removed from the process. Applying the halal, *tayyib*, and *khabith* concepts denotes the rules of thumb for HSC, and their values and relationship must be galvanized in HSCM (Alzeer et al., 2018). Hence, HSCM needs to manage all the activities of HSC to extend halal and *tayyib* from production to the consumption point with improved performance (Khan et al., 2018).

4.3.2 Halal Logistics

Halal logistics are critical for HSCM (Handayani et al., 2022). Quality of personnel, information, halal assurance, order quantity, and correction actions are crucial for halal logistics (Zailani et al., 2018). Trust in the halal provider services significantly impacts the satisfaction of halal entrepreneurs. Further, halal assurance and diversified halal services by the third-party logistics providers (Selim et al., 2022) and training to the halal logistics personnel (Haleem & Khan, 2017) are significant for HSCM.

4.3.3 Stakeholders' Affiliation in HSCM

A firm's internal integration, suppliers' integration, and consumer integration are needed for HSC (Ali et al., 2017). Coercive pressure from halal certifiers, the government, and markets shape the HSC (Zulfakar et al., 2018). The government must ensure regulation, financial incentives, taxation, infrastructure, guidance, education, and labor supply (Talib et al., 2020).

4.3.4 Halal Integrity

Researchers strongly urge the integration of halal norms from the point of origin to the destination for halal products. Soon et al. (2017) and Handayani et al. (2022) focus on halal integrity in the supply chain to avoid haram contamination. Further, Mohamed et al. (2020) opine on measuring the effectiveness of halal integrity assurance for HSCM. Again, Ali and Suleiman (2018) concentrated on raw materials, production, service, and the consumer to strengthen halal integrity.

4.3.5 Technology for Halal Traceability

Researchers have also stressed testing halal products in case of suspicion by technological assistance. Ab Rashid and Bojei (2020) relate halal traceability and halal integrity with the halal supply chain, arguing that halal traceability is significantly associated with halal integrity for HSC. Then, Fernando et al. (2022) add that halal traceability and halal traceability training can foster HSC. Also, Rejeb (2018) aimed at the halal critical control point, blockchain, and the Internet of Things can help traceability in the HSCM.

4.3.6 A Model of SHSC

Figure 3 shows an Islamic model of SHSC that emphasizes the Islamic principles, the Quran and Sunnah, as the rules of thumb. Particularly, halal entrepreneurs must galvanize *halal* and *tayyib* norms in production, distribution, and management.

At the same time, *khabith* or impurity must be removed. Even *mushabbah* or suspicion must be avoided for better purity or wholesomeness. In case of testing halal status, management must utilize relevant technologies and use blockchain Internet

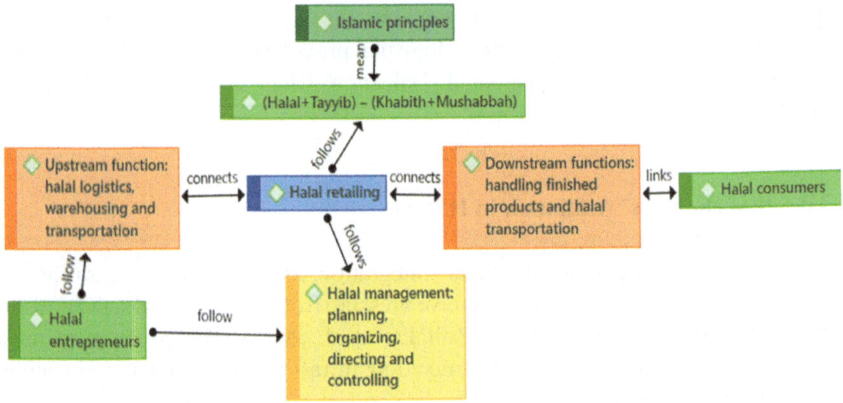

Fig. 3 A model of SHSC (Original)

on Things (IoT) for halal integrity. Islamic principles term science and technologies as *Hikma*.

In other words, Islamic HSCM is the summation of three 'S', Shariah (*Halal*), System (*Toyyib*), and Science (*Hikma*). In addition, a more profound sensation toward the verses related to halal business and consumption must broaden and strengthen the HSCM. For instance, verses 168 and 172 of the second chapter in the Noble Quran outline halal consumption for halal consumers. Then, verse 275 of the second chapter depicts halal business for halal producers. The duties and responsibilities of halal entrepreneurs are to ensure halal integrity until the products reach halal consumers' hands. Halal entrepreneurs will source the managerial principles from Shariah. Also, halal certifiers and policymakers must devise halal standards and other guidelines from the Noble Quran to foster HSC.

The government and other legislators must look into the upstream and downstream supply chains so that unintentional contamination with haram and *khabith* is avoided. For the betterment, all the halal stakeholders must avoid suspicion as halal is not only a business phenomenon but also a spiritual issue, the words of Allah, and a great responsibility.

4.4 Sustainable Halal Standards (SHS)

Halal standards refer to the guiding principles to set the halal certification, like MS1500:2019 for Malaysian halal standards, GSO993:2015 for Gulf countries' halal standards, HAS23103:2012 for Indonesian halal standards, and OIC/SMIIC1:2019 for OIC member countries' standards (Abdallah et al., 2021). Most Muslim-majority countries do not have halal standards. They either copy other standards or use other accredited standards. However, halal standards for individual Muslim nations must be the resource base for halal entrepreneurs and a key to the sustainability of halal entrepreneurship.

Halal entrepreneurs are primarily worried about the variation of halal standards in different countries that impede the growth of the halal business (Fuseini et al., 2021; Haleem et al., 2020; Johan & Schebesta, 2022). Halal entrepreneurs use some of the production inputs that contrast with halal standards. Some of the critical issues include pig, and its by-products (Nikzad et al., 2017), haram (prohibited) gelatin (Ali et al., 2018), risks associated with the contamination of halal with haram (Ab Rashid & Bojei, 2020), genetically modified organisms (GMOs) issues, and alcoholic treatment (Alzeer et al., 2020). Hence, sourcing halal factors of production is a crucial challenge to halal standards for halal entrepreneurs. Sustainable halal standards (SHS) are the protective gear and backups for halal entrepreneurship that must address halal entrepreneurs' challenges. Against this backdrop, Islamic scholars are critical stakeholders in forming halal standards, and government, policymakers, and other legal authorities are the users of the halal standards.

4.4.1 Basics of Halal Standards

Halal and *tayyib* are the two Arabic words centered on Muslims' lives. *Halal* is permissible, and *tayyib* is good. Muslims believe that the ticket to hereafter success depends on passing lifestyle as per the *halal* and *tayyib* guidelines. These guidelines are equally crucial for Muslim certifiers, producers, and consumers. Adhering to the explicit *halal* and *tayyib* guidelines will tranquilize the Muslims' hearts and achieve ultimate success hereafter. Therefore, though Muslims play their due roles as producers, certifiers, and consumers, they must design their way of passing life in the world according to halal and *tayyib* norms.

The opposite of *halal* and *tayyib* is haram and *khabith. Haram* means forbidden, and *khabith* indicates impure. Though the quantity of *khabith* is abundant, *khabith* and *tayyib* are not similar; The Quran says in verse 100 of the chapter Al-Ana'm. Hence, Muslims should accept *halal* and *tayyib* and reject *haram* and *khabith.* Regarding suspicion about *halal* and *haram, halal* must get priority. Between *tayyib* and *khabith,* the latter must be omitted. Thus, Muslims should give up *haram* and *khabith* in producing, consuming, certifying, and acknowledging halal and *tayyib.* Besides, certifiers and policymakers must be cautious in defining and labeling *halal.*

The bindings that Allah has imposed upon the Muslims are for their well-being. This feeling of well-being must tranquilize Muslims' hearts to motivate them to avail *halal* and *tayyib.* Hence, entrepreneurs can follow the business process according to the *halal* and *tayyib* process, and certifiers can supervise the process in the right direction. Moreover, certifiers, policymakers, and governments harmonize and facilitate the *halal* and *tayyib* process. Eventually, the valued consumers will receive the fruits of the harmonious relationship between producers and certifiers resulting from the institutionalization of halal entrepreneurship with Islamic norms.

4.4.2 Few Specific Issues with Halal Standards

Stunning Debates

Making birds and animals immobile before slaughter is a requirement in non-Muslim majority countries. Islamic slaughter principles imply that the animals and birds must be halal, and the name of Allah must be pronounced before slaughter (The Noble Quran, 2: 173; 5: 3; 22: 36). The Sunnah dictates that the knife must be appropriately sharpened, and the animals should not see the knife. Then, the animals must be slaughtered perfectly (Sahi Muslim, book of slaughtering animals and sacrifice).

Islamic principles have specified the slaughtering process. Muslims typically do not make slaughtering animals senseless since the objects may die. Since dead animals are haram, stunning animals before slaughter increases doubt. Islamic rulings also imply avoiding suspicion regarding halal and haram. Therefore, many Islamic scholars are opposed to stunning animals before slaughter. Based on the cautious scholars' opinions, halal standards and certification rulings on halal meat differ. However, leading halal standards have allowed stunning if it is obligatory to access the non-Muslim country for international marketing. Notably, the animals must be alive after stunning and before slaughtering and mentioning Allah's name.

Questionable Ingredients Used in Halal Business

Islamic principles in using ingredients imply that Allah created all the items on the earth for humans (The Noble Quran, 2: 29). The objects include animals and plants, and humans must use halal and *tayyib* (purified) from the objects. The cattle live on grass and are domestic; having different verities are permissible (The Noble Quran, 6: 142–144), but dead cattle, their running blood, pork, and what are sacrificed for others, rather than Allah, are prohibited (The Noble Quran, 6: 145). The *tayyib* state is essential for plant ingredients, although they are halal.

Halal Ruling on Istihalah

Islamic principles imply adhering to the *halal* and *tayyib* (The Noble Quran, 2: 168,172) and forbid mixing impurity with halal (The Noble Quran, 5: 100; 4: 2; 2: 42). Thus, genetically modified organisms (GMOs) used in halal products must abide by the Islamic rulings. The origin of the GMO objects must be halal, and the process must be pure or *tayyib*; then, the output of the GMO-led products will be halal.

Few processed products labeled as halal require gelatin, solvent, and other additives. Halal ruling (*istihalah*) for the finished products associated with GMOs and their ingredients differ. For instance, Islamic ruling about modifying genes is questionable according to the Quranic verse 30 of chapter 30. As such, the verse prohibits changes in Allah's creation resulting in different opinions of the Islamic scholars leading to various standards.

Alcoholic Ruling

Islamic principles prohibit alcohol from causing drunken/addiction and harm (The Noble Quran, 5: 90–91; 4: 43; 2: 219). Prophet Muhammad (Peace be upon him) said:

"Every intoxicant is *Khamr* (intoxicant), and every intoxicant is forbidden" (Sahi Muslim, Book 23, Number 4965).

As such, the basic and specific Islamic principles can guide the formation of a sustainable halal standard to sustain and safeguard halal entrepreneurship. Governments, policymakers, and other stakeholders concerned with halal standards must seek help from mainstream Islamic scholars to shape accepted and global halal standards. Further, Islamic scholars can clarify any critical Islamic issues on halal standards according to Muhammad's prescriptive Quranic verses and authentic Prophetic traditions (May Allah Be Peace Upon him).

4.5 Sustainable Halal Certification (SHC)

A halal certification refers to a license for producers guaranteeing that the products are halal (Islam, 2021). Halal certification significantly differentiates between halal-certified and non-halal-certified products, resulting in competitive advantages (Salindal, 2019). Thus, halal-certified producers enjoy economic advantages (Talib et al., 2017). Perceiving economic benefits, non-Muslim producers pursue halal certification (Rosnan et al., 2015). Resultantly, halal certification is a strategic tool that helps increase sales (Islam, 2022b). Moreover, entrepreneurs perceive halal certification as an ethical guideline and responsibility (Majdina & Jasimah, 2021).

Halal entrepreneurs must consider halal certification as a spiritual, legal, and profit-making tool for halal entrepreneurship. The government and other legislative authorities must ensure that the halal certification management process is user-friendly, rigorous, and authentic. Some Islamic principles can guide halal entrepreneurs for sustainable halal certification.

4.5.1 Authority

The Holy Quran instructs entrepreneurs to follow government authority, and the manufacturers must entertain the government's instruction. Therefore, coercive pressure from the government may result in accepting halal certification (The Noble Quran, 4: 59; 5: 165). Thus, the above two verses can guide the government to pressure entrepreneurs to follow halal certification.

4.5.2 Volunteerism and Cooperation

To accept halal certification, entrepreneurs intentionally can go ahead. Entrepreneurs voluntarily can take the halal certification, halal supply chain, and other halal norms (The Noble Quran, 67: 2). Alternatively, halal entrepreneurs can help cooperate and replicate halal certification with one another in accepting halal notions (The Noble Quran, 5: 2; 16: 90).

The institutionalization of halal certification in the industry may undergo a slow and steady process. The government can accelerate the halal adaptation process by governing the authority, and industry players must cooperate with the government.

Alternatively, industry players will devise halal certification and supply chains, which the government will facilitate. Also, the individual farm can proceed with halal certification and a halal supply chain, and the government and the other farms can collaborate. On top of that, halal entrepreneurs' spiritual motivations can help institutionalize the halal certification process.

4.5.3 Trust in the Certification Board

Halal certifications and logos symbolize a trusting place for consumers who depend on the certifiers. Certifiers and Shariah board act as agents that consumers can rely on (The Noble Quran 16: 43; 21: 7). Mass people need to depend on knowledgeable and authoritarian people regarding halal status. The Shariah board includes Islamic experts and governments. Then, general people can ask the board for further clarification by putting their trust.

Under Islamic principles, Members of the Shariah board must verify the halal production process, and the mass people can rely on the halal certification. Islam outlines guidelines to form the board by *Shura* to certify halal (The Noble Quran 3: 159; 48: 38). Regarding halal and haram concerns, the certification board must avoid suspicion (The Noble Quran, 2: 147).

Shura means consultation, and the stakeholders can form a Shariah board in line with the root word (Islam, 2021). The halal certification counseling board may comprise government representatives, product experts, and academicians of halal marketing. Halal certification, the source of resources, trust, and spirit, emerges from Shariah. So, sustainable halal certification (SHC) can give halal entrepreneurship longevity.

5 Discussion and Conclusion

Figure 4 illustrates the key variables of halal entrepreneurship (HE). Taken together, the individual inputs of institutionalization of HE in a sustainable economy (SE) are SHCA, SHSC, SHS, and SHC. Islamic principles (IP) must govern the inputs to attain institutionalization. Further, halal entrepreneurs are responsible for SHCA collaborating with supply chain members for SHSC. The government and other legislative bodies must look for SHS and SHC.

Hence, halal entrepreneurship institutionalization can partly result from sustainable halal competitive advantage and supply chain from the business stakeholders. The government and other legal entities must input sustainable halal standards and certification to institutionalize halal entrepreneurship. Based on accepted standards, halal certification can gift a nation sustainable halal entrepreneurship where Islamic principles are the keys to institutionalization variables.

The stakeholders of halal entrepreneurship must work for *Tawhid* (monotheism) followed by *Taqwa* (consciousness of Allah) as the shield of refraining entrepreneurship from any unethical and fraudulent activities. Importantly, the upstream and downstream supply chain members and halal entrepreneurs must concentrate on core business functions. Then, the government is primarily responsible for bonding with the other stakeholders to attain the goal of institutionalization. Shariah guidelines on halal and haram must be the rules of thumb or mixing halal and haram will not be sustainable. Eventually, the sustainability of people's welfare must center on the planet with the help of the profit of halal entrepreneurship.

Halal entrepreneurship is encouraged for the believers in the Holy Quran (Chapter 2, verse 275; Chapter 4, verse 29). Also, the Arabs traditionally traveled for business (Chapter 106, verses 1–2). Prophet Muhammad (May Allah Be Peace Upon Him) was engaged in business, and Mother Khadija (May Allah Be Satisfied with her) was a renowned businessperson in Arab. When the companions of the Prophet (May Allah Be Satisfied with them) migrated empty hands from Mecca to Madina, they were engaged in halal entrepreneurship. Engagement with halal entrepreneurship changed the economic condition in Mecca and Medina's golden era, resulting in a sustainable economy. Consequently, finding people seeking charity in that golden regime was not easy.

Similarly, halal entrepreneurship in the present time can result in a sustainable economy if the institutionalization process is shariah compliant. Government, policymakers, Islamic scholars, entrepreneurs, and suppliers must work together hand in

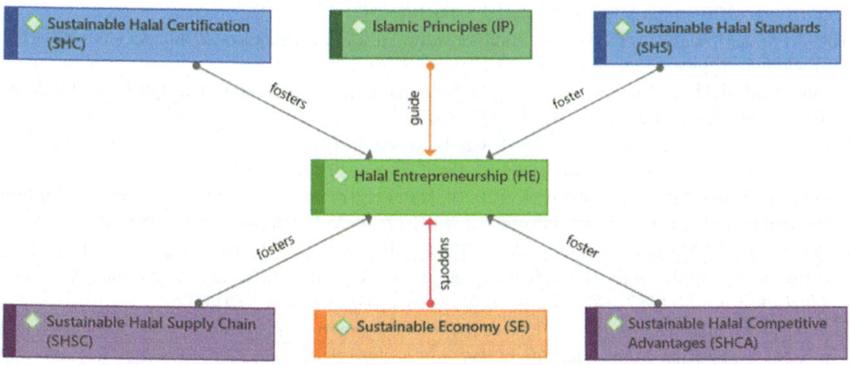

Fig. 4 Halal entrepreneurship institutionalization in a sustainable economy (Original)

hand to get back to the golden era of halal entrepreneurship. All the agents of halal entrepreneurship must hold conscious of Allah to refrain from unethical practices and fraudulent activities. Establishing *Tawhid* by *Sunnah* (Prophetic tradition) must be the fundamental principle of halal entrepreneurship in a sustainable economy.

References

Ab Rashid, N., & Bojei, J. (2020). The relationship between halal traceability system adoption and environmental factors on halal food supply chain integrity in Malaysia. *Journal of Islamic Marketing, 11*(1), 117–142. https://doi.org/10.1108/JIMA-01-2018-0016

Abdallah, A., Mohammed, R. A., & Pasqualone, A. (2021). The multiplicity of *halal* standards: A case study of application to slaughterhouses. *Journal of Ethnic Food, 8*(7), 2–15.

Ali, M. H., & Suleiman, N. (2018). Eleven shades of food integrity: A Halal supply chain perspective. *Trends in Food Science & Technology, 71*, 216–224.

Ali, M. H., Zhan, Y., Alam, S. S., Tse, Y. K., & Tan, K. H. (2017). Food supply chain integrity: The need to go beyond certification. *Industrial Management & Data Systems, 117*(8), 1589–1611. https://doi.org/10.1108/IMDS-09-2016-0357

Ali, E., Sultana, S., Hamid, S. B. A., Hossain, M., Yehya, W. A., Kader, A., & Bhargava, S. K. (2018). Gelatin controversies in food, pharmaceuticals, and personal care products: Authentication methods, current status, and future challenges. *Critical Reviews in Food Science and Nutrition, 58*(9), 1495–1511.

Alzeer, J., Rieder, U., & Hadeed, K. A. (2018). Rational and practical aspects of Halal and Tayyib in the context of food safety. *Trends in Food Science and Technology, 71*, 264–267.

Alzeer, J., Ulrike, R., & Khaled, A. H. (2020). Good agricultural practices and its compatibility with Halal standards. *Trends in Food Science & Technology, 2*, 237–241.

Anwar, I., Thoudam, P., & Saleem, I. (2021). Role of entrepreneurial education in shaping entrepreneurial intention among university students: Testing the hypotheses using mediation and moderation approach. *Journal of Education for Business, 97*(1), 1–13.

Chigunta, F. (2017). Entrepreneurship as a possible solution to youth unemployment in Africa. *Laboring and Learning, 10*, 433–451.

DiMaggio, P. J., & Powell, W. W. (2000). *The iron cage revisited institutional isomorphism and collective rationality in organizational fields* (pp. 143–166). Emerald Group Publishing Limited.

Fernando, Y., Wahyuni-TD, I. S., Zainul Abideen, A., & Mergeresa, F. (2022). Traceability technology, halal logistics brand and logistics performance: Religious beliefs and beyond. *Journal of Islamic Marketing*. https://doi.org/10.1108/JIMA-06-2020-0183

Fikru, M. G. (2014). Firm-level determinants of international certification: Evidence from Ethiopia. *World Development, 64*, 286–297.

Fuseini, A., Phil, H., & Toby, K. (2021). Halal food marketing: An evaluation of UK halal standards. *Journal of Islamic Marketing, 12*(5), 977–991.

Haleem, A., & Khan, M. I. (2017). Towards successful adoption of Halal logistics and its implications for the stakeholders. *British Food Journal, 119*(7), 1592–1605.

Haleem, A., Khan, M. I., & Shahbaz, K. (2020). Halal certification, the inadequacy of its adoption, modelling and strategising the efforts. *Journal of Islamic Marketing, 11*(2), 384–404.

Handayani, D. I., Masudin, I., Haris, A., & Restuputri, D. P. (2022). Ensuring the halal integrity of the food supply chain through halal suppliers: A bibliometric review. *Journal of Islamic Marketing, 13*(7), 1457–1478. https://doi.org/10.1108/JIMA-10-2020-0329

Hashim, P., & Mat Hashim, D. (2013). A review of cosmetic and personal care products: Halal perspective and detection of ingredient. *Pertanika Journal of Science & Technology, 21*, 281–292.

Hashim, N. A. M. K., Aziz, R. C., Yusoof, A. M., et al. (2020). The success of Halal supply chain management practices in Malaysia. *Journal of Advanced Research in Dynamical and Control Systems, 12*(8), 232–236. https://doi.org/10.5373/JARDCS/V12I8/20202469

Hassan, Y., & Sengupta, A. (2019). India—an untapped market for halal products. *Journal of Islamic Marketing, 10*(3), 981–1002. https://doi.org/10.1108/JIMA-09-2018-0179

Islam, M. M. (2018). Islamic marketing practice as a panacea to social marketing criticism. *International Journal of Islamic Marketing and Branding, 3*(2), 104–115.

Islam, M. M. (2021). Segmenting, targeting and positioning in Islamic marketing. *Journal of Islamic Marketing, 12*(7), 1385–1404. https://doi.org/10.1108/JIMA-10-2018-0181

Islam, M. M. (2022a). Evaluating negative attitudes of the students and shoppers towards halal cosmetics products. *Journal of Islamic Marketing, 13*(3), 565–585. https://doi.org/10.1108/JIMA-03-2020-0067

Islam, M. M., & Reza, A. (2021). COVID-19 and Islamic doctrine: Service marketing opportunities to address mental health. *International Journal of Islamic Marketing and Branding, 6*(1), 1–13.

Islam, M. M., Ab Talib, M. S., & Muhamad, N. (2023). Developing theoretical lenses for upstream halal businesses. *Journal of Islamic Marketing*. https://doi.org/10.1108/JIMA-05-2022-0156

Islam, M. M. (2019). Halal management: Translating its principles into branding. *ICBM conference proceedings*, 426–431. ISBN 978-984-344-3540.

Islam, M. M. (2022b). Strategic perspectives of Islamic entrepreneurship and marketing. In *Strategic Islamic marketing*, Chap. 13 (pp. 183–200). Springer.

Islam, M. M. (2022c). Reaching Halal and Islamic market segments: tapping marketing opportunities beyond the borders. In *Handbook of research on ethnic and intra-cultural marketing*, Chap. 15 (pp. 200–212). Edward Elgar Publishing, Inc.

Johan, E., & Schebesta, H. (2022). Religious regulation meets international trade law: Halal measures, a trade obstacle? Evidence from the SPS and TBT committees. *Journal of International Economic Law, 25*(1), 61–73.

Khan, M. H., Haleem, A., & Khan, S. (2018). Defining Halal supply chain management. *Supply Chain Forum: An International Journal, 19*(2), 122–132.

Khan, S., Khan, M. I., & Haleem, A. (2019). Evaluation of barriers in the adoption of halal certification: A fuzzy DEMATEL approach. *Journal of Modelling in Management, 14*(1), 153–174.

Khan, M. I., Khan, S., & Haleem, A. (2022). Analysing barriers towards management of Halal supply chain: A BWM approach. *Journal of Islamic Marketing, 13*(1), 66–80.

Majdina, N. F. N., & Jasimah, W. M. R. C. W. (2021). Religion and cosmetics: Guidelines for preparing products aimed at the Muslim world based on the interpretation of halal cosmetics in Malaysia. *Journal of Cosmetic Science, 72*(2), 139–154.

Mariotti, F., Kadasah, N., & Abdulghaffar, N. (2014). Motivations and barriers affecting the implementation of ISO 14001 in Saudi Arabia: An empirical investigation. *Total Quality Management & Business Excellence, 25*(11/12), 1352–1364.

Mohamed, Y. H., Abdul Rahim, A. R., & Ma'aram, A. (2020). The effect of halal supply chain management on halal integrity assurance for the food industry in Malaysia. *Journal of Islamic Marketing, 12*(9), 1734–1750. https://doi.org/10.1108/JIMA-12-2018-0240

Nikzad, J., Soraya, S., Maryam, T., Nastaran, N.-V., & Maryam, T. (2017). Simultaneous detection of bovine and porcine DNA in pharmaceutical gelatin capsules by duplex PCR assay for halal authentication. *DARU, Journal of Pharmaceutical Sciences, 25*(1), 146–71.

Rejeb, A. (2018). Halal meat supply chain traceability based on HACCP, blockchain and internet of things. *Acta Technica Jaurinensis, 11*(4), 218–247.

Rosnan, R., Osman, I., Nor, N., & Aminuddin, A. (2015). Halal certification: An exploratory study on non-certified restaurants. *Advanced Science Letters, 21*(6), 1854–1857.

Salindal, N. A. (2019). Halal certification compliance and its effects on companies' innovative and market performance. *Journal of Islamic Marketing, 10*(2), 591–605.

Selim, N. I. I. B., Zailani, S., Aziz, A. A., & Rahman, M. K. (2022). Halal logistic services, trust and satisfaction amongst Malaysian 3PL service providers. *Journal of Islamic Marketing, 13*(1), 81–99. https://doi.org/10.1108/JIMA-05-2018-0088
Soon, J. M., Chandia, M., & Regenstein, J. M. (2017). Halal integrity in the food supply chain. *British Food Journal, 119*(1), 39–51. https://doi.org/10.1108/BFJ-04-2016-0150
Talib, M. S. A. (2021). Identifying halal logistics constraints in Brunei Darussalam. *Journal of Islamic Marketing, 12*(6), 1145–1158. https://doi.org/10.1108/JIMA-09-2019-0189
Talib, M. S. A., Ai Chin, T., & Fischer, J. (2017). Linking Halal food certification and business performance. *British Food Journal, 119*(7), 1606–1618.
Talib, M. S. A., Pang, L. L., & Ngah, A. H. (2020). The role of government in promoting Halal logistics: A systematic literature review. *Journal of Islamic Marketing, 12*(9), 1682–1708.
Tarí, J. J., Iñaki, H.-S., & Gavin, D. (2014). Internal and external drivers for quality certification in the service industry: Do they have different impacts on success? *Service Business, 8*(2), 337–354.
Wilson, J. A. J., & Liu, J. (2010). Shaping the Halal into a brand? *Journal of Islamic Marketing, 1*(2), 107–123.
Zailani, S., Iranmanesh, M., Aziz, A. A., & Kanapathy, K. (2017). Halal logistics opportunities and challenges. *Journal of Islamic Marketing, 8*(1), 127–139.
Zailani, S., Jafarzadeh, S., Iranmanesh, M., Nikbin, D., & Selim, N. I. I. (2018). Halal logistics service quality: Conceptual model and empirical evidence. *British Food Journal, 120*(11), 2599–2614. https://doi.org/10.1108/BFJ-07-2017-0412
Zulfakar, M. H., Chan, C., & Jie, F. (2018). Institutional forces on Australian halal meat supply chain (AHMSC) operations. *Journal of Islamic Marketing, 9*(1), 80–98.

Development of Halal Entrepreneurship Framework Through Business Incubator Service for Sustainability Using PRISMA

Nurudeen Babatunde Bamiro, Zainizam Bin Zakariya, and Basit Adekunle Nasiru

Abstract The halal industry is growing swiftly, and halal has become a crucial barometer for Muslim consumers' acceptability. As a result, aspiring business owners wishing to break into the halal goods sector must actively hunt for business mentoring opportunities in order to flourish in the competitive business environment. This study investigates the development of a halal entrepreneurship framework through a business incubator service for sustainability using the PRISMA protocol for systematic review. The Scopus and Google Scholar databases are employed in this review. A rigorous keyword search of the online databases produced 103 research papers from 2014 to 2023, 20 of which were research that was relevant to the issue. The findings revealed that halal entrepreneurship plays a crucial role in driving innovation, job creation, societal well-being, and global economic growth. It has the potential to support sustainable development by integrating ecological and socioeconomic considerations into business practices. Using the Viable Systems Model (VSM), the halal sector can adapt to its environment, meet stakeholder interests, and uphold Islamic ideals.

Keywords Halal entrepreneurship · PRISMA · Systematic Review · Viable system model · Business incubator · Incubatee

N. B. Bamiro · B. A. Nasiru
Department of Language, Arts and Social Science Education, Faculty of Education, Lagos State University, Lagos, Nigeria
e-mail: nurudeen.bamiro@lasu.edu.ng

N. B. Bamiro · Z. B. Zakariya (✉)
Department of Economics, Faculty of Management and Economics, Universiti Pendidikan Sultan Idris (UPSI), Perak, Malaysia
e-mail: zainizam@fpe.upsi.edu.my

L. Raimi et al. (eds.), *Contemporary Discourse of Halal and Islamic Entrepreneurship*,
https://doi.org/10.1007/978-981-99-6427-7_6

1 Introduction

Global economic growth, job creation, innovation, and societal well-being all depend heavily on entrepreneurship. The halal sector is expanding significantly, with a value of $560 billion and a projected annual growth rate of 20% (Abdullah & Azam, 2020). The estimated value of the worldwide halal market in 2017 was US$4.54 trillion, and by 2025, it is anticipated to grow to US$9.71 trillion (Thomson Reuters, 2018). The halal industry's prospective client base now includes non-Muslim consumers in addition to the 2.8 billion Muslims who now make up its core market.

Halal products have evolved as a result of rising demand, striving to provide reliable and satisfying consumption and guaranteeing excellence and safety (Haleem et al., 2020). These goods have the power to influence people's attitudes, tastes, and morals. Despite the misconception that Halal is only required of a particular religious sect, it is actually a requirement that applies to all parts of life, including relationships, revenue-generating, and consumption (Haleem et al., 2020).

The early 2000s witnessed the start of the study of halal, which has continued to advance since 2015 till the present. A significant amount of research is required to provide new insights and discoveries that can advance the Halal business as it continues to expand and flourish (Shamsudin et al., 2022). According to Shamsudin et al.'s bibliometric analysis of 879 halal research publications published in 2022, researchers have paid significant attention to halal management, halal consumerism, and halal tourism.

Also, Mohd Nawawi et al. (2019), Nur Sa'adah et al. (2019), Abdullah and Dzuljastri (2019) argued further that aspects like halal logistics and supply chain management, the halal market and its expansion, halal certification, and halal tourism are some of the more specialized topics covered in the existing literature on the halal sector. There is, however, a glaring absence in the systematic analysis of the halal business or in the explanation of the connections and partnerships among its constituent parts (Khairul Akmaliah et al., 2020). This divide makes it difficult to comprehend how the sector can be long-term managed and sustained.

Also, studies that have already been done on business incubation have mostly concentrated on how it supports the expansion of businesses and the economy (Khairul Akmaliah et al., 2019). The potential for it to be a social innovation, where incubators act as platforms for simultaneous advancement in business, the economy, and society, is less well studied. More specifically, nothing is known about how social-based incubators operate. The operations and effects of these types of incubators, which prioritize social development alongside corporate and economic objectives, need to be explored and understood more thoroughly (Khairul Akmaliah et al., 2019). It is based on this that the study seeks to provide the answer to the following questions;

1. What is the impact of halal incubators on the environment, economy and society?
2. What are the factors that can promote the success of Halal business incubators?
3. How can the Viable System Model (VSM) serve as a Sustainable Framework for the Development of Halal Entrepreneurship?

2 Halal Entrepreneurship

Halal, as used in Islamic law, includes deeds or goods that are allowed, required, or not forbidden (Hasan et al., 2020). Halal has changed from being a term that was historically associated with religion to a branding tool that company owners may use to grow their operations. Muslims are encouraged by Islamic teachings to follow Halal laws and engage in business. Halal entrepreneurship entails creatively grasping chances to build a just society while making money (Khalek, 2018).

Halalpreneurs, who make up a sizable number of enterprises in Muslim nations, are important for the development and prosperity of the Halal sector (Abdullah & Azam, 2020). Entrepreneurship is a notion that is broadly acknowledged and described by academics and professionals around the world. But in the Islamic economy, entrepreneurship is seen differently and is known as "Halalpreneurship." Although this term is used, it has not yet been given a precise definition. Muslim business owners must comprehend Halalpreneurship from the standpoint of Maqasid-al-Shariah in order to defend its application in the Halal market and set it apart from traditional entrepreneurship. Halalpreneurship, which includes endeavours to respect Islamic beliefs and benefit society. It is regarded as a type of religious responsibility (jihad fi sabilillah) that aims to battle social and criminal concerns while also supplying livelihoods, generating goods, giving services, and opening up employment opportunities. Additionally, it is regarded as a way to improve the bond between people and Allah (SWT) through worship and good deeds (Kedah et al., 2015).

In Muslim nations, halal business, also known as halal-minded business, has become more popular and has spread beyond the food industry to include industries like cosmetics, drugs, travel, and banking (Khalek, 2018). With intents based on scripture sources and a specific metaphysical goal, it is influenced by Islamic practices and ideals (Tok & Kaminski, 2018). Islamic entrepreneurship affects a range of levels of analysis, including organizations, people, and institutions. It is supported by three pillars: entrepreneurial, religious-spiritual, and socioeconomic/ethical. Muslim company owners are expected to respect moral standards and assure the authenticity of their operations. It is essential to create a thorough model that incorporates the complexities of Halal entrepreneurship in the complex and dynamic global economy (Salaheldeen et al., 2023).

Halal entrepreneurship has the ability to serve as a catalyst for transformational change by promoting sustainable development principles and actively aiding in the attainment of Sustainable Development Goals (Chapra, 1993; Youssef et al., 2018). If Halal entrepreneurs follow the principles of Halal business, they would have a good understanding of their ecological and societal settings, be aware of environmental threats, and behave with compassion, they will be better able to identify chances for sustainable development (Chapra, 1993; Youssef et al., 2018).

The administration of halal in countries like Indonesia, Malaysia, and Qatar to mention a few shows the commitment of a Muslim country to advance the halal idea and carry out its social obligation grounded in religious beliefs. The development of a robust ecosystem is essential for the expansion of the halal business because of the complexity of halal rules. Due to the lack of information and resources in Muslim-majority cultures, building an entire halal industry ecosystem from scratch is frequently necessary (Khairul Akmaliah et al., 2020). Therefore, it is difficult for any industry to ignore the profitable and quickly growing worldwide halal market. Numerous Muslim-minority countries have become interested in this industry due to its extensive influence and significant growth potential (Fazira, 2020).

3 Business Incubator

Business incubation is the process of using an incubator as a start-up company's support network. The incubator provides a range of services, such as space rents, legal and accounting counsel, and links to suppliers and customers. Since incubators' rental prices are often lower than market rates, they offer businesses a safe and supportive environment that improves their chances of expansion and sustainability (Khairul Akmaliah et al., 2019). The primary goal of business incubator programs is to support local economic development and business expansion. Incubators provide new businesses with a secure environment in which to thrive, and investors benefit from a steady rental income that supports the incubator's expansion and operations (Khairul Akmaliah et al., 2019).

Young entrepreneurs can get support from business incubators. Surprisingly, 87% of firms that have graduated from business incubators still successfully run their companies (Jimainal et al., 2022). Additionally, more than 80% of business owners who got resources from these incubators succeeded, demonstrating the value of such support for young firms (National Business Incubation Association, 2007).

Incubators are essential for promoting the growth and development of new businesses, which can boost innovation systems within a cluster or a particular geographic area. Incubators increase the possibility of economic success in that area by offering assistance and resources. The expansion of enterprises assisted by incubators is consistent with the societal objective of creating wealth for business owners and supporting local economic growth. Numerous studies have emphasized the beneficial effects of incubators on local economies and wealth development (Mohd Fuaad et al., 2012).

Incubators are companies that offer a range of assistance to business owners at the beginning of their ventures. Coworking areas, education, workshops, coaching, networking, technological advice, and capital access are some of these offerings (Handoyo et al., 2021). By encouraging innovation and promoting the formation of new businesses, incubators promote government programs aimed at attaining economic growth (McIver-Harris & Tatum, 2020; OECD, 2019).

4 Methodology

The PRISMA technique was utilized for a thorough literature research of halal business incubators in the halal industry in the study. The PRISMA statement, which offers instructions for performing systematic reviews (Enrico, 2021; Yusuf et al., 2022), was used to conduct the review. PRISMA statement is a standardized and stringent set of instructions for performing systematic literature reviews (Costan et al., 2021). In order to find halal business incubators, a search procedure that included choosing a search database, employing keywords to search, gathering reference materials, and doing the content analysis was used. The review's results were then presented using descriptive statistics.

4.1 Search Strategy

The writers extracted a wide range of peer-reviewed literature from well-known sources using the Scopus and Google Scholar databases to ensure comprehensive coverage of publications related to halal business incubators. Then, only the most pertinent journal articles were carefully chosen for their review. The two databases, Scopus and Google Scholar, are frequently used to conduct searches across a variety of fields, including the sciences, the humanities, medicine, and the arts (Yusop et al., 2022). In addition, the researchers manually searched these databases for pertinent papers using keywords like "Halal business incubators," "Business incubator in Muslim countries," and "Halal business incubator and business performance."

4.2 Screening Phase

In this stage, five duplicate articles were found and eliminated from the data gathered from SCOPUS and Google Scholar databases. So, on the leftover were 98 distinct articles, of which 47 satisfied their precise requirements and were chosen for additional examination. These requirements included elements like the nature of the research papers, the language, and the period of publishing. The study specifically focused on articles released between 2014 and 2023, a 10-year time frame.

4.3 Eligibility

At this point, the titles and abstracts of the papers were reviewed to determine whether they were still appropriate for the review. Researchers only chose publications that satisfied the eligibility standards and fulfilled all of the requirements in the two rounds. Books, non-English language articles, and conference proceedings satisfy the exclusion criteria and other works published after 2013 are included to acquire accurate and high-quality data. About 20 publications, total were included in these systematic reviews' final articles (Table 1). The below PRISMA flowchart shows the step-by-step approach employed in the scientific review.

Table 1 Data extraction

Serial number	Authors and year	Method	Sector	Country
1	Handoyo et al. (2021)	Qualitative	ICT	Indonesia
2	Ahwarumi et al. (2018)	Qualitative	Social entrepreneurship	Indonesia
3	Jimainal et al. (2022)	Quantitative	Business	Malaysia
4	Khairul Akmaliah et al. (2019)	Qualitative	Business	Malaysia
5	Hendratmi et al. (2022)	Quantitative	Social entrepreneurship	Indonesia
6	Dawood et al. (2014)	Qualitative	Business	Malaysia
7	Hadiningrum et al. (2021)	Qualitative	Social entrepreneurship/ financing	Indonesia
8	Vanderstraeten et al. (2020)	Quantitative	Administrative support service	Indonesia
9	Khairul Akmaliah et al. (2020)	Qualitative	Business	Taiwan
10	Hendratmi et al. (2019)	Qualitative	Financing	Indonesia
11	Jamil et al. (2016)	Qualitative	Business	Malaysia
12	Indiran et al. (2021)	Qualitative	Business	Malaysia
13	Sukhur et al. (2018)	Qualitative	Technology	Malaysia
14	Baskaran et al. (2019)	Qualitative	Social entrepreneurship	Malaysia
15	Gozali et al. (2018)	Quantitative	Business	Indonesia
16	Amiruddin et al. (2021)	Quantitative	Social entrepreneurship	Malaysia
17	Gozali et al. (2015)	Qualitative	Social entrepreneurship	Indonesia
18	Ayatse et al. (2017)	Qualitative	Business	Nigeria
19	Rusmana et al. (2021)	Qualitative	Business	Indonesia
20	Sariningsih et al. (2023)	Qualitative	Social entrepreneurship	Indonesia

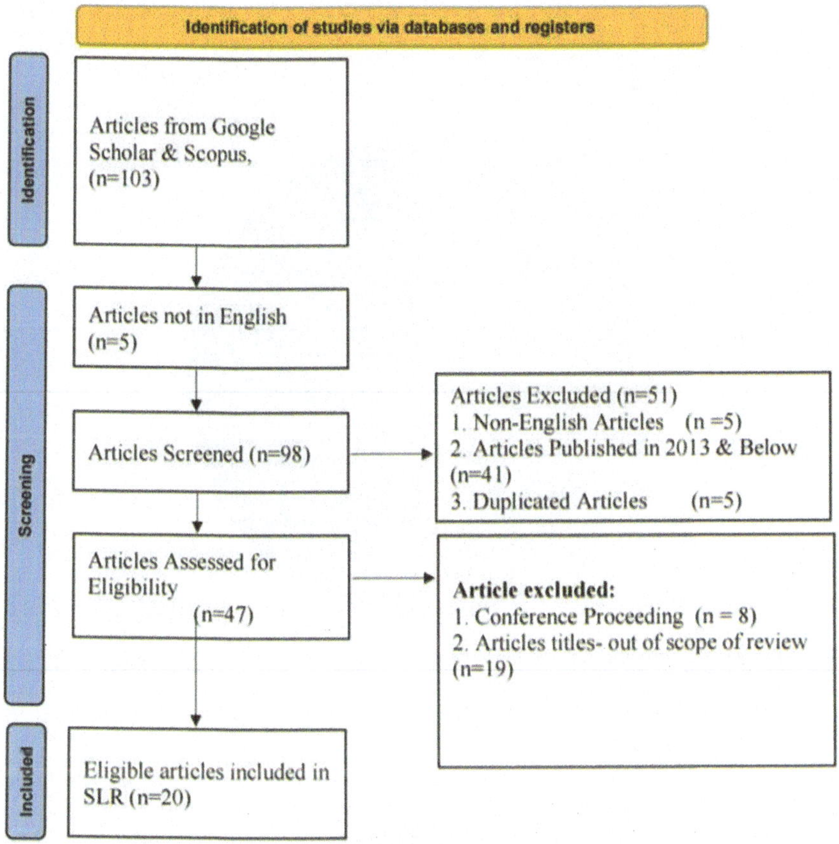

Source Page et al. (2020)

Figure 1 shows that most publications on halal incubators are based in Indonesia and Malaysia while 5% of the publications are from Taiwan and Nigeria.

Figure 2 shows that the highest number of publications centred around business incubators' services on business and social enterprises, respectively. Forty-three per cent of the studies focus on halal incubators promoting start up businesses through effective business management and mentoring of their incubatees while 33% of the studies are directed towards halal incubators that have been instrumental in driving social enterprise and supporting poverty reduction business initiatives for young graduates and the unemployed. 10% of the studies centred around halal incubators' services promoting halal financing for young entrepreneurs to survive in the industry. Equally, the least of the studies posited that 9 and 5% of the studies focus on how halal incubators impact the ICT infrastructures and administrative support services of the young start-up.

Figure 3 indicated that 75% of the publications used in the study are qualitative while 25% are quantitative.

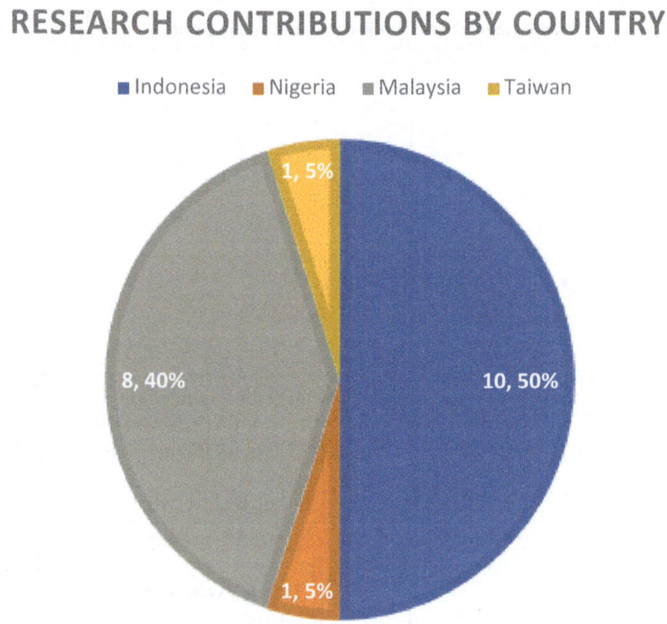

Fig. 1 Research contributions by country

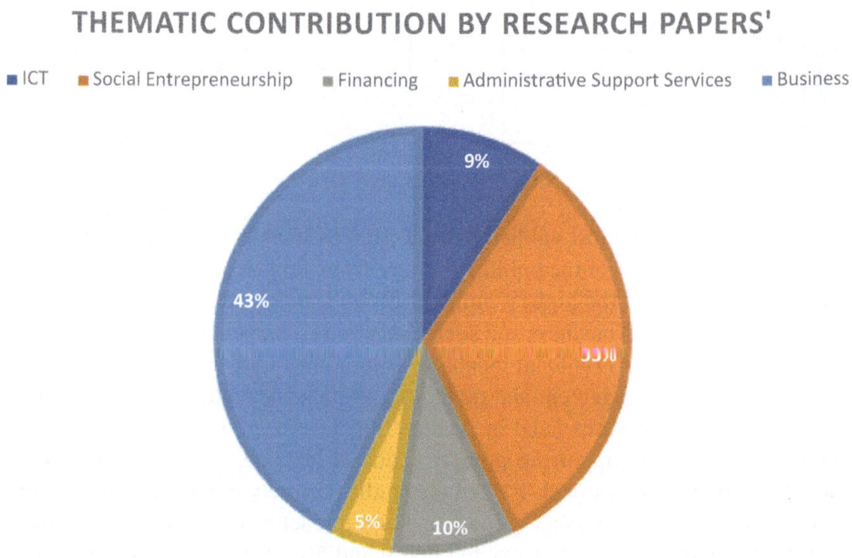

Fig. 2 Thematic contribution by research papers

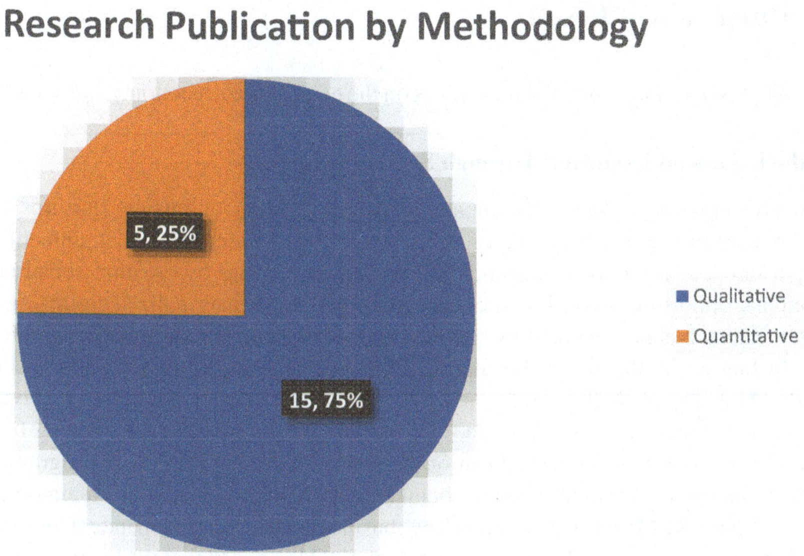

Fig. 3 Research publication by methodology

Figure 4 indicates that largest number of publications used in the review are published in year 2021 and 2018, respectively.

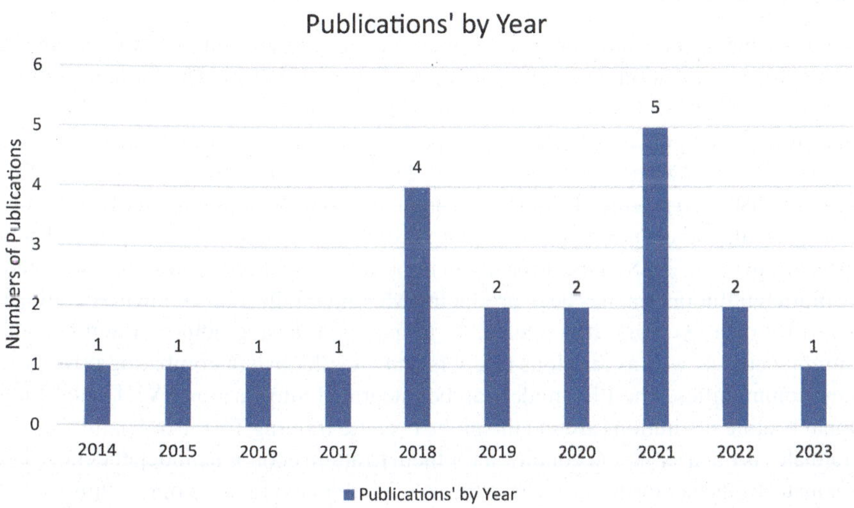

Fig. 4 Publications by year

5 Discussion of Result

1. What is the impact of halal incubators on the environment, economy and society?

Reducing Social Exclusion Through Social Protection

Ethical incubator services encompass economic criteria of raising start-ups for economic gains alone. Its mode of operation has also promoted the attainment of the sustainable development agenda of the United Nations by creating social and economic opportunities for low-income earners and other marginalized groups. With this, the halal business incubators are reducing social exclusion through social safety net. In Indonesia, the Social Entrepreneurial Programme (ProKUS) was launched by the Ministry of Social Affairs in 2020 to give KPMs (poor families receiving state assistance) company capital, advice on social enterprise, and mentoring from business incubators in higher education (Sariningsih et al., 2023). The programme seeks to increase their innovation in social entrepreneurship. ProKUS's main objective is to help KPMs who are starting new businesses become independent and stop relying on government aid. Hadiningrum et al. (2021) posited that the business incubator at Tabungan Wakaf Indonesia is an incubator that is directed towards social entrepreneurship and poverty reduction strategy through the management of educational establishments for the benefit of the children of the poor. Also, the incubator managed health facilities in order to benefit the poor and equally managed retail outlets called Daya Mart on behalf of the shareholders that are poor.

Poverty Reduction

Halal business incubator ethical business strategy has continuously promoted employment generation and created more employers of labour. The Pesantren Business Incubator model has been an anti-poverty agent that converts it graduates to employers of labour in order to reduce poverty and create opportunities for youth and families of low socioeconomic status. The Pesantren Business Incubator (PBI) was established to produce Islamic entrepreneurs from Pesantren by integrating religious, social, and economic knowledge to promote personal independence in Islam (Ahwarumi et al., 2018). Pesantren, as an important educational and socio-economic institution in Indonesia, has been producing Muslim intellectuals known as graduate Santri for over 40 years. It is interesting to note that these graduates often become entrepreneurs as well as religious teachers and are effective in combating poverty in their communities. The PBI model can be integrated into various TVET and Traditional Islamic institutions around the globe because training TVET or Islamic school graduates is not a sufficient condition for them to attain economic independence. The graduate needs mentoring services in the area of advisory, funding opportunities, and administrative services to be able to translate their knowledge into solving societal problems.

Islamic Crowdfunding as Economic Empowerment Strategy

Even when they have great ideas or initiatives, young entrepreneurs frequently have trouble getting funding for their micro or small business ventures (Cosh et al., 2009). Startups may find it challenging to obtain funding or draw in investors due to a lack of collateral, weak cash flow, and information asymmetry with investors (Hendratmi et al., 2019). In order to overcome these obstacles, entrepreneurs are increasingly looking at new finance sources (Hendratmi et al., 2019). Through Islamic crowdfunding, young startups with original concepts have the potential to receive funding from Shariah-compliant fintech companies like ALAMI in Indonesia. With an average amount of $75,000, ALAMI has assisted more than 150 SMEs in obtaining funding (ALAMI Press, 2023). Through the company's mobile app, users from other nations can make financial contributions to Indonesian SMEs on the platform. This website-based Islamic crowdfunding approach provides a cutting-edge way for start-ups to obtain alternative capital that can aid in their growth into long-lasting firms by bringing together investors from various locations and business founders in Indonesia (Hendratmi et al., 2019).

2. What are the factors that can promote the success of Halal business incubators?

a. Halal Business Incubator

Gozali et al. (2018) contend that a number of crucial variables have a substantial impact on how well business incubators work. These elements include physical infrastructure, entrance and exit standards, and financial backing. The actual resources and amenities, such as office space, furniture, and utilities, that the incubator offers to its tenants are referred to as infrastructural facilities. The appeal of the incubator to potential entrepreneurs may depend on the availability and calibre of these amenities. Entrepreneurs who match the criteria will be given consideration for the incubator program. The stage of the firm, the industry sector, and the experience and credentials of the entrepreneur are only a few examples of these characteristics. Exit criteria are requirements that must be satisfied in order for a company to "graduate" from the incubation program. The market's preparedness, profitability, and income creation are a few examples of these. Financial resources including seed money, mentorship, and connection to investors are examples of the funding help that the incubator offers to its residents. The success of the firms that take part in the program might be affected by the quantity and quality of funding support. The paper emphasizes the significance of these elements in business incubator effectiveness overall. Incubators can boost their appeal to entrepreneurs and raise the success rates of the businesses they support by taking these aspects into account and enhancing them.

According to Baskaran et al. (2019), there are a number of ways to make an incubator's business model more efficient. Developing more effective value chain models, specializing in particular markets or industries, maintaining a flat organizational structure, and having a qualified management team are some of these tactics. The business incubator places a strong emphasis on the benefits of offering incubators' resources beyond merely furniture and office space. To draw and keep entrepreneurs, incubators should provide extra services like mentoring, networking opportunities, and financial availability.

Effective value chain models optimize operations at the incubator to cut costs and boost value for incubatees. This can involve utilizing technology, reducing administrative procedures, and collaborating with other organizations to provide more resources and services. Specializing in particular markets or industries might aid incubators in developing expertise and gaining a competitive edge. Incubators can provide specialized programmes and resources that address the particular needs of the entrepreneurs they support by concentrating on a particular industry or market. Incubators can function more successfully and efficiently if they keep an open organizational structure and have a qualified management team. This can be done by assigning decision-making responsibility to others, employing seasoned experts with the necessary skills, and promoting a culture of cooperation and innovation. The studies emphasize how crucial effective management and strategic planning are to the success of business incubators. Incubators can increase the value they offer their incubates while also enhancing their own performance and sustainability by putting these techniques into practice.

Amiruddin et al. (2021) conducted research on the success determinants for business incubators. Factors from outside the organization: financial resources, mentoring, networking, government policies, access to research, infrastructure, and technical assistance. Internal determinants include education, experience in the family business, and entrepreneurial knowledge and abilities. The success of an incubator depends on both internal and external factors. Resources and assistance are provided by external variables, but internal elements provide entrepreneurs with the ability to use those resources wisely.

In order to manage the intricate nature of halal business development, Adham et al.'s (2019) emphasize the necessity for halal business incubators to be extremely responsive to the dynamic business environment. Incubators must quickly adjust to these developments in order to promote the expansion and development of Halal enterprises since the Halal industry operates in a dynamic environment. In order to successfully negotiate the difficulties and complexities of the global Halal market, the study emphasizes the significance of flexibility and adaptability in Halal business incubators.

When developing an effective strategy and value proposition for incubators, Indiran et al.'s (2021) emphasize the significance of taking current demands, trends, difficulties, and possibilities within the startup setting into account. In order to successfully help startups, incubators must possess a solid awareness of the current entrepreneurial ecosystem, including the unique requirements and needs of startups, emerging market trends, the difficulties they encounter, and the opportunities open to them. Incubators can increase their chances of success by adjusting their tactics and value offerings to suit the particular needs of startups by taking these aspects into account.

Sukhur et al. (2018) emphasize in their study that a number of factors affect the success of technology incubators in Malaysia. These elements consist of the management team's competence and competence, the scope and efficacy of services offered to incubatees, the selection procedure for startups accepted into the incubator programme, the accessibility of funding sources to support the growth of the startups, and the networking opportunities offered by the incubator. The study emphasizes the importance of these elements in figuring out the general efficacy and success of technology incubators in Malaysia.

b. Halal Business Incubatee

Ayatse et al. (2017) suggest that aspiring business owners who wish to enrol in incubator programmes to concentrate on creating their management, market, and financial plans in order to improve their chances of getting accepted into the incubator programme. The significance of having a comprehensive and realistic plan that includes accurate financial estimates, competent management techniques, and in-depth knowledge of the market and competition is to enhance the success of the incubator-incubator programme.

In order to flourish in this market, Rusmana et al. (2021) suggest that business owners of young halal start-up enterprises combine positioning, differentiation, and branding techniques. By discovering and concentrating on a certain market niche, an entrepreneur can position themselves as superior to their rivals. For instance, a halal fashionpreneur can concentrate on creating apparel to satisfy the demands of Muslim customers who desire modest yet stylish clothing options. Differentiating a product or service from its rivals includes developing special characteristics or advantages. For a halal fashionpreneur, this can entail the use of premium components, creative designs, or ethical and sustainable production techniques. In order to build and preserve a company's reputation and client loyalty, branding is a crucial aspect of the halal fashion sector. Halal fashionpreneurs can promote their ideals, such as a devotion to humanitarian issues or ethical and sustainable production practices, through branding.

3. How can the Viable System Model (VSM) serve as a Sustainable Framework for the Development of Halal Entrepreneurship?

The Viable System Model (VSM) is a framework that emphasizes the stability or sustainability of a system within its environment and employs a systems approach. The VSM offers a structured method for ensuring a system's viability and independence by focusing on control and information flow through five pillars of systemic management, which are implementation, coordination, control, intelligence, and policymaking (Khairul Akmaliah et al., 2020). According to Khairul Akmaliah et al. (2015), the Viable System Model (VSM) can be used as a modelling and diagnosing tool for diverse areas of human endeavour due to its capability to evaluate and enhance complex systems. VSM has been used to model social incubator's operation, the adoption of biotechnology, IT sector development plans and conceptualize a workable research university and monitor the activities associated with policy execution have all been the subject of prior research that used the VSM for diagnostic purposes (Khairul Akmaliah et al., 2020).

Implementing the five principles of recursiveness, complexity, coherence, responsiveness, and variety is essential for system viability (Khairul Akmaliah et al., 2020). Recursiveness describes the existence of sub-systems within a system, each of which is made up of more sub-systems. Subsystems inside a system, all the way down to the level of an individual, are said to be recursive. For a system to function, each subsystem must be functional. For a system to be viable, its components must work cohesively. Cohesion is crucial for system viability, and it involves the cohesive relationships among all five system functions: implementation, coordination, control, intelligence, and policymaking. By balancing internal and external variety, cohesive operations allow the system to handle internal and external complexity with a high degree of responsiveness (Espejo & Gill, 1997).

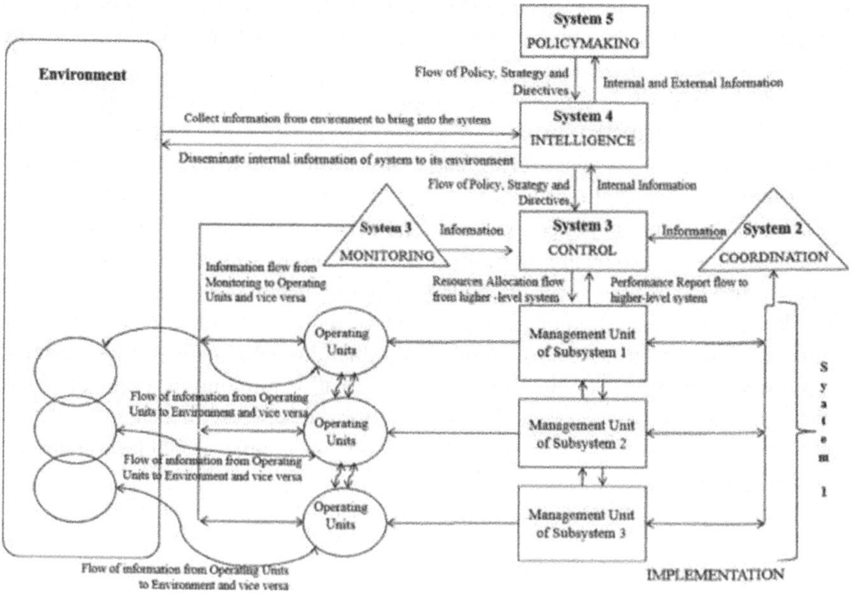

Source Khairul Akmaliah et al. (2018).

Khairul Akmaliah et al. (2019) explained further the interaction of the system 1–5 in the VSM model. The primary production unit is the implementation function, whereas the control function relays instructions from higher-level management (policymaking and intelligence). The coordination function makes sure that all functions are able to communicate and exchange information effectively. The main decision-making function is policy-making, and through the control function, intelligence collects data from both internal and external sources. The policy-making function then uses this knowledge to make decisions. Additionally, the intelligence function shares internal data with the system's environment and uses the control function to transmit policymaking decisions to the operational unit (Espejo & Gill, 1997).

The five interconnected halal industry functions of policymaking, intelligence, control and monitoring, coordination, and implementation should all work together. The halal industry may respond to its environment and meet stakeholder needs while upholding Islamic principles and the halal standard if it meets these requirements (Khairul Akmaliah et al., 2020). It is crucial for the system's application of principles and functions to comprehend Islamic teachings and the halal market. Also, an incubation model that emphasizes the importance of selection practices in the incubation process was created by Hackett and Dilts (2004). The model advises that while vetting prospective incubators, management, market, product, and financial considerations should be taken into account. According to Aerts et al. (2007) and Bergek and Norrman (2008), incubators that follow these standards are thought to be following best practices in the field of business incubation.

According to Porter's Diamond Model (Porter, 1990), an incubator must meet four requirements in order to guarantee the competitiveness of its tenant businesses and sector. First, it should create favourable conditions so that tenants may quickly access resources and take advantage of cost advantages due to location and logistics. It also needs to have favourable demand circumstances so that tenants' products can be successfully sold and satisfy consumer demand. Third, the incubator ought to have an industry rivalry, strategy, and structure that gives tenants a competitive edge. In order to help tenants grow their businesses, it should, fourth, provide favourable access to relevant industries and supporting organizations. In order to facilitate connections between tenants and clients, suppliers, and other pertinent organizations, the incubator should have a concentration of firms. These four elements ensure survival.

An incubator that satisfies the four competitiveness conditions can successfully align its variety with that of the surrounding environment when examined through the lens of the Viable Systems Model (VSM). This makes it possible for the incubator to manage complexity both inside and outside of its operations (Khairul Akmaliah et al., 2019). These standards must be met for the incubator to be responsive to the needs of tenants and other stakeholders. These four conditions serve as the internal elements or necessary variety of the incubator in the VSM framework to successfully negotiate the complexity of the external world. Although Porter's Diamond Model can be used to deduce the requirements of variety, VSM does not state them directly.

The creation of a competitive halal business necessitates that the factor conditions concur with the tenets of Islamic teachings in order to encourage the incubation of halal enterprises (Khairul Akmaliah et al., 2019). The firm's resources, such as its buildings, machines, and knowledge, as well as resources obtained through suppliers and other value chain participants, are included in these factor conditions. Islamic teachings place a strong emphasis on making the best use of resources possible while protecting justice and worker welfare in all facets of business management. Islamic teachings play a crucial role in providing the incubator and its tenant businesses with the necessary variety from the standpoint of the Viable Systems Model (VSM). This guarantees the creation of halal goods that satisfy Muslim customers' needs, representing the exterior variety of the system. The external variety also includes the market circumstances for the tenants' goods as well as the competitive environment on both a national and international scale.

6 Conclusion

Innovation, job creation, societal well-being, and global economic growth all depend heavily on entrepreneurship. By integrating ecological and socioeconomic issues into business practices, halal entrepreneurship has the potential to support sustainable development and help achieve Sustainable Development Goals. The halal sector can adapt to its surroundings, satisfy the interests of stakeholders, and respect the Islamic ideals of the nascent halal start-up by using the Viable Systems Model (VSM). If a business incubator's tenant companies have the following advantages, such as resource access, demand conditions, industry competition and strategy, and access to key industries and support organizations, they will be more competitive. The incubator can handle complexity, align with the external environment, and assure the survival of tenant firms by fulfilling these requirements. Islamic teachings are essential for providing the required variety, ensuring the production of halal products that satisfy Muslim consumers' expectations, and taking into account market dynamics and rivalry.

7 Theoretical and Managerial Implication of the Study

The study offers valuable insights into the influence of a halal business incubator on the effective development of the halal industry. Furthermore, it highlights the need for additional research to explore the role of halal incubator services in areas such as ICT, financing, and administrative support services. The managerial implications of the study emphasize the sustainable growth of the halal industry through the implementation of the VSM model. By considering the business environment, leveraging business intelligence, and establishing effective internal business coordination mechanisms, the adoption of the VSM model ensures the growth and success of halal businesses.

8 Limitation and Direction for Future Study

The study conducted a review of research articles gathered from the Scopus and Google Scholar databases within the limited timeframe of 2014–2023. This serves as one of the limitations of the study. Future research should consider utilizing other databases, such as Web of Science, to obtain more relevant research papers. Additionally, expanding the years of publication beyond 2014 would allow for a wider coverage of papers and a more comprehensive analysis. Furthermore, future studies should explore the application of the VSM model in the context of specific country business scenarios, considering the unique challenges and opportunities present in those settings.

References

Abdullah, M. A., & Azam, M. S. E. (2020). Halal entrepreneurship from Maqasid-al-Sharia'h perspective: Inseparable concept for Halalpreneurs. *Food Research, 4*, 34–42.

Aerts, K., et al. (2007). Critical role and screening practices of European business incubators. *Technovation, 27*(5), 254–267.

Ahwarumi, B., Sawarjuwono, T., & Mawardi, I. (2018), Roles of business incubator in Sunan Drajat Pesantren in generating Islamic entrepreneurs. In *International conference on Islamic finance, economics and business* (pp. 351–362), KnE Social Sciences. https://doi.org/10.18502/kss.v3i8.2519

Alami, F. S. (2023). Indonesian Islamic crowdfunding fintech has very global ambitions. https://alamisharia.co.id/press/indonesian-islamic-crowdfunding-fintech-has-very-global-ambitions/ retrieved July 10, 2023.

Amiruddin, M. H., Suib, S. N., Sri Sumarwati R. N., & Hamzah, U. (2021). A framework of entrepreneurship incubator for indigenous youth to become successful entrepreneurs. *Online Journal for TVET Practitioners, 6*(2), 1–10. https://publisher.uthm.edu.my/ojs/index.php/oj-tp/article/view/8671

Ayatse, F. A., Kwahar, N., & Iyortsuun, A. (2017). Business incubation process and firm performance: An empirical review. *Journal of Global Entrepreneurship Research, 7*, 2. https://doi.org/10.1186/s40497-016-0059-6

Baskaran, A., Chandran, V., & Ng, B.-K. (2019). Inclusive entrepreneurship, innovation and sustainable growth: Role of business incubators, academia and social enterprises in Asia. *Science, Technology and Society, 24*(3), 385–400.

Bergek, A., & Norrman, C. (2008). Incubator best practice: A framework. *Technovation, 28*(1–2), 20–28.

Chapra, M. U. (1993). *Islam and economic development: A strategy for development with justice and stability* (Vol. 14). International Institute of Islamic Thought (IIIT).

Cosh, A., Cumming, D., & Hughes, A. (2009), "Outside entrepreneurial capital." *The Economic Journal, 119*(540), 1494–1533, available at: https://doi.org/10.1111/j.1468-0297.2009.02270.x

Costan, E., Gonzales, G., Gonzales, R., Enriquez, L., Costan, F., Suladay, D., Atibing, N. M., Aro, J. L., Evangelista, S. S., Maturan, F., et al. (2021). Education 4.0 in developing economies: A systematic literature review of implementation barriers and future research agenda. *Sustainability, 13*, 12763. https://doi.org/10.3390/su132212763

Dawood, S. R., Leng, K. S., & Nooriah Yusof, N. (2014). Regional Halal clusters in the Ncer Region: Revisiting the role of institutional thickness. *International Journal of Environment, Society and Space, 2*(1), 47–60.

Enrico, M. A. (2021). Una bussola per le revisioni sistematiche: La versione italiana della nuova edizione del PRISMA statement. *BMJ, 372*, 71.

Espejo, R. & Gill, A. (1997). *The Viable system model as a framework for understanding organizations*. Phrontis Limited & SYNCHO Limited.

Fazira, E. (2020). Olympics in Japan and South Korea: The symbiosis of halal food with the travel industry. *Euromonitor International.* https://blog.euromonitor.com/olympics-in-japan-and-south-korea-thesymbiosis-of-halal-food-with-the-travel-industry/

Gozali, L., Masrom, M., Haron, H. N., & Zagloel, T. Y. M. (2015). A framework of successful e-business incubator for Indonesian public universities. *The Asian Journal of Technology Management, 8*(2), 120–134.

Gozali, L., et al. (2018). Critical success and moderating factors effect in Indonesian public universities' business incubators. *International Journal of Technology, 5*, 1049–1060.

Hackett, S. M., & Dilts, D. M. (2004). A real options-driven theory of business incubation. *Journal of Technology Transfer, 29*(1), 41–54.

Hadiningrum, L. P., Karnawijaya, N., & Rokhaniyah, S. (2021). NAZHIR'S development of fundraising and business incubators through the development of Wakaf villages assisted. In *Proceeding of 1st International Conference on Research and Development ICORAD* (218–235).

Haleem, A., Khan, M. I., Khan, S., & Jami, R. (2020). Research status in Halal: A review and bibliometric analysis. *Emerald Journal of Modern Supply Chain Research and Applications*, 2631–3871.

Handoyo, S., Firdaussy, U. F., & Kholiyah, S. (2021). Technology business incubator service challenges during the Covid-19 pandemic: Traditional incubator versus virtual incubator. *Wacana, 24*(2), 80–89.

Hasan, H., Sulong, R. S., & Tanakinjal, G. H. (2020). Halal certification among the SMEs in kinabalu. *Journal of Consumer Sciences, 5*(1), 16–28.

Hendratmi, A., Ryandono, M. N. H., & Sukmaningrum, P. S. (2019). Developing an Islamic crowdfunding website platform for startup companies in Indonesia. *Journal of Islamic Marketing, 11*(5), 1041–1053.

Hendratmi, A., Sukmaningrum, P., & Ryandono, M. N. H. (2022). The role of university resource support and entrepreneurial characteristics on Halal startup businesses. *Indonesian Journal of Business and Entrepreneurship (IJBE), 8*(3), 363. https://doi.org/10.17358/ijbe.8.3.363

Indiran, L., Nallaluthan, K., Baskaran, S., & Dalayga, B. (2021). Business incubator: The genesis, evolution, and innovation invigoration. *International Journal of Academic Research in Business and Social Sciences, 11*(7), 342–354.

Jamil, F., Ismail, K., Siddique, M., Khan, M. M., Kazi, A. G., & Qureshi, M. I. (2016). Business incubators in Asian developing countries. *International Review of Management and Marketing, 6*(4S), 291–295.

Jimainal, M. N. H., Hassan, R. A., Kalimin, K. M., Ansar, R., Chekima, B., & Fook, L. M. (2022). The effect of business support from business incubator towards the performance of entrepreneurs in the early start-up companies in Malaysia with the moderating effect of risk-taking propensity. *Journal of Entrepreneurship and Business Innovation, 9*(2), 16–31.

Kedah, Z., Adamu, I. M., Kadir, M. A. B. A., & Anwar, M. A. (2015). Effect of business Jihad on entrepreneurs' ethical behavior and corporate social responsibility: A qualitative study. *International Journal of Business and Globalization, 15*, 425–442.

Khairul Akmaliah, A., Hasmiah, K., Rosmah, M., Fatimah, O., & Faizah, A. (2015). Developing a framework for a viable Research University. *Systemic Practice and Action Research, 28*(5), 503–525.

Khairul Akmaliah, A., Muhamad, N. S., Mohd Fuaad Said, M. F., Abdul Sarhadat, S., Ismail, H. A., & Mohd Nasir, M. F. A. (2019). Diagnosing business incubation for social purpose: A viable system model approach. *Systemic Practice and Action Research, 32*(2), 219–238.

Khairul Akmaliah, A., Muhamad, N. S., & Said, M. F. (2020). Diagnosing the Halal industry of Taiwan: A viable system model approach. *Jurnal Pengurusan, 58*, 169–179. https://doi.org/10.17576/pengurusan-2020-58-14

Khalek, A. A. (2018). Entrepreneurship and the Halal wave in Malaysia. In *Global entrepreneurship and new venture creation in the sharing economy, IGI Global* (pp. 191–205).

McIver-Harris, K. D., & Tatum, A. (2020). Measuring incubator success during a global pandemic: A rapid evidence assessment. USA. (Working Paper).

Mohd Fuaad, S., Khairul Akmaliah, A., Nur Atiqah, A., Hänninen, S., & Walsh, S. T. (2012). Incubators and government policy for developing IT industry and region in emerging economies. *Asian Academy of Management Journal, 17*(1), 65–96.

Mohd Nawawi, M. S. A., Abu-Hussin, M. F., Faid, M. S., Pauzi, N., Man, S. & Mohd Sabri. N. (2019). The emergence of halal food industry in non-Muslim countries: A case study of Thailand. *Journal of Islamic Marketing, 11*(4), 917–931.

National Business Incubation Association (NBIA). (2007). Business Incubation FAQ. [Online]: http://www.nbia.org/resource_center/bus_inc_facts/index.php

Nur Sa'adah, M., Syahnaz S., Khairul Akmaliah, A., & Mohd, F. S. (2019). Halal tourism: Literature synthesis and direction for future research. *Pertanika Journal of Social Sciences and Humanities, 27*(1), 729–745.

OECD and European Commission. (2019). Policy brief on incubators and accelerators that support inclusive entrepreneurship. OECD SME entrepreneurship papers. 13 (Report). http://europa.eu

Porter, M. E. (1990). Clusters and the new economics of competition. *Harvard Business Review, 76*(6), 77–90.

Rusmana, I., Maulana, R, Baihaqi, A., Vikanda, V., & Ramadhan, A. (2021). The urgency of Indonesian Islamic fashionpreneur as part of the world's Halal Industry. *Journal of Business and Entrepreneurship, 1*(4), 21–28.

Salaheldeen, M., Battour, M., Nazri, M. A., Bustamam, U. S. A., & Mohd Hashim, A. J. C. (2023). The perception of success in the halal market: Developing a halal entrepreneurship success scale. *Journal of Islamic Marketing, 14*(3), 799–825.

Sariningsih, Y., Albert, W. K. G., & Mariane, I. (2023). Strategy to improve KPM's start-up business creativity in the context of social entrepreneurship program. *International Journal of Professional Business Review, 8*(4), e0590.

Shamsudin, S. N., Abu Bakar, E., Osman, S., et al. (2022). Research trend in HalalStudies: A bibliometric analysis using the Scopus database. *Journal of Halal Industry & Services, 5*(1), a0000300.

Sukhur, S. S., & Abu Bakar, S. (2018). Factors contributing to the incubation performance of Malaysian technology incubators. *Economic and Technology Management Review, 13*, 33–43.

Thomson Reuters. (2018). State of the Global Islamic Economy Report 2018/19. Retrieved from Haladinar website: https://haladinar.io/hdn/doc/report2018.pdf

Tok, M. E., & Kaminski, J. (2018). Islam, entrepreneurship, and embeddedness. https://doi.org/10.1002/tie.21970

Vanderstraeten, J., van Witteloostuijn, A., Matthyssens, P. (2020). Organizational sponsorship and service co-development: A contingency view on service co-development directiveness of business incubators. *Technovation,* 102154. https://doi.org/10.1016/j.technovation.2020.102154

Youssef, A. B., Boubaker, S., & Omri, A. (2018). Entrepreneurship and sustainability: The need for innovative and institutional solutions. *Technological Forecasting and Social Change, 129*, 232–241.

Yusop, S. R. M., Rasul, M. S., Mohamad Yasin, R., Hashim, H. U., & Jalaludin, N. A. (2022). An assessment approaches and learning outcomes in technical and vocational education: A systematic review using PRISMA. *Sustainability, 14*, 5225. https://doi.org/10.3390/su14095225

Yusuf, M., Mai, M. Y. M., Al Maki, S. H., Shaffeei, K., Folashade, A. T., Bamiro, N. B., & Shittu, M. A. (2022). A systematic review of pedagogical practices in the Education 4.0. *Hong Kong Journal of Social Sciences,* 504–514. https://doi.org/10.55463/hkjss.issn.1021-3619.60.49

Designing Sustainable Business Models for Islamic Entrepreneurship

Amal A. M. Elgharbawy, Avicenna Yuhan, Mariam Kotachi, and Erry Yulian Adesta

Abstract To address the high failure rate of Muslim enterprises caused by the absence of such models, this chapter discusses the crucial importance of sustainable business models in Islamic entrepreneurship. Islamic entrepreneurship is a specific type of business endeavor that needs a special strategy because it has the dual objectives of profitability and Al-Falah (success in this life and the afterlife). The failure rate of Muslim-owned firms is greater than usual because many of them find it difficult to remain profitable while upholding Islamic ideals. To solve this problem, this chapter examines how Islamic and Halal business owners might create and employ sustainable business strategies. It goes into detail on the fundamentals of Islamic entrepreneurship, the significance of sustainable business models, and the particular difficulties experienced by Muslim-owned enterprises. The chapter emphasizes the necessity for a change to sustainable business models that agree with Islamic values by conducting a thorough analysis of the common causes of these failures. It gives Islamic and Halal company owners a manual for understanding and successfully implementing these models, resulting in enterprises that are lucrative and favorably impacting society in accordance with the principles of Al-Falah. In the chapter on future trends and prospects in Islamic entrepreneurship, it is emphasized how important innovation and technology will be in determining this future. It goes into detail on the fundamentals of Islamic entrepreneurship, the significance of sustainable business models, and the challenges faced by Muslim-owned enterprises. The chapter emphasizes the necessity for a change to sustainable business models that agree with Islamic values by conducting a thorough analysis of the common causes of these failures. It gives Islamic and Halal company owners a manual for understanding and successfully implementing these models, resulting in enterprises that are lucrative

A. A. M. Elgharbawy (✉)
International Institute for Halal Research and Training (INHART), International Islamic University Malaysia, Kuala Lumpur, Malaysia
e-mail: amalgh@iium.edu.my

A. Yuhan · E. Y. Adesta
Universitas Indo Global Mandiri (UIGM), Jl. Jendral Sudirman No. 629 Km. 4, Palembang 30129, Indonesia

M. Kotachi
School of Business, Shenandoah University, Winchester, VA 22601, USA

L. Raimi et al. (eds.), *Contemporary Discourse of Halal and Islamic Entrepreneurship*,
https://doi.org/10.1007/978-981-99-6427-7_7

and favorably impacting society in accordance with the principles of Al-Falah. In the chapter on future trends and prospects in Islamic entrepreneurship, it is emphasized how important innovation and technology will be in determining this future.

Keywords Business model · Islamic entrepreneurship · Halal entrepreneurship · Sustainability · Dual goal

JEL classification G0 · G1 · F6 · M2

1 Introduction

A distinctive and important segment of the world economy is Islamic entrepreneurship. With its roots in Islamic ideas, it aims to strike a balance between the pursuit of profit and the accomplishment of Al-Falah, a notion that denotes success in both this life and the hereafter (Mokhtar et al., 2023; Molla, 2012). Islamic entrepreneurship differs from traditional business models because of its dual purpose, which gives it a sense of meaning that goes beyond purely materialistic gain.

The path to establish this equilibrium, nevertheless, is not without obstacles. The absence of viable and long-term business models in the industry has become a major problem. Muslim-owned firms have a higher-than-average failure rate because they frequently find it difficult to remain profitable while upholding Islamic beliefs (Wilson & Grant, 2013). Islamic entrepreneurship is a unique subject that needs a distinctive methodology and not merely a subset of entrepreneurship. Islamic marketing should not be considered as a footnote or addition to the canon of traditional marketing, according to Wilson and Grant (2013). Instead, it symbolizes a distinct consumer and marketing wave that is being led by both Muslims and non-Muslims.

By examining how Islamic and Halal business owners may create and deploy sustainable business models to accomplish their dual objectives, this chapter seeks to solve this issue. Muslim company owners may build lucrative enterprises that uphold the ideals of Al-Falah and contribute positively to society by comprehending the tenets of Islamic entrepreneurship and incorporating them with contemporary business practices.

2 Brief Overview of Islamic Entrepreneurship

The issue of unbearable economic and social duality in economies is addressed by the distinctive style of business initiative known as Islamic entrepreneurship, which is inherently community-centric (Molla, 2012). As a natural response to all types of capitalist exploitation, it aims to maintain control over resources and address issues such as economic inequality, wealth concentration, and social differences. *Maqasid Al-Shari'ah*, the goals of Islamic law, which include the protection of religion, life, intellect, offspring, and property (Shehu & Al-Aidaros, 2015) serve as the foundation for Islamic business. These goals offer a moral and ethical foundation for corporate operations, guaranteeing that the pursuit of profit does not jeopardize societal well-being. *Maqasid Al-Shari'ah*, the goals of Islamic law, which include the preservation of religion, life, intellect, offspring, and property, serve as the foundation for Islamic entrepreneurship (Shehu & Al-Aidaros, 2015). These goals give corporate operations a moral and ethical context, guaranteeing that the pursuit of profit does not jeopardize society's well-being.

The idea of Waqf, which in Islam refers to a type of social entrepreneurship model, is one of the distinctive aspects of Islamic entrepreneurship. Waqf, which entails donating a portion of one's money or property to public causes and social welfare, exemplifies the importance that Islamic businesses place on volunteer work and social duty (Salarzehi et al., 2010). Gender concerns and business in Islam are intertwined. Muslim women entrepreneurs serve as an example of how Islamic principles may empower women in the business sector by using many facets and teachings of Islam to make sense of their entrepreneurial decisions (Tlaiss & McAdam, 2021). Islamic business is not only about turning a profit, in essence. It involves developing companies that follow Islamic ideals, benefit society, and pursue both financial success and Al-Falah.

3 The Significance of Sustainable Business Models

The importance of sustainable business models (SBMs) in attaining sustainability performance in enterprises is becoming more widely acknowledged (Geissdoerfer et al., 2018). A key source of long-term competitive advantage and a key lever for improving an organization's sustainability performance is the capacity to swiftly and successfully transition into new business models. However, many attempts to innovate business models fall short frequently because of a lack of knowledge on how to incorporate sustainability into business models.

SBMs employ a triple bottom-line strategy that considers the interests of various stakeholders, including the environment and society. They play a crucial role in promoting and putting into practice corporate innovation for sustainability, may assist in integrating sustainability into organizational goals and operational procedures, and act as a major source of competitive advantage (Bocken et al., 2014). SBMs go beyond just enhancing social and environmental responsibility while preserving profitability. They signify a fundamental change in how companies conduct their operations, moving away from the conventional profit-driven business model and toward one that places equal emphasis on social and environmental results as it does on financial ones. To achieve long-term social and environmental sustainability, this change is required (Upward & Jones, 2016). SBMs are significant because of their potential to revolutionize organizations and sectors, spurring sustainability and innovation while also providing value to a wide variety of stakeholders. They stand for a brand new approach to conducting business that is not only successful but also beneficial to both society and the environment.

4 The Dual Goals of Islamic Entrepreneurship: Profitability and Al-Falah

The Islamic entrepreneurship, which aims to control resources and address issues of economic inequality, wealth concentration, and social divisions, is primarily community-centered and is considered as a tactic against all types of capitalist exploitation (Molla, 2012). Profitability and Al-Falah, which stands for prosperity in this life and the afterlife, serve as its dual guiding principles. Islamic business success involves more than simply monetary gain. It involves developing companies that maintain Islamic beliefs, benefit society, and experience sustainable growth. The fundamentals of Islamic law, which place a premium on moral behavior in business and the need to strike a balance between monetary goals and spiritual and moral commitments, conform to this strategy for prosperity.

Al-Falah, on the other hand, stands for the objective of Islamic business. It is a comprehensive idea that includes not only material success but also moral and spiritual fulfillment. Success in all facets of life, both in this world and the afterlife, is the meaning of achieving Al-Falah. It involves striking a balance between monetary prosperity and societal welfare and between spirituality and physical health. In essence, the two objectives of Islamic business demonstrate the distinctiveness of this type of enterprise. It involves more than simply generating a profit; it also entails respecting Islamic ideals and improving society. Islamic entrepreneurship differs from traditional business models due to its simultaneous emphasis on profitability and Al-Falah, which highlights the potential for it to produce sustainable and socially responsible firms.

Islamic entrepreneurship is furthermore viewed as a workable and essential economic model to secure the achievement of economics' core objective, which is to promote human welfare on a national and international scale. The welfare (*falah*) of all people is its main objective, and it is devoted to justice and fraternity. This wellness is the harmonious satisfaction of the requirements of the human psyche, both material and spiritual (Shehu et al., 2016).

The notions of profitability and Al-Falah are firmly ingrained in the Hadith and the teachings of the Quran in the context of Islamic entrepreneurship. For instance, the Quran promotes profit-making and commerce, but it also stresses that it must be done in a just and moral way. According to Surah Al-Isra (17:35),

> *Give in full when you measure, and weigh with an even balance. That is fairest and best in the end.*
>
> [Al-Quran, 17:35]

Additionally, Al-Falah, or achievement in this life and the hereafter, is a recurrent idea in the Quran. In Surah Al-Baqarah (2:201–202), there is a dua'a (prayer) that supports this idea:

Yet there are others who say, "Our Lord! Grant us the good of this world and the Hereafter, and protect us from the torment of the Fire. It is they who will receive a ˹heavenly˺ reward for the good they have done. Surely Allah is swift in reckoning."*

In terms of Hadith, the Prophet Muhammad (PBUH) has underlined the significance of moral business conduct as well as the pursuit of prosperity in this life and the hereafter:

Abu Sa'eed narrated that the Prophet ((ﷺ)) said:

The truthful, trustworthy merchant is with the Prophets, the truthful, and the martyrs. [Jami' at-Tirmidhi 1209].

The Prophet Muhammad (PBUH) once remarked "*The world is a prison-house for a believer and Paradise for a non-believer.*" [Sahih Muslim 2956].

This Hadith highlights Al-Falah's perception and advises believers to work toward achievement in the hereafter, even if it means to overcome difficulties in this life.

These examples emphasize the significance of striking a balance between profit and moral behavior and the pursuit of success in this life and the next, which are fundamental Islamic entrepreneurial ideals.

5 The Challenge: Why Do Muslim Businesses Fail

5.1 The High Failure Rate of Muslim Businesses

Several variables may be responsible for Muslim firms' high failure rates. The lack of a sustainable business plan is one of the main causes. According to Geissdoerfer et al. (2018), many Muslim-owned firms fail to include sustainability concepts in their business models, which can cause financial instability and eventually cause the demise of the company. A key source of long term competitive advantage and a key lever for improving an organization's sustainability performance is the capacity to swiftly and successfully transition into new business models. However, many attempts to innovate business models frequently fall short because of a lack of knowledge on how to incorporate sustainability into business models. The high failure rate of Muslim enterprises is significantly attributed to this lack of knowledge and application of sustainable business concepts. Additionally, the lack of comprehension and application of the two objectives of Islamic entrepreneurship—profitability and Al-Falah—can be blamed for the failure of Muslim firms. Many Muslim businesses ignore the spiritual and moral tenets of Al-Falah in favor of maximizing profits. Due to this mismatch, commercial decisions may be made that are contrary to Islamic law and may result in failure (Malhotra, 2005; Murphy & Smolarski, 2018).

Further investigation into the prevalent causes of the high failure rate of Muslim-owned enterprises, specifically the absence of viable business models, reveals some important elements:

a. First the idea of sustainable business models has become more well-known recently due to its potential to enhance an organization's sustainability performance. These models take a long-term view and involve proactive multi-stakeholder management and the generation of financial and non-financial value for a wide variety of stakeholders. However, many business model improvements fall short frequently because their incorporation of sustainability concepts is not well understood.
b. Second, a key source of the long-term competitive advantage is the capacity to quickly and successfully adopt new business models. However, many businesses struggle to reach their sustainability goals, indicating that business model innovation is necessary to align incentives and income streams to utilize sustainable solutions.
c. Third, compared to other nations, the United States has more research on sustainable business strategies. This implies that local or cultural variables may impact the viability of sustainable business strategies, which may be especially important for Muslim-owned enterprises.
d. Finally, as the utilization of cutting-edge technology has grown, so too has the success of sustainable business models across all application sectors. This implies that a crucial element in the viability and success of business models may be the incorporation of technology (Bocken et al., 2014; Nosratabadi et al., n. d.).

The high failure rate of Muslim-owned firms is mostly due to the absence of viable business strategies. Islamic and Halal business owners must comprehend how to create and use sustainable business models in order to accomplish their twin objectives of profitability and Al-Falah in order to handle this issue.

5.2 Examination of the High Failure Rate of Muslim Businesses

It is essential to concentrate on the absence of viable business strategies while examining the high failure rate of Muslim-owned enterprises. A sustainable business model depicts the interconnections between value components and the flow of value within an organizational unit. The relationship and purpose of these components, which are crucial to the success of any firm, are communicated in a more straightforward manner. The idea of sustainable business models has become more well-known in recent years because of its potential to increase an organization's sustainability performance. These approaches include proactive multi-stakeholder management, value generation for a wide variety of stakeholders in both monetary and non-monetary terms, and a long-term outlook. The failure of several business model innovations, however, has negative economic repercussions for organizations and causes significant delays in the adoption of sustainable solutions. This is especially important for Muslim-owned firms because they often fail miserably due to a lack of viable business concepts (Schaltegger et al., 2016).

6 Understanding Business Models

6.1 Explanation of What a Business Model Is

In the past, organizations have unintentionally developed business models. However, in the last few years with the advancements in computing technology, business models have become popular because they can be represented and evaluated using computers (Andrea, 2015). After further research into the definition of a business model, scholars have not yet settled on a definition for a business model (Hakanen, 2021) and that the interpretation can depend on the application context (Andrea, 2015). But mostly developing a business model is all about creating and capturing value (Hakanen, 2021). Some scholars have defined a business model as a profit-making plan for an organization (Andrea, 2015) and others as a method for identifying customers for an organization while providing value and meeting their needs (Hakanen, 2021). Business models usually focus on the exploration of two fundamental organizational principles: value generation and design. Business models are linked to the method and purpose of creating value and how organizations operate about structures and relationships. Thus, a business model can be defined as a plan for a business that projects the next few years and outlines the path the business intends to take to meet customer needs while making money and growing revenue (Bock & George, 2017). Essentially, every organization, regardless of its size, type, purpose, or location, can benefit from and should have a business model (Bock & George, 2017).

6.2 The Importance of a Business Model to the Success of Business

A business model is a foundation for the organization and a roadmap that guides the business and keeps everyone focused and on track. It plays an important role in understanding the purpose and vision of a business and guiding it toward success.

A good business model distinguishes an organization by identifying exceptional selling points, such as excellent customer service, reduced costs, convenience, accessibility, and innovative features. All of these can give an organization or business competitive advantage that enables business to outperform competitors and succeed while capturing a larger market share. A business model also highlights creating value to meet customer needs. Identifying and understanding customer needs help the organization design products, services, or experiences that will fulfill those needs. In turn, this will satisfy and retain customers while attracting new customers at the same time, which leads to business success (Bock & George, 2017). Having a business model can also help effectively allocate resources to reduce waste, optimize utilization, and maximize the efficiency. It can also create revenue to cover expenses by aligning revenue generation with value creation. In addition, having a business plan can help identify potential risks, opportunities, and challenges, which gives the organization time to create a risk management plan and proactively address them (Hakanen, 2021).

Overall, a great business model ties together value creation, resources, and activities and helps guide decision-making. This will help the organization adapt to change and generate revenue, in addition to attracting stakeholders and standing out. Thus, by recognizing the importance of a business model, an organization can achieve sustainable growth and profitability.

6.3 Introduction to the Concept of Sustainability in Business Models

The definition of sustainability in the context of a business model is "a model that will last over time" (Bock & George, 2017). Having a sustainable business model means understanding that value creation and long-term success do not rely on profitability alone but also on making responsible decisions that will reduce negative environmental impacts and help create a more sustainable future (DeThomas et al., 2015).

Accounting for sustainability within a business model is optional and depends on the values of managers and entrepreneurs. Scholars have used sustainability within business models to emphasize the competitive advantage of an organization, yet some organizations choose to incorporate sustainability, while others ignore sustainability elements in their business model (Barrow et al., 2015).

Having a sustainable business model means being environmentally responsible, for example: reducing resource consumption and waste generation while adopting environmentally friendly practices. Typical goals of a sustainable business model are mitigating the negative ecological impacts of operations, such as reducing carbon emissions, waste and pollution, while conserving energy. Other sustainable business model characteristics are avoiding supply chain distruptions, using renewable energy resources and embracing new technologies. Such models are adaptable and can encourage innovation and creativity and has the capacity to address current and future sustainability challenges (Urmetzer, 2021).

Additionally, sustainable models also actively engage with stakeholders in their business. This includes employees, customers, investors and the surrounding communities. It is important to nurture positive social relationships with stakeholders so that business models can have the support of the community and local customers while having employees with good morals (Ortuño & Dentchev, 2021).

Incorporating sustainability in business models is about widening the organization's scope to consider environmental, social, and economic aspects. Integrating sustainability within a business model emphasizes the organization's competitiveness, reputation, and resilience (Parry, 2014).

7 Islamic and Halal Business Models

Sustainable business models are important in the context of Islamic entrepreneurship because they connect with Islamic ethical and social responsibility values and being financially sustainable. For instance, a study discusses how Islamic banks such as Islamic Bank Bangladesh Limited have shifted their focus to more universal disclosures such as sustainability, charity, employees, and community-related disclosures (Belal et al., 2015). This shift signals responsible conduct and the bank's adoption of a "wider stakeholder approach", which aligns with the Islamic principles of equity, justice, and fairness (Rahman, 2014).

Islamic banking has a significant potential for implementing sustainable business models by applying the principles of green banking, according to research by Solekah (2019). The Islamic values of social responsibility and environmental care conform to this strategy. The report emphasizes the need for Islamic banking to develop its core business competencies and not just be restricted to corporate social responsibility (CSR) programs (Solekah, 2019).

In the framework of Islamic entrepreneurship, sustainable business models focus on social responsibility and Islamic ethical standards and financial sustainability. An illustration of how Islamic banking products and corporate practices may directly affect customer happiness and loyalty is given in a paper by Khan and Mohamed (2017) and Ahmed (2010). To achieve customer happiness, the study emphasizes the value of green banking products and corporate green images. Given that money is not viewed as a commodity in Islam and that any profit made should be the result of a shared risk or venture between the lender and the borrower, this agrees with the Islamic ideals of justice and avoiding exploitation (Ahmed, 2010; Khan & Mohomed, 2017). This argues that sustainable business models for Islamic entrepreneurship should not only prioritize profitability but also the development of goods and services that benefit both the target market and society at large. This is in accordance with the Islamic Al-Falah concept, which urges companies to strive for prosperity in this life and the next by making a beneficial contribution to society. Additional research by Belal et al. (2015) expands on the idea of accountability in Islamic principles. The report emphasizes that people and organizations have a social responsibility to one another and that full disclosure of information is crucial to meeting Islamic Financial Institutions (IFIs') accountability. This implies that accountable and transparent business practices should be fundamental components of Islamic entrepreneurship (Belal et al., 2015).

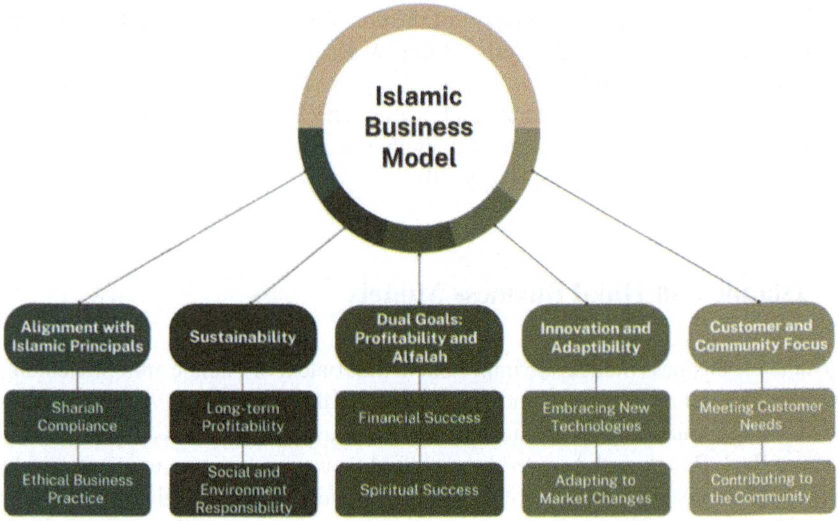

Fig. 1 Elements of the Islamic business model

Creating ethical business practices, social responsibility, customer happiness, and transparency all go hand in hand with building financially successful business models for Islamic entrepreneurship. When used properly, these components can aid Islamic business owners in achieving their dual objectives of Al-Falah and profitability. Figure 1 proposes the elements of Islamic business models.

The figure outlines the salient features emphasizing the significance of sustainable business models in the contemporary business climate.

a. Long-term Profitability: Sustainably minded company strategies are built to guarantee long-term profit. This is accomplished by having stable finances, which enable the company to withstand economic ups and downs, and development prospects, which enable the company to develop and boost its market share over time (Scott, 2017; Strine Jr, 2010).
b. Social Responsibility: Organizations using sustainable business strategies frequently place a high priority on social responsibility. They want to have a beneficial influence on society, which can help their brand's reputation. This not only aids in winning the trust of customers but also improves the company's reputation, which may result in more devoted customers and commercial chances (Du et al., 2010; Scott, 2017).
c. Environmental Responsibility: Environmental responsibility is considered in sustainable business concepts. Businesses implement eco-friendly practices to lessen their negative environmental effects. Additionally, adherence to environmental standards is essential to avoid legal problems and possibly reputational harm to the business (Mishra & Sharma, 2010).

d. Innovation and adaptability: Innovative and adaptable company concepts are encouraged. While innovation can result in the creation of new goods, services, or processes that can offer a firm a competitive edge, the capacity to adapt to market changes is what allows a corporation to remain competitive (Chiva et al., 2014; Okpara, 2007).

In conclusion, profitable business models are not the only consideration for sustainable ones. They also consider the company's effects on the environment and society. In addition, they encourage creativity and adaptability, two qualities necessary for prospering in the constantly shifting corporate environment.

8 Case Studies: Successful Islamic Entrepreneurs

This section will look at actual cases of prosperous Islamic business people and the lessons that may be drawn from them. These real-world examples will put the preceding theoretical ideas into context and show how Islamic principles can be incorporated into effective business strategies.

8.1 Presentation of Real-Life Examples of Successful Islamic Entrepreneurs and Enterprises

a. **The Jerusalem Interest-Free Microfinance Fund (JIMF)** is one of the successful examples of Islamic business. By offering training and loans to members of any Jerusalem community who lack access to bank financing and who want to launch or grow small businesses, the Jerusalem Interest-free Microfinance Fund aims to reduce poverty and ease tensions between communities in the city. The goals of JIMF include reducing poverty, creating a stable basis for peace and community cohesion, and offering interest-free loans to company owners with viable ideas but little capital (Jerusalem Interest-Free Microfinance, n. d.).
b. **Zero Interest Microfinance (ZiM)**, which consists of young professionals from various ethnic backgrounds, cultures, and job objectives, is such. By developing social business ventures, ZiM seeks to raise social responsibility and awareness. ZiM's goal is to find Non-Governmental Organizations (NGOs) that want to include a microfinance component into their current activities. ZiM and NGOs can work together to boost the efficacy of the NGO by giving its clients direct, dependable loans with no interest (ZIM, n. d.). ZIM strive to empower small business owners who are at or near the poverty line by promoting financial literacy and provide essential banking services to their borrowers in more than 10 countries.
c. **Amana financing consultant:** Amanah Finance Consultancy is a renowned Middle Eastern consultant for Islamic financing. Their entire business strategy

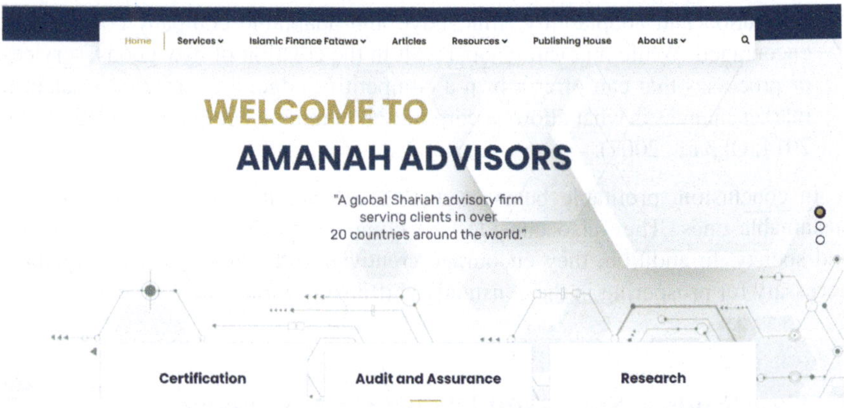

Fig. 2 Amanah Consultancy website. *Source* https://amanahadvisors.com/

is focused on offering enterprises, organizations, and financial institutions full Islamic financial advice services. Among the many services they provide are corporate finance, wealth management, and Islamic financial planning. Their ability to succeed is a result of their dedication to conducting all of their financial transactions in accordance with Islamic principles and the knowledge of their team of professionals in both conventional and Islamic finance (Fig. 2).

d. **HalalBooking:** For halal-aware travelers, HalalBooking is a comprehensive travel search and booking service. Their distinctive business strategy is built on meeting the special requirements of Muslim travelers. They provide a variety of "halal-friendly" lodgings that adhere to Islamic values, such as halal cuisine, non-alcoholic settings, and privacy for women, all over the world. Customers may filter lodgings using their user-friendly website according to their own halal criteria. HalalBooking's success may be credited to their knowledge of the unique market of Muslim tourists and dedication to providing top-notch, halal-compliant travel alternatives (Fig. 3).

These firms have proven that it is feasible to build successful companies that uphold Islamic ideals by effectively incorporating them into their business structures. They act as fantastic role models for ambitious Islamic businesspeople.

Amana financing consultant: Amanah Finance Consultancy is a renowned Middle Eastern consultant for Islamic financing. Their entire business strategy is focused on offering enterprises, organizations, and financial institutions full Islamic financial advice services. Among the many services they provide are corporate finance, wealth management, and Islamic financial planning. Their ability to succeed is a result of their dedication to conducting all financial transactions in accordance with Islamic principles and the knowledge of their team of professionals in both conventional and Islamic finance.

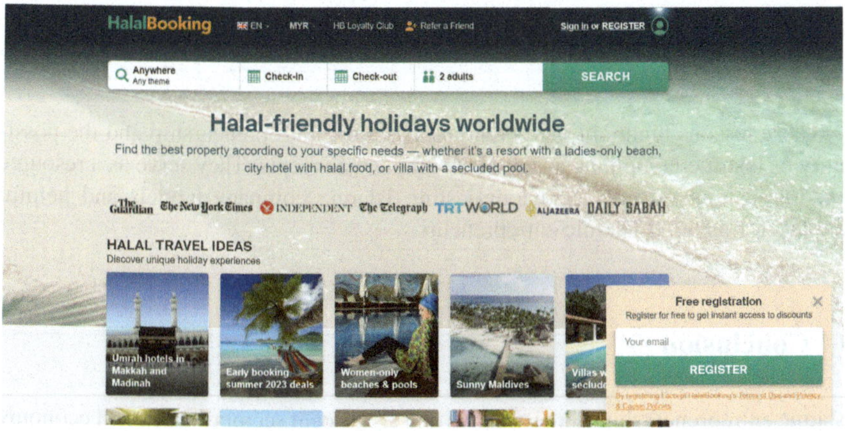

Fig. 3 HalalBooking. *Source* https://en.halalbooking.com/

8.2 Lessons Learned from the Success Stories

The success tales of these Islamic and Halal businesses provide insightful information and important lessons for both prospective company owners and well-established organizations.

a. Market opportunities: Businesses like Saffron Road, Crescent Foods, and HalalBooking have shown the value of comprehending the particular requirements and preferences of the Muslim market. Their success has largely been attributed to the way in which they have adapted their goods and services to fulfill these demands.
b. Adherence to Islamic values: All of these companies have demonstrated a strong adherence to Islamic values, which has drawn customers from both their core Muslim clientele and a wider market seeking morally and environmentally responsible goods and services. Their commercial practices, which range from providing Halal-certified goods to guaranteeing Sharia-compliant banking services, reflect this dedication.
c. Innovation and Adaptability: These companies have also demonstrated a great deal of creativity and flexibility. For instance, HalalBooking's user-friendly website illustrates their creative approach to satisfying consumer demands by enabling clients to filter lodgings depending on certain Halal standards.
d. Quality and Excellence: These companies all share dedication to quality and excellence. These companies have worked hard to provide their clients with the best, whether that means selling premium Halal-certified goods or first-rate financial advising services.
e. Community Engagement: These companies have demonstrated a significant commitment to the local community. They have placed a strong emphasis on both generating money and making a beneficial impact on the neighborhood.

This agrees with the Islamic value of Al-Falah, which urges companies to work toward prosperity in this life and the next by making a beneficial contribution to society.

These lessons highlight the potential of Islamic entrepreneurship and the possibility of Islamic-compliant sustainable company concepts. They serve as a resource for establishing effective and long-lasting Islamic company models and helpful insights for aspiring Islamic entrepreneurs.

9 Conclusion

Islamic entrepreneurship is a distinctive and significant sector of the world economy that aims to strike a balance between the pursuit of profit and the achievement of Al-Falah, which stands for success in this life and the hereafter. However, a change in strategy is required due to the high failure rate of Muslim-owned enterprises, which is sometimes linked to a lack of viable business ideas. The key factors in the competitive advantage and sustainability performance are sustainable business models that incorporate a triple bottom line approach and take a wide variety of stakeholder interests into account. They signify a fundamental change in how businesses operate, moving away from a paradigm that prioritizes financial gains at the expense of social and environmental impacts. Saffron Road, Crescent Foods, Amanah Finance Consultancy, and HalalBooking are just a few examples of prosperous Islamic businesses and entrepreneurs that offer useful case studies. They show the potential of Islamic business when it is in line with the values of sustainability and success. These examples demonstrate that it is feasible to develop an effective company strategy that abides by Islamic principles and is also financially viable. To achieve the dual objectives of profitability and Al-Falah, it is essential for Islamic entrepreneurship to create and implement sustainable business models. When these models agree with Islamic teachings, they can assist Islamic company owners in developing lucrative ventures that also benefit people and the environment.

References

Ahmed, A. (2010). Global financial crisis: an Islamic finance perspective. *International Journal of Islamic and Middle Eastern Finance and Management.*

Andrea, O. (2015). What is a business model? *Harvard Business Review*. https://hbr.org/2015/01/what-is-a-business-model

Barrow, C., Barrow, P., & Brown, R. (2015). *The business plan workbook: A practical guide to new venture creation and development*. Kogan Page Publishers.

Belal, A. R., Abdelsalam, O., & Nizamee, S. S. (2015). Ethical reporting in Islami bank Bangladesh limited (1983–2010). *Journal of Business Ethics, 129*, 769–784.

Bock, A. J., & George, G. (2017). *The business model book: Design, build and adapt business ideas that drive business growth*. Pearson.

Bocken, N. M. P., Short, S. W., Rana, P., & Evans, S. (2014). A literature and practice review to develop sustainable business model archetypes. *Journal of Cleaner Production, 65*, 42–56.

Chiva, R., Ghauri, P., & Alegre, J. (2014). Organizational learning, innovation and internationalization: A complex system model. *British Journal of Management, 25*(4), 687–705.

DeThomas, A. R., Derammelaere, S., & Fox, S. (2015). *Writing a convincing business plan*. Barrons Educational Services. https://books.google.com.my/books?id=Cm67oQEACAAJ

Du, S., Bhattacharya, C. B., & Sen, S. (2010). Maximizing business returns to corporate social responsibility (CSR): The role of CSR communication. *International Journal of Management Reviews, 12*(1), 8–19.

Geissdoerfer, M., Vladimirova, D., & Evans, S. (2018). Sustainable business model innovation: A review. *Journal of Cleaner Production, 198*, 401–416.

Hakanen, E. (2021). What is a business model-for products, platforms or ecosystems? *Journal of Business Models, 9*(4), 1–12.

Jerusalem Interest-Free Microfinance. (n.d.). Retrieved June 1, 2023, from https://www.jerusalemmicrofinance.com/

Khan, T., & Mohomed, A. B. R. N. (2017). Ethical banking and Islamic banking: A comparison of Triodos Bank and Islami Bank Bangladesh Limited. *Islamic Economic Studies, 130*(5377), 1–45.

Malhotra, Y. (2005). Integrating knowledge management technologies in organizational business processes: Getting real time enterprises to deliver real business performance. *Journal of Knowledge Management*.

Mishra, P., & Sharma, P. (2010). Green marketing in India: Emerging opportunities and challenges. *Journal of Engineering, Science and Management Education, 3*(1), 9–14.

Mokhtar, S., Thia, K., Esa, M. S., Ibrahim, M. A., & Mohd Talib, M. N. (2023). Revealing the veil of alms culture as an approach in the concept of al-falah Islamic entrepreneurship. *International Journal of Education, Psychology and Counseling, 8*(49), 110–124. https://doi.org/10.35631/IJEPC.849008

Molla, R. I. (2012). *Mainstreaming the third sector economics by adopting the principles of Islamic entrepreneurship: For development with equity and social justice* (Issue 9).

Murphy, M. J., & Smolarski, J. M. (2018). Religion and CSR: An Islamic "Political" model of corporate governance. *Business & Society, 59*(5), 823–854. https://doi.org/10.1177/0007650317749222

Nosratabadi, S., Mosavi, A., Shamshirband, S., Kazimieras Zavadskas, E., Rakotonirainy, A., & Wing Chau, K. (n.d.). *Sustainable business models: A review*.

Okpara, F. O. (2007). The value of creativity and innovation in entrepreneurship. *Journal of Asia Entrepreneurship and Sustainability, 3*(2), 1.

Ortuño, C. A., & Dentchev, N. A. (2021). We need transdisciplinary research on Sustainable Business Models. *Journal of Business Models, 9*(2), 72–86.

Parry, Z. (2014). *Book review: Business model generation: A handbook for visionaries, game changers, and challengers*. SAGE Publications.

Rahman, S. (2014). *Relationship between Employee Corporate Social Responsibility (CSR) Attitudes, Job Satisfaction and Organisational Commitment in Bangladesh*.

Salarzehi, H., Armesh, H., & Nikbin, D. (2010). Waqf as a social entrepreneurship model in Islam. *International Journal of Business and Management, 5*(7), 179.

Schaltegger, S., Lüdeke-Freund, F., & Hansen, E. G. (2016). Business models for sustainability: A co-evolutionary analysis of sustainable entrepreneurship, innovation, and transformation. *Organization & Environment, 29*(3), 264–289.

Scott, J. T. (2017). *The sustainable business: A practitioner's guide to achieving long-term profitability and competitiveness*. Routledge.

Shehu, F., Hayati, N., Ahmad, B., & Al-Aidaros, A.-H. (2016). Islamic entrepreneurship in the Light of Maqasid Al-Shari'ah: A critical review. *Journal of Social and Development Sciences, 6*, 6–14.

Shehu, F. M., & Al-Aidaros, A.-H. (2015). Islamic entrepreneurship in the Light of Maqasid Al-Shariâ€™ ah: A critical review. *Journal of Social and Development Sciences, 6*(4), 6–14.
Solekah, N. A. (2019). The effect of green banking product and green corporate image on green customers loyality in green customers satisfaction Syariah banking mediation. *Management and Economics Journal.*
Strine, L. E. Jr. (2010). One fundamental corporate governance question we face: Can corporations be managed for the long term unless their powerful electorates also act and think long term? *The Business Lawyer*, 1–26.
Tlaiss, H. A., & McAdam, M. (2021). Unexpected lives: The intersection of Islam and Arab women's entrepreneurship. *Journal of Business Ethics, 171*, 253–272.
Upward, A., & Jones, P. (2016). An ontology for strongly sustainable business models: Defining an enterprise framework compatible with natural and social science. *Organization & Environment, 29*(1), 97–123.
Urmetzer, S. (2021). Dedicated business models: Connecting firms' values with the systemic requirements of sustainability. *Journal of Business Models, 9*(2), 87–108.
Wilson, J. A. J., & Grant, J. (2013). Islamic marketing—A challenger to the classical marketing canon? *Journal of Islamic Marketing, 4*(1), 7–21. https://doi.org/10.1108/17590831311306327
ZIM. (n.d.). Retrieved June 1, 2023, from https://www.zimbank.org/

Halal Entrepreneurship in Islamic Digital Economy from a Cultural Perspective

Lukman Raimi, Ibrahim Adeniyi Abdur-Rauf, and Basirat Olaide Raimi

Abstract This chapter discusses the link between Halal Entrepreneurship (HE) and the Islamic Digital Economy (IDE) from a cultural perspective. Using a qualitative research method, we provide answers to the research questions through critical discourse analysis (CDA). We selected 76 scholarly articles and texts from the Google Scholar database using a perfect blend of the purposive sampling technique and inclusion/exclusion criteria. Three findings emerged from the CDA. First, HE in Islamic discourse refers to an alternative way of establishing and running a business in accordance with Shari'ah principles to provide Halal products and services, while IDE refers to all Shari'ah-compliant economic activities in the regulated digital space. Second, the relationship between HE and IDE is complementary; the latter provides a digital backbone through e-commerce, e-wallet transactions, and fintech for the former to operate effectively and achieve the double prosperity of Al-Falah. Third, from four cultural perspectives, the interconnectedness of HE and IDE is expected to have a positive impact on the production of Halal products and services, sales and marketing, internationalization, market visibility, the ability to reach broader customer segments, and better access to fintech, leading to the achievement of Al-Falah (double prosperity) and economic growth. The originality of this chapter stems from the fact that there are very few academic resources that discuss HE and IDE from cultural perspectives. Arguably, the chapter offers relatively new insights and implications.

Keywords Culture · Halal ecosystem · Halal entrepreneurship · Islamic digital economy

L. Raimi (✉)
Universiti Brunei Darussalam, Bandar Seri Begawan, Brunei
e-mail: Luq_man2001@yahoo.com

I. A. Abdur-Rauf
Department of Shariah, Universiti Sultan Zainal Abidin, Kuala Terengganu, Terengganu, Malaysia

B. O. Raimi
School of Social Entrepreneurship, Roxbourg Institute of Social Entrepreneurship, La Sarraz, Switzerland

L. Raimi et al. (eds.), *Contemporary Discourse of Halal and Islamic Entrepreneurship*,
https://doi.org/10.1007/978-981-99-6427-7_8

1 Introduction

In the fast-growing Halal ecosystem, Halal entrepreneurship (HE) and the Islamic digital economy (IDE) have clearly emerged as ultra-religious alternatives to conventional entrepreneurship and digitalization, respectively. Both valuable concepts are driven by powerful forces of faith, entrepreneurship, and digitalization with the intent to create value, transform lives, provide goods and services, and create jobs for people and prosperity for communities and even nations in consonance with the five fundamental principles of Islamic law (Maqasid-ul Shari'ah). The five principles of Maqasid-ul Shari'ah or Islamic law include guarding religion (hifz al-din), guarding the soul (hifz al-nafs), guarding reason (hifz al-'aql), guarding property (hifz al-mal), and guarding offspring/descendants (hifz al-nasl) responsibly and sustainably (Raimi et al., 2013; Muhammad et al., 2020). The concepts of HE and IDE have advanced in different parts of the world and are fast becoming the bedrocks of the economies of Muslim countries. For instance, 1.9 billion Muslims (knowingly or unknowingly) spent USD 2 trillion on food, pharmaceuticals, cosmetics, fashion, travel, media, and recreation sectors in 2021, leading to 8.9% year-over-year growth. The trend is projected to grow further because the Muslim population is expected to grow up to 3 billion by 2060, covering 30% of the global population (Malaysia Digital Economy Corporation, 2022). Moreover, the growing awareness of halal concepts among 2.18 billion Muslims, the value of the global halal industry is estimated at around US$2.3 trillion, coupled with increased global demand for halal products, services, and user-based technologies (Azam & Abdullah, 2020).

In retrospect, Muslim theorists and practitioners, through pragmatic research and business model innovation, have proposed HE and IDE as new ultra-religious models offering faith-based entrepreneurship and Islamic-oriented digitalization, respectively (Abdullah & Azam, 2020; Barata, 2019; Salaheldeen, 2022). While the HE concept connotes an alternative way of starting and managing a business in accordance with Shari'ah rules and principles to provide halal products and services (Kayed & Hassan, 2010; Ramadani et al., 2015), the concept of IDE, on the other hand, refers to any Sharia-compliant socio-economic activities undertaken by Muslim entrepreneurs and companies within the digital space (Salaheldeen, 2022).

The nexus of HE and IDE is imperative in a globalized world because digitalization has become a catalyst for all human activities, including Islamic social and economic practices. Therefore, IDE has emerged in the domains of e-commerce, e-wallet transactions, and Fintech due to the convergence of digital technology and Islamic values and practices (Bakar et al., 2020; Barata, 2019). In the Halal ecosystem, IDE provides a digital backbone for HE, as market visibility, ease of payment, payment safety, and product-service-process awareness have the propensity to stimulate an increase in demand for halal products, services, technologies, and business solutions in business contexts where customers attach importance to Islamic ethics (Salaheldeen, 2022). Unlike the traditional economy, IDE covers a wide range of sectors such as fintech, blockchain, e-commerce, digital marketing, and mobile applications that facilitate the design, creation, production, and delivery of halal products and services to households (B2C), business organizations (B2B), and governments (B2G). Furthermore, the relationship between HE and IDE, as explained above, is catalytic and complementary, as both pursue the goal of Al-Falah (success) within the Halal ecosystem. The former conducts entrepreneurship by creating, delivering, and capturing Shariah-compliant values (products, services, and other solutions) to customers to gain Al-Falah, while the latter deploys Shariah-compliant digitalization platforms to aid the delivery of digital products, services, and other solutions to end-users to gain Al-Falah (the economic goal of eternal prosperity) (Rafiki & Wahab, 2013; Suselo, 2018).

Despite the interdependence of both religious concepts, they have not been sufficiently researched in the emerging plural economic landscape. Therefore, this exploratory chapter discusses HE and IDE from a cultural perspective. Specifically, this chapter aims to make a comprehensive contribution to the theory and practice of HE and IDE by addressing the following thematic research questions (TRQs):

- RQ1: What are the conceptual definitions of HE and IDE in the existing literature?
- RQ2: What are the complementary relationships between the concepts of HE and IDE in the existing literature?
- RQ3: In what way can culture strengthen the nexus of Halal entrepreneurship and IDE to create a strong Halal ecosystem?

We aim to address the existing knowledge gap regarding Halal entrepreneurship (HE) and Islamic digital economy (IDE) through two approaches. Firstly, by examining these concepts within the context of existing literature, this chapter enhances the conceptual understanding of a wide range of Halal stakeholders and professionals. Secondly, by elucidating how culture strengthens the connection between HE and IDE to foster a robust Halal ecosystem, this chapter emphasizes the importance of cultivating an enabling and supportive culture to facilitate the development of a functional Halal ecosystem. In the absence of an enabling and supportive culture for IDE in Muslim nations, the growth of HE will be hindered, as the Halal culture plays a significant role in moderating performance outcomes (Zailani et al., 2020). Similarly, the absence of a nurturing and supportive culture for entrepreneurship and digitization would impede the ability of Muslim entrepreneurs to establish businesses, generate employment, create wealth, improve the gross domestic product, achieve sustainable growth, and attain al-Falah.

Apart from the aforementioned introduction (Sect. 1), this paper is divided into five sections. Section 2 provides an explanation of the methodology employed. Section 3 focuses on the application of critical discourse analysis to three themes: HE, IDE, and four cultural perspectives. Section 4 elucidates cultural perspectives in relation to HE and IDE, including the modeling of the impact of culture on shaping the Halal ecosystem. Finally, Sect. 5 concludes with a summary of the discussion, implications, and limitations.

2 Methodology

In writing this chapter, we have followed the methodology of qualitative research. To obtain answers to our research questions, we reviewed academic papers using critical discourse analysis (CDA) to understand the language and communication of higher education (HE), international development education (IDE), and cultural perspectives in the existing literature (Mayr & Machin, 2012). CDA is an interdisciplinary approach that focuses on analyzing language in texts and discourses to recognize, assess, and combat perceived power imbalances, injustices, and social inequalities (Briant Carant, 2017; Mullet, 2018). In this chapter, we specifically apply CDA to Halal research, with a particular focus on HE and IDE. We follow the CDA approaches of Briant Carant (2017) on Sustainable Development Goals (SDGs) and George Mwangi et al. (2018) on the internationalization of higher education. Using CDA, we explore the construction of HE, IDE, and cultural perspectives within and across scholarly documents to understand how language and communication are used, maintained, or transformed through discourses. Our application of CDA also extends to examining the underlying ideologies, assumptions, and values embedded in the language of HE, IDE, and cultural perspectives, and how these themes shape our understanding of entrepreneurship and digitalization in the Halal ecosystem.

The assumption behind our use of CDA in this chapter is based on two best practices. First, adopting CDA can play a critical role in defining, understanding, and analyzing the ways in which language and communication are used to construct and reinforce values, norms, and power relations in HE, IDE, and cultural perspectives in Halal research. Second, the use of CDA helps uncover areas where HE and IDE can be challenged and transformed, and it can aid in developing more Sharia-compliant business models. To apply CDA, we selected 76 articles and texts from the Google Scholar database using a purposive sampling technique and specific selection/inclusion criteria (relevance, language, and recency). We systematically analyzed the selected papers using CDA. This approach allows us to identify the strengths and limitations of Halal entrepreneurship and Islamic finance and contributes qualitatively to theoretical advancements in both fields. The current study followed a five-step approach to conduct CDA, as depicted in Fig. 1.

3 Critical Discourse Analysis

In this section, the conceptual definitions, scope, and significance of Halal entrepreneurship, the Islamic digital economy (IDE), and the Halal ecosystem are critically dissected and discussed.

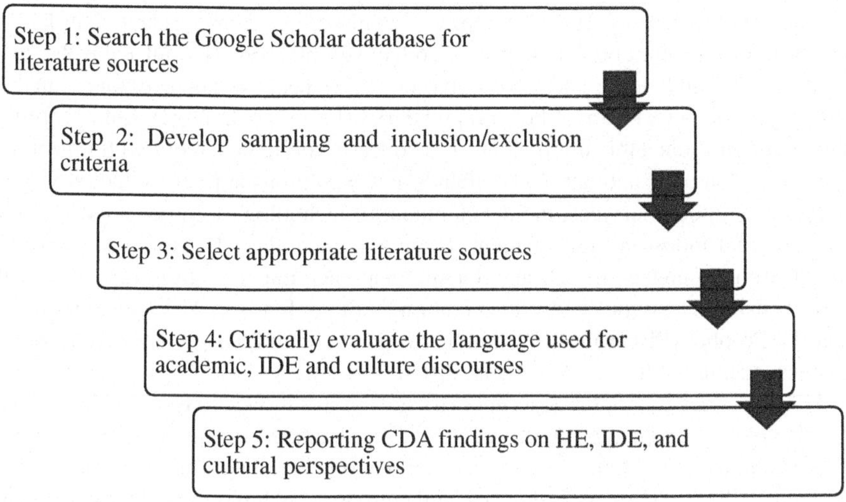

Fig. 1 Conducting CDA through a six-step approach (Author's Creation, 2023)

3.1 Halal Entrepreneurship and Its Significance

Halal entrepreneurship is an amalgamation of two words: halal and entrepreneurship. Although entrepreneurship is not a new concept, as it exists across countries, cultures, and contexts, it has been present even before and during the era of Prophet Muhammad (PBUH). Halal entrepreneurship (HE) is an alternative way of incorporating and running a business in accordance with Shari'ah rules and principles. The objective of HE is to provide halal products and services to customers and other end-users, with the ultimate goal of creating an Islamic economy. Muslim entrepreneurs, through the entrepreneurial process, create business value, offer goods and services, generate employment, and provide socio-economic benefits to diverse consumers and communities. HE can be described as the integration of Islamic ethics (halal and toyyib) into mainstream entrepreneurship, aiming to produce halal products and conduct business in a Sharia-compliant manner. In Islam, halal refers to what is permissible or generally allowed, while toyyib refers to what is good, high-quality, healthy, and sustainable. HE is a distinct form of entrepreneurship that is inseparable from Islam and follows a different business model. The uniqueness of HE lies in its representation of an alternative approach to creating and managing a business in compliance with the Islamic principles of Halal (permissible) and Haram (prohibited). In other words, HE is a faith-based concept rooted in the belief that Muslim entrepreneurs should conduct businesses and commercial activities in a manner consistent with Islamic values. This includes abstaining from unlawful and illegal commercial activities such as the production and sale of alcohol, drugs, usury, gambling, pornography, and immoral practices.

The significance of Halal entrepreneurship stems from the fact that Islam views and treats entrepreneurship as a collective obligation (Farḍul Kifayah), not a compelling individual obligation (Farḍul 'Ain) because not everyone can be entrepreneurs, but we can all be entrepreneurial (Faizal et al., 2013). Entrepreneurship, built on sound ethical principles, is a collective obligation required for meeting societal, communal, and national demands and aspirations in terms of the provision of products/goods, services, the development of technologies, job creation, wealth creation, and industrial development. Islam has unequivocally expressed the need for Muslims to engage in entrepreneurship and encouraged them to take an active part in business activities and value creation. Nu'aym Ibn Abd Al-Rahman narrated that the Prophet (PBUH) said: "Nine-tenths of livelihood (rizq) comes from trade/business ventures" (Kayed & Hassan, 2010).

Halal products, as a generic term in HE, are not just limited to food and beverages but also include cosmetics, pharmaceuticals, architecture, tourism, aesthetics, logistics, warehouses, and financial products, among others (Abdul Rahman et al., 2018; Mohamed, 2023; Selim et al., 2022). Halal entrepreneurship is thriving and growing massively among Muslims and non-Muslims around the world. The global halal market is worth over US$2.3 trillion, with the food and beverage sector accounting for the bulk of the halal market (Husin et al., 2021). Even non-Muslim entrepreneurs are allowed to practice halalpreneurship if they follow Sharia law in producing and providing products and services for the benefit of the ummah (Muslim community) and mankind. This is permissible based on the concept of maslahah or public interest (Abdullah & Azam, 2020, 2021).

3.2 *Islamic Digital Economy (IDE) and Its Significance*

The concept of the Islamic economic system is broad and represents a collection of rules, values, and standards of behavior that organize economic life and establish production relations in Islamic society (Ishak & Man, 2011). These rules and standards are based on the Islamic order as recognized in the Qur'an and Sunna, the body of jurisprudence developed by thousands of jurists over the past 1400 years, and the changing circumstances and evolving lives of Muslims around the world (Aouissi, 2023; Ishak & Man, 2011). IDE is simply an aspect of the Islamic economic system that refers to an emerging ultra-religious economy that uses digital technology to facilitate the creation, production, and distribution of halal products, services, business processes, and solutions that respect the ethics, values, standards, and principles of Islamic law (Za'aba et al., 2020; Zuhriatusobah & Rahayu, 2022). Moreover, IDE refers to any Shari'ah-compliant or Sharia-neutral commercial activity undertaken by individual and corporate entrepreneurs in the digital space at national, regional, and international levels (Salaheldeen, 2022). All the above definitions show that Islamic law, values, and culture play a crucial role in shaping the Halal ecosystem, IDE, and the behavior of Halal entrepreneurs towards customers and other stakeholders.

The business model of the digital economy is based on digital goods and services, and its outputs are mainly or exclusively based on digital technologies (Bukht & Heeks, 2017). The scope of the digital economy includes both the core digital sector and the broader range of large-scale digital activities in the halal ecosystem but does not include all digitized activities in the market. IDE, like traditional digital platforms, offers significant advantages over traditional commercial platforms. The advantages of IDE include lower transaction costs, the removal of barriers to entry, easy access to domestic and international markets, the opening of new markets, attracting peers and non-professionals, and access to new sources of funding for small start-ups (Battour et al., 2021; Salaheldeen et al., 2019).

Arguably, HE and IDE are inseparable in the globalized and interconnected world that is technology-driven. The commitment of HE within the IDE extends to providing high-quality and innovative Halal products, services, processes, business solutions, and technologies to meet the changing needs of customers and corporate users. Therefore, Halal businesses are at the forefront of the IDE that provides e-commerce, a virtual marketplace, fintech, blockchain, Islamic finance, and crowdfunding, among others, following Shari'ah-compliant standards, while driving innovation in the sector (Biancone, Secinaro & Kamal, 2019; Mohamed & Ali, 2018). These businesses are using technology to develop new products and services, and they are leveraging social media to reach out to their customers. The products, services, and business models of HE face serious challenges competing with non-Halal businesses, which often have a competitive advantage as they are not restricted by Halal laws and principles. To survive the competition posed by non-Halal entrepreneurship, the IDE serves as a powerful enabler and solution. In other words, IDE has the propensity to resolve the three major competitive challenges facing the growth of the halal industry and aspiring halal entrepreneurs. The first challenge is the lack of awareness of halal products, services, household technologies, and business solutions, as many people assume that halal only applies to food and beverages and are unaware that halal products and services also apply to other industries (Damit et al., 2017; Elasrag, 2016).

Functionally, an IDE provides a strong platform for creating awareness among Halal entrepreneurs, allowing them to market their products and services to a wider audience both within and outside of Muslim communities. One challenge associated with this is the limited market for Halal products and services, as many potential Muslim and non-Muslim consumers are unaware of the principles and practices of Halal entrepreneurship. This ultimately makes it difficult for Halal entrepreneurs and Halal-certified companies to reach a larger customer base (Elasrag, 2016; Nurhayati & Hendar, 2020). Furthermore, IDE backbones such as e-commerce and virtual marketplaces offer unlimited market potential for Halal products and services. These platforms allow entrepreneurs to market their offerings at a lower cost and with greater ease of entry. The third challenge for Halal entrepreneurship is the lack of access to finance in an economy that is dominated by conventional financial institutions. As a result, many well-intentioned Halal entrepreneurs are unable to secure funding for their start-ups and scale-ups from Islamic institutions and mainstream financial institutions (Abdullah & Oseni, 2017). This is where IDE comes in to address the challenges faced by the functionality of Halal entrepreneurship. IDE offers a unique opportunity for start-ups and scale-ups to raise funds through fintech platforms, crowdsourcing, and digital crowdfunding options.

3.3 Mapping the Halal Ecosystem in Relation to HE-IDE Nexus

This section examines the relationship between Halal Economy (HE) and Islamic Digital Economy (IDE) in the Halal ecosystem. It highlights the mutual influence between these two concepts, emphasizing that HE goes beyond mere profitability and encompasses a commitment to environmental issues and making a positive impact on society. HE involves incorporating ethical and sustainable practices, such as reducing carbon emissions, promoting social justice, and contributing to community well-being. This commitment is particularly relevant in the fast-growing digital economy, which emphasizes standards, compliance, and transparency. Numerous businesses operating in the IDE are Halal-oriented and certified, adhering to the principles of Maqasid-ul Shari'ah. These businesses span various sectors, including Halal food, cosmetics, banking and finance, tourism, media, arts, and entertainment. Figure 4 provides a comprehensive overview of the key players, products, and services within the Halal ecosystem (Fig. 2).

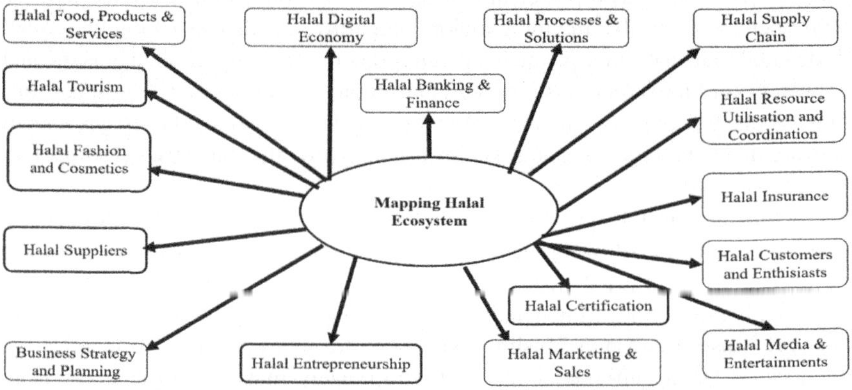

Fig. 2 Mapping the Halal ecosystem in relation to HE-IDE nexus (Author's creation, 2023)

4 Cultural Perspectives in Relation to HE and IDE

The HE and IDE are not only important from a religious perspective but also from a cultural perspective. Culture, from multidisciplinary boundaries, explains a set of values, traditions, ethical rituals, ideas, artifacts, and other symbols, material objects, and services produced and valued by a group of people in different social contexts (Parameswara et al., 2023; Shepherd et al., 2023). The understanding of culture extends to different factors that influence how people, groups, organizations, and countries behave and react in a particular context or situation. It also regulates what, how, and when to act and react in different situations (Bermeo & Perez, 2023; Ng, 2023). Other studies describe culture as the contextual characteristics of a group of people, such as the language, religion, cuisine, and social habits of people, as well as their shared patterns of behaviors and interactions, cognitive constructs, and understandings that are learned through the process of orientation and socialization (Arafah et al., 2023; Quinn et al., 2023). The understanding of culture covers a set of basic assumptions and values, orientations to life, beliefs, policies, procedures, and behavioral conventions that are shared by a group of people, which subsequently influence their behavior and interpretations of other people's behavior (Hill et al., 2023; Zort et al., 2023).

Cultural theories have been used in secular studies to explain the relationship between culture and conventional entrepreneurship. These theories suggest that culture, along with its associated values and norms, can influence entrepreneurial behavior and business performance. For instance, it has been found that entrepreneurs are influenced by the national and contextual culture in which they operate. Consequently, their business practices reflect the values and culture of their society (Ausat et al., 2023; Bate, 2023). Some other studies have also reported that national culture is one of the predominant predictors and moderators of entrepreneurial performance metrics such as sales growth, growth in profits, and market share of firms (Saeed et al., 2014; Watson et al., 2019). Therefore, the notions of HE and IDE in Muslim countries are classic examples of how culture influences entrepreneurship and digitalization. Cultural perspectives are diverse, but the four dominant cultural perspectives that provide analytical frameworks for discussing the nexus of HE and IDE are depicted in Fig. 3.

Geert Hofstede's cultural perspective is the first paradigm for understanding national culture. The perspective identifies six dimensions of culture that are relevant to entrepreneurship, namely: (a) power distance, (b) individualism vs. collectivism, (c) masculinity vs. femininity, (d) uncertainty avoidance, (e) long-term vs. short-term orientation, and (f) indulgence vs. restraint. These six dimensions of culture manifest in varying degrees in different countries (Malik & Huo, 2023; Matharu et al., 2023). The influence of national, regional, and international cultural dimensions affects entrepreneurship and industry practices such as cross-border mergers, acquisitions, joint ventures, and alliances (Brannen & Peterson, 2009; Campagnolo & Vincenti, 2022; Irwin et al., 2022). Hofstede offers a cross-cultural view of national culture and its impact on organizational processes.

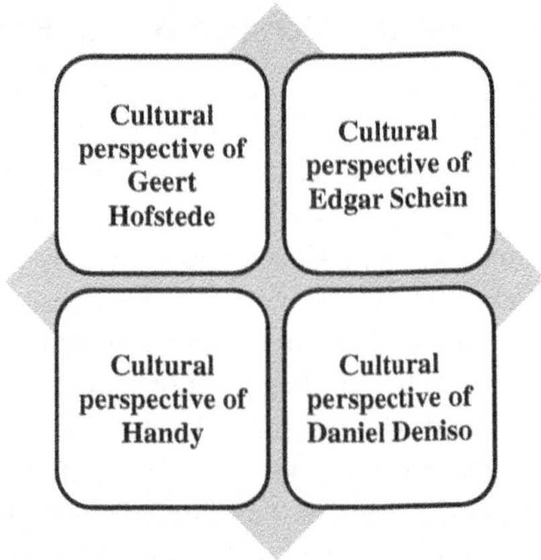

Fig. 3 Dominant culture perspectives that provide analytical frameworks for HE-IDE nexus (Author's creation, 2023)

Edgar Schein's cultural perspective is the second paradigm for cultural discourse, which explains that organizations learn and adopt a culture over time through past experiences, incremental learning, and habitual practice (El-Masri & Matkó, 2022; Khripunov, 2023). The iterative process of incremental learning and habitual practice leads to the formation of an organizational culture.

Schein's three hierarchical levels of culture are (a) artifacts, (b) espoused values, and (c) underlying assumptions underlying organizational formation (Khripunov, 2023; Steiber et al., 2023). This is largely a cognitive view of organizational culture and social reality with an emphasis that culture can be learned over time and inherited from past experiences at three hierarchical levels of culture formation.

Charles Handy's cultural perspective offers a third paradigm for explaining organizational culture. He postulates that culture within an organizational context can be classified into four basic typologies based on the organization's characteristics and structures, namely: (a) power culture, (b) role culture, (c) task culture, and (d) person culture (Handy, 1993, 2007; Malagas et al., 2022; Sokolović et al., 2022). Handy's cultural perspective represents a cognitive view of organizational culture and its impact on changing social realities, people, and processes (Handy, 2007).

Daniel Denison's cultural perspective offers a fourth paradigm for explaining culture and how cultural traits influence organizational effectiveness. According to Denison, the type of culture exhibited by an organization and its members largely determines its functional effectiveness because culture is adaptive by nature (Fey & Denison, 2003; Opoku et al., 2022). Functional culture promotes organizational effectiveness, while dysfunctional culture does not. Furthermore, Denison's culture model, which influences organizational values, beliefs, and assumptions, is broken down into four cultural traits: Mission, Adaptability, Commitment, and Durability (Jahan et al., 2022). Operationally, each of the four cultural traits has three smaller subdivisions (indices), for a total of 12 cultural indices (Denison, 2014). Based on the explanation above, Denison presents a behavioral view of organizational culture that impacts internal integration and external adaptation through performance effectiveness.

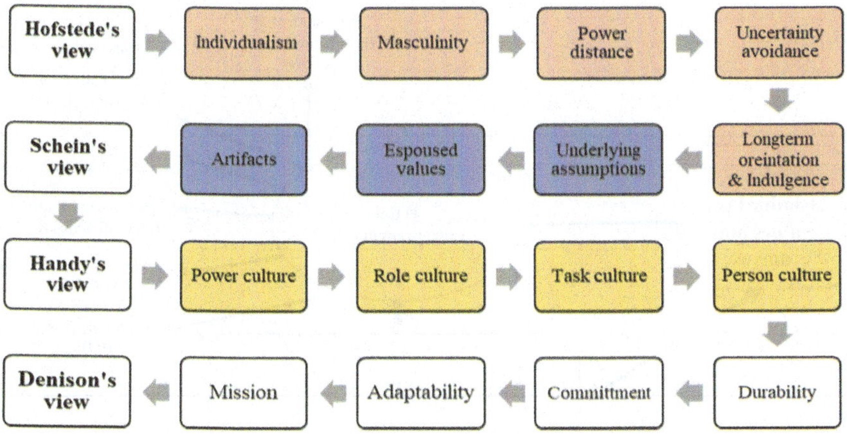

Fig. 4 Seventeen culture enablers of HE-IDE nexus (Author's Creation, 2023)

From the foregoing, the four cultural perspectives enriched the Islamic faith-based literature with a total of 17 culture enablers (dimensions, traits, and characteristics) as depicted in Fig. 3. These 17 culture enablers have the propensity to influence and shape the HE-IDE nexus in Muslim countries and contexts. The first cultural perspective suggests six national culture dimensions; the second cultural perspective identifies three hierarchical culture levels; the third perspective suggests four cultural traits and structures; and the fourth cultural perspective prescribes four culture traits. Consequently, the activities of HE and IDE in the Halal ecosystem are largely determined by the prevailing cultures in Muslim countries. When the culture in the Halal ecosystem influences both HE and IDE, it also influences people and other stakeholders to accept, adopt, and disseminate Halal products, services, digital technologies, and digital solutions, including increasing performance outcomes (Fig. 4).

4.1 *Modeling Impact of Culture in Shaping Halal Ecosystem*

Undoubtedly, cultural factors play a crucial role in shaping the context of the Halal ecosystem, as well as the interaction and behavior of Halal entrepreneurs, Halal-certified companies, and regulators in the market in Muslim-dominated countries (Addiarrahman, 2022; Salaheldeen, 2022). The important cultural factors in the Halal ecosystem include the religious, social, and economic norms, ethics, standards, and values of Muslims and Muslim countries that influence the way Halal entrepreneurs think, act, manage, and communicate with multiple stakeholders in the Halal ecosystem (Hoque et al., 2022). Figure 5 shows the conceptual model of how culture shapes the Halal ecosystem and the interplay between elements (HE and IDE) and entrepreneurial outcomes.

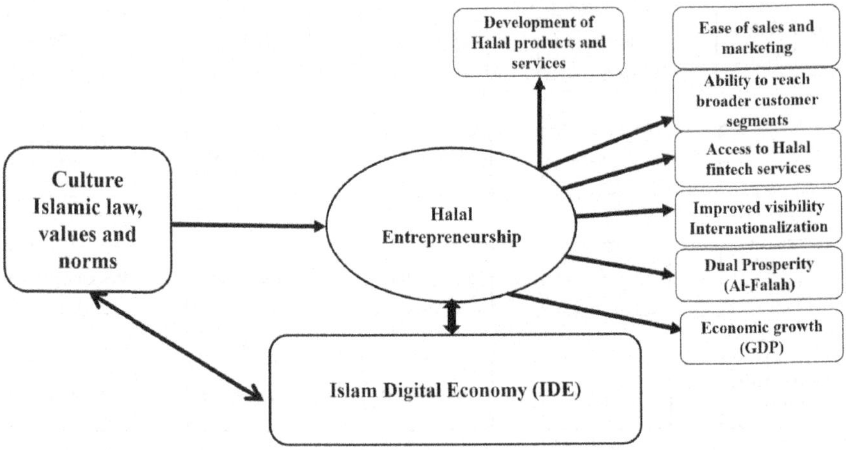

Fig. 5 Modeling impact of culture in Halal ecosystem (Author's Creation, 2023)

The conceptual model explains the development of the halal ecosystem in accordance with the Islamic principles of justice, kindness, fairness, and social responsibility to achieve performance results. The halal ecosystem does not come about automatically (Nisha & Iqbal, 2017). The arrow from Islamic culture to HE shows how culture influences the way entrepreneurs conduct business relations with stakeholders, including customers, suppliers, and employees. The Islamic culture in the Halal ecosystem is comprised of social norms and values, as well as economic norms and values. Social norms and values of Islamic culture include family life, community relations, marriage, and other socio-cultural issues (Amrin et al., 2022). They shape the social context in which entrepreneurs and stakeholders (customers, suppliers, and employees) operate, as well as their attitude towards digitalization and technology (Hoque et al., 2022; Mukherjee & Palit, 2022).

Economic norms and values of Islamic culture influence the level of compliance with the principles of market competition, profit maximization, and economic efficiency in accordance with Islamic law. This plays a critical role in the relationship between halal entrepreneurship (HE) and Islamic digital economy (IDE) (Rahajeng, 2022; Zsolnai, 2022). Halal entrepreneurs and other stakeholders operating in Muslim countries must strike a balance between capitalist economic norms and values and Islamic law, norms, and values in order to create a sustainable business model that combines worldly gains and spiritual prosperity (Amir & Abdukic, 2021).

In the above model, IDE is depicted as a powerful enabler that impacts both HE and culture by providing halal entrepreneurs and halal-certified enterprises with the tools and platforms to create, produce, and distribute various halal products, services, and business solutions more efficiently and effectively. By leveraging different digital infrastructural backbones such as e-commerce, fintech, digital marketing tools, and mobile applications, the players within the IDE will be able to drive entrepreneurship, financial development, and economic growth (Aziz et al., 2022; Barata, 2019).

Specifically, the e-commerce/digital marketplace platforms provided by IDE ultimately facilitate the sale and distribution of halal products, services, and business solutions to a global audience. Fintech solutions provide halal financial services, such as Islamic banking, crowdfunding, and investment, to halal entrepreneurs and investors. Moreover, digital marketing tools enable halal entrepreneurs and halal-certified firms to reach wider customer segments and provide flexible technology for effectively engaging with existing customers and prospective ones. The various mobile applications in the IDE provide accessible, easy, and effective platforms for advertising, marketing, booking, and delivering halal products and services to global customers and clients (Al Amin et al., 2020; Salaheldeen, 2022).

5 Conclusion

The study examines the link between Halal Economy (HE) and the Islamic Digital Economy (IDE) from a cultural standpoint. The critical discourse analysis (CDA) yielded three main findings. Firstly, HE within Islamic discourse refers to an alternative approach to establishing and operating a business in accordance with Shari'ah principles, while IDE encompasses all Shari'ah-compliant businesses and economic activities in the digital sphere. Secondly, the complementary nature of HE and IDE lies in IDE providing a digital infrastructure through e-commerce, e-wallet transactions, and fintech, enabling HE to function and achieve the dual prosperity of Al-Falah. Lastly, from four cultural perspectives, the interconnection between HE and IDE is anticipated to have a positive impact on the production of halal products and services, sales and marketing, internationalization, market visibility, the ability to reach a wider customer base, and improved access to fintech, all contributing to the attainment of Al-Falah (double prosperity) and economic growth.

5.1 Theoretical Implications

The first theoretical implication of this paper is that it offers researchers, halal entrepreneurs, IDE experts, and policymakers relatively new insights into the link between HE and IDE, based on cultural perspectives. The second theoretical implication is that HE and IDE are likely to have a positive impact on empowerment, Islamic digital literacy, balanced gender digital access, entrepreneurship development, poverty alleviation through wealth creation, and the realization of Al-Falah (double prosperity). Additionally, it can contribute to the creation of new businesses and jobs, provision of halal products and services, and economic growth. The third implication stems from the fact that the chapter provides researchers with valuable theoretical models that logically discuss HE in the Islamic digital economy through multiple cultural theories.

5.2 *Managerial Implications*

The first implication for management is that cultural factors play a crucial role in shaping the context of the Halal ecosystem and the interaction and behavior of Halal entrepreneurs, Halal-certified companies, and regulators in Muslim countries or Islamic markets. Second, the connection between HE and IDE serves as a catalyst for the production of Halal products and services, sales and marketing, the ability to reach broader customer segments, access to Halal fintech services, increased visibility and internationalization, as well as the achievement of goals like Al-Falah (double prosperity) and economic growth. Third, non-Muslim entrepreneurs and digital solution providers are permitted to participate in the opportunities of the sector, but Islamic culture requires the actors and stakeholders within the Halal ecosystem to conduct their business activities in accordance with Islamic principles of justice, equality, friendliness, fairness, and social responsibility. Finally, this novel academic effort offers researchers, Halal entrepreneurs, Islamic digital practitioners, and policymakers relatively new insights into the relationship between academia and the Islamic digital economy, based on cultural perspectives.

5.3 *Limitations and Future Research Directions*

While the findings of this chapter are remarkable, it is important to note that this represents only a preliminary examination of the relationship between HE and IDE in the culture-driven halal ecosystem. Therefore, the conclusions drawn in this chapter are based on a limited body of scholarly work. Given the exploratory nature of this study, it is crucial to conduct a more specific field investigation for future studies. As a result, the extensive qualitative results of the current study need to be empirically verified using comprehensive theoretical models and frameworks. For future researchers, it is recommended to consider options such as surveys, interviews, ethnographies, focus groups, and case studies to validate the insights presented in this chapter.

References

Abdul Rahman, N. A., Mohammad, M. F., Abdul Rahim, S., & Mohd Noh, H. (2018). Implementing air cargo halal warehouse: Insight from Malaysia. *Journal of Islamic Marketing, 9*(3), 462–483.

Abdullah, M. A., & Azam, M. S. E. (2020). Halal entrepreneurship from Maqasid-al-Sharia'h perspective: Inseparable concept for Halalpreneurs. *Food Research, 4*(1), 34–42.

Abdullah, M. A., & Azam, M. S. E. (2021). Halal entrepreneurship: Concept and business opportunities. In *Entrepreneurship*. IntechOpen. https://doi.org/10.5772/intechopen.93657

Abdullah, S., & Oseni, U. A. (2017). Towards a shari'ah-compliant equity-based crowdfunding for the halal industry in Malaysia. *International Journal of Business and Society, 18*(S1), 223–240.

Addiarrahman, I. Y. (2022). Halal industry in Javanese culture: Yogyakarta regional government policy in obtaining its economic values. *Inferensi, 16*(1), 151–174.

Al Amin, M., Arefin, M. S., Sultana, N., Islam, M. R., Jahan, I., & Akhtar, A. (2020). Evaluating the customers' dining attitudes, e-satisfaction and continuance intention toward mobile food ordering apps (MFOAs): Evidence from Bangladesh. *European Journal of Management and Business Economics, 30*(2), 211–229.

Amir, H., & Abdukic, A. (2021). The spiritual nature based on ethics in the halal entrepreneurial industry. *Turkish Online Journal of Qualitative Inquiry, 12*(10), 6212–6236.

Amrin, A., Priyono, A., Supriyanto, S., & Nurrahmania, N. (2022). Analysis of local wisdom in Bima community marriage (study of socio-cultural values). *Legal Brief, 11*(4), 2418–2425.

Aouissi, A. (2023). The Islamic economic system from a normative point of view design based on questionnaire tool. *Journal of Islamic Economics, 3*(1), 1–30.

Arafah, B., Hasjim, M., & Arafah, A. N. B. (2023). Cultural relations among speakers of south halmahera languages. *Theory and Practice in Language Studies, 13*(1), 168–174.

Ausat, A. M. A., Al Bana, T., & Gadzali, S. S. (2023). Basic capital of creative economy: The role of intellectual, social, cultural, and institutional capital. *Apollo: Journal of Tourism and Business, 1*(2), 42–54.

Azam, M. S. E., & Abdullah, M. A. (2020). Global halal industry: Realities and opportunities. *IJIBE (international Journal of Islamic Business Ethics), 5*(1), 47–59.

Aziz, T., Khan, M. G. U., Islam, M. T., & Pradhan, M. A. H. (2022). An analysis on the relationship between ICT, financial development and economic growth: Evidence from Asian developing countries. *The Journal of International Trade & Economic Development*, 1–17.

Bakar, N. A., Rosbi, S., & Uzaki, K. (2020). E-wallet transactional framework for digital economy: A perspective from Islamic financial engineering. *International Journal of Management Science and Business Administration, 6*(3), 50–57.

Barata, A. (2019). Strengthening national economic growth and equitable income through sharia digital economy in Indonesia. *Journal of Islamic Monetary Economics and Finance, 5*(1), 145–168.

Bate, A. F. (2023). Unearthing the contextual influence of national culture on entrepreneurship: Systematic literature review. *Research Square, 1*(1), 1–31. https://doi.org/10.21203/rs.3.rs-2420126/v1

Battour, M., Salaheldeen, M., & Mady, K. (2021). Halal tourism: exploring innovative marketing opportunities for entrepreneurs. *Journal of Islamic Marketing, Ahead-of-Print (Ahead-of-Print)*. https://doi.org/10.1108/JIMA-06-2020-0191

Bermeo, J. O., & Perez, M. A. (2023). Trends in human talent management of and impact on inclusive organizational culture. In *Handbook of Research on Promoting an Inclusive Organizational Culture for Entrepreneurial Sustainability* (pp. 241–263). IGI Global.

Biancone, P. P., Secinaro, S., & Kamal, M. (2019). Crowdfunding and Fintech: Business model sharia compliant. *European Journal of Islamic Finance* (12).

Brannen, M. Y., & Peterson, M. F. (2009). Merging without alienating: Interventions promoting cross-cultural organizational integration and their limitations. *Journal of international business studies, 40*, 468–489.

Briant Carant, J. (2017). Unheard voices: A critical discourse analysis of the Millennium Development Goals' evolution into the Sustainable Development Goals. *Third World Quarterly, 38*(1), 16–41.

Bukht, R., & Heeks, R. (2017). Defining, conceptualising and measuring the digital economy (Development Informatics working paper no. 68).

Campagnolo, D., & Vincenti, G. (2022). Cross-border M&As: The impact of cultural friction and CEO change on the performance of acquired companies. *Journal of International Management, 28*(4), 100942.

Damit, D. H. D. A., Harun, A., & Martin, D. (2017). Key challenges and issues consumer face in consuming halal product. *International Journal of Academic Research in Business and Social Sciences, 7*(11), 590–598.

Denison, D., Nieminen, L., & Kotrba, L. (2014). Diagnosing organizational cultures: A conceptual and empirical review of culture effectiveness surveys. *European Journal of Work and Organizational Psychology, 23*(1), 145–161.

Elasrag, H. (2016). Halal industry: Key challenges and opportunities. MPRA Paper No. 69631. Munich Personal RePEc Archive. https://mpra.ub.uni-muenchen.de/69631/1/MPRA_paper_69631.pdf

El-Masri, J. A., & Matkó, A. (2022). The importance of Toyota Kata in organizational development and sustainable improvement. *Network Intelligence Studies, 10*(19), 35–51.

Faizal, P. R. M., Ridhwan, A. A. M., & Kalsom, A. W. (2013). The entrepreneurs characteristic from al-Quran and al-Hadis. *International Journal of Trade, Economics and Finance, 4*(4), 191.

Fey, C. F., & Denison, D. R. (2003). Organizational culture and effectiveness: Can American theory be applied in Russia? *Organization Science, 14*, 686–706.

George Mwangi, C. A., Latafat, S., Hammond, S., Kommers, S., Thoma, H., Berger, J., & Blanco-Ramirez, G. (2018). Criticality in international higher education research: A critical discourse analysis of higher education journals. *Higher Education, 76*, 1091–1107.

Handy, C. (1993). *Understanding Organizations* 4th Edition. Penguin, London-UK.

Handy, C. (2007). *Understanding organisations*. Penguin.

Haque, M., Muniruzzaman, M., & Haque, I. E. (2022). The changing pattern of intimate relationship and the influence of technology on youth in socio-cultural attachment of Bangladesh. *International Journal of Social Science Research and Review, 5*(3), 52–66.

Hasan, K. S., & Pasyah, T. (2022). Challenges of Indonesian Halal industry in the digital economic era. *Sriwijaya Law Review, 6*(2), 319–335.

Hill, C., Lin, C. Y., Wan, Y. T., & Chen, Y. W. (2023). Understanding the role of culture in teaching. In *Supporting and Learning from Academics: EMI Toolkit* (pp. 45–57). Singapore: Springer Nature Singapore.

Hoque, M. N., Rahman, M. K., Said, J., Begum, F., & Hossain, M. M. (2022). What factors influence customer attitudes and mindsets towards the use of services and products of Islamic Banks in Bangladesh? *Sustainability, 14*(8), 4703.

Hunter, M. (2014). Entrepreneurship as a means to create Islamic economy. *Economics, Management, and Financial Markets, 9*(1), 75–100.

Husin, M. M., Kamarudin, S., & Rizal, A. M. (2021). Food and beverage industry competitiveness and halal logistics: Perspective from small and medium enterprises in Malaysia. *Asian Journal of Islamic Management (AJIM)*, 1–10.

Irwin, K., Gilstrap, C., McDowell, W., Drnevich, P., & Gorbett, A. (2022). How knowledge and uncertainty affect strategic international business investment decisions: Implications for cross-border mergers and acquisitions. *Journal of Business Research, 139*, 831–842.

Ishak, F. I., & Man, Y. C. (2011). Halal economy: Proof from Al-Quran and as-Sunnahand demands to utilize it in parallel. In *International Islamic Banking, Finance and Investment Conference*. Kuala Lumpur, Malaysia.

Ismaeel, M., & Blaim, K. (2012). Toward applied Islamic business ethics: Responsible halal business. *Journal of Management Development, 31*(10), 1090–1100.

Jahan, I., Huynh, T., & Mass, G. (2022). The influence of organisational culture on employee commitment: An empirical study on civil service officials in Bangladesh. *South Asian Journal of Human Resources Management, 9*(2), 271–300.

Karim, A. A. (2016) Rancang bangun ekonomi islam. Karim Consulting.

Kayed, R. N., & Hassan, M. K. (2010). Islamic entrepreneurship: A case study of Saudi Arabia. *Journal of Developmental Entrepreneurship, 15*(04), 379–413.

Khripunov, I. (2023). National and organizational culture. *Human Factor in Nuclear Security: Establishing and Optimizing Security Culture* (pp. 13–30). Springer International Publishing.

Malagas, K., Kontos, G., Yilmaz, A. K., & Nikitakos, N. (2022). Organizational culture: Types and critical success factors for organizational excellence. *Advances in Sociology Research*, 75–109.

Malaysia Digital Economy Corporation (2022). Islamic Digital Economy (IDE)—Driving investments through Islamic digital economy. https://mydigitalinvestment.gov.my/islamic-digital-economy

Malik, T. H., & Huo, C. (2023). National cultural moderates the link between work stress and depression: An analysis of clinical trial projects across countries. *Cross-Cultural Research, 57*(1), 23–55.

Matharu, G. K., von der Heidt, T., Sorwar, G., & Sivapalan, A. (2023). The moderating role of Hofstede's cultural dimensions on consumer purchasing of organic food. *Journal of international consumer marketing*, 1–20.

Mayr, A., & Machin, D. (2012). How to do critical discourse analysis: A multimodal introduction. *How to Do Critical Discourse Analysis*, 1–240.

Mohamed, E. S. H. (2023). Aesthetics of Islamic architecture and its application to printed hotel furnishing fabrics. *International Design Journal, 13*(2), 151–160.

Mohamed, H., & Ali, H. (2018). Blockchain, Fintech, and Islamic Finance. In Blockchain, Fintech, and Islamic Finance. de Gruyter.

Muhammad, N., Alwi, S. F. S., & Muhammad, N. (2020). Credit management in full-fledged Islamic bank and Islamic banking window: Towards achieving Maqasid Al-Shariah. *International Journal of Financial Research, 11*(3), 92–99.

Mukherjee, Y., & Palit, S. (2022). Digitalisation and revitalisation of cultural heritage through information Technology. In *Digitalization of Culture Through Technology* (pp. 44–49). Routledge.

Mullet, D. R. (2018). A general critical discourse analysis framework for educational research. *Journal of Advanced Academics, 29*(2), 116–142.

Ng, K. Y. N. (2023). Effects of organizational culture, affective commitment and trust on knowledge-sharing tendency. *Journal of Knowledge Management, 27*(4), 1140–1164.

Nisha, N., & Iqbal, M. (2017). Halal ecosystem: Prospect for growth in Bangladesh. *International Journal of Business and Society, 18*(S1), 205–222.

Nurhayati, T., & Hendar, H. (2020). Personal intrinsic religiosity and product knowledge on halal product purchase intention: Role of halal product awareness. *Journal of Islamic Marketing, 11*(3), 603–620.

Opoku, E. O., Hongqin, C., & Aram, S. A. (2022). The influence of organizational culture on employee performance in the banking sector: Evidence from GCB Bank, Ghana. *European Journal of Business and Management Research, 7*(2), 168–175.

Parameswara, A., Saskara, I. A. N., Utama, I. M. S., & Setyari, N. P. W. (2023). Exploring cultural value and its sustainability of Balinese handwoven textiles. *TEXTILE, 21*(1), 174–197.

Quinn, J. M., Freeland, R. E., Rogers, K. B., Hoey, J., & Smith-Lovin, L. (2023). How cultural meanings of occupations in the US changed during the covid-19 pandemic. *American Behavioral Scientist, 67*(1), 125–147.

Rafiki, A., & Wahab, K. A. (2013). Influences of Islamic practices on small firm performance: A study in North Sumatera, Indonesia. *Islamic Management and Business, 5*(11), 64–82.

Rahajeng, D. K. (2022). The ethical paradox in Islamic cooperatives: A lesson learned from scandalous fraud cases in Indonesia's Baitul Maal Wat Tamwil. *Cogent Business & Management, 9*(1), 2090208.

Raimi, L., Shokunbi, M. O., Suara, I. B., & Fadipe, A. O. (2013). Embedding Islamic Financial System (IFS) in the curricula of schools in Nigeria. *Journal of Business Administration and Education, 2*(2), 65–84.

Ramadani, V., Dana, L. P., Ratten, V., & Tahiri, S. (2015). The context of Islamic entrepreneurship and business: Concept, principles and perspectives. *International Journal of Business and Globalisation, 15*(3), 244–261.

Saeed, S., Yousafzai, S. Y., & Engelen, A. (2014). On cultural and macroeconomic Contingencies of the entrepreneurial orientation-performance relationship. *Entrepreneurship Theory and Practice, 38*(2), 255–290. https://doi.org/10.1111/etap.12097

Salaheldeen, M. (2022). Opportunities for Halal Entrepreneurs in the Islamic digital economy: future and trends from a cultural entrepreneurship perspective. In *Cultural Entrepreneurship: New Societal Trends* (pp. 95–107). Singapore: Springer Nature Singapore.

Salaheldeen, M., Battour, M., & Nazri, M. A. (2019). Halal entrepreneurship and its role in sustainable development goals 2030 (SDGs). In *Paper presented at the International Conference on Dakwah and Islamic Management (IC-DAIM 2019)*. Malaysia.

Salaheldeen, M., Battour, M., Nazri, M. A., Ahmad Bustamam, U. S., & Hashim, A. J. C. M. (2023). The perception of success in the halal market: Developing a halal entrepreneurship success scale. *Journal of Islamic Marketing, 14*(3), 799–825. https://doi.org/10.1108/JIMA-10-2021-0341

Selim, N. I. I. B., Zailani, S., Aziz, A. A., & Rahman, M. K. (2022). Halal logistic services, trust and satisfaction amongst Malaysian 3PL service providers. *Journal of Islamic Marketing, 13*(1), 81–99.

Shepherd, D. A., Breugst, N., & Patzelt, H. (2023). A founding-team model of creating a venture's culture. *Journal of Business Venturing, 38*(2), 106286.

Sokolović, B., Katić, I., Nešić, L. G., Ivanišević, A., & Pavlović, A. (2022). The specific role of the transformational leadership in the organizational culture of service organizations. *Anali Ekonomskog fakulteta u Subotici, 58*(47), 131–145.

Steiber, A., Corvello, V., & Ghosh, S. (2023). International acquisition processes: A cultural analysis of GE Appliances' business transformation. *Business Horizons, 66*(2), 171–180.

Suselo, D. (2018). Business and religiosity: Review of business ethics Mayangkara group. *Jurnal Pendidikan Ekonomi Dan Bisnis (JPEB)*

Watson, A., Dada, O., Wright, O., & Perrigot, R. (2019). Entrepreneurial orientation rhetoric in franchise organizations: The impact of national culture. *Entrepreneurship Theory and Practice, 43*(4), 751–772. https://doi.org/10.1177/1042258717738519

Wilson, J. A. (2014). The halal phenomenon: An extension or a new paradigm? *Social Business, 4*(3), 255–271.

Za'aba, N. S., Zanorrain, S. M., Isa, N. A. M., & Raziman, N. (2020). Islamic digital economy: The role of Islamic Fintech as economy driver. *Journal of Islamic Economics and Law (JIEL), 1*(2).

Zailani, S., Iranmanesh, M., Jafarzadeh, S., & Foroughi, B. (2020). The influence of halal orientation strategy on financial performance of halal food firms: Halal culture as a moderator. *Journal of Islamic Marketing, 11*(1), 31–49.

Zort, Ç., Karabacak, E., Öznur, Ş, & Dağlı, G. (2023). Sharing cultural values and heritage through storytelling in digital environments. *Frontiers in Psychology, 14*, 225.

Zsolnai, L. (2022). Spirituality and economics. *Journal for the Study of Spirituality, 12*(2), 131–145.

Zuhriatusobah, J., & Rahayu, Y. (2022). Millenials In Islamic digital economy sustainability. *Academy of Strategic Management Journal, 21*, 1–9.

Nexus of Halal Entrepreneurship and Islamic Finance for the Creation of a Strong Halal Ecosystem

Saheed Adebowale Nurein

Abstract Islamic finance is essential for halal entrepreneurship because both are business processes that operate based on the Shariah and are integral part of the halal industry. Integrating Islamic finance with halal industry enhances the growth of halal entrepreneurship and its ecosystem. This chapter aims to create awareness on the nexus of halal entrepreneurship and Islamic finance for creating a strong halal ecosystem. This awareness creates a better understanding of the contribution of both halal entrepreneurship and Islamic finance to the halal ecosystem and proffer basis for further research. This study reviewed that halalpreneuers ecosystem must be fully enhanced by Islamic finance through integration to achieve a strong halal ecosystem, which offers significant benefits, including improved access to capital, ethical financing practices, market integration, product development, capacity building, and branding opportunities. In spite of its challenges like lack of awareness of Islamic finance products, its fragmentation across different borders regulatory frameworks among many few, such integration could still strengthen the overall halal ecosystem, foster entrepreneurship, and drive sustainable economic growth.

Keywords Halal entrepreneurship · Islamic finance · Halalpreneurship · Sharīah-compliant

JEL Classification G2 · G21 · G23 · G24 · J23 · L26

1 Introduction

Having access to income is one of the essential human rights that every human being should be entitled to. According to the theory of "social equilibrium", socio-economic justice requires that individuals have equal opportunity but does not require equality of outcomes (Chapra, 1985). It is possible to earn a halal (lawful) living either by being employed and working for others, or by being self-employed and employing

S. A. Nurein (✉)
American University of Nigeria, Yola, Nigeria
e-mail: nurein.adebowale@aun.edu.ng

L. Raimi et al. (eds.), *Contemporary Discourse of Halal and Islamic Entrepreneurship*,
https://doi.org/10.1007/978-981-99-6427-7_9

others. The latter case constitutes entrepreneurial activity. Though, working for others for a fixed compensation is supported by Islam, but it motivates Muslims to become entrepreneurs, as entrepreneurship is the ideal means of halal earnings (Hassan, 2015). The Islamic teachings encourage Muslims to find ways of benefiting each other (Sarker et al., 2019). Thus, they must engage in activities that must be beneficial and valuable to themselves and the society. It can be concluded that the Islamic view of social entrepreneurship is related to the early social awareness concept of being beneficial to others (Gümüsay, 2015; Sarker & Rashid, 2015). Also, religious entrepreneurs have the self-assured of their entrepreneurial idea since they believe that their goals will be achieved with the help of divine powers (Ashraf, 2021; Gümüsay, 2015), which inspires them to strive hard because it provides them with significance for their existence; accordingly, this helps them to be successful (Hassan, 2020).

Not only does Islam encourages entrepreneurship; it further requires entrepreneurs to work diligently to earn *halal* income that will fulfill the entrepreneur's needs as well as help support the Muslims and the community at large (Beg, 1979). This type of responsible entrepreneurship aids others and deters people from exploiting public wealth. It also discourages individuals from becoming reliant on the government. Public wealth is associated with the Muslims, thus, it should be appropriated to projects that will be beneficial to the community (Hassan, 2015).

Entrepreneurship, in the view of Islamic ontology, is regarded as a social procedure that is entrenched in various scopes outside the view of the economic scope (Hassan, 2020; Sarker et al., 2015; Tok & Kaminski, 2018). Halal entrepreneurship intentions are significantly inspired by Islamic practices and values (Hassan, 2021; Rehan et al., 2019) because Islam view entrepreneurship as an argued concept (Hassan, 2021; Tok & Kaminski, 2018). Nevertheless, it is laid on three interweaving pillars, which include entrepreneurial, socioeconomic/ethical and religion-spiritual (Gümüsay, 2015; Hassan, 2020). It is contrast to ethical entrepreneurship since it has distinct practices, which are derived from on scriptural sources and a unique metaphysical objective (Gümüsay, 2015; Ramadani et al., 2015). Similarly, Islamic entrepreneurship influences the macro- and micro-levels of analysis in many ways, through shaping the individual, the organization, and numerous institutions, which include the market and the government (Gümüsay, 2015; Khalek, 2018; Tok & Kaminski, 2018). It is expected that Muslim entrepreneurs must continue espouse good deeds and uphold uprightness in all their business dealings (Hassan, 2021).

Halal entrepreneurship is an entrepreneurship concept in which halal is viewed as "entrepreneurial process for innovatively using opportunities to obtain economic gains and society equity on an equal footing" (Battour et al., 2021). Halal entrepreneurship is also called "halal driven entrepreneurship" and "halal minded entrepreneurship" (Gümüsay, 2015; Khalek, 2018; Ramadani et al., 2015; Soltanian et al., 2016). The halal food industry is first known with practicing halal entrepreneurship before other industries, which include logistics and banking, pharmaceuticals, personal care, cosmetics, tourism, and hospitality (Ashraf, 2021; Battour et al., 2021). Halal entrepreneurs always creatively exploit various opportunities available in the halal industry in accordance with the Islamic principles to attain financial returns.

Thus, the halal entrepreneurship complexity requires integration to a holistic model, which will balance its explanatory parsimony and richness (Ashraf, 2021; Bennani Khouloud, 2020; Gümüsay, 2015; Khalek, 2018; Liu et al., 2018; Salaheldeen et al., 2022; Ratten et al., 2017; Tlaiss & McAdam, 2021).

An integral part of the halal industry is halal entrepreneurship. The halal industry has been growing very fast as a business industry in the contemporary business world, which include the increasing demand of halal products and goods by the non-Muslims. There is an increase in expectation that halal market will grow from $1.4 trillion as at 2020 to $2.6 trillion in 2024 (Dinar Standard, 2020). Muslims' consumers are demanding for halal products not only to fulfill their faith obligations but also to fulfill their worldly interests (Hassan, 2020; Utomo et al., 2020). Recently, halal industry is the new paradigm shift in the business world (Wilson et al., 2013), and its recent utmost growth can be traced to the increase of the population of Muslims in Europe as well as in other western countries, which has contributed to the globalization of the halal market (Fuseini, 2017; Hassan, 2021). As the sensitization of halal increases among consumers and the halal market, halal entrepreneurs face more challenges and sensitivity to run their businesses (Ashraf, 2021; Khan et al., 2020; Salaheldeen et al., 2022; Tlaiss & McAdam, 2021). The focus of halal industry is not only on production and selling of halal goods and services but also focuses on establishing an all-inclusive business strategy (Ashraf, 2021; Bennani Khouloud, 2020; Gümüsay, 2015; Khalek, 2018; Liu et al., 2018; Ratten et al., 2017; Wilson & Liu, 2010, 2011).

The globalization and liberalization of global economy in line with the growing Muslim population also contributed to the growth of the halal industry (Ashraf, 2021; Gümüsay, 2015; Hamid et al., 2019). This has created opportunity for the multinational companies to reach out to the implausible Muslim consumers and provide them various Shariah-compliant products and services (Hassan, 2020; Nisha & Iqbal, 2017). Essentially, the Islamic finance industry and the halal industry are the two sectors which play key roles in providing and ensuring Muslim consumers enjoys variety of halal products and services (Thomas & Selimovic, 2015).

On the other hand, Islamic finance is described as the financing or business action that is in accordance with the principles set by the Shariah and its applications through the growth of comprehensive Islamic economics (Hassan, 2020; Kayed & Hassan, 2013; Hassan & Rabbani, 2021). The basic Shariah principles are based on the principles of ownership, principles of equity as well as principles of participation (Bekele et al., 2016; Hassan, 2020; Wilson et al., 2013; Yusof et al., 2018). With the paradigm recently shifting towards halal industry and halal entrepreneurship, it can be concluded that Islamic finance is the future financial system that has the possibility of emerging as the biggest threat to the conventional financial system (Ashraf, 2021; Hassan, 2020; Kayed & Hassan, 2013; Khan & Rabbani, 2020a; Khan et al., 2021a, 2021b; Moh'd Ali et al., 2020; Rabbani et al., 2021; Sun et al., 2020a).

Thus, both the halal industry and Islamic finance industry complement each other because Islamic finance has proven to be the most sustainable and robust financial system that can survive the test of time, such as the global financial crisis and COVID-19 pandemic (Hassan & Kayed, 2009; Kayed & Hassan, 2013; Kayed et al., 2015;

Khan & Rabbani, 2020a; Khan et al., 2021a, 2021b; Moh'd Ali et al., 2020; Sun et al., 2020a). The integration of halal industry (which halal entrepreneurship is a major determinant) with Islamic finance industry can be regarded as the method to improve the trust and confidence of consumers in the halal industry through their products and services (Ismaeel & Blaim, 2012). However, it is not without some challenges that may stand on the way of successful integration of the two concepts in real life. Challenges such as universality of halal products that align different regulatory frameworks in different nations may affect businesses that operate in multiple countries. There are many of such challenges which will be discussed in detail as we progress in the chapter.

2 Literature Review

2.1 Nexus of Halal Entrepreneurship and Islamic Finance

As shown in Fig. 1, ideal entrepreneurial ecosystem has five pillars that nurture the development of entrepreneurial ventures, and one of these pillars is access to funding (Ernst & Young, 2015). In a halal entrepreneurial ecosystem, Islamic finance is the major source of funding.

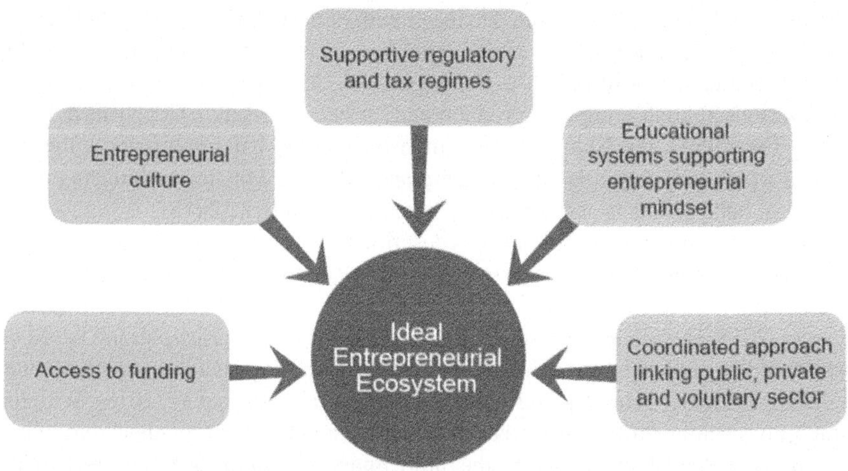

Fig. 1 Ideal entrepreneurial ecosystem pillars. *Source* Ernst & Young, *Megatrends 2015: Making Sense of a World in Motion*, Ernst and Young (2015)

2.2 *Raising Funds Through Islamic Finance for Halalpreneuers*

a. Islamic Capital Markets: The Islamic capital market (ICM) has huge potential needed to raise capital and manage risk. Table 1 depicts various potential levels in various Islamic financial products available under ICM. Different bonds issued by SME which include lenders bonds, covered bonds, and private placement bonds are huge prospective for Islamic finance. However, those bonds issued through banks, or by SMEs through alternative markets, bond funds as well as loan securitizations provide moderate prospective for Islamic finance. Meanwhile, those SME funds that include loan funds and receivables provide low prospective. Therefore, high and moderate prospective instruments of Islamic finance should be a priority for Halalpreneuers.

Table 1 Prospective mobilization of institutional investors for Halalpreneuers via Islamic finance

Product/Instrument	Depiction	Prospect for Islamic finance
Bonds issued via banks	The bonds issued either by private or public offerings	Moderate
Bonds issued via other SME lenders	Corporate bonds issued by SME lenders as a refinancing instrument	High
Bonds issued via SMEs through alternative markets	These are SMEs' alternative markets for retail debt financing and investing with proportionate framework and easy disclosure requirements	Moderate
Bonds issuance through SMEs as private placement	Using private offerings and ideal private offers regime for SME bonds, mostly focused on institutional investors	High
SME bond funds	Mutual investment structures that put together bond issued via SMEs, typically organized as closed-end funds	Moderate
SME funds via factoring and receivables	Funds invested in factoring firms. The funds usually purchase receivables from the SMEs, offering them with instant financing at an implicit interest rate which is lower compared to bank rates	Low
SME covered bonds	Debt securities issued by credit institutions that are covered by a group of high-quality assets	High
SME loan securitizations	Securitizing SME loans (transforming illiquid instruments to liquid tradable securities)	Moderate
SME loan funds	Mutual investment structures that put together SME-related assets (e.g., receivables and loans) and provide returns to the fund investors	Low

Source Joint World Bank Group–Islamic Development Bank G20 Islamic Finance Policy Paper, *Leveraging Islamic Finance for SMEs*, Istanbul, 2015

b. Venture capitals and private equity funds: they are important source funds because they promote development of growth-oriented and innovative start-ups. The halalpreneurs are structured for private equity funds and venture capital due to the profit and loss sharing (PLS) model of Islamic finance.
c. Angel investors: offer funds to halalpreneurs, specifically during seed and early growth stages, while venture capital funds can be provided in the other stages. Moral and value-oriented approach are taken by Islamic finance with aim of fulfilling social and material necessities of a society through utilization of financial and economic resources. Through this, they can utilize numerous non-interest crowdfunding models.
d. Crowdfunding: this is an encouraging financing method as it includes coming together of numerous individuals over the social media and internet to each contribute their preferred amount as investment. With crowdfunding, various small are pooled, which allowed bypassing of institutional investors. In addition, potential investors that have thought their limited means are insufficient for investment would appreciate that they contribute to a proposed start-up. Extension of the "investor" definition through its scope increases the funds available for investment. SMEs have been boosted with the creation of non-banking financing options like crowdfunding which banks have ignored. Provided that these are Sharī'ah-compliant funds that can be attained with a bit of planning and effort, halalpreneurship will be able to generate their needed funds. Some proposed crowdfunding models that are *Sharī'ah*-compliant are addressed in Table 2. Halalpreneurs can use these models as funding alternatives. These funding include equity-and asset-based models and reward-based models for product financing. Existing and potential halalpreneurs with high potential for growth will benefit more on these types of funding.

Table 2 *Sharī'ah*-compliant crowdfunding models and instruments

Financing for	Crowd model	Potential beneficiary	Instrument with end client
Products	Reward-based	i. Existing halalpreneuer businesses ii. Start-ups halalpreneuer businesses	Sale
Investments	Asset-based	Existing halalpreneuer businesses	*Murābahah* *Ijārah*
	Equity-based	Existing halalpreneuer businesses	*Diminishing Mushārakah* *Mushārakah and Qarḍ* *Muḍārabah*
		Start-ups halalpreneuer businesses	*Mushārakah and Qarḍ* *Muḍārabah*

Source Joint World Bank Group–Islamic Development Bank G20 Islamic Finance Policy Paper, *Leveraging Islamic Finance for SMEs*, Istanbul, 2015

3 Methodology

3.1 Benefits of Halal Entrepreneurship Integration with Islamic Finance

Fully enhancing the halal entrepreneurship ecosystem through integration with Islamic finance can bring numerous benefits and contribute to the development of a strong halal ecosystem. Some of the key benefits include:

Access to Capital: Islamic finance provides a unique avenue for halalpreneurs to access capital and funding that aligns with Shariah principles. Islamic finance instruments such as Islamic banking, sukuk (Islamic bonds), and venture capital funds can provide halalpreneurs with the necessary financial resources to start and expand their businesses. This access to capital can foster entrepreneurship, promote business growth, and create employment opportunities.

Ethical and Responsible Financing: Islamic finance operates on the principle of avoiding interest (riba) and adheres to ethical and responsible financing practices. Integrating Islamic finance into the halal entrepreneurship ecosystem ensures that businesses operate in accordance with Islamic principles, promoting transparency, fairness, and social responsibility. This alignment with ethical standards can enhance the reputation and credibility of halal entrepreneurship and the overall halal ecosystem.

Market Integration: Islamic finance can facilitate the integration of halal entrepreneurship into wider markets, both locally and globally. Islamic financial institutions have networks and expertise that can assist halalpreneurs in accessing new markets, establishing trade links, and forging partnerships. This integration can expand the reach and market share of halalpreneurs, leading to increased business opportunities and growth.

Product Development and Innovation: Integration with Islamic finance can support the development of innovative halal products and services. Islamic financial institutions can provide research and development support, investment in product innovation, and guidance on Shariah compliance. This collaboration between halal entrepreneurship and Islamic finance can drive the creation of new and unique offerings that cater to the needs of the global halal market.

Capacity Building and Knowledge Sharing: Islamic financial institutions have expertise in finance, investment, and risk management. Through collaboration, they can contribute to the capacity building of halalpreneurs by providing training, mentorship, and advisory services. This knowledge sharing can enhance the skills and capabilities of halal entrepreneurship, enabling them to build sustainable businesses and contribute to the growth of the halal ecosystem.

Branding and Marketing Opportunities: Integration with Islamic finance can provide halalpreneurs with branding and marketing opportunities. Islamic financial institutions often have extensive networks and customer bases, which can be leveraged to promote halal products and services. This collaboration can enhance the visibility and market positioning of halal entrepreneurship, leading to increased consumer awareness and demand.

It is important to note that these are views of the author(s) of this chapter that it was a general overview of the potential benefits of integrating Islamic finance into the halalpreneurs ecosystem, which was based on common knowledge and general information. As there are fewer or no extant literature on the said integration.

3.2 Challenges of Integrating Halal Entrepreneurship with Islamic Finance

The challenges of integrating halal entrepreneurship with Islamic financing are based on common knowledge. These challenges can include:

Limited Awareness and Understanding: One challenge is the limited awareness and understanding of Islamic finance among halalpreneurs. Many entrepreneurs may not be familiar with the principles and mechanisms of Islamic finance, making it difficult for them to effectively integrate it into their business operations.

Complexity and Compliance: Islamic finance operates on specific principles and guidelines derived from Shariah law. Ensuring compliance with these principles can be complex and require specialized knowledge and expertise. The additional requirements and processes associated with Islamic financing can pose challenges for halalpreneurs.

Limited Availability of Islamic Financial Products: In some regions or markets, the availability of Islamic financial products and services may be limited compared to conventional financial options. This can make it challenging for halalpreneurs to access the necessary financing solutions that align with their ethical and religious requirements.

Cost and Efficiency: Islamic financial products may involve additional costs compared to conventional financing due to the structures and mechanisms involved. The higher costs and potentially longer processing times can present challenges for halalpreneurs seeking affordable and efficient financing options.

Fragmentation of the Islamic Finance Industry: The Islamic finance industry is fragmented, with different countries and regions having their own regulatory frameworks and standards. This fragmentation can create challenges for halalpreneurs operating in multiple markets or seeking cross-border financing.

4 Conclusion

Both halal entrepreneurship and Islamic finance encompasses business processes that based their operations on Shariah, which is crucial to the halal industry (Hassan et al., 2020, 2021a, b; Hassan & Salman, 2017). This makes Islamic finance the natural fit for halapreneurship. Integrating halal industry with Islamic financing enhances the growth of halal entrepreneurship (Khan & Rabbani, 2020b, 2021a, b). In addition, the Shariah-compliant funds for the halalpreneuers can improve their ethical and operational integrity since Islamic financing is regarded as being transparent, ethical, and economical. Integration of the two industries will be a "holistic branding" where halal financing methods will be used to finance halal products (Wilson, 2014; Wilson & Liu, 2011).

Halal ecosystem is essential for Muslims and Islamic economy. This halal ecosystem is regarded as the complete atmosphere halal industry that consists of the production of goods (foods, beverages, drugs, vaccines and cosmetics etc.), halal services (travels and tours, media and recreation, Islamic financial services, etc.), halal capital and government support (executives, academicians, executives, etc.) (Anwer, 2019; Shahzad et al., 2020). Thus, to achieve halal entrepreneurship success under the halal industry, Islamic finance must enhance halal entrepreneurship to create a supply chain of halal products and services for a strong halal ecosystem (Kaliszewska, 2020; Shafie & Othman, 2006, Zakaria & Kaushal, 2017).

References

Anwer, Z. (2019). Islamic venture capital investment style—Opportunities and challenges. *Journal of Islamic Marketing, 10*(3), 848–859 [online]. https://doi.org/10.1108/JIMA-02-2018-0046

Ashraf, M. A. (2021). Determinants of Islamic entrepreneurial intentions: An analysis using SEM. *Journal of Islamic Marketing, 12*(1), 20–40. https://doi.org/10.1108/JIMA-05-2019-0116

Battour, M., Salaheldeen, M., & Mady, K. (2021). Halal tourism: Exploring innovative marketing opportunities for entrepreneurs. *Journal of Islamic Marketing*. https://doi.org/10.1108/JIMA-06-2020-0191

Beg, T. (1979). Promotion of Muslim entrepreneurship under state support. *Journal of Objective Studies, 2*(1), 95–106.

Bekele, G., Chowdhury, R. H., & Rao, A. (2016). Analysis of default behavior of borrowers under Islamic versus conventional banking. *Review of Behavioral Finance, 8*(2), 156–173 [online]. https://doi.org/10.1108/RBF-06-2015-0025

Bennani Khouloud, S. (2020). Is Islam associated with business success? In T. Khaled & S. Anis Ben (Eds.), *Understanding the relationship between religion and entrepreneurship* (pp. 51–78). IGI Global.

Chapra, M. U. (1985). *Towards a just monetary system*. The Islamic Foundation.

Dinar Standard. (2020). *State of the global Islamic economy report 2020/21*. Dubai International Financial Centre [online]. Retrieved June 13, 2021, from https://haladinar.io/hdn/doc/report2018.pdf

Ernst & Young. (2015). *Megatrends 2015: Making sense of a world in motion*. Ernst & Young.

Fuseini, A. (2017). Halal food certification in the UK and its impact on food businesses: A review in the context of the European Union. *CAB Reviews: Perspectives in Agriculture, Veterinary*

Science, Nutrition and Natural Resources, 12 [online]. https://doi.org/10.1079/PAVSNNR201712007

Gümüsay, A. A. (2015). Entrepreneurship from an Islamic perspective. *Journal of Business Ethics, 130*(1), 199–208.

Hamid, A., Said, M., & Meiria, E. (2019). Potency and prospect of halal market in global industry: An empirical analysis of Indonesia and United Kingdom. *Business and Management Studies* [online]. https://doi.org/10.11114/bms.v5i2.4167

Hassan, K. (2015). Entrepreneurship, Islamic finance and SME financing. In *IFSB 7th Public Lecture on Financial Policy and Stability*, Jakarta, Indonesia (pp. 1–46).

Hassan, Y. (2020). A decade of research on Muslim entrepreneurship. *Journal of Islamic Marketing*. https://doi.org/10.1108/JIMA-12-2019-0269

Hassan, Y. (2021). A decade of research on Muslim entrepreneurship. *Journal of Islamic Marketing*. https://doi.org/10.1108/JIMA-12-2019-0269

Hassan, M. K., & Kayed, R. N. (2009). The global financial crisis, risk management and social justice in Islamic finance. *ISRA International Journal of Islamic Finance, 1*(1), 33–58.

Hassan, M. K., & Rabbani, M. R. (2021). *Islamic fintech, blockchain & crowdfunding: Current landscape & path forward.* Under review (unpublished source).

Hassan, M. K., Rabbani, M. R., & Abdullah, Y. (2021a). Socioeconomic impact of COVID-19 in MENA region and the role of Islamic finance. *International Journal of Islamic Economics and Finance, 4*(1), 51–78.

Hassan, M. K., Rabbani, M. R., & Ali, M. A. (2020). Challenges for the Islamic finance and banking in post COVID era and the role of fintech. *Journal of Economic Cooperation and Development, 43*(3), 93–116.

Hassan, M. K., Rabbani, M. R., Khan, S., & Ali, M. A. M. (2021b). *An Islamic finance perspective of crowdfunding and peer to peer lending.* Under review (unpublished source).

Hassan, R., & Salman, S. A. (2017). Guiding principles in developing Shari'ah governance framework for Islamic capital market. *International Journal of Economic Research, 14*(6), 27–38 [online]. https://www.scopus.com/inward/record.uri?eid=2-s2.0-85019561222&partnerID=40&md5=7a3c960a5bf0211140f44acef6bf1c74

Hayat, R., Den Butter, F., & Kock, U. (2013). Halal certification for financial products: A transaction cost perspective. *Journal of Business Ethics* [online]. https://doi.org/10.1007/s10551-012-1534-9

Ismaeel, M., & Blaim, K. (2012). Toward applied Islamic business ethics: Responsible halal business. *Journal of Management Development, 31*(10), 1090–1100 [online]. https://doi.org/10.1108/02621711211281889

Kaliszewska, I. (2020). Halal landscapes of Dagestani entrepreneurs in Makhachkala'. *Ethnicities, 20*(4), 708–730 [online]. https://doi.org/10.1177/1468796820905692

Kayed, R. N., & Hassan, M. K. (2013). *Islamic Entrepreneurship* [online]. https://doi.org/10.4324/9780203840801

Kayed, R. N., Mahlknecht, M., & Hassan, M. K. (2015). The current financial market crisis: Lessons learned, risks and strengths of Islamic capital markets compared to the conventional system. *Islamic Capital Markets* [online]. https://doi.org/10.1002/9781119206040.ch17

Khalek, A. A. (2018). *Entrepreneurship and the halal wave in Malaysia. Global entrepreneurship and new venture creation in the sharing economy* (pp. 191–205). IGI Global.

Khan, S., Al-Dmour, A., Bali, V., Rabbani, M. R., & Thirunavukkarasu, K. (2021b). Cloud computing based futuristic educational model for virtual learning. *Journal of Statistics and Management Systems, 24*(2), 357–385.

Khan, A., Arafat, M. Y., & Azam, M. K. (2020a). Role of halal literacy and religiosity in buying intention of halal branded food products in India. *Journal of Islamic Marketing* [online]. https://doi.org/10.1108/JIMA-08-2019-0175

Khan, S., Hassan, M. K., & Rabbani, M. R. (2021a). An artificial intelligence-based Islamic fintech model on Qardh-Al-Hasan for COVID 19 affected SMEs. In *Islamic perspective for sustainable financial system.* Istanbul University Press.

Khan, S., & Rabbani, M. R. (2020a). Artificial intelligence and NLP based chatbot as Islamic banking and finance expert. In *2020 International Conference on Computational Linguistics and Natural Language Processing (CLNLP 2020)*, Seoul, South Korea, 20–22, July.

Khan, S., & Rabbani, M. R. (2020b). Chatbot as Islamic finance expert (CaIFE): When finance meets artificial intelligence. In *2020 International Conference on Computational Linguistics and Natural Language Processing (CLNLP 2020)*, Seoul, South Korea (pp. 1–5).

Khan, S., & Rabbani, M. R. (2021a). In depth analysis of blockchain, cryptocurrency and Sharia compliance. *International Journal of Business Innovation and Research* [online]. https://doi.org/10.1504/ijbir.2020.10033066

Khan, S., & Rabbani, M. R. (2021b). Artificial intelligence and NLP based chatbot as Islamic banking and finance expert. *International Journal of Information Retrieval Research (IJIRR), 11*(3), 65–77.

Liu, Z., Guo, Q., Sun, P., Wang, Z., & Wu, R. (2018). Does religion hinder creativity? A national level study on the roles of religiosity and different denominations. *Frontiers in Psychology, 9*, 1912.

Moh'd Ali, M. A., Basahr, A., Rabbani, M. R., & Abdulla, Y. (2020). Transforming business decision making with internet of things (IoT) and machine learning (ML). In *2020 International Conference on Decision Aid Sciences and Application (DASA)* (pp. 674–679).

Nisha, N., & Iqbal, M. (2017). Halal ecosystem: Prospect for growth in Bangladesh. *International Journal of Business and Society, 18*(S1), 205–222.

Rabbani, M. R., Bashar, A., Nawaz, N., Karim, S., Ali, M. A. M., Rahiman, H. U., & Alam, M. S. (2021). The Response of Islamic financial service to the COVID-19 pandemic: The open social innovation of the financial system. *Journal of Open Innovation: Technology Market and Complexity, 7*(2), 136.

Ratten, V., Ramadani, V., Dana, L.-P., & Gërguri-Rashiti, S. (2017). Islamic entrepreneurship and management: Future research directions. In V. Ramadani, L.-P. Dana, S. Gërguri-Rashiti, & V. Ratten (Eds.), *Entrepreneurship and management in an Islamic context* (pp. 227–242). Springer International Publishing.

Ramadani, V., Dana, L.-P., Ratten, V., & Tahiri, S. (2015). The context of Islamic entrepreneurship and business: Concept, principles and perspectives. *International Journal of Business and Globalisation, 15*(3), 244–261.

Rehan, M., Block, J., & Fisch, C. (2019). Entrepreneurship in Islamic communities: How do Islamic values and Islamic practices influence entrepreneurship intentions? *Journal of Enterprising Communities People and Places in the Global Economy*. https://doi.org/10.2139/ssrn.3405196

Salaheldeen, M., Battour, M., Nazri, M. A., Bustamam, U. S. A., & Hashim, A. J. C. M. (2022). The perception of success in the halal market: Developing a halal entrepreneurship success scale. *Journal of Islamic Marketing.*

Sarker, M. N. I., & Rashid, M. H. O. (2015). An impact of banking activities of private commercial Islamic bank to economic development in Bangladesh: A case study on First Security Islami Bank Limited (FSIBL). *Journal of Investment and Management, 4*(5), 264–272.

Sarker, M. N. I., Khatun, M. N., & Alam, G. M. (2019). Islamic banking and finance: Potential approach for economic sustainability in China. *Journal of Islamic Marketing, 11*(6).

Shafie, S., & Othman, M. N. (2006). Halal certification: An international marketing issues and Challenges. In *Proceeding at the International IFSAM VIIIth World Congress.*

Shahzad, M. A., Jun, D., Noor, G., & Zubair, A. (2020). Causation of halal food consumption in China. *Journal of Islamic Marketing* [online]. https://doi.org/10.1108/JIMA-07-2019-0153

Soltanian, M., Zailani, S., Iranmanesh, M., & Aziz, A. A. (2016). Motivations of SME entrepreneurs to become halal entrepreneurship. *Journal of Science and Technology Policy Management, 7*(2), 173–189.

Sun, H., Rabbani, M. R., Sial, M. S., Yu, S., Filipe, J. A., & Cherian, J. (2020a). Identifying big data's opportunities, challenges, and implications in finance. *Mathematics, 8*(10) [online]. https://doi.org/10.3390/math8101738

Thomas, P., & Selimovic, A. (2015). Sharia on a plate? A critical discourse analysis of halal food in two Norwegian newspapers. *Journal of Islamic Marketing, 6*(3), 331–353.

Tlaiss, H. A., & McAdam, M. (2021). Islam, Arab women's entrepreneurship and the construal of Success. *International Journal of Entrepreneurial Behavior and Research, 27*(3), 821–844. https://doi.org/10.1108/IJEBR-08-2020-0523

Tok, M. E., & Kaminski, J. (2018). Islam, entrepreneurship, and embeddedness. https://doi.org/10.1002/tie.21970

Utomo, S. B., Sekaryuni, R., Widarjono, A., Tohirin, A., & Sudarsono, H. (2020). Promoting Islamic financial ecosystem to improve halal industry performance in Indonesia: A demand and supply analysis. *Journal of Islamic Marketing* [online]. https://doi.org/10.1108/JIMA-12-2019-0259

Wilson, J. A. J. (2014). The *Halal* phenomenon: An extension or a new paradigm? *Social Business, 4*(3), 255–271 [online]. https://doi.org/10.1362/204440814x14103454934294

Wilson, J. A. J., & Liu, J. (2010). Shaping the halal into a brand? *Journal of Islamic Marketing* [online]. https://doi.org/10.1108/17590831011055851

Wilson, J. A. J., Belk, R. W., Bamossy, G. J., Sandikci, Ö., Kartajaya, H., Sobh, R., Liu, J., & Scott, L. (2013). Crescent marketing, Muslim geographies and brand Islam: Reflections from the JIMA Senior Advisory Board. *Journal of Islamic Marketing, 4*(1), 22–50 [online]. https://doi.org/10.1108/17590831311306336

Wilson, J. A. J., & Liu, J. (2011). The challenges of Islamic branding: Navigating emotions and halal. *Journal of Islamic Marketing* [online]. https://doi.org/10.1108/17590831111115222

Yusof, S. A., Budiman, M. A., & Amin, R. M. (2018). Relationship between religiosity and individual economic achievement: Evidence from South Kalimantan, Indonesia. *Journal of King Abdulaziz University, Islamic Economics, 31*(2), 3–16 [online]. https://doi.org/10.4197/Islec.31-2.1

Zakaria, N., & Kaushal, L. A. (2017). *Global entrepreneurship and new venture creation in the sharing economy.* IGI Global.

Halalisation: Challenges and Opportunities in Halal Food and Beverages Industry for Halalpreneurs

Naelati Tubastuvi and Yan Aldo Wiliantoro

Abstract The Halal food and beverage industry presents a dynamic landscape with both challenges and opportunities for aspiring entrepreneurs in this emerging sector. Against the backdrop of the Indonesian halal market, this chapter discusses the concept of halalization and the associated challenges and opportunities that halal entrepreneurs face when entering this lucrative market. It also examines Halal certification using regular and self-declaration systems and describes the intricacies of obtaining Halal certification, dealing with complex regulatory frameworks, and addressing the changing needs of discerning consumers. It also explores the emerging trends in the industry, such as plant-based and organic halal products, which are opening new avenues for innovation in the halal business landscape. The chapter concludes by highlighting the promising prospects for micro, small and medium enterprises (MSMEs) in the halal food and beverage sector and highlights the importance of understanding and adapting to the ever-growing halal consumer market. Halalpreneurs must be well prepared to meet the unique demands of this niche industry while leveraging the immense economic potential it offers.

1 Introduction

According to the Indonesia Halal Market report in 2021/2022, the world's Muslim population spent US$ 1.9 trillion in 2020 on various lifestyle products such as food, beverages, fashion, and tourism. The food and beverage sector has the highest expenditure compared to other industries. Spending on this sector reached US$ 1,185 billion in 2020 and is predicted to rise to US$ 1,668 billion in 2025.

Even for the halal food product sector, Indonesia is ranked second in the world based on the State of the Global Islamic Economy (SGIE) Report 2022, released

N. Tubastuvi (✉) · Y. A. Wiliantoro
Faculty of Economics and Business, Universitas Muhammadiyah Purwokerto Jalan KH. Ahmad Dahlan Dukuhwaluh, Central Java, Purwokerto, Indonesia
e-mail: naelatitubastuvi@ump.ac.id

Y. A. Wiliantoro
Litera, Business School, Purwokerto, Indonesia

L. Raimi et al. (eds.), *Contemporary Discourse of Halal and Islamic Entrepreneurship*,
https://doi.org/10.1007/978-981-99-6427-7_10

by DinarStandard, on March 31, 2022. Malaysia occupies the first position in the halal food and beverage category. As for the modest fashion, pharmaceutical, and cosmetic categories, Indonesia is ranked third and ninth.

Indonesia has experienced significant progress, especially in developing the Sharia ecosystem and providing halal products since the enactment of the halal product guarantee law in 2014, which came into force in 2019. The Indonesian government's desire to become number one in providing halal food has encouraged the government to perfect all the necessary regulations so that the target of mandatory halal certification for all products circulating in Indonesia can be achieved.

As is known that the issuance of law Number 33 of 2014 concerning halal product guarantees aims to provide security and comfort for the Muslim community in particular. Based on this law in 2017, a halal product guarantee organizing agency was formed or commonly abbreviated as BPJPH. The establishment of this BPJPH aims to implement the implementation of halal product guarantees, and this law also regulates all forms of halal product guarantees.

In 2021 the Indonesian government issued Government Regulation 39 of 2001, which regulates that products that enter, circulate, and are traded in the territory of Indonesia must be halal certified. The products in question include goods or services related to food, beverages, cosmetics, medicines, and valuable goods used, used, or utilized by the public. Besides that, products derived from prohibited materials must be given a non-halal statement.

Halal certification will also provide added value for business actors in selling and producing their products. With this halal product guarantee law, it is hoped that all imported and circulating products in Indonesia will have halal certificates.

The halal product guarantee law changes halal certification obligations from voluntary to mandatory. Halal certification has since been carried out by BPJPH as the leading sector administratively by involving the Halal Examining Agency (LPH), which is authorized to inspect and test the halalness of products, as well as the Indonesian Ulema Council (MUI), which determines the fatwa on product halalness.

2 Staging of Halal Certification

Law Number 33 of 2014 concerning Halal Product Guarantee regulates that products that enter, circulate, and are traded in the territory of Indonesia must be halal certified. The obligation to be halal certified by BPJPH has been in effect since October 17, 2019. This obligation applies to food, beverages, and slaughter products and services in the first stage.

In the second stage, halal certification obligations will apply to cosmetic medicine products and utility goods. This is stated in government regulation number 39 of 2001 concerning implementing the halal product guarantee sector; the second stage will be implemented from October 17, 2021, to the nearest October 17, 2026.

According to the Minister of Religion, it was conveyed that this staging aims to make halal-certified obligations for products as stipulated in the regulations well implemented and avoid potential difficulties, especially for business actors in maintaining the sustainability and development of their business. The scope of products in the Halal Product Guarantee is comprehensive, including food, beverages, drugs, cosmetics, chemical products, biological products, genetically modified products, and goods used, used, or utilized by the public. This staging policy is a necessity in implementing mandatory halal certification.

The phasing of halal certification obligations allows business actors to prepare the entire production process to comply with established halal standards. One of the obstacles faced by business actors is providing halal-certified raw materials that still need to be made available in large quantities. This means that business actors have few choices regarding the ingredients used. This is a problem because if you continue to use other ingredients even though they are halal certified, it will impact the taste of the products produced. Another obstacle faced by business actors who use raw materials derived from meat is the need for halal-certified slaughterhouses, even though meat products are one of those required in the halal certification process.

3 Self-Declare Halal Certification Mechanism and Regular Scheme

Apart from the regular mechanism in the process of applying for halal certification. In 2021, the Indonesian government issued Minister of Religious Affairs regulation number 20 of 2021 concerning halal certification for micro and small business actors based on a statement from the micro and small business actors (self-declare) scheme.

In general, the differences between halal certification with regular and self-declare schemes are described in the figure and table below:

The step of Self-Declare Halal Certification (Fig. 2).

Regular scheme	Self-declare scheme
• The business actor bears the service fee for applying for halal certification	• The application fee for halal certification is zero Rupiah (free)
• A halal inspection agency carries out inspection activities (audits), and business actors can choose LPH (Halal Inspection Agency) registered with BPJPH	• Verification and validation activities are carried out by a companion institution for the halal product process where business actors choose a PPH Companion Institution registered with BPJPH, such as Islamic organizations and accredited universities

(continued)

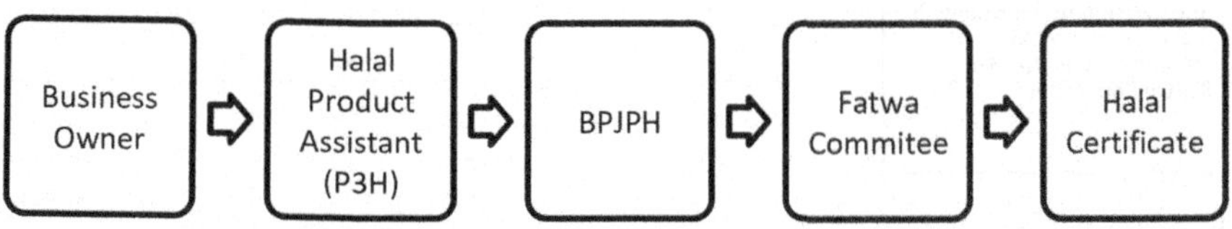

Fig. 1 The step of self-declare halal certification

(continued)

Regular scheme	Self-declare scheme
Mechanism: 1. Business actors apply for halal certification to BPJPH online through the halal website 2. BPJPH checks and completeness of business documents and issues an inspection fee bill based on the LPH determined by the applicant 3. Business actors make payments and obtain documents Document receipt letter 4. LPH conducts product inspection and testing 5. The MUI Fatwa Commission holds a fatwa session and issues a decision to issue a product halal determination decision 6. BPJPH issues halal certification based on the decision to determine the halalness of the Product by MUI	**Mechanism:** 1. Business actors apply for halal certification through halal by selecting the self-declaration scheme and entering the facilitation code 2. PPH assistants will verify and validate the submission of business actors 3. Document verification by BPJPH 4. BPJPH issues document receipt letter 5. MUI Fatwa Commission or BPJPH fatwa committee conducts a fatwa hearing 6. BPJPH issues halal certification that business actors can download

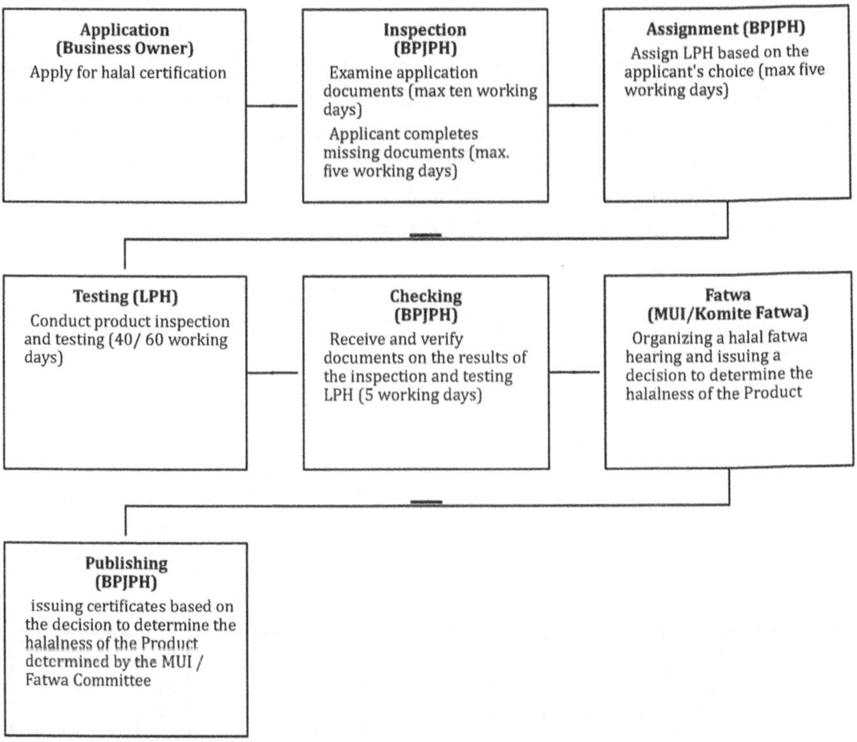

Fig. 2 The flow of self-declare halal certification

4 The Latest Halal Certification Mechanism

The Indonesian government issued Government Regulation instead of Law (Perppu) No. 2 of 2022 concerning Job Creation on December 30, 2022. According to BPJPH, there are changes in the provisions of halal products regulated in Perppu 2/2022 compared to Law 11/2020 on Job Creation, among others:

No	Matters regulated	Explanation
1	Regular halal certification	• Determination of Product halalness is carried out by MUI, Provincial MUI, Regency/City MUI, or Consultative Assembly of Aceh Ulama • If the time limit for determining the halalness of the Product is carried out by the MUI, Provincial MUI, Regency/City MUI, or the Aceh Ulama Consultative Assembly is exceeded, the determination of the halalness of the Product is carried out by the Halal Product Fatwa Committee, based on the provisions of Halal Fatwa • Determination of Product halalness by the Halal Product Fatwa Committee is done within 2 working days
2	Certification by halal declaration (self declare)	• In the application for halal certification carried out by micro and small business actors through a halal statement, the determination of the halalness of the Product is carried out by the Halal Product Fatwa Committee based on the provisions of Halal Fatwa • Determination of Product halalness by the Halal Product Fatwa Committee is carried out by 1 working day from the receipt of the results of PPH assistance
3	Halal product fatwa committee	• The Halal Product Fatwa Committee is formed and is responsible to the Minister • The Halal Product Fatwa Committee consists of the following elements • Ulama; and academics
4	Halal certification validity period	• Halal Certificate is valid since BPJPH issues it and remains valid as long as there is no change in the composition of ingredients and PPH • If there is a change in the composition of ingredients and PPH, Business Actors must renew the Halal Certificate
5	Electronic-based halal product guarantee implementation services	• JPH implementation services must use an integrated electronic system • The integrated electronic system connects the halal certification service process carried out by • BPJPH; LPH; MUI, Provincial MUI, Regency/City MUI, and Aceh Ulama Consultative Assembly; Halal Product Fatwa Committee; and PPH assistants • BPJPH manages the integrated electronic system

5 Halal Product Assurance System and Micro-Small-Medium Enterprises (MSME's) Progress

Along with the implementation of halal certification obligations, the term halal lifestyle is increasingly popular in society. This lifestyle refers to one part of Islamic sharia, namely, the obligation for Muslims to consume and use everything that has been proven halal.

Product halalness is very important, considering Indonesia is the world's fourth most populous Muslim country. For a Muslim, consuming food and drinks with a halal certificate can guarantee cleanliness and hygiene, which leads to product safety; this is in line with the willingness to increase awareness of the importance of healthy living.

For consumers, halal has now become the foremost preference. There is much evidence that shows people prefer halal products. Not only Muslims but also non-Muslims. For example, New Zealand is one of the world's largest exporters of halal meat. Sixty-five percent of the halal meat is exported to non-Muslim countries.

The halal lifestyle has become a trend. The halal lifestyle is gaining ground. From food and other aspects, people are paying more attention. So that everything is made into a lifestyle, including shoes. In Singapore, shoes are sold, and the lining is made of pig skin. This attention shows awareness of the halal lifestyle in various aspects of life.

The halal lifestyle is accompanied by the industry, which is also increasingly mushrooming. The halal industry is an industry of activities or activities that are based on the provision of sharia-compliant goods and services or under Islamic rules.

The halal industry covers many aspects; if, in the past, people talked about the halal sector more than the food industry or the food industry, then as awareness increased, people started to look at all other aspects.

However, the food industry accounts for less than a quarter of the halal industry. At the same time, half of it is almost contributed by cosmetics, pharmaceuticals, personal cases, and all kinds of things, while another quarter is from services. In this sense, services are halal logistics, such as the halal supply chain.

In Indonesia, the halal industry has the potential to grow well. This is because Indonesia is a large country with at least 225 million Muslim population.

With such a market supported by extraordinary natural resources, Indonesia can lead in the halal industry. The key to achieving that is to raise awareness at all levels of society.

For companies or business actors, halal certification is not only a guarantee of halal to consumers but more than that, the Consumer Halal label will provide added value to the product value, then become a point in penetrating the global market to increase the product market in the market and so on.

6 Halal Product Assurance System

Definition of Halal Product Guarantee System

Halal Product Guarantee System (SJPH) is an integrated system compiled, implemented, and maintained to regulate materials, production processes, products, resources, and procedures to maintain the sustainability of PPH. (Article 65 PP 39/2021 Chapter Explanation).

In the regulation of halal certification, Halal is not only seen from substances such as carrion, blood, pork, and so on, but the concept of halal also includes how the process or method of obtaining it or making it, which is referred to as the concept of traceability or traceability of halalness from upstream to downstream, from the provision of ingredients to products ready for consumption.

Producers are obliged to fulfill the needs/rights of consumers. The form of producer responsibility towards consumers, especially Muslim consumers, is to produce halal food products. To give consumers confidence that the products they have created are halal, MSME business actors need to have halal certificates. MSME business actors who have certified the halalness of their food products are required (mandatory) to prepare a system to consistently ensure the halal production process's continuity, which is referred to as the halal assurance system.

Objectives of the Halal Product Assurance System

The Halal Assurance System (SJH) aims to maintain the continuity of the halal production process so that the products produced can always be guaranteed halal under LP-POM regulations (Ariny, 2020). The Halal Assurance System (HAS) also aims for businesses to get added value for producing halal products under Law No. 33 of 2014 concerning the Halal Product Guarantee (BSN, 2017). Based on "Article 4 of Law Number 33 of 2014," products that enter, circulate, and are traded in the territory of Indonesia must be halal certified.

Legal Basis for the Halal Product Guarantee System

Strengthening and regulating halal regulations are regulated in a progressive and responsive legal institution, Law Number 33 of 2014 concerning Halal Product Guarantee. The most crucial objective of the government to pass Law Number 33 of 2014 concerning Halal Product Guarantee is legal certainty; Radbruch argues that there are four things related to the meaning of legal certainty (Fig. 3).

The government is responsible for the halal guarantee system organized by the Minister of Religion by establishing the Halal Product Guarantee Agency (BPJPH), which is domiciled under and responsible to the Minister of Religion (Article 6 of the Halal Product Guarantee Law). The Halal Product Guarantee Organizing Agency (BPJPH) has the following authorities: (a) Formulate and establish JPH policies; (b) Establish JPH norms, standards, procedures, and criteria; (c) Issue and revoke Halal Certificates and Halal Labels on Products; (d) Register Halal Certificates on foreign products; (e) Conduct socialization, education, and publication of Halal Products; (f) Accreditation of LPH (Halal Examining Institution); (g) Registration of Halal

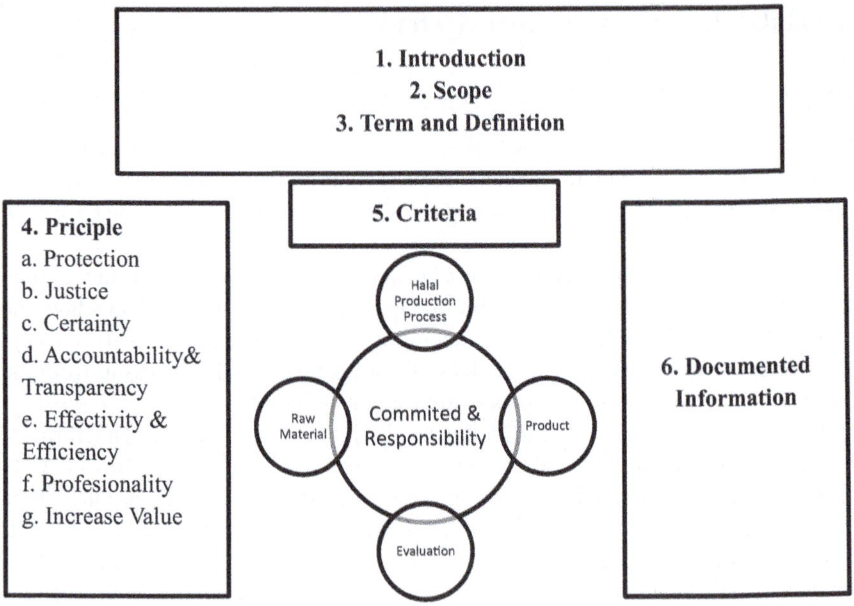

Fig. 3 System of halal product assurance

Auditors; (h) Supervise JPH; (i) Conducting guidance for Halal Auditors; and (j) Cooperating with domestic and foreign institutions in the field of organizing JPH (Article 10 of the Halal Product Guarantee Act).

7 Progress of MSMEs

Business actors in the Law of the Republic of Indonesia Number 8 of 1999 concerning Consumer Protection Article 1 Paragraph (3) is every individual or business entity, both in the form of a legal entity and not a legal entity established and domiciled or conducting activities in the jurisdiction of the Republic of Indonesia, either alone or jointly through agreements organizing business activities in various economic fields.

Micro, small, and medium enterprises are the leading players in economic activities in Indonesia (Suri, 2023). In realizing national development goals, MSMEs have an essential role in national business and have a strategic position, position, and role (Gunawan et al., 2020). The revival of MSMEs cannot only be done by providing funds from the government but must also improve the quality of MSME products themselves (Donny & Kurniawan, 2023). In order to improve the competitiveness of MSME products, it is necessary to take strategic steps under the capabilities and resources of MSMEs. One of the strategic steps that can be taken is through the halal certification program. Islamic teachings are no longer just beliefs and rituals; Islamic teachings function as a symbol of a product (identity). Regarding the symbols listed on the packaging of a product that shows products in the form of food and drinks with halal labels, it gives consumers and the broader community confidence that the Product is safe and healthy for consumption.

Micro, small, and medium enterprises (MSMEs) are improving the quality of their products by developing registration to obtain products with halal labels. The Indonesian Halal Label has been determined by the Ministry of Religion's Halal Product Guarantee Agency (BPJPH) and applies nationally. This determination is contained in the Decree of the Head of BPJPH Number 40 of 2022 concerning the Determination of Halal Label as the implementation of the mandate of Article 37 of Law Number 33 of 2014.

With the presence of Law No. 33 of 2014, the atmosphere or business climate will improve, especially for the halal industry in Indonesia. A good ecosystem is needed for halal industry players in this country (Fatima et al., 2023) because the halal product guarantee system involves many parties who can collaborate. Law Number 33 of 2014 is related to several policy target groups originating from business actors, the public as consumers, the Halal Inspection Institute, MUI, and BPJPH.

8 Halal and Its Components

Muslims comprise about 67% of the world's population, mainly in Asia (Pradana et al., 2023). Muslims are obliged to follow a halal lifestyle, including halal food, clothing, media, entertainment, cosmetics, medicine, and hospitals (Adinugraha et al., 2019).

9 Halal Food and Beverages

World food consumers consider the ethics and sustainability of food consumption (Nazaruddin et al., 2023). Some religions have rules, such as halal rules for Jews and halal rules for Muslims (Corte et al., 2018).

Food that has been certified halal can embed the halal logo on the packaging. This confirms that the Product is suitable for consumption. Embedding the halal logo on the packaging provides legal certainty to consumers that these foods and beverages have passed the halal test, are safe for consumption, and are guaranteed health and hygiene (Fathoni et al., 2023). Embedding the halal logo on the packaging also serves to help simplify the consumer decision-making process.

10 Halal Fashion

Halal fashion trends are in demand by the majority Muslim Indonesian community and are coupled with the awareness of Muslim women today to perfect their star's appearance (Lukmana, 2023). Halal fashion is a set of tools to beautify one's appearance under Islamic teachings. The development of Muslim fashion has recently proliferated and advanced; this can be seen in many teenagers and adult women wearing sari clothing (Lukmana, 2023).

The halal fashion industry aims to maintain halal integrity in halal fashion products to eliminate Muslim consumers' doubts about using them (Sumarliah et al., 2021). The halal fashion halal supply chain also has challenges that can be divided into three aspects, namely, (1) the lack of halal certification that is globally recognized as a disparity in criteria indicating product processing regulations in Muslim societies; (2) the absence of internationally agreed halal criteria related to the integrity of halal products; (3) technological advances distort halal raw materials and non-halal raw materials, requiring additional expert resources and time to provide decisions based on Islamic law regarding these raw materials (Poniman et al., 2015).

11 Halal Tourism

The global Halal tourism market has been proliferating recently, driven by the increasing demand for Halal travel options among Muslim travelers. According to a recent report, The global Halal tourism market was valued at over $200 billion in 2020 and is expected to grow at a Compound Annual Growth Rate of over 6% between 2021 and 2028 (Azam et al., 2022).

Some of the common facilities and services offered by halal tourism providers include (Gündüz & Topaloğlu, 2021):

1. Halal Food Options

Halal food options include access to halal-certified restaurants, cafes, and food stalls and providing halal food in hotels and other accommodations.

2. Prayer Facilities

Prayer facilities include the provision of prayer mats, Qibla (Mecca direction), and designated prayer areas in hotels and other public spaces.

3. Separate Swimming and Recreation Areas for Men and Women

This aligns with traditional Islamic modesty guidelines, which require separate spaces for men and women in some activities and situations.

4. Modest Dress Code

Many halal travel providers have dress codes that align with Islamic principles, such as covering the head and avoiding tight and revealing clothing.

5. Alcohol-Free Environment

Usually, halal tourism facilities are free from alcohol and other intoxicants under Islamic principles.

6. Religious and cultural tourism: Halal tourism providers often offer tours that focus on Islamic history and culture, such as visits to mosques, Islamic art museums, and historical sites.

The halal tourism industry is dynamic and growing, with excellent market potential. The halal tourism market industry worldwide will continue to make a significant contribution and provide economic benefits for countries that can provide a comprehensive halal tourism experience (Gunduz, 2023).

12 Halal Certification Procedures for Food and Beverages, Halal Fashion, and Halal Tourism

The stages that business actors must pass are: (1) Sign Up at e-lppommui.org; at this stage, business actors create a cerol account before the next stage. (2) after creating a Carol account, business actors register to apply for halal certification. (3) Pay the halal certification registration contract fee of Rp. 200,000 in cash or transfer to LPPOM MUI. (4) Upload documents and submit a Halal Assurance System (HAS) questionnaire. (5) Pre-audit monitoring and payment of certification contracts. (6) Submission of an audit schedule, after passing or meeting all the criteria during the pre-audit, the following procedure is to submit an audit schedule conducted by LPPOM MUI. (7) Auditors will conduct audits according to a predetermined schedule; auditing is also guided by data uploaded by businesses when registering their products for certification. (8) Auditor Meeting. (9) Post-audit monitoring, at this stage, business actors are advised to carry out daily monitoring to find any discrepancies in the audit results so that they can be immediately corrected and completed. Post-audit monitoring also includes four things, namely, halal documents, products, materials, and matrices. (10) Pass all approval auditing & SJH; at this stage, the business actor corrects and completes all documents as requested by the halal auditor from the audit results to carry out a fatwa by MUI. (11) MUI Fatwa Commission Meeting, The MUI Fatwa Commission conducts a meeting on documents from the results of the halal auditor, and a fatwa is given on whether the Product is halal or not according to the MUI Fatwa Commission. (12) Issuance of Halal Certification, if the results of the MUI Fatwa Commission state that the registered product is Halal based on the results of the audit by the halal auditor, then the halal certification will be issued by LPPOM MUI, but on the other hand, if according to the Fatwa Commission, the product is not halal, halal certification will not be issued. Halal Certificate from LPPOM MUI is valid for 4 years from its issuance (Fig. 4).

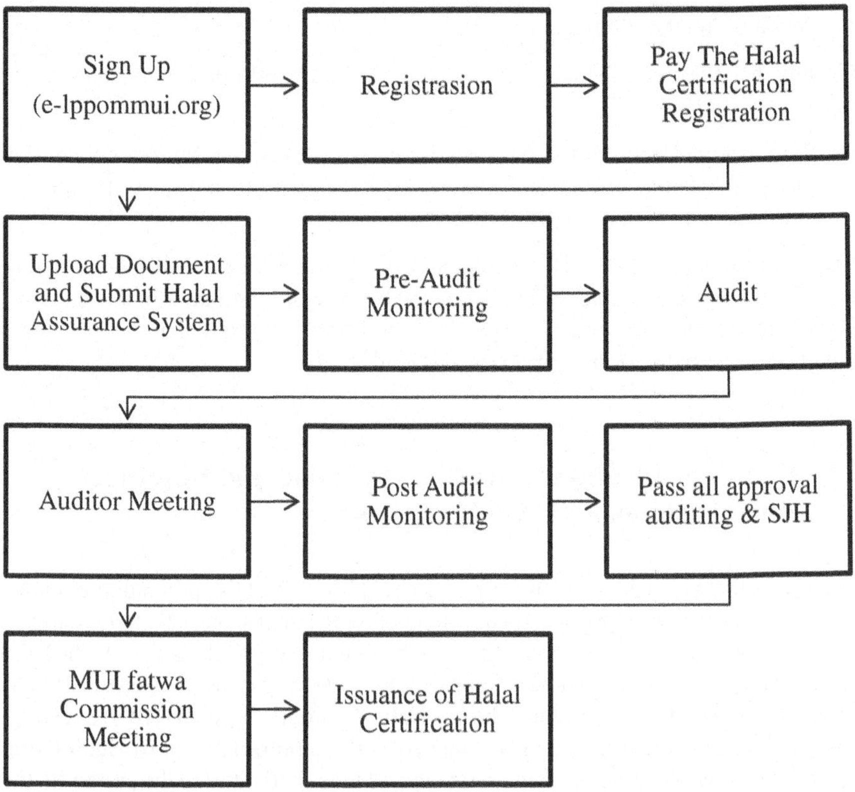

Fig. 4 Halal certification procedures

13 New Risk of Halal Fraud

The actions of food manufacturers are part of a fraud that is very detrimental to consumers, especially Muslim consumers who expect to buy halal food but are deceived by the MUI halal logo that is not actually on the food packaging. The case of traders adding their halal logos to their products is alarming (LPPOM MUI, 2018). Attempts to install halal logos on products sold by small traders are called acts of fraud.

As of September 2021, a total of 63,599 halal products with 1,510 active halal certificates from 1,291 companies circulating in Indonesia have carried out the halal certification process through the Halal Examining Agency (LPH) of the Indonesian Ulema Council's Food, Drug and Cosmetics Assessment Institute (LPPOM MUI). With this large number, preventive action is undoubtedly needed to minimize fraud or counterfeiting of products on the market, especially those related to using the halal logo.

It is hoped that the public will be more careful in consuming the products offered by entrepreneurs. The public can also ensure the correctness of the halal logo on a product through the official website of LPPOM MUI.

LPPOM MUI has regulated the use of the halal logo. Here are the provisions and procedures for its use:

1. Organizations that already have a halal decree for their products can only use the halal logo for these products according to the scope listed in the halal decree and only apply to the manufacturer's factory location listed in the halal decree.
2. The affixing of the halal logo depends on the type and nature of the product, and the marking must be such that it is straightforward to read.
3. The halal logo must be affixed directly on the product unless this is not possible either because the size of the product is too small or because of the nature of the product; in such cases, the halal logo must be affixed to the smallest packaging used in marketing the product.
4. The affixation of the halal logo is placed in a place that is easily visible with a size such that the halal logo and its complementary information can be read easily without tools.
5. Business actors can change the green color of the logo but are not allowed to change the shape of the halal logo.

LPPOM MUI will suspend or revoke the license to use the halal logo if the business actor is proven negligent or fails to meet the terms and conditions of halal product certification. Business actors are also required to publish the granting, cancellation, suspension, and revocation of certificates through public media so that the public can find out the halal status of their products.

Further actions include stopping the halal logo on products and publication in brochures or advertisements accompanied by cancellation, suspension, revocation, or return of halal provisions.

References

Adinugraha, H. H., Sartika, M., & Ulama'i, A. H. A. (2019). Halal lifestyle di Indonesia. *An-Nisbah: Jurnal Ekonomi Syariah, 5*(2), 57–81. https://doi.org/10.21274/an.2019.6.1.57-81.

Ariny, B. D. (2020). Dampak Positif Undang-Undang Nomor 33 Tahun 2004 Tentang Jaminan Produk Halal Dalam Menciptakan Sistem Jaminan Produk Halal di Indonesia. *Syar'ie: Jurnal Pemikiran Ekonomi Islam, 3*(2), 198–218.

Azam, M. S. E., & Abdullah, M. A. (2020). Global halal industry: Realities and opportunities. *IJEBI (International Journal of Islamic Business Ethics), 5*(1), 47–59

Badan Standarisasi Nasional. (2017). UndangUndang Republik Indonesia Nomor 33 Tahun 2014 tentang Jaminan Produk Halal.

Corte, V. D., Gaudio, G. D., & Sepe, F. (2018). Ethical food and the kosher certification: A literature review. *Br. Food J., 120*, 2270–2288.

Donny, A., & Kurniawan, B. (2023). EVALUASI PELAKSANAAN KEBIJAKAN SERTIFIKASI JAMINAN PRODUK HALAL DALAM MENDORONG PERKEMBANGAN USAHA MIKRO, KECIL, DAN MENENGAH PASCA COVID-19. *Publika* (1965–1982).

Fathoni, M. A., Faizi, F., & Sari, R. (2023). Determinasi Pembelian Makanan Halal Melalui Platform Digital: Kesadaran Halal Sebagai Variabel Mediasi. *Jurnal Ilmiah Ekonomi Islam, 9*(1), 45–54.

Fatima, N., Jumiati, I. E., & Yulianti, R. (2023). Implementasi Undang-Undang Nomor 33 Tahun 2014 Tentang Jaminan Produk Halal. *JDKP Jurnal Desentralisasi Dan Kebijakan Publik, 4*(1), 40–51.

Gunawan, S., Darmawan, R., Qadariyah, L., Wirawasista, H., Firmansyah, A. R., Hikam, M. A., & Ardhilla, M. F. (2020). Pendampingan produk UMKM di sukolilo menuju sertifikasi halalan thayyiban. *Sewagati, 4*(1), 14–19.

Gunduz, C. (2023). *An evaluation of the structure of the halal tourism market and its current situation in Europe.* Multifaceted Research in the Field of Tourism.

Gündüz, C., & Topaloğlu, C. (2021). Helal otellerde Porter'in jenerik rekabet stratejilerinin tespiti: Yöneticiler üzerine bir araştırma. *Balıkesir Üniversitesi Sosyal Bilimler Enstitüsü Dergisi, 24*(45), 557–579.

Lukmana, A. (2023). Analysis of service quality and customer satisfaction on repurchase halal fashion products: Study on Akhwat bone sewing house customers. *Economics and Business Journal (ECBIS), 1*(2), 65–72.

Nazaruddin, L. O., Gyenge, B., Fekete-Farkas, M., & Lakner, Z. (2023). The future direction of halal food additive and ingredient research in economics and business: A bibliometric analysis. *Sustainability, 15*(7), 5680. https://doi.org/10.3390/su15075680.

Poniman, D., Purchase, S., & Sneddon, J. (2015). Traceability systems in the Western Australia halal food supply chain. *Asia Pacific Journal of Marketing and Logistics, 27*(2), 324–348.

Pradana, M., Elisa, H. P., & Syarifuddin, S. (2023). The growing trend of Islamic fashion: A bibliometric analysis. *Cogent Social Sciences, 9*(1), 2184557.

Sumarliah, E., Li, T., Wang, B., Moosa, A., & Sackey, I. (2021). The impact of customer halal supply chain knowledge on customer halal fashion purchase intention. *Information Resources Management Journal, 34*(3), 79–100.

Suri, A. (2023). Sosialisasi Sertifikasi dan Labelisasi Halal pada UMKM DAPUR J24 di Kecamatan Tambun. *Kabupaten Bekasi. Jurnal Pelita Pengabdian, 1*(1), 102–108.

Influence of Religious and Health Factors on the Halal Cosmetics Industry

Nabila Huda Ibrahim

Abstract The halal cosmetics industry has seen exponential growth in recent years due to rising demand for halal products. Halal cosmetics adhere to Islamic principles, such as the prohibition of alcohol and non-halal animal-derived ingredients in their formulation. The competitive pricing, ethical standards, and natural ingredients of halal cosmetics have made them increasingly popular among Muslim and non-Muslim consumers alike. In addressing the growing industry of halal cosmetics, this study scrutinizes the influence of religious and health factors on Halal cosmetics and identifies the success stories of *halalpreneurship* in the areas of cosmetics and pharmaceuticals. Through the documents analysis method, this study reveals that religion and health are two significant factors that influence the purchasing and development of halal cosmetics. Successful *halalpreneurship* stories not only inspire but also impact consumers and the environment positively. Thus, the future of halal cosmetics is undeniably bright.

Keywords Halal cosmetics · Religious · Health · *Halalpreneurship* · Halal success story

1 Introduction

Halal cosmetics have become a significant segment in the halal industry as Muslim women are required to maintain their beauty with halal products. Halal cosmetics are gaining popularity due to their high-quality and cruelty-free products, which are permissible under Islamic *Shariah* law. Globally, the halal cosmetics market size reached US$30.3 Billion in 2022, which is not surprising due to its size (*Top halal cosmetics companies, manufacturers and brands*, 2022). A halal paradigm is a way of bringing halal to Muslim consciousness. Halal cosmetic products include anti-aging creams, skin moisturizers, perfumes, lipsticks, eye and face makeup, shampoo, hair color, toothpaste, and deodorants (Handriana et al., 2021). These products are usually

N. H. Ibrahim (✉)
University of Malaya, Kuala Lumpur, Malaysia
e-mail: s2003937@siswa.um.edu.my

L. Raimi et al. (eds.), *Contemporary Discourse of Halal and Islamic Entrepreneurship*,
https://doi.org/10.1007/978-981-99-6427-7_11

free from non-halal animal-derived ingredients and alcohol and are made from natural ingredients safe for human use. Halal cosmetics are different from normal cosmetics as they need to meet Islamic requirements for purity and cleanliness. They are widely accepted in Muslim countries and are gaining popularity globally. Providing a safe and effective way to maintain beauty and personal care without compromising religious beliefs, Halal cosmetics are a great alternative to traditional cosmetics due to their high quality and long-lasting effects. The use of Halal cosmetics offers everyone an opportunity to look and feel their best without compromising their convictions. As a result, the Halal industry has contributed trillions of dollars to the economy, and consumers are becoming more aware of the quality of the goods they consume and value-added products (Rahim, 2017).

Statistics show that the number of Muslims in the world is estimated to be over 2.01 billion by 2023, making Islam the second-largest religion in the world. Islam is an official religion in 26 countries in Asia, Africa, the Middle East, and sub-Saharan Africa. Muslims are the fastest-growing religion in the world, making them a diverse and dynamic group spread out across the globe (*Global Muslim Population*, 2023). The global halal cosmetics market size is expected to reach US$38,217 Mn in 2022 and surpass a valuation of US$114,524 Mn by 2032. Popular types of halal cosmetics include fragrances, color cosmetics, personal hygiene items, and skin care goods. Consumers are shifting towards chemical-free and natural ingredient-based cosmetics and personal care products, which are driving the market expansion. Halal items are on a rise in Muslim-majority countries (*Halal cosmetics market share to thrive at a CAGR of 11.6% through 2032*, 2022). It is estimated that between 2022 and 2031, the halal cosmetic market will increase by over 15.6% (Elabed, 2023). The demand for halal cosmetic products among the 2.4 billion Muslim consumers worldwide is increasing, but production is dominated by non-halal cosmetic manufacturers (Sugibayashi et al., 2019).

Halal cosmetics consists of two important aspects of a Muslim which are religion and health. It is compulsory for Muslim consumers to know the origin of raw materials and the production process of cosmetic ingredients as obligated in the Holy Quran:

> O humanity! Eat from what is lawful and good on the earth and do not follow Satan's footsteps. He is truly your sworn enemy (2: 168).
>
> O believers! Eat from the good things We have provided for you. And give thanks to Allah if you ⌜truly⌝ worship Him ⌜alone⌝ (2: 172).

Every Muslim needs to make sure their food intake or any consumption is lawful and permissible as in a hadith reported by Anas ibn Malik:

The Prophet, peace and blessings be upon him, said, "**Seeking the lawful is a duty upon every Muslim.**"

Source: al-Mu'jam al-Awsaṭ lil-Ṭabarānī 8610 (Elias, 2022).

The concept of halal means the products that is allowed by God to be consumed and do not impact sin and torture which also include purity (Tayyib) (Nurhayati & Hendar, 2020). Halal is used to identify the way an animal is slaughtered, which involves killing through a cut to the jugular vein, carotid artery, and windpipe. Other halal choices of consumption include abstaining from alcoholic beverages or pork

(*What is halal beauty?*, 2023). Purchasing food with the halal certification can help to ease some of the worries about food additives, as there is a growing list that is approved and aligned with halal practices of being wholesome and permitted, and a list of those that are considered harmful and forbidden. This same goes to halal cosmetics as halal guarantees the healthy, safe, and good quality products as the regulations ensure that animals used for products are treated humanely, and they are prepared in a way that is hygienic and wholesome (Elabed, 2023). Purchasing and consuming halal cosmetics indicate the significance of religion and health factors were taken into account. Most importantly, halal obligation has led to the growing trends of halal industry, and it is imperative to identify the success factors in the *halalpreneurship.* Thus, the objective of this chapter is:

1. To scrutinize the influence of religious and health factors on the Halal cosmetics.
2. To identify the success stories of *halalpreneurship* in the areas of cosmetics and pharmaceuticals.

2 Literature Review

2.1 Halal Cosmetics

Cosmetics are treatments intended to improve the appearance of a person. The term refers to any preparation applied to the skin, eyes, mouth, hair, or nails for cleansing, beautifying, enhancing attractiveness, or altering appearance. In response to Muslim demand for halal, high-quality, and safe cosmetics, the market for halal cosmetics is growing (Shahid et al., 2018). Previous studies show that Muslim consumers are becoming increasingly aware of halal cosmetics and personal care products. Despite this, Halal products are perceived differently by consumers for both food and cosmetics. In accordance with Islamic guidelines, halal cosmetics should not contain any traces of porcine by-products and their derivatives, alcohol, and other prohibited materials (Ishak et al., 2020). Halal cosmetic ingredients are any constituents derived from plants, soil, water, permissible animals slaughtered according to Islamic law, marine animals deemed halal, and synthetic materials that are safe for consumers and unadulterated with filth. For halal cosmetics to gain consumer acceptance and diminish doubt, plant-derived components and chemical synthesis are replacing non-halal animal-derived ingredients ones. Each ingredient must be certified halal by suppliers before it can be used by manufacturers (Sugibayashi et al., 2019).

Halal cosmetic products are an innovation and revolution in the cosmetic industry due to their high quality and compliance with Sharia. Halal cosmetics go beyond religious requirements and have to follow strict scientific investigation to come up with a product that is pure, safe and uses the best natural ingredients. Non-Muslims can be attracted to consume the halal cosmetics products (Khan et al., 2021). It should exclude alcohol, any human tissue, any part of prohibited animal and animal-derived ingredients categorized as non-halal by Islamic Sharia law or fatwa. Also, it must not contain substances that endanger health while it must be prepared with approved, clean tools and must avoid contact or proximity to any materials that fail to satisfy Islamic Sharia law or fatwa (Herjanto et al., 2023). As cosmetics often use animal fats as emulsifiers and alcohols as solvents, both of which cannot be used in halal cosmetics, it is possible to minimize toxicity when using an alcohol solvent by using organic or food-grade alcohols (Elabed, 2023). This is another reason why Halal Cosmetics are usually organic and high quality.

In purchasing the halal cosmetics products, there are many factors that contribute including Halal logo, halal brand image and halal awareness and attitudes. The Halal logo is a sign of trust and quality in the consumer market, which guarantees that the product has been prepared in accordance with Islamic laws and traditions. The Halal logo is present on food products, cosmetics, and other items that are safe for Muslim consumers. Meanwhile, attitudes describe consumer confidence in an object's benefits and attributes, as well as awareness of its environment (Septiarini et al., 2023). Brand perception helps the consumers to identify a brand under different conditions. It is affected by factors such as previous experience, education level, perceived risk, and situational factors (Rahim, 2017).

2.2 *Religion Factor in Halal*

Religion, particularly Islam, has significant influences on the production and consumption of halal products as it affects consumer decision-making behavior, influences attitude and behavior towards products (Abdullah et al., 2021). Muslim consumers are becoming more aware of halal cosmetic products, which are considered more important and meaningful than products carrying international certification. Halal certification endorses a product as religiously compliant with Islamic requirements. The market for halal cosmetics is large, but most of them are produced by non-Muslim manufacturers, leading to suspicion among Muslim consumers about the use of non-halal raw materials. However, non-Muslim consumers also buy halal products due to the perception that they are safer to use (Briliana & Mursito, 2017). Halal trust is crucial to Muslim consumers when purchasing products or services. Halal products indicate conformity to Islamic values, including being lawful, pure, and healthy (Suhartanto et al., 2022).

The religion factor depends on religiosity which is a measure of the degree to which people hold and practice beliefs in certain religious values and ideas (Nurhayati & Hendar, 2020). It is a system of faith and one's belief concerning the truthfulness and intrinsic qualities of a person's religious teachings and scriptures. It is considered a key factor controlling individuals' behavior and is the essential element influencing consumers' attitude and behavior toward consumption. Religiosity is the driving force for many consumers to purchase halal products, as it is an important part of life, adherence to Islam and its teachings. Muslim prioritize being faithful to their religion which made it essential for them to search for halal ways life for future rewards. Religiosity acts as antecedents of halal purchase consumption and influences alternative evaluation and final purchase (Shahid et al., 2018). Studies reveal that religion is among the factors that influence intention to purchase halal cosmetics (Hussain, 2022; Majid et al., 2015).

2.2.1 Health Factor in Halal Cosmetics

Accordingly, the demand for halal requirements has changed how business operators process halal certifications. The increasing demand for halal cosmetics due to safe, healthy, and clean food has led to the development of halal as a common term among both Muslim and non-Muslim communities worldwide (Katuk et al., 2021). The nutritious products in halal cosmetics have increased, leading to the growth of Halal products beyond religious boundaries. It is becoming a core competitive business strategy, with strict requirements minimizing production, thereby minimizing the risk of contamination. This is the reason why Multinational Companies (MNC) are investing heavily in assimilating the values, standards, and guidelines about Halal to increase their market base and high-return prospects (Khan et al., 2022).

When halal labels are placed on halal products, Muslims have the knowledge of their contents and can use them without caution as Halal products are free of toxic substances as well as harmful chemicals (Arrifin et al., 2016). This is because, non-halal cosmetic products are at high risk of leaving side effects to their consumers, including mercury and hydroquinone. Mercury is a substance that easily penetrates the skin and reaches into the blood, causing physical weakness, emotional instability, and poor memory problems. Hydroquinone is another chemical that is widely used in cosmetic creams to act as a whitener, but it has been linked to the occurrence of cancer in humans. For example, ochronosis, a skin disease known as thick and black, is also among the effects of hydroquinone use (Zakaria et al., 2022). This is among the reasons why people's health factor is significant in purchasing or consuming the halal cosmetics. As revealed in the study by Zakaria et al. (2022), the respondents show the highest mean for choosing clean, pure and healthy cosmetics products, which indicates the knowledge of the consumer. Other studies also indicate that consumers prioritize the ingredients in choosing the halal cosmetics (Che Mohd Hashim & Musa, 2014; Ishak et al., 2020).

2.2.2 Halal Entrepreneurship

In Islam, entrepreneurship is considered Halalpreneurship, which is an essential aspect of life. *Halalpreneurship* conforms to the Shari'ah ("*Aqidah, Fiqh, Akhlaq*") and ensures that its activities do not deviate from Islam's guidelines. *Halalpreneurship* is regarded as being the role of a Khalifah (Caliph). Khalifah's mission is to worship Allah Subhanahu Wa Taala (SWT) and to develop and prosper the world. As such, entrepreneurship is a role that contributes to society, world, and humanity's welfare (Abdullah & Azam, 2020). Halal entrepreneurship and Halal-minded entrepreneurship are used interchangeably by researchers. Malaysia ranked first in the global Halal food indicator in 2015, followed by the United Arab Emirates and Australia. Halal entrepreneurship is a social process embedded in different scopes outside the purview of what is generally conceived of as the purely economic scope. It is grounded on three interlinking pillars of entrepreneurial, religion-spiritual, and socioeconomic/ethical. Muslim entrepreneurs are expected to continuously promote good deeds and ensure legitimacy in their business practices. Halal entrepreneurs exploit opportunities in the Halal industry according to Islamic teachings to obtain financial gains. The complexity of Halal entrepreneurship needs to be integrated into a holistic model that balances explanatory richness and parsimony (Salaheldeen et al., 2022). Hence, the success of *halalpreneruship* is not dependent on the success of the business itself, but how it positively impacts the stakeholders and the surroundings.

3 Research Methodology

This study is a qualitative content analysis that involves secondary data analysis. Document analysis is a systematic procedure for reviewing or evaluating documents, which requires the data to be examined and interpreted. To develop empirical knowledge, it is necessary to analyze and interpret data in order to understand them and elicit meanings from them (Bowen, 2009). Data collections are divided into two parts: studies on Halal Cosmetics; websites and reports of successful halal entrepreneurship. For the studies on Halal Cosmetics, only the studies that used health and religion among the determinants for the intention to purchase halal cosmetics will be used. Meanwhile, for the halal entrepreneurship, this study identifies companies that have successfully developed the halal cosmetics and pharmaceuticals.

4 Research Findings and Discussion

The growing demands of Halal beauty products indicate the awareness of the user about the ingredient and safety of the cosmetics. This is because, Muslim consumers must ensure that products or services must meet hygiene and health standards, derived from ethical sources and not contrary to Islamic teachings which only can be offered by Halal products (Sobari et al., 2022). Religion and health are two significant factors in halal products as every Muslim is obligated to obtain and consume lawful and permissible products that could guarantee safety. Thus, the consumption is not only dependent on the individuals but also on the company and the authority. This study looks at both individual consumption and halal entrepreneurship for promoting halal, high quality, and safe products. The research findings consist of two parts: reviewed studies on Halal cosmetics purchase and consumptions; and successful Halal Entrepreneurship companies.

4.1 Studies Review

This study has identified ten studies from Malaysia, Indonesia, India, and Pakistan on Halal cosmetics purchase and consumption as Table 1. Studies in Malaysia show that the consumers prioritize the ingredients over the halal approval in order to purchase Halal cosmetics. Meanwhile, studies in Indonesia show that the consumers will be influenced by their attitudes, knowledge and trust in order to purchase the halal cosmetics products. Religiosity and Halal awareness are among other factors that influence the consumer to purchase the Halal cosmetics products exhibited in the studies in India and Pakistan. Although religion and health factors are two significant factors in halal cosmetics, the studies review indicates otherwise for Malaysia and Indonesia as accessibility of Halal logo product is high. Meanwhile, religion is still one of determinants to purchase halal cosmetics and products in India and Pakistan.

The probable reasons both studies in Malaysia and Indonesia indicate that Halal was not a priority in purchasing or consuming cosmetics are the fact that these countries have very stringent Halal procedures and vast availability or access to the products. Malaysia has been ranked number one in the Global Islamic Economy Indicator (GIEI) Score for 9 consecutive years, proving that it is a leading light in the halal economy (Bernama, 2022). Therefore, Malaysians have no problem obtaining halal products, causing priority to be given to other things. Malaysians are well versed in halal products and their awareness is no longer a priority. This same applies to Indonesia that (in order to impose halal products) have a specific law that requires that halal products need to be declared in accordance with Islamic law (Nurhayati & Hendar, 2020). Hence, the halal logo already provides a guarantee that the cosmetics do not contain prohibited materials and are processed in a manner in compliance with Islamic law (Handriana et al., 2021). Furthermore, Malaysians and Indonesians belong to Imam Shafii school of jurisprudence, which indicates that their level of halal awareness (religion) should be the same. Hence, it is not surprising why halal awareness is not an issue for them.

Meanwhile, religious factors or determinants play a significant role in purchasing and consuming halal cosmetics in India and Pakistan. Since Pakistan and India belong to the Imam Hanafi School of Jurisprudence, Muslims in both countries should have similar understandings. In other words, the level of halal awareness within both countries is the same. India is not a Muslim majority country like Pakistan, so the availability of halal could be limited, making religion and awareness of halal priorities over other things. As a result, Muslim consumers in this region are highly religious in respect of their beliefs and practice of certain religious values. This has to do with one's faith in God and how far they follow God's path (Nurhayati & Hendar, 2020). This has to do with one's faith in God and how far they follow God's path (Nurhayati & Hendar, 2020).

Other than religion and health, the other factors that influence halal consumptions in these countries are attitudes, brand image, knowledge, and others. These factors could also be considered by manufacturers or halal industry in producing and promoting halal products.

Table 1 Studies review on halal cosmetics purchase and consumptions

Number	Author(s)	Objective	Methodology	Country	Findings
1	Che Mohd Hashim and Musa (2014)	To identify the factors considered in making a decision to consume cosmetic products	Focus groups: Group A: (users) among those who are using Halal cosmetic products Group B: (non-users) among those who are not using halal cosmetic products	Malaysia	The result shows that Halal is not the main factor that they considered before they consume the cosmetic product. However, the content/ingredient of the product is the most important factor that both respondents (user and non-user) considered in making the decision to buy a cosmetic product
2	Khan et al.	To propose a model to reveal the distinctive factors that influence the purchase intention of halal cosmetics among Generation Y in Malaysia	Quantitative method: 262 respondents (Generation Y consumer)	Malaysia	This study discovered that ingredient safety followed by the halal logo, promotional and religious beliefs are the predictors for the purchase intention of halal cosmetic products among Generation Y consumers
3	Ishak et al. (2020)	To describe cosmetics purchase behavior of young, educate Muslim females in Malaysia and to explore its relationship with certain potential antecedents	Quantitative method: 250 respondents (female consumers from four higher education institutions)	Malaysia	The study revealed that the consumers are selective and prudent for the ingredients of halalness, country of origin, health safety guarantee and the benefits of the products

(continued)

Table 1 (continued)

Number	Author(s)	Objective	Methodology	Country	Findings
4	Briliana and Mursito (2017)	To provide an improved understanding of the influential factors on attitudes toward halal cosmetic products	Mixed method: in-depth interviews and survey with 350 respondents	Indonesia	The results indicated that attitudes towards halal cosmetic products were important antecedents of intention to purchase halal cosmetic products and mediated the influence of knowledge, religiosity and subjective norm
5	Putri et al. (2019)	To increase awareness of the society about the importance of halal products, not only for internal use but also external use	Quantitative method: 354 respondents over the age of 18 years old and who purchased halal cosmetics in the last 6 months	Indonesia	Neither religiosity nor knowledge has a significant result in the intention to repurchase halal cosmetics
6	Handriani et al. (2021)	To analyze millennial generation purchase behavior on halal cosmetic products in Indonesia	Quantitative method: 206 respondents (Muslim females of the millennial generation)	Indonesia	The study shows that trust of the product is influenced by the perceived value and brand image. The attitude of the users is influenced by the brand image, and religious belief. Halal awareness is influenced by halal certification but not religious belief. Attitude is influenced by trust and halal awareness. Trust, attitude, and halal awareness influenced the intention to purchase the products

(continued)

Table 1 (continued)

Number	Author(s)	Objective	Methodology	Country	Findings
7	Shahid et al. (2018)	To present a framework of halal consumers' purchase and explore the factors that Indian consumers consider while buying halal cosmetics	Qualitative method: focus group discussion and in-depth interviews in Delhi, Mumbai and Hyderabad	India	The study found that religiosity and increasing awareness about halal products influenced individuals' halal product consumption along with halal certification and growing education level of Muslim consumers
8	Sama and Trivedi (2019)	To observe the effect of consumers' beliefs and subjective norms on attitude towards halal cosmetics products	Quantitative method: 418 respondents (Muslims respondents of Juhapura area of Ahmedabad in India)	India	The results indicate that Muslim consumers' beliefs have the most significant effect on attitude towards halal products, which leads to brand love. Further, brand love leads to brand loyalty for halal cosmetics. Religiosity moderates the relationship between consumers' beliefs, subjective norms, and the dependent variable- attitude towards halal products

(continued)

Table 1 (continued)

Number	Author(s)	Objective	Methodology	Country	Findings
9	Majid et al. (2015)	To check the relationship between awareness, religious belief, and halal product certification towards consumer purchase intention particularly in geographical region of Sahiwal, Pakistan	Quantitative method: 300 respondents (female students)	Pakistan	The findings revealed that awareness, religious belief, and halal certified brands of cosmetics positively influence the intention of cosmetic consumer females towards halal brands
10	Hussain (2022)	To determine the impact of Muslim customers' purchases of halal cosmetic products in Pakistan	Quantitative method: 223 respondents (Muslims who were all over the age of 18.)	Pakistan	The study shows that the purchase intention was influenced by product quality, personal social perception, religious belief, halal awareness, and halal certification, but not brand awareness

4.2 *Success Stories of* Halalpreneurship

The second objective of this study is to identify success stories and companies that have brought the halal entrepreneurship to a different level. There are two categories of halal entrepreneurship identified in this study, namely, (1) cosmetic and (2) pharmaceuticals.

4.2.1 Cosmetics

Table 2 shows seven successful Halal Cosmetics Brands that have been recognized around the world. The first is Simply Siti, a Malaysian brand that was established in 2010. Simply Siti is owned by the first Malaysian singer, Datuk Seri Siti Nurhaliza Taruddin. The focus of Simply Siti is to produce the premium products at the local level but to be at the same par as the international level. The range of Simply Siti products are cosmetic, skincare, fragrance, and wellness. Simply Siti's products are designed and manufactured in South Korea and use premium ingredients such as red ginseng (Izzah, 2019).

Second brand is Wardah, an Indonesian brand that was established in 1995 by PT Paragon Technology and Innovation. Wardah not only focuses on Halal cosmetics but also natural, alcohol-free, and cruelty-free products. Wardah uses three branding approaches to attract consumers to its products; Pure and Safe, Beauty Expert, and Inspiring Beauty. The most important aspect of Wardah branding is 'Pure and Safe'. According to the Pure and Safe Principle, the products are made of safe materials and are halal according to Islam, so Indonesian Muslim women can use them with no concerns (Sukesi & Akhbar Hidayat, 2019).

Third brand is CHOBS, a South Korean brand that is owned by CH Harmony Co. Ltd. It has been established since 2006. The focus of CHOBS is not only organic and natural but green and sustainability. CHOBS aspires to become a leader in spearheading initiatives related to climate change mitigation and the promotion of low-carbon movements. The range of CHOBS products includes skincare, hair and cooking utensils. They strived to get their products certified as vegan, organic, natural & halal whenever possible. The nature conscious trendsetters are best suited for CHOBS (*Chobs Certified Organic Natural Vegan Skincare—official distributor SG*, 2021).

Fourth brand is INIKA Organic, an Australian brand established in 2006 focusing on Certified Organic, Cruelty-Free, Halal and Vegan values. The philosophy of INIKA is 'Pure with Purpose', including pure products, pure planet and pure performance. The products are not only natural and effective but they also take into account the impact to the environment, which makes them focus on sustainable materials. The range of products is skincare and cosmetics.

Fifth brand is Amara Beauty, a USA brand established in 2011. The brand is the first brand that obtained halal certification in the US market. The focus of this brand is the highest quality of skincare products. As the ultimate goals, AMARA Beauty

Table 2 The successful halal cosmetics brands

Number	Brand/ Company	Year of establishment	Range of products	Country	Key point	Website
1	Simply Siti-Simply SS Trading Sdn. Bhd.	2010	Cosmetic, skincare, fragrance, and wellness	Malaysia	Premium local brand and at the same par of international level	https://simplysiti.com.my
2	Wardah-PT Paragon Technology and Innovation	1995	Cosmetics and skincare	Indonesia	Halal green beauty	https://www.wardahbeauty.com/en
3	CH Organic Beauty Store (CHOBS)-CH Harmony Co., Ltd.	2006	Skincare, hair, and cooking utensils	South Korea	Organic and natural	http://www.chharmony.com/
4	Inika Organic-Inika Organic Australia	2006	Cosmetics and skincare	Australia	Certified organic, cruelty-free, halal and vegan values	https://www.inikaorganic.com/pages/our-story
5	Amara Beauty	2011	Skincare	USA	Highest quality of skincare products (first-US Halal certified)	https://amarabeauty.com/pages/about
6	Halal Beauty Cosmetics	2010	Cosmetics	Birmingham, United Kingdom	Halal cosmetics (first halal-certified store in the United Kingdom)	https://halalbeautycosmetics.com/pages/about-us
7	Saaf Organic Skincare	2008	Skincare and cosmetics	Manchester, United Kingdom	Natural sources, 100% organic and halal-certified	https://www.saafbeauty.com

provides premium quality products at affordable prices and is accessible to everyone. Prohibited ingredients such as petrochemicals, parabens, artificial colors, and others will not be found in their range of products that include skincare.

Sixth brand is Halal Beauty Cosmetics, a United Kingdom brand established in 2010. Aisha is the CEO and founder of Halal Beauty Cosmetics, a family-owned business that strives to bring healthy, halal cosmetics to women worldwide. The motivation to open her own beauty salon was driven by her faith and family, but it was hard to find halal products. Her dream is to give back to the community by providing strength and confidence to other women in the community. This brand is not only focusing on the halal cosmetics, but they want to help women to find the strength and confidence in facing their struggle with both beauty and grace. It is not just cosmetic, but humanity.

Seventh brand is Saaf Organic Skincare, a United Kingdom brand established in 2008. Dr. Mah, Saaf's founder, is a pharmaceutical scientist who formulated the Saaf range using her knowledge of natural ingredients (*Saaf organic skincare for halal-conscious minds*, 2023). The Saaf Beauty skincare line is formulated with the latest skincare innovations for advanced noticeable results. Premium ingredients are used to produce luxury and effective skincare products. Providing long-term skincare that leaves you looking and feeling good is one of their core values. Their range of products is skincare and cosmetics.

Overall, based on these seven successful stories of halal cosmetic entrepreneurship, it shows that halal cosmetics brands could share common values such as halal, purity, high-quality, vegan, cruelty-free, organics, and others. It shows that halal cosmetics have different qualities compared to common cosmetics products. Hence, it is not surprising why the demands for halal cosmetics are showing growing trends.

4.2.2 Pharmaceuticals

1. AJ Pharma

Striving for an innovation for an upgraded quality of life, AJ Pharma translating customer and end-user insights into meaningful solutions. AJ Pharma Holding was established in 2012 by the Aljomaih Group of Saudi Arabia as a dedicated healthcare investment company in Malaysia. Since then, they have been putting the building blocks in place to become a significant contributor to the nation's economic growth, technological advancements, and overall community well-being. They set themselves apart from their peers and competitors by identifying the unmet needs of the communities they operate in and working towards highly beneficial outcomes for society. The starting point for AJ Pharma was identifying major barriers to the effective delivery of vaccines. In order to increase collective awareness and knowledge of critical issues affecting Muslims around the world, such as immunization and the need for (affordable) halal medicines, AJ Pharma has reached out and made important connections and partnerships with key Islamic Economic stakeholders. Among the accomplishments of AJ Pharma established a global footprint through the acquisition of Danish medical laboratory Statens Serum Institut (SSI); Secured seed investment of $100 million to launch the first-ever vaccine facility in Malaysia and the first-ever halal vaccine globally; and initiated the development of vaccines against hand, foot and mouth disease and meningococcal meningitis in 2016. AJ Pharma addressed affordable pharma globally with 400 million individuals who are without access to healthcare and have been left behind by the existing pharmaceutical industry. This provides an opportunity for new players to make pharmaceutical products more affordable. The other motivation was to have access to a polio vaccine and to develop new formulations and expand its reach to contribute to the World Health Organization's objective of eradicating polio.

2. Ain Medicare Sdn Bhd.

As a trusted name in the pharmaceutical industry, Ain Medicare Sdn Bhd is located in Kelantan, Malaysia. The company operates from a multi-million-dollar state-of-the-art pharmaceutical complex that was inaugurated by former Prime Minister Tun Dr. Mahathir Mohamad in 1997. The company has achieved numerous remarkable achievements through this forward-looking leadership and strategic management system. As of today, AIN MEDICARE has an authorized share capital of RM 20 million and a paid-up share capital of RM 20 million. The company's products are used by both the private and public healthcare sectors, as well as non-profit health care providers in Malaysia and abroad.

3. Pharmaniaga Berhad

Founded in 1994, Pharmaniaga Berhad is Malaysia's largest listed integrated pharmaceutical company. Research and development, pharmaceutical manufacturing, logistics and distribution, sales and marketing, as well as retail pharmacy are all parts of Pharmaniaga Berhad's pharmaceutical value chain. It is the first Malaysian pharmaceutical company to fill, and finish manufacturing a human vaccine in 2021. Pharmaniaga Berhad is expanding its global presence strategically as one of the major players on the domestic market. It is the company's mission to provide Malaysians with high-quality pharmaceutical products at affordable prices.

4. Hasmats Health

Established in 2019, Hashmats Health aims to improve the quality of life of its customers through wellness and healthcare. This company offers a range of products that promote physical and mental well-being. Together with doctors, scientists, and nutritionists, the brand creates products that are safe, effective, and of the highest quality. The range includes products for immunity, digestion, sleep, and personal care such as haircare and skin care. It strives to create sustainable, eco-friendly, and cruelty-free products. Bringing decades of healthcare expertise and experience to the healthcare industry, Hashmats Health is poised to become a trusted name in the healthcare industry (*Hashmats*, 2023).

5. Viva Pharmaceuticals

Viva is the biggest GMP-certified pharmaceutical and natural health food products manufacturer in British Columbia, Canada. It is dedicated to improving its facilities to ensure all products are made using advanced manufacturing equipment. It has been certified by government officials since 2000 and by the Natural Health Products Directorate since 2004. Viva Pharmaceutical offers manufacturing of natural health products using pharmaceutical standards, a full on-site laboratory, quick turnaround time and one-stop shop for all raw material sourcing. It also engages in manufacturing, coating, testing, R&D, packaging and shipping needs, FDA, Health Canada, NSF, Halal audited, and large production capacity of 40 million softgels, 25 million tablets, and 10 million capsules daily.

Overall, these five companies are the evidence on the importance of *halalpreneurship*. They not only focus on the profit, but how the consumers and other stakeholders will benefit from consuming their products (Table 3).

Table 3 The successful halal pharmaceuticals

Number	Brand/Company	Year of establishment	Range of products	Country	Key point	Website
1	AJ Pharma	2012	Vaccines	Malaysia	First halal vaccines	https://www.ajpharmaholding.com
2	AIN Medicare	1993	Pharmaceutical	Malaysia	Affordable and high-quality pharmaceutical products	https://www.ainmedicare.com.my
3	Pharmaniaga Berhad	1994	Pharmaceutical value chains	Malaysia	Halal pharmaceuticals	https://pharmaniaga.com
4	Hashmats Health	2019	Vitamins and supplement	United Kingdom	Halal and vegetarian certified for high-quality vitamins and supplements	https://www.hashmatshealth.com
5	Viva Pharmaceutical Inc.	1994	Vitamins and supplement	Canada	Natural health products	https://www.vivapharm.com

5 Conclusion

The demand for halal cosmetics has seen significant growth in recent years. It has become an increasingly important part of the halal industry and is embraced by an ever-growing consumer base. With the rise in demand and the development of various products, the halal industry is growing more competitive and dynamic. This sector offers multiple opportunities for businesses and consumers alike, and the potential for growth is tremendous. As the industry matures and regulations become increasingly stringent, the halal industry promises to grow into an even more critical part of the global halal industry. As the industry matures, halal certification is becoming more widely accepted and respected and is becoming a key factor in many business decisions. This made religion and health factors an important factor in the development of halal industry. The preference between these two factors could, however, be influenced by consumer demographics. Furthermore, the growing halal industry shows that *halalpreneurs* are addressing the needs of consumers for halal products. Halal products promote safety, organic, free of chemicals, and cruelty-free environment. Therefore, the halal cosmetics are projected to continue growing in the coming years.

References

Abdullah, J. B., Abdullah, F., & Bujang, S. B. (2021). Muslim religiosity and its impact on purchase intention. *Journal of Advanced Management Science, 9*(1).

Abdullah, M. A., & Azam, M. S. E. (2020). Halal entrepreneurship: Concept and business opportunities. In *Entrepreneurship*. IntechOpen.

Ariffin, A., Noor, M. A. M., & Wahid, H. (2016). *Faktor-faktor Yang Mempengaruhi Permintaan Produk Kosmetik Halal*. Prosiding Seminar Kebangsaan Tamadun & Warisan Islam (TAWIS). Universiti Kebangsaan Malaysia.

Bernama. (2022, October 19). Malaysia has much to offer in halal economy, other areas in Muslim world—Mustapa. Retrieved April 28, 2023, from https://www.bernama.com/en/business/news.php?id=2130344#:~:text=The%20country%20is%20a%20role,one%20for%20nine%20years%20consecutively

Briliana, V., & Mursito, N. (2017). Exploring antecedents and consequences of Indonesian Muslim youths' attitude towards halal cosmetic products: A case study in Jakarta. *Asia Pacific Management Review, 22*(4), 176–184.

Bowen, G. A. (2009). Document analysis as a qualitative research method. *Qualitative Research Journal, 9*(2), 27–40.

Che Mohd Hashim, A. J., & Musa, R. (2014). Factors influencing attitude towards halal cosmetic among young adult Urban Muslim women: A focus group analysis. *Procedia-Social and Behavioral Sciences, 130*, 129–134.

Elabed, F. (2023). *The benefits of halal certification for cosmetics and food products* ... Inc.com. Retrieved April 24, 2023, from https://www.inc.com/inc-masters/benefits-of-halal-certification-for-cosmetics-and.html

Elias, A. A. (2022, September 13). *Hadith on halal: Seeking lawful is an obligation on all Muslims*. Daily Hadith Online. Retrieved April 28, 2023, from https://www.abuaminaelias.com/dailyhadithonline/2022/09/13/halal-food-wajib/#:~:text=Anas%20ibn%20Malik%20reported%3A%20The,a%20duty%20upon%20every%20Muslim

Future Market Insights Global and Consulting Pvt. Ltd. (2022, September 8). *Halal cosmetics market share to thrive at a CAGR of 11.6% through 2032*. GlobeNewswire News Room. Retrieved April 24, 2023, from https://www.globenewswire.com/en/news-release/2022/09/08/2512122/0/en/Halal-Cosmetics-Market-Share-to-Thrive-at-a-CAGR-of-11-6-Through-2032-Future-Market-Insights-Inc.html

Handriana, T., Yulianti, P., Kurniawati, M., Arina, N. A., Aisyah, R. A., Ayu Aryani, M. G., & Wandira, R. K. (2021). Purchase behavior of millennial female generation on halal cosmetic products. *Journal of Islamic Marketing, 12*(7), 1295–1315.

Herjanto, H., Amin, M., & Karmagatri, M. (2023). A systematic review on halal cosmetic consumption: Application of theory method context–attributes decision outcome framework. *Journal of Islamic Accounting and Business Research, 14*(1), 148–163.

Hussain, Z. (2022). Intention to purchase halal cosmetic products in an Islamic Pakistani culture. *Journal of Islamic Economics and Finance Studies, 3*(1), 1–11.

IMARC Group. (2022, September 29). *Top halal cosmetics companies, manufacturers and brands*. Top Halal Cosmetics Companies, Manufacturers and Brands. Retrieved April 28, 2023, from https://www.imarcgroup.com/halal-cosmetics-companies-brands

Ishak, S., Che Omar, A. R., Khalid, K., Ab Ghafar, I. S., & Hussain, M. Y. (2020). Cosmetics purchase behavior of educated millennial Muslim females. *Journal of Islamic Marketing, 11*(5), 1055–1071.

Izzah, A. (2019, December 30). *Cover story: Dato' sri siti nurhaliza on her Beauty Empire, Simplysiti*. Tatler Asia. Retrieved April 28, 2023, from https://www.tatlerasia.com/lifestyle/entertainment/dato-sri-siti-nurhaliza-simplysiti

Katuk, N., Ku-Mahamud, K. R., Kayat, K., Abdul Hamid, M. N., Zakaria, N. H., & Purbasari, A. (2021). Halal certification for tourism marketing: The attributes and attitudes of food operators in Indonesia. *Journal of Islamic Marketing, 12*(5), 1043–1062.

Khan, M. I., Haleem, A., & Khan, S. (2022). Examining the link between Halal supply chain management and sustainability. *International Journal of Productivity and Performance Management, 71*(7), 2793–2819.

Khan, N., Sarwar, A., & Tan, B. C. (2021). Determinants of purchase intention of halal cosmetic products among Generation Y consumers. *Journal of Islamic Marketing, 12*(8), 1461–1476.

Majid, M. B., Sabir, I., & Ashraf, T. (2015). Consumer purchase intention towards halal cosmetics & personal care products in Pakistan. *Global Journal of Research in Business & Management, 1*(1).

MyNaturalStory.com. (2021). *Chobs certified organic natural vegan skincare—Official distributor SG*. My Natural Story Singapore. Retrieved April 28, 2023, from https://mynaturalstory.com/sg/brand/chobs/

Nurhayati, T., & Hendar, H. (2020). Personal intrinsic religiosity and product knowledge on halal product purchase intention: Role of halal product awareness. *Journal of Islamic Marketing, 11*(3), 603–620.

Putri, I. S., Daryanti, S., & Ningtias, A. R. (2019, March). The influence of knowledge and religiosity with mediation of attitude toward the intention of repurchasing halal cosmetics. In *12th International Conference on Business and Management Research (ICBMR 2018)* (pp. 172–177). Atlantis Press.

Prayer Times. (2023, April 27). *Global Muslim population*. Retrieved April 27, 2023, from https://timesprayer.com/en/muslim-population/#:~:text=The%20growth%20of%20Islam%20is,second%20largest%20religion%20after%20Christianity

Rahim, N. F. B. (2017). Consumer behaviour, perception and planning towards halal marketing. *Advances in Islamic Finance, Marketing, and Management: An Asian Perspective*.

Salaheldeen, M., Battour, M., Nazri, M. A., Bustamam, U. S. A., & Hashim, A. J. C. M. (2022). The perception of success in the halal market: Developing a halal entrepreneurship success scale. *Journal of Islamic Marketing*.

Sama, R., & Trivedi, J. P. (2019). Factors affecting consumers' loyalty towards halal cosmetics: An emerging market perspective. *International Journal of Business and Emerging Markets, 11*(3), 254–273.

Septiarini, D. F., Ratnasari, R. T., Salleh, M. C. M., & Herianingrum, S. (2023). Drivers of behavioral intention among non-Muslims toward halal cosmetics: Evidence from Indonesia, Malaysia, and Singapore. *Journal of Islamic Accounting and Business Research, 14*(2), 230–248.

Shahid, S., Ahmed, F., & Hasan, U. (2018). A qualitative investigation into consumption of halal cosmetic products: The evidence from India. *Journal of Islamic Marketing.*

Sobari, N., Kurniati, A., & Usman, H. (2022). The influence of Islamic attributes and religious commitments toward halal wellness services customer satisfaction and loyalty. *Journal of Islamic Marketing, 13*(1), 177–197.

Sugibayashi, K., Yusuf, E., Todo, H., Dahlizar, S., Sakdiset, P., Arce, F. J., & See, G. L. (2019). Halal cosmetics: A review on ingredients, production, and testing methods. *Cosmetics, 6*(3), 37.

Suhartanto, D., Djatnika, T., Suhaeni, T., & Setiawati, L. (2022). Halal trust during the COVID-19 outbreak: The role of quality, perceived benefit and health risk evidence from mobile food purchasing. *Journal of Islamic Accounting and Business Research* (ahead-of-print).

Sukesi, S., & Akbar Hidayat, W. G. P. (2019). Managing the halal industry and the purchase intention of Indonesian Muslims the case of Wardah cosmetics. *Journal of Indonesian Islam, 13*(1), 200–229.

TheEcoMuslim. (2023). *Saaf organic skincare for halal-conscious minds.* Retrieved April 28, 2023, from https://www.theecomuslim.co.uk/2015/06/saaf-organic-halal.html

Welzo. (2023). *Hashmats.* Retrieved April 28, 2023, from https://welzo.com/collections/hashmats

What is halal beauty?. (2023). *MEIYUME.* Retrieved April 24, 2023 from https://meiyume.com/what-is-halal-beauty-the-future-of-halal-certified-cosmetics/

Zakaria, N. H., Busu, Z. M., Nordin, B., Yusuf, N., & Ahmad, M. M. A. (2022). Halal cosmetic products: Analysis of the level of understanding and awareness among Uitm Cawangan Kelantan Staff. *International Journal of Academic Research in Business and Social Sciences, 12*(10), 1131–1145.

Halal Digital Entrepreneurship and Disruptive Technologies from the Lenses of *Maqasid al-Shari'ah*

Amal A. M. Elgharbawy, Md Siddique E Azam, and Betania Kartika

Abstract Digital entrepreneurship has become a popular field with the infusion of disruptive technologies, creating new opportunities for start-ups. However, the mechanism of start-ups' disruptive innovation in the context of digital economy remains unclear. Halal digital entrepreneurship is a relatively new field that has not been fully explored, creating a gap in understanding the challenges and opportunities that halal digital entrepreneurs face in the context of disruptive technologies. The principles of *Maqasid al-Shari'ah* provide a framework for ethical and sustainable digital entrepreneurship that aligns with the values and principles of Islam. Nonetheless, their application to the context of halal digital entrepreneurship has not been fully explored. The intersection of halal digital entrepreneurship and disruptive technologies was the focus of a comprehensive literature review that placed an emphasis on *Maqasid al-Shari'ah*. The chapter is significant, providing an insight into halal digital entrepreneurship and disruptive technologies through the lens of *Maqasid al-Shari'ah*. The study also sheds light on the opportunities and threats that disruptive technologies present to halal digital entrepreneurs. The importance of *Maqasid al-Shari'ah* in guiding the creation of game-changing technologies for halal business owners is also emphasised in this chapter. Additionally, some successful examples of halal digital entrepreneurship have been demonstrated along with future research recommendations and prospects.

Keywords Halal digital entrepreneurship · Disruptive technologies · *Maqasid al-Sharia'h*

JEL Classification L26 · I15 · G20 · G30 · G4

A. A. M. Elgharbawy (✉) · M. S. E Azam · B. Kartika
International Institute for Halal Research and Training (INHART), Kuala Lumpur, IIUM, Malaysia
e-mail: amalgh@iium.edu.my

L. Raimi et al. (eds.), *Contemporary Discourse of Halal and Islamic Entrepreneurship*,
https://doi.org/10.1007/978-981-99-6427-7_12

1 Introduction

Disruptive technology and halal digital entrepreneurship are two fields that are expanding quickly and have the potential to change society and the economy. As stated in *Maqasid al-Shari'ah*, it is crucial to make sure that these technologies are in line with Islamic norms and principles. The application of *Maqasid al-Shari'ah* to disruptive technologies and halal digital entrepreneurship offers innovators, business owners, and policymakers a framework to guarantee that these innovations are created and used in a way that benefits society (Shehu et al., 2016). Islam is a comprehensive religion, and halalpreneurship includes entrepreneurship as a component that is inextricably linked to Islam. Halalpreneurship is the term for entrepreneurship that falls under the purview of Shari'ah (*'Aqidah, Fiqh,* and *Akhlaq*) so that its actions do not conflict with Islamic duties. To grow and prosper around the globe, a person must play the role of *Khalifah* (Caliph), which implies that entrepreneurial endeavours must benefit society, the Ummah, and all of mankind (Abdullah et al., 2022). Halalpreneurship is a recently created notion that is neither well recognised nor completely understood yet. It connects halal development to commercial endeavours carried out in a halal entrepreneurial manner. It involves all the functions, events, and actions associated with the perception of opportunities and the creation of organisations to pursue them.

Disruptive technologies can have ethical implications, and halal entrepreneurship is the practise of creating and managing a business venture for the purpose of addressing a social or environmental problem while also generating a profit. The ethics of disruptive technologies is an emerging topic of academic interest. Scholarly initiatives that bear testimony to this claim include the overarching project in which the present research has been undertaken, the Dutch interuniversity research project, "Ethics of Socially Disruptive Technologies (ESDiT) 2020–2029" (Nickel et al., 2022). Additionally, studies show that when innovative technologies challenge long-held moral norms without establishing their own, they can have a profound effect on society's moral fabric. This can affect our intellectual capacity and others' moral duties and lead to moral dissonance (Nickel, 2020).

Maqasid al-Shari'ah offers a framework for making sure that disruptive technologies and halal digital entrepreneurship are created and employed in ways that are in line with Islamic values and principles. *Maqasid al-Shari'ah* can be interpreted as a group of goals or aims that serve as the foundation for Islamic law and direct Muslim jurists and scholars in their interpretation and application of Islamic teachings (Binti Alli & bin Usop, 2022). In recent years, researchers and practitioners have begun to pay more attention to the *Maqasid al-Shari'ah's* concept as they have realised its applicability to modern challenges, such as the advancement and usage of technology. The protection of religion, life, intellect, property, and lineage are the five goals of *Maqasid al-Shari'ah* (Kamali, 2008). These goals do not conflict with one another; rather, they operate in tandem to ensure that disruptive technologies and halal digital entrepreneurship are consistent with Islamic values and principles (Yousufzai et al., 2021).

As the concept of halal digital entrepreneurship is so new, limited research has been done in relevant fields. As a result, halal digital entrepreneurs lack awareness of the opportunities and challenges that exist in the era of disruptive technologies. Although the principles of *Maqasid al-Shari'ah* provide a framework for ethical and sustainable digital entrepreneurship consistent with the values and principles of Islam, their application in the context of halal digital entrepreneurship has not been thoroughly explored. Therefore, it is essential to weigh the challenges and opportunities of being a halal digital entrepreneur in the age of disruptive technologies and to determine how far halal entrepreneurs can go by adhering to the principles of *Maqasid al-Shari'ah*. In this regard, this chapter aims to achieve the following objectives:

1. To learn about halal digital entrepreneurship and how it relates to disruptive technologies.
2. To use *Maqasid al-Shari'ah* as a lens for exploring the intersection of halal digital entrepreneurship and disruptive technologies.
3. To realise the opportunities and threats that disruptive technologies pose to halal digital entrepreneurs.

The halal entrepreneurial process is a complex phenomenon; however, this process is important in understanding Halalpreneurial growth. In this chapter, we shall examine how *Maqasid al-Shari'ah*, disruptive technologies, and halal digital entrepreneurship may be combined to advance economic growth and societal advancement while respecting Islamic values and principles.

2 Literature Review

2.1 An Overview of Maqasid al-Shari'ah

The concept of *Maqasid al-Shari'ah* is founded on the concept of human needs, and its principles are derived from the Quran and hadith as the primary sources. Initially, the needs were categorised into four levels by Al-Juwayni (Labbani & Mohammed, 2011), which were later refined into three levels by Al-Ghazali (1901). The three levels of needs are: (i) *Daruriyat* (necessities), (ii) *Hajiyat* (needs), and (iii) *Tahsiniyat* (luxuries). Figure 1 is an illustration of *Maqasid al-Shari'ah* showing the three levels of needs. To fulfil the first level of need, which is *daruriyat* (necessities), Muslim scholars came up with the five elements or objectives (Al-Raysuni, 1992). *Maqasid al-Shari'ah,* or the five objectives of *Shari'ah,* form the basis of Islamic law and instruct Muslims on how to act in all spheres of society and in all positions of authority. The five main goals are as follows:

(a) *Hifz al-Din* (preservation of faith or religion) is the first objective that safeguards Islam as a faith and religion, and all its tenets and practises. This objective has a strong association with entrepreneurship and business management as

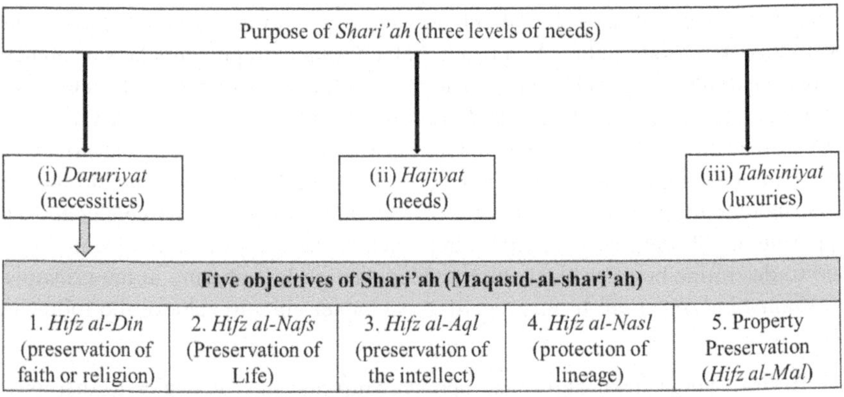

Fig. 1 Overview of Maqasid al-Shari'ah showing three levels of needs. Adapted from Mohamed Azmi et al. (2019)

a way of earning a livelihood (Normaaruf et al., 2020). Entrepreneurship and digital entrepreneurship can be related to *Hifz al-Din* by creating businesses that adhere to Islamic law, operate with honesty, and do not engage in any form of prohibited activity in Islam. Digital entrepreneurship research includes those studies exploring and theorising on entrepreneurial processes, outcomes, and agencies transformed by digitization. By creating digital businesses that adhere to Islamic law, entrepreneurs can contribute to preserving faith and religion while also taking advantage of the opportunities provided by digitization.

(b) *Hifz al-Nafs*, or preservation of life, is the second objective. This objective is to ensure serving the basic necessities (e.g. food, clothing, shelter, medical care, etc.) of human beings that are required for maintaining health, safety, and security. Halal entrepreneurs can significantly contribute to this goal by creating businesses that provide products or services that improve people's health and well-being. For example, entrepreneurs can create businesses that provide healthy food options, medical devices, or fitness equipment. However, halal entrepreneurs care about more than just making people healthier and happier; they also consider things like environmental impact, animal welfare, and social responsibility. In their roles as *khalifas* (leaders) on Earth, halal business owners have a special obligation to work for the benefit of future generations.

(c) *Hifz al-Aql*, or the preservation of the intellect, is the third goal of Islam. Its tenets include the encouragement of lifelong learning and the cultivation of an analytical mindset while protecting mental health and intellect. In Islam, any consumption that may affect human intellect is prohibited. For example, alcohol drinking, weed smoking, taking drugs, etc. Likewise, activities like gambling are also prohibited, which becomes an addition in most cases and has a strong influence on causing high depression and affecting mental health (Awaworyi Churchill & Farrell, 2018). Overall, *Hifz al-Aql* emphasises the importance of maintaining a healthy and sharp mind, free from any substances or activities that may harm it. By promoting lifelong learning and critical thinking, Islam encourages individuals to continuously improve and strengthen their intellect while safeguarding their mental health.

(d) *Hifz al-Nasl* is the fourth goal, and it entails safeguarding lineage and marriage as a social institution, regulating sexual behaviour, and preventing harm to individuals and communities. Several aspects of halal business and halal digital entrepreneurship relate to this goal. Establishing a business, for instance, may provide family members with stable employment and a source of income. Growth and stability in the economy are beneficial not just to people but also to companies and communities. People with more spare money may decide to invest in themselves by, for example, furthering their education or investing in their health. This has the potential to start a cycle of enhanced wealth for all those involved. The development of leadership, communication, and problem-solving abilities are only some of the transferrable talents that may benefit from participating in entrepreneurial endeavours. These skills are valuable in other fields outside of business. Therefore, supporting halal business practises may be beneficial for more than just the business owner.

(e) Property Preservation (*Hifz al-Mal*): This goal stresses the regulation of economic activity and the prevention of theft, fraud, and exploitation of private and public property. Property Preservation (*Hifz al-Mal*): This goal stresses the regulation of economic activity and the prevention of theft, fraud, and exploitation of private and public property. For example, in Islamic finance, *Hifz al-Mal* is one of the most important objectives of the *Shari'ah.* The preservation of wealth is achieved through various means, such as *Zakat* (charity), Waqf (endowment), and other social finance instruments. In addition, *Hifz al-Mal* also involves the prevention of money laundering and other financial crimes. The significance of this goal is realised in the detailed guidelines for wealth management in the Quran. For example, guidelines on property distribution (4:11–14, 176); managing any financial contracts or agreements (2:272–292); all the products in Islamic finance are derived from the principles of the Quran and Hadith and focused on achieving this objective of *Shari'ah.* These guidelines ensure that wealth is distributed fairly and that financial transactions are conducted ethically, in accordance with Islamic principles. As a result, Islamic finance products are designed to promote social justice and economic stability while also providing financial services to individuals and businesses. Halal entrepreneurs who start enterprises that make and sell halal goods and services may help regulate the global halal economy. This may assist entrepreneurs in preventing theft and fund misuse. Hence, halal entrepreneurship may increase economic growth, job creation, and social welfare by eliminating poverty. This is in line with the objective, *Hifz al-Mal.*

3 Halal Digital Entrepreneurship

3.1 The Significance of Halal Digital Entrepreneurship

The pursuit of possibilities based on the use of digital media and other information and communication technology is referred to as digital entrepreneurship. To seek prospects, digital entrepreneurs rely on the features of IT and digital media. By trying to take advantage of the opportunities, they might accelerate the process of creative destruction in the digital economy, aggravating changes in the competitive landscape. Depending on the types of possibilities the entrepreneur is seeking, the value gained via digital initiatives might vary substantially (Gregor, 2006).

What happened during the COVID-19 pandemic resulted in new entrepreneurial opportunities. For instance, the US reported an 82% increase in new business applications, which was the highest since 2020. Digital entrepreneurs are self-employed, with the addition of operating via digital platforms. They rely on information technology (IT) and digital media tools to find potential customers. These tools have given digital entrepreneurs the opportunity to promote their business outside of their local communities. It saves them the money they would need to spend on a physical office space and replaces it with a more affordable online storefront. In addition, throughout 2021, Google Trends recorded significant upticks in searches like "how to start a business," "how to start a business at home," and "how to start a business online." Additionally, as e-commerce sales rise, more business owners are turning to online sales for their products and services. E-commerce sales in the US increased by 3.3% from the first quarter of 2021 to $222.5 billion from April to June of 2021 alone. Additionally, it is predicted that m-commerce (mobile commerce) sales will surpass $432 billion by 2022, up from $148 billion in 2018 ("The rise of digital entrepreneurship", n.d.).

The COVID-19 epidemic has had an impact on international businesses and cultures, and this is also true of the environment for digital entrepreneurship. The epidemic has sped up the process of digitization and increased demand for digital goods and services. The pandemic has thus produced both possibilities and difficulties for the development of digital enterprises. Demand for digital goods and services has grown because of COVID-19, which is one of its most important forces for digital entrepreneurship. Businesses and customers have been forced to extensively rely on digital platforms for communication, e-commerce, and remote labour due to lockdowns and social isolation policies in place (Sedera et al., 2022). Digital entrepreneurs now have a new opportunity to offer creative solutions that address the evolving demands of consumers and enterprises. For instance, the usage of telemedicine and online fitness courses has increased, opening new business prospects for those in the health and wellness industries. The epidemic has, however, also made it more difficult for digital businesses to develop. Due to the economic depression brought on by the epidemic, many entrepreneurs struggle to get capital. New entrepreneurs may find it challenging to obtain funding since investors are becoming more careful and selective about where they invest their money. Additionally, the pandemic has presented

Fig. 2 Advantages of digital entrepreneurship

businesses with substantial operational difficulties, such as supply chain interruptions, shipping delays, and cybersecurity hazards (Almeida et al., 2020; Modgil et al., 2022). Despite these obstacles, COVID-19 has also provided new chances for businesses to work together and create. Many company owners have modified their business strategies to address the pandemic's demands, such as by inventing new contact tracking tools or starting new online markets for tiny firms. With many businesspeople attempting to address the social and economic effects of the epidemic via creative solutions, the pandemic has also emphasised the significance of social entrepreneurship (Almeida et al., 2020).

As a result, COVID-19 has significantly influenced the development of digital entrepreneurship, posing both difficulties and possibilities. While the epidemic has presented enterprises with operational and financial difficulties, it has also opened them to new possibilities for cooperation and innovation (Modgil et al., 2022). Entrepreneurs will need to adapt and innovate to thrive in the post-epidemic era as the pandemic continues to impact the landscape of digital enterprise. There are several advantages to the emergence of digital entrepreneurship, for conventional and halal digital entrepreneurship, which can be summarised in Fig. 2.

An emerging notion called "halal digital entrepreneurship" describes digital business practises that adhere to Islamic beliefs and principles. For Muslim businesspeople and businessmen who want to build wealth while upholding their Islamic principles, it is a crucial idea. The potential for halal digital businesses to foster economic growth, provide jobs, and advance society while preserving Islamic beliefs and principles is what makes them so significant. The importance of halal digital entrepreneurship cannot be overstated (Ridhani, 2022). First, it gives Muslim business owners a chance to develop avant-garde goods and services that are consistent with Islamic beliefs and values. This can include halal food delivery services and platforms for Islamic financial technology (fintech), which allow Muslims to invest their money in accordance with Islamic financial principles. Second, halal digital entrepreneurship may stimulate economic growth and provide employment, especially in nations with a large percentage of Muslims and low unemployment rates. Policymakers can foster a climate for innovation and entrepreneurship, which may lead to job creation and economic growth, by encouraging halal digital entrepreneurship. Thirdly, by tackling social concerns in a way that is compliant with Islamic beliefs and principles, halal digital entrepreneurship may help to improve society. By giving people access to reasonably priced healthcare, education, and other necessary services, for instance, halal digital entrepreneurship may advance social welfare. The growth of ethical, sustainable, and socially responsible company practises that are in line with Islamic values can also be facilitated through halal digital entrepreneurship (Salaheldeen, 2022).

Halal digital entrepreneurship also offers the ability to advance social and cultural integration in addition to these advantages. Halal digital entrepreneurship may assist Muslims in integrating into the global economy while keeping their religious identity by developing goods and services that are in line with Islamic values and principles. Increased collaboration and understanding across cultures may result from this, which is crucial in the linked world we live in today.

It should be noted that digital entrepreneurs differ from entrepreneurs in many ways. We can present those in a diagram (Fig. 3).

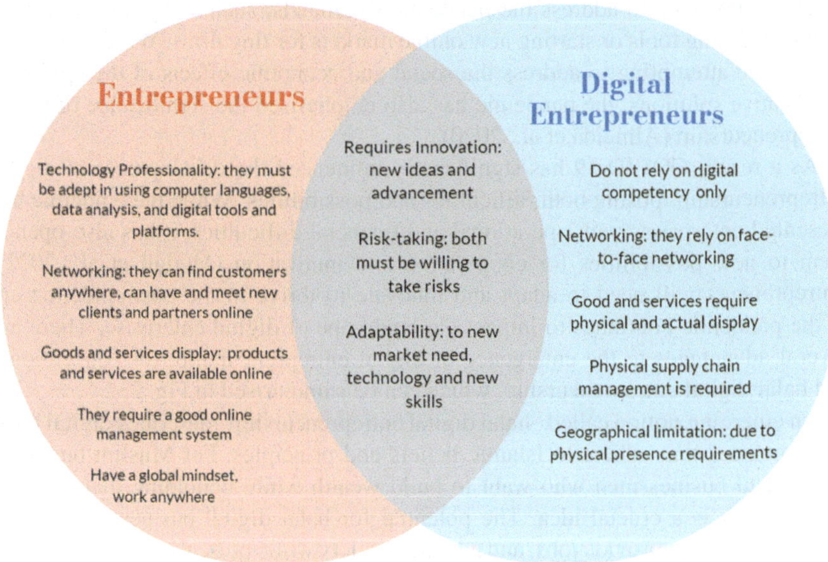

Fig. 3 Similarities and differences between digital entrepreneurs and entrepreneurs. Summarised from several references and sources, including Abdullah et al. (2022), Baierl et al. (2019), Barigozzi and Tedeschi et al. (2019), Sahut et al. (2021), Sedera et al. (2022), Yousufzai et al. (2021)

3.2 *Applications of* Maqasid al-Shari'ah *in Halal Digital Entrepreneurship*

The framework outlining the goals and guiding principles of Islamic law is known as *Maqasid al-Shari'ah.* In many facets of life, including business and entrepreneurship, it offers instructions on how Muslims should behave. An increasing number of people are now interested in using *Maqasid al-Shari'ah* principles in the area of halal digital entrepreneurship.

The protection of life, which includes fostering health and wellness, is one of *Maqasid al-Shari'ah's* main goals. By encouraging the creation of goods and services that improve the health and welfare of people and communities, this purpose may be applied to halal digital entrepreneurship. Halal digital entrepreneurs, for instance, can develop goods that promote physical activity or give underprivileged areas access to healthcare services.

The propagation of Islamic ideals and principles is included in one of the *Maqasid al-Shari'ah,* which is the safeguarding of religion. The promotion of the creation of goods and services that maintain Islamic values and principles might serve this purpose in the context of halal digital business. Halal digital entrepreneurs, for instance, can design items that meet halal certification requirements or online markets that support moral and environmentally friendly business practises.

The preservation of wealth, which includes the encouragement of economic expansion and prosperity, is another goal of Maqasid al-Shari'ah. This goal may be achieved through halal digital entrepreneurship by encouraging the creation of goods and services that foster business possibilities and promote economic expansion. Halal digital entrepreneurs, for instance, can develop fintech systems that support Islamic financial concepts like profit-sharing and moral investing.

Protecting the intellect, which involves advancing education and knowledge, is *Maqasid al-Shari'ah's* third goal. By encouraging the creation of goods and services that grant access to education and training, this purpose may be applied to halal digital entrepreneurship. Halal digital business owners could develop e-learning platforms that provide programmes on Islamic business, entrepreneurship, and other pertinent subjects, as an illustration.

The preservation of lineage, which encompasses the advancement of familial and communal values, is *Maqasid al-Shari'ah's* fifth goal. This goal may be achieved through halal digital entrepreneurship by encouraging the creation of goods and services that support the preservation of family values and the advancement of society. Halal digital entrepreneurs, for instance, can develop social media sites that help local communities and small enterprises, or they might develop online markets that do the same (Battour et al., 2021; Fisol et al., 2019; Rahman et al., 2017).

Maqasid al-Shari'ah's goals can, in general, offer direction and advice for halal digital entrepreneurs who wish to generate wealth while respecting Islamic values and precepts. Entrepreneurs may improve society, foster economic expansion and prosperity, and respect the tenets of Islamic law by adopting these aims.

3.3 *Successful Halal Digital Entrepreneurship: Examples that Align with* Maqasid al-Shari'ah

Digital entrepreneurship that adheres to Islamic values has grown in popularity in recent years as businesspeople seek out methods to cater to the demands of Muslim customers. In line with the goals of *Maqasid al-Shari'ah*, a large number of prosperous halal digital entrepreneurial projects have evolved. Halaltrip (Fig. 4), a Singapore-based business that offers travel services for Muslim customers, is one such. The website provides travel itineraries that emphasise well-known halal locations across the world as well as lodging, dining, and prayer alternatives that are halal-friendly. The service supports *Maqasid al-Shari'ah's* goals of promoting life and religion by giving Muslim travellers access to secure, pleasant lodging that complies with their religious requirements.

Wahed Invest, a New York-based digital investing company that provides Sharia-compliant investment portfolios, is another such. The portal offers access to halal investment solutions that follow Islamic ideals of ethical and responsible investing, such as Sukuk and Islamic bonds. The programme supports *Maqasid al-Shari'ah's* goal of asset protection by offering halal investment alternatives that foster economic development and prosperity. A smartphone app called Muslim Pro (Fig. 5), which offers information on Islamic prayer hours, Qibla directions, and other Islamic resources, serves as a third example. The software has been hailed for its precision and usability and has received over 100 million downloads globally. The programme supports the *Maqasid al-Shari'ah* goal of defending religion by giving users access to Islamic knowledge and education-promoting materials.

Another example is Zilzar, an online marketplace located in Malaysia that links halal providers with customers from all over the world. The portal gives users access to a huge selection of halal goods, including anything from food and drinks to clothing

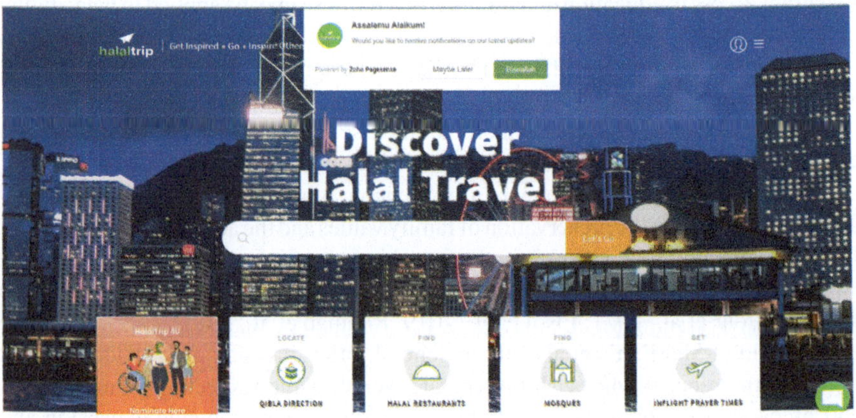

Fig. 4 The homepage of the Halaltrip website as an example of halal digital entrepreneurship. *Source* https://www.halaltrip.com/

Fig. 5 Muslim Pro mobile App as an example of halal digital entrepreneurship. *Source* https://www.muslimpro.com/en/about-us

and cosmetics. Additionally, Zilzar provides a Halal Digital Chain solution that enables vendors to monitor the halal status of their goods all the way through the supply chain. The service supports the *Maqasid al-Shari'ah* goal of asset protection by fostering economic development and prosperity while respecting Islamic values of moral and ethical conduct in business ("Malaysia's Zilzar.com", 2014). Furthermore, users of the UK-based app Halal Dining Club may look for halal restaurants nearby, make bookings, and provide reviews of their dining experiences. Additionally, the website has a loyalty programme that gives users points for eating at partner establishments. The service is in line with *the Maqasid al-Shari'ah* goal of improving life by giving Muslim customers access to satisfying eating experiences and by supporting halal eateries, which in turn promotes economic growth and prosperity (Halal Dinner Club, n.d.).

There is an overall message of hadiths in the encouragement for Muslims to learn, invent, and develop fresh concepts and goods that are both beneficial to society and consistent with Islamic teachings.

Allah's Messenger (ﷺ) said:

> *He who introduced some good practise in Islam that was followed after him (by people) would be assured of reward like one who followed it, without their rewards being diminished in any respect. And he who introduced some evil practise in Islam which had been followed subsequently (by others), he would be required to bear the burden like that of one who followed this (evil practise) without theirs being diminished in any respect.* [Sahih Muslim, Hadith 1017e]

Digital entrepreneurship, a type of innovation with the potential to promote economic growth and social welfare, can benefit from the application of these concepts.

4 Disruptive Technologies

This chapter's section focuses on disruptive technologies, their effects on society, and how they relate to *Maqasid al-Shari'ah* principles. New and current markets are disrupted by disruptive technologies, which are inventions that radically alter how people live and work. These technologies have significantly changed how people interact, obtain information, and conduct business. They do, however, also bring up issues related to data ethics, security, and privacy. In this part, we shall examine the effects of disruptive technologies on society as well as how they might support *Maqasid al-Shari'ah's* goals of encouraging moral and responsible usage.

4.1 The Impact of Disruptive Technologies on Society

Innovations that radically alter how people live and work are referred to as disruptive technologies. They may develop new markets while upending those that already exist, presenting both possibilities and difficulties for society. The internet, mobile phones, social media, cloud computing, and artificial intelligence are a few examples of disruptive technology.

Disruptive technologies have had a profound influence on society. They have changed how people interact, get information, and do business. In addition, they have rendered certain sectors and jobs obsolete while developing new ones. However, they have also brought up issues with data ethics, security, and privacy (Kasinathan et al., 2022).

Finance is one industry where disruptive technologies have made a big difference. For instance, the advent of fintech firms has challenged traditional banking by providing cutting-edge financial services that are more easily and affordably available. Previously, traditional financial institutions neglected many people, who have now been financially included as a result of this. Disruptive technologies have a wide-ranging and complicated influence on society. Although they have the potential to have huge positive effects, they also bring up substantial moral and societal challenges that need to be resolved. The employment of *Maqasid al-Shari'ah* principles can aid in directing the creation and implementation of disruptive technologies in a way that is consistent with Islamic values and tenets (MIT Professional Education, 2022).

4.2 Applications of Maqasid al-Shari'ah to Disruptive Technologies

The guidelines of *Maqasid al-Shari'ah* can direct the creation and usage of disruptive technologies in a way that is consistent with Islamic morals and values. For instance, the preservation of intellect is one of *Maqasid al-Shari'ah's* fundamental principles. This implies that while ensuring that they are utilised for ethical goals, technologies should be created and used in a way that encourages knowledge, innovation, and creativity. Protecting money is another fundamental principle; thus, disruptive technology should not be employed for dishonest or unethical financial gain (Ahmed, 2011; Laldin & Furqani, 2013).

Some of the ethical issues posed by disruptive technologies, such as privacy and data security, can be addressed by using *Maqasid al-Shari'ah* principles. They can be in line with *Maqasid al-Shari'ah* principles by making sure that these technologies are created and applied in a way that respects individual privacy and data protection.

There are a number of verses in the Quran and also in the prophetic hadiths that highlight how crucial it is to respect privacy and safeguard personal data. Allah SWT, for instance, declares in the Qur'an:

> *O believers! Avoid many suspicions, for indeed, some suspicions are sinful. And do not spy or backbite one another. Would any of you like to eat the flesh of your dead brother? You would despise that! And fear Allah. Surely Allah is the Accepter of Repentance, Most Merciful.* [Al-Quran, 49-12]

This verse accentuates the significance of avoiding presumptions about other people and refraining from backbiting or eavesdropping, which can be viewed as a violation of privacy.

In the Hadith, on the authority of Abu Hurayrah (may Allah be pleased with him), who said: The Messenger of Allah (peace and blessings of Allah be upon him), said:

> *Part of the perfection of one's Islam is his leaving that which does not concern him.* [Hadith 12, 40 Hadith an-Nawawi]

The significance of keeping one's own affairs in order and refraining from meddling in other people's issues, including respecting their privacy and personal information, is underlined in this hadith.

These Islamic teachings place a strong emphasis on the value of protecting individual privacy and data security, and they may be used to solve the moral dilemmas raised by disruptive technologies like data security and privacy. Individuals and organisations may make sure they are employing these technologies in an ethical and responsible way while preserving significant Islamic values and ethics by adhering to these teachings and concepts.

A fundamental principle of *Maqasid al-Shari'ah* is the protection of life, and this principle may be applied to disruptive technologies by creating tools that increase public safety or improve health results. Furthermore, the preservation of wealth may be achieved by ensuring that disruptive technologies are created, deployed, and used in an ethical, open, and transparent manner, without causing harm to people, communities, or the environment. In the context of disruptive technologies, this implies that technologies should be created and utilised in a way that encourages knowledge, innovation, and creativity while simultaneously making sure that they are used ethically. Making sure that disruptive technologies do not conflict with Islamic principles and values and are not employed to further immoral practises or ideologies is another way to defend religion. Disruptive technologies may be developed and used in ways that encourage moral and responsible behaviour while also guaranteeing that they are in line with Islamic values and principles by applying *Maqasid al-Shari'ah* principles. Technology users and developers may provide solutions that help society as a whole while also respecting significant Islamic values and ethics by taking into account the principles of *Maqasid al-Shari'ah* (Khalish et al., 2020a; Rosidi et al., 2022).

Applying *Maqasid al-Shari'ah* principles to disruptive technologies may assist in directing their development and usage in a way that encourages moral and responsible use, as well as ensuring that they are consistent with Islamic values and principles.

4.3 Disruptive Technologies: Examples that Align with Maqasid al-Shari'ah

Several disruptive technologies align with *Maqasid al-Shari'ah's* ideals and precepts. These technologies not only provide creative answers to numerous societal issues but also encourage moral and responsible usage. For instance, halal food traceability systems leverage blockchain technology to give complete food product traceability, guaranteeing that they are manufactured, stored, and transported in line with Islamic rules. As it helps to assure the safety and authenticity of halal food items, this technology is in line with the protection of life and religion. Furthermore, green technologies—technologies that minimise carbon emissions and encourage sustainable behaviour—are in line with *Maqasid al-Shari'ah's* core value of protecting the environment (Khalish et al., 2020b; Sarkawi et al., 2017). For instance, fossil fuel dependence is reduced by solar and wind energy technologies. Fossil fuel is a contributing factor in climate change. Protection of the environment for future generations can cover several objectives such as life, lineage and resources (wealth). Another example is healthcare technologies, as they aid in the prevention and treatment of illnesses. Technologies that provide access to healthcare and encourage preventative care are consistent with the protection of life and lineage. Telemedicine technology, for instance, improves patients' access to treatment by enabling them to obtain medical services from a distance. In addition to that, digital health care facilities, such as at home AI monitoring and sensors, help to protect the elderly and facilitate their compliance.

Overall, these examples show how disruptive technologies may be in line with *Maqasid al-Shari'ah's* principles and values to encourage moral and responsible usage while also advancing social welfare.

5 Insights into the Interaction Between Halal Digital Entrepreneurship and Disruptive Technologies from the Lenses of *Maqasid* al-Shari'ah

The tenets of *Maqasid al-Shari'ah* serve as a guide for halal entrepreneurship. When it comes to adopting digital technologies, halal entrepreneurs ought to consider aligning with the five objectives of *Shari'ah* while conducting their businesses. In the case of disruptive technologies, the preservation of intellect is particularly relevant, as these technologies often involve the development and application of new knowledge and ideas. Digital entrepreneurs should ensure that their activities contribute positively to the pursuit of knowledge and the development of critical thinking.

Additionally, disruptive technologies may have an impact on the preservation of life, property, and lineage. For example, the development of autonomous vehicles could improve road safety and reduce the number of accidents, thereby contributing to the preservation of life. However, if these technologies lead to job losses or the displacement of workers, they may have negative consequences for the preservation of property and lineage.

To sum up, from the vantage point of *Maqasid al-Shari'ah*, the connection between halal digital entrepreneurship and disruptive technologies can be understood by looking at how their activities help to preserve the five objectives. Entrepreneurs in the digital space should create and employ tools that adhere to Islamic halal principles and encourage the pursuit of knowledge, all the while keeping in mind the effects that such tools may have on individuals and communities. Digital entrepreneurship that adheres to Sharia law and disruptive technologies share all of *Maqasid al-Shari'ah*'s goals. However, the goals of intellectual preservation (*Hifz al-Aql*) and material preservation (*Hifz al-Mal*) are especially pertinent to these domains, and here is why.

(a) **Intellectual preservation (*Hifz al-Aql*)**

Techno-moral change is a process that explains how new technologies and moral values influence each other (Nickel et al., 2022). The study by Nickel et al. (2022) suggests two important accounts: the ethics of technology and responsible innovations, which are two important criteria that have been suggested to evaluate techno-moral change and its disruptiveness. Disruptive technologies and digital entrepreneurship frequently necessitate the development and implementation of new knowledge and approaches. Simultaneously, innovation and creative thinking are the aspects that define entrepreneurship. Therefore, protecting one's mind is crucial for making sure that these pursuits help one grow in wisdom and critical thinking. Entrepreneurship in the halal digital space should prioritise protecting people's mental health without sacrificing their ability to use technology to advance knowledge and spark new ideas.

Halal digital entrepreneurship and disruptive technologies can help promote innovation and creativity by enabling entrepreneurs to develop new products and services that are compliant with Islamic law and principles. They can also help improve access to education and knowledge by providing new tools and platforms for learning and research. In addition, halal digital entrepreneurship and disruptive technologies can help promote critical thinking and analysis by providing new ways of analysing data and information. This can help individuals make more informed decisions about their lives and businesses. Disruptive technologies may also pose a threat to existing knowledge systems and paradigms. As a result, it's crucial to check that these innovations don't go against Islamic principles. For instance, artificial intelligence (AI) and machine learning (ML) algorithms should be developed in a way that they don't violate *Shari'ah* principles like respect for human rights and personal autonomy. Strong data privacy and security measures can guarantee intellectual preservation for halal digital entrepreneurship and disruptive technologies. Encryption, firewalls, and secure servers are all options for warding off cybercriminals and protecting private data. They are also useful for keeping proprietary and sensitive company data safe from scammers and hackers.

Open-source software and knowledge sharing within the halal digital space are also ways to promote intellectual preservation. With open-source software, business owners have access to the source code and can make changes to it to create new goods and services. The halal digital space can benefit from entrepreneurs collaborating and learning from one another by sharing knowledge and resources. Halal digital entrepreneurship should prioritise ethical and socially responsible innovation. Disruptive technology and digital entrepreneurship must not endanger Islamic ideals like justice, equality, and human dignity. Entrepreneurs should prioritise halal and eco-friendly innovations.

In conclusion, there are many prospects for development and progress in the fields of halal digital entrepreneurship and disruptive technologies. If the halal digital space is going to survive and thrive, entrepreneurs need to make protecting intellectual property and creating new products with integrity their top priorities. This will help them grow as individuals and professionals while also benefiting society at large.

(b) **Preservation of wealth (*Hifz al-Mal*)**

The development of innovative products, services, and business practises is a common by-product of digital entrepreneurship and disruptive technologies. Therefore, protecting property is critical to guaranteeing that these actions accord with people's and organisations' legal rights to the resources they manage.

In order to be deemed halal, a halal entrepreneur's use of technology must be economically beneficial to society and must not violate the rights of others' property. A halal food delivery service, for instance, might employ such technologies to speedily serve customers while adhering to Islamic dietary regulations. The halal business must also treat its customers, vendors, and employees with honesty and integrity. Additionally, disruptive technologies have the potential to reshape established markets and industries. Many people may lose their jobs or be forced to relocate as a direct result of the uncertainty caused by disruptive technologies. For this reason, halal digital entrepreneurs must prioritise the use of technology to increase employment and reduce disruptions in the workplace.

Halal digital entrepreneurs can help create new opportunities for wealth creation and preservation by enabling entrepreneurs to develop innovative products and services that are compliant with Islamic law and principles. They can also help reduce costs and increase efficiency, which can lead to greater profitability and wealth creation. In addition, halal digital entrepreneurship and disruptive technologies can help promote transparency and accountability in financial transactions by providing more accurate and timely information about business operations and financial performance. This can help prevent fraud and other unethical practises that can lead to the loss of wealth.

Overall, halal digital entrepreneurship and disruptive technologies can play an important role in promoting the fifth objective of *Shari'ah,* preservation of wealth (Hifz al-Mal), by creating new opportunities for wealth creation and preservation, reducing costs and increasing efficiency, and promoting transparency and accountability in financial transactions.

6 Conclusions

Halal digital entrepreneurship and disruptive technologies can both be guided by the principles and values of *Maqasid al-Shari'ah,* helping to uphold fundamental Islamic values and ethics while promoting ethical and responsible practises. In addition to ensuring that goods and services are created and provided in a manner that is consistent with Islamic beliefs and principles, halal digital entrepreneurship may play a significant role in fostering economic growth and the creation of jobs. Halal digital entrepreneurs may develop solutions that are socially responsible and in line with the larger aims and purposes of Islamic teachings by applying the concepts of *Maqasid al-Shari'ah* to their work. The same is true for disruptive technologies; by applying *Maqasid al-Shari'ah* principles, they may be developed and used in a way that encourages moral and responsible behaviour while also guaranteeing that they are in line with Islamic values and principles. This might lead to the development of technologies that advance society as a whole while respecting crucial Islamic principles and ethics. When creating new enterprises or technologies, it is crucial for entrepreneurs and innovators to keep *Maqasid al-Shari'ah's* guiding principles and values in mind. Doing so can help to guarantee that these developments are made and used in a way that is morally and responsibly responsible. This involves protecting private and personal information as well as factors such as protection of life, money, intelligence, religion, and ancestry. In order to ensure that moral and responsible behaviour is upheld, there is a need for ongoing study and innovation in Halal digital entrepreneurship and disruptive technologies. This involves looking into fresh approaches to integrating *Maqasid al-Shari'ah* principles into the creation and application of technology as well as encouraging moral and socially conscious business practises.

References

Abdullah, M. A., Elgharbawy, A. A., & Azam, M. S. E. (2022). *Halal entrepreneurship* (1st ed.). IIUM Press.

Ahmed, H. (2011). Maqasid al-Shari'ah and Islamic financial products: A framework for assessment. *ISRA International Journal of Islamic Finance, 3*(1), 149–160.

Al-Ghazali, A. H. (1901). *Al-Mustasfa min 'Ilm al-U l.* Egypt. Al-Matba'ah al-Amiriyyah.

Almeida, F., Santos, J. D., & Monteiro, J. A. (2020). The challenges and opportunities in the digitalization of companies in a post-COVID-19 World. *IEEE Engineering Management Review, 48*(3), 97–103.

Al-Raysuni, A. (1992). *Nazariyat Al-Maq id 'Inda al-Imam al-Shatibi.* Herndon, International Institute of Islamic Thought.

Awaworyi Churchill, S., & Farrell, L. (2018). The impact of gambling on depression: New evidence from England and Scotland. *Economic Modelling, 68*, 475–483. https://doi.org/10.1016/J.ECONMOD.2017.08.021

Baierl, R., Behrens, J., & Brem, A. (2019). *Digital entrepreneurship.* Springer.

Barigozzi, F., & Tedeschi, P. (2019). On the Credibility of ethical banking. *Journal of Economic Behavior & Organization, 166*, 381–402.

Battour, M., Salaheldeen, M., & Mady, K. (2021). Exploring innovative marketing opportunities for Halal entrepreneurs in hospitality and tourism industry. *SHS Web of Conferences, 124*, 10001.

binti Alli, Z. N. A., & bin Usop, R. (2022). Understanding the relation of Maqasid al-Shari'ah and Islamic Economic Development to develop a better Islamic Entrepreneurial Culture in Schools. *Conference Proceeding*, 54–57. https://oarep.usim.edu.my/jspui/handle/123456789/15674.

Fisol, W. N. M., Suid, I. S., Saufi, M., & Bahari, A. (2019). Islamic tourism development based on the scientific of the maqasid shari'ah framework. *International Journal of Academic Research in Business & Social Sciences, 9*(5), 784–795.

Gregor, S. (2006). The nature of theory in information systems. *MIS Quarterly*, 611–642.

Kamali, M. H. (2008). *Maqāṣid Al-Sharīāh Made Simple* (Vol. 13). International Institute of Islamic Thought (IIIT).

Kasinathan, P., Pugazhendhi, R., Elavarasan, R. M., Ramachandaramurthy, V. K., Ramanathan, V., Subramanian, S., Kumar, S., Nandhagopal, K., Raghavan, R. R. V., & Rangasamy, S. (2022). Realization of sustainable development goals with disruptive technologies by integrating industry 5.0, society 5.0, smart cities and villages. *Sustainability, 14*(22), 15258.

Khalish, N., Purwanto, M. R., Supriadic, T. M., & Marazie, H. (2020a). The significance of maqasid Syariah principles in improving Islamic economics and finance. *International Journal of Innovation, Creativity and Change, 13*(3). www.ijicc.net.

Khalish, N., Purwanto, M. R., Supriadic, T. M., & Marazie, H. (2020b). The significance of maqasid Syariah principles in improving Islamic economics and finance. *International Journal of Innovation, Creativity and Change, 13*(3). www.ijicc.net

Labbani, M., & Mohammed, M. O. (2011). Decision making tools for resource allocation based on Maq id Al-Shar'ah. *Islamic Economic Studies Journal, 19*(2), 51–67.

Laldin, M. A., & Furqani, H. (2013). Developing Islamic finance in the framework of maqasid al-Shari'ah: Understanding the ends (maqasid) and the means (wasa'il). *International Journal of Islamic and Middle Eastern Finance and Management, 6*(4), 278–289.

Modgil, S., Dwivedi, Y. K., Rana, N. P., Gupta, S., & Kamble, S. (2022). Has Covid-19 accelerated opportunities for digital entrepreneurship? An Indian perspective. *Technological Forecasting and Social Change, 175*, 121415.

Mohamed Azmi, A. S., Hanif, N. R., Mahamood, S. M., & Mohd Ali, S. N. (2019). Synthesizing the Maqasid al-Syariah for the waqf property development. *IOP Conference Series: Earth and Environmental Science, 385*(012051), 1–7. https://doi.org/10.1088/1755-1315/385/1/012051

Nickel, P. J. (2020). Disruptive innovation and moral uncertainty. *NanoEthics, 14*(3), 259–269. https://doi.org/10.1007/s11569-020-00375-3

Nickel, P. J., Kudina, O., & van de Poel, I. (2022). Moral uncertainty in technomoral change: Bridging the expl anatory gap. *Perspectives on Science, 30*(2), 260–283. https://doi.org/10.1162/posc_a_00414

Normaaruf, M., Hamid, A., & Yunus, A. M. (2020). Application of the concept of hifz al-din in shariah-compliant business management. *International Journal of Islamic Studies and Social Sciences, 2*(1), 111. https://doi.org/10.56613/islam-universalia.v2i1.150

Rahman, F. K., Tareq, M. A., Yunanda, R. A., & Mahdzir, A. (2017). Maqashid Al-Shari'ah-based performance measurement for the halal industry. *Humanomics*.

Ridhani, D. (2022). Digital entrepreneurship of MSME Nagari Kamang Hilia. *Enrichment: Journal of Management, 12*(2), 2074–2078.

Rosidi, M. H., Mokhtar, Wifaq, A., & Majid, M. N. B. A. (2022). The role of Maqasid al-Shari'ah as a fundamental ethics in social media use. *International Journal of Academic Research in Business and Social Sciences*.

Sahut, J.-M., Iandoli, L., & Teulon, F. (2021). The age of digital entrepreneurship. *Small Business Economics, 56*, 1159–1169.

Salaheldeen, M. (2022). Opportunities for Halal Entrepreneurs in the Islamic digital economy: future and trends from a cultural entrepreneurship perspective. In *Cultural entrepreneurship: New societal trends* (pp. 95–107). Springer.

Sarkawi, A. A., Abdullah, A., Dali, N. M., & Khazani, N. A. M. (2017). The philosophy of Maqasid Al-Shari'ah and its application in the built environment. *Journal of Built Environment, Technology and Engineering, 2*(3), 215–222.

Sedera, D., Tan, C.-W., & Xu, D. (2022). Digital business transformation in innovation and entrepreneurship. In *Information & management* (p. 103620). Elsevier.

Shehu, F., Hayati, N., Ahmad, B., & Al-Aidaros, A.-H. (2016). Islamic entrepreneurship in the light of Maqasid Al-Shari'ah: A critical review. *Journal of Social and Development Sciences, 6*, 6–14.

Yousufzai, S. F., Hayat, A., & Abbas, M. H. (2021). Digital transformation of value-based intermediation-a risk-based perspective. *Journal of Contemporary Business and Islamic Finance (JCBIF), 1*(1), 23–31.

Other References

Halal Dinner Club. (n.d.). Halal Dinner Club. https://www.halaldinnerclub.com.

"Malaysia's Zilzar.com" (2014) *aims to become Alibaba for Muslim consumer market*. https://www.business-standard.com/article/news-ani/malaysia-s-zilzar-com-aims-to-become-alibaba-for-muslim-consumer-market-114110400743_1.html.

MIT Professional Education. (2022). *Top 5 Disruptive Technologies to Change the World|MIT Professional Education*. MIT Professional Education. https://professionalprograms.mit.edu/blog/technology/top-disruptive-technologies/.

Muslim Pro for iPhone and Android. (n.d.). https://www.muslimpro.com.

Plan your Halal Travel Holiday Experience|Halal Trip. HalalTrip. https://www.halaltrip.com.

Population Size and Annual Population Growth Rate. (2022). *Strategic communication and international division*. Retrieved March 22, 2023, from https://www.dosm.gov.my/v1/index.php?r=column/cthemeByCat&cat=155&bul_id=dTZXanV6UUdyUEQ0SHNWOVhpSXNMUT09&menu_id=L0pheU43NWJwRWVSZklWdzQ4TlhUUT09.

The rise of digital entrepreneurship. (n.d.). WThe rise of digital entrepreneurship: Tips for how to start a business online. Retrieved fromhttps://www.adobe.com/acrobat/resources/digital-entrepreneurship-starting-a-business-online.html.

Innovative Opportunities for Halal Entrepreneurs in the Tourism Sector

Siti Nur Azizah

Abstract This chapter discusses various innovation opportunities for halal entrepreneurs, especially in tourism. This innovation opportunity includes four discussion sections: demand and supply of halal products and standard services and how it has developed so far. Some countries' backgrounds will undoubtedly have differences in demand and supply for halal products and services. This chapter also explains the innovative opportunities in the neglected tourism Sector apart from Hajj and Umrah. Recently, people only know Hajj and Umrah as potential halal tourism sectors, but many other innovations can still be developed. Furthermore, this chapter reveals the point of view of halal entrepreneurs regarding medical, space, education, and sports as some of the tourism innovation issues currently developing.

1 Introduction

Many industries, including tourism, have transformed due to technology to become more innovative. Halal tourism is one of the subcategories classified explicitly into various subcategories. Halal entrepreneurs play a crucial role in this innovation, particularly in Muslim nations. The Islamic heritage of a country impacts how innovative halal entrepreneurs are in the travel industry. The invention responds to the supply and demand for conventional services and halal goods.

Additionally, the extent of innovation has only grown in specific areas like the Hajj and Umrah. The halal tourist industry can offer a lot of innovative opportunities. Halal tourism can be produced from a variety of tourism innovation prospects. Technology's influence on tourism sheds light on various travel-related industries, including sports, medical, space, and educational tourism.

S. N. Azizah (✉)
Universitas Muhammadiyah Purwokerto, Purwokerto, Indonesia
e-mail: sitinurazizah@ump.ac.id

L. Raimi et al. (eds.), *Contemporary Discourse of Halal and Islamic Entrepreneurship*,
https://doi.org/10.1007/978-981-99-6427-7_13

2 Demand for Halal Products and Standard Services

The worldwide halal market is exhibiting encouraging fast and steady growth, particularly for the Halal food industry. Over 2.1 trillion USD worth of goods and services are being traded internationally (Elasrag, 2022). The rapid spread of Islam worldwide, the rising purchasing power of the Muslim population, and the rapidly expanding Muslim tourism industry sector in the West are numerous factors contributing to this growth rate. In recent years, Muslim residents and visitors have significantly increased worldwide, particularly in Western Europe. This growth increases awareness of the demand for halal goods and services (Halkias et al., 2014).

Halal goods and services are in high demand in nations with a predominately Muslim population. However, nations with a small Muslim population or none are exempt from this need (Jia & Chaozhi, 2020). There is no remarkable trend to utilize it in nations having a Muslim minority. Food items are currently in high demand as halal products (Aniqoh & Hanastiana, 2020). Financial products are a category of halal services that have shown recent growth in demand. However, when adhering fully to its Sharia, Sharia financial services only occasionally function effectively. Halal product and service companies face difficulties as a result of this circumstance. Furthermore, some requirements must be upheld for halal goods and services. As a result, halal goods and services have more extraordinary operating expenses than their non-halal rivals that use comparable ingredients. Therefore, the number of Muslims living in the country continues to affect the daily expansion of halal goods and services (Cetin & Dincer, 2016).

The demand between halal products and services has a significant difference (Hong et al., 2019). Financial items are currently the halal services that are in high demand. However, when adhering strictly to its Sharia, Sharia financial services only seldom perform effectively. Halal product and service companies face difficulties as a result of this circumstance. Furthermore, some requirements must be upheld for halal goods and services. Therefore, halal goods and services have more significant operational expenses than non-halal rivals using comparable ingredients. The number of Muslims living in the country determines how quickly halal goods and services are growing daily (Halkias et al., 2014). In contrast, halal services are exempt from this. Except for financial services, no particular legal suggestion outlines the necessity of halal services or the repercussions of non-halal services. The demand for halal goods and services differs significantly because of this difference in legality. Demand for halal goods is more significant than that for halal services (Danjuma, 2021).

3 Supply of Halal Products and Services

The supply of goods or services must be following with its demand (Hidayat et al., 2022). High demand is only sometimes met by high supply, but low demand is typically followed by low supply. Lack of products or services is a result of it. There needs to be more supply and demand for halal goods and services. Halal goods are more readily available than financial services, especially non-financial ones (Ikram & Ali, 2020).

The corporation must consider its products' availability because this factor significantly impacts consumer purchase decisions (Husnain et al., 2019). Product availability refers to the assortment of goods a store or supermarket has (Rachmawati et al., 2019). Product availability comprises variants within each kind and the breadth of each product category. The business uses Product availability marketing tactics to hasten and simplify product storage. Product availability is a reliable and effective technique to provide customers with what they desire and anticipate will be well-received by customers (Kotler et al., 2019).

Except for Islamic finance, most halal goods and services are still available on a limited basis (Ameraldo et al., 2019; Utomo et al., 2021). The majority of halal services are still run on a local scale by families, especially in the tourism industry. Family businesses, or firms owned by one's own family members, are sometimes categorized as tiny or micro businesses. Family-owned enterprises have few employees, a modest market share, a low yearly revenue, and a sparse infrastructure and asset base. Family enterprises are less successful than other firms (Ganesan & Varkkey, 2022).

People are encouraged to start enterprises and become entrepreneurs for various reasons. Family enterprises have a long history of being created to achieve individual and familial objectives. Family-run companies are commonplace in the tourist and hospitality sectors, a global phenomenon (Arcese et al., 2021; Kallmuenzer, 2018; Peters & Kallmuenzer, 2018). For instance, rural farmers initially let visitors into their homes in order to support their families and care for the family's land. The more time the company spends expanding, the more customers it attracts. One of the earliest methods of implementing this innovation in rural areas was the emergence of "bed and breakfast" (B&B) enterprises to balance work and family. Modern family enterprises are also becoming more profit- and growth-oriented entrepreneurs, aside from social and cultural factors. For instance, the idea of a tourist village provides tourists visiting the village with local knowledge, customs, and traditions (Peters & Kallmuenzer, 2018).

People who want to establish a family business can take advantage of tourism opportunities and conveniences. The tourism industry is very appealing due to its inexpensive startup costs, low operating expenses, and straightforward management. According to lifestyle, geography, and recreational inclinations, family companies can accomplish economic success through tourism. Additionally, research explains why family business managers favour operating in the tourism industry. Some people opt to work for themselves because they despise their current position, want a better lifestyle, need a change for personal reasons, and prefer a particular location or semi-retirement while establishing a new source of income (Kallmuenzer, 2018).

Small businesses and families dominate some tourist destinations, especially in rural or remote areas (Arcese et al., 2021). The tourism industry's success can also help the local economies of popular tourist locations. Small business family networks play a crucial role in destination development. Additionally, the authors contend that the local community must support and preserve family businesses because they can serve as pillars of development in rural and isolated locations (Halkias et al., 2014).

There are disadvantages to running a family business in the tourism industry, such as seasonal demand and cycles. The tourism industry must adapt to these cycles' demand patterns, which vary significantly throughout national holidays, school breaks, and regular working days (Arcese et al., 2021). Weekday travel is prevalent during the busiest travel season, whereas weekday travel is less prevalent. Cash flows and overall profitability, which are only partially stable, are critical issues for enterprises in these locations. It might jeopardize their company's ability to survive (Kallmuenzer, 2018). To get around this problem, business owners frequently put in extra time and engage temporary workers to handle the high volume of business during the peak season. Obtaining additional work during the off-season to increase income is another choice for many people (Peters & Kallmuenzer, 2018). Another significant obstacle is the need for small or family enterprises to reconcile performance and economic sustainability while competing with larger firms with access to more resources and cash. These restrictions frequently coexist with poor management by firm owners who need proper business or marketing backgrounds or prior experience in the tourism sector (Kallmuenzer, 2018). However, only some studies have examined family-owned businesses in the tourism and hospitality sectors.

4 The Innovative Opportunities in the Neglected Tourism Sector Apart from Hajj and Umrah

Muslim visitors typically favour services that adhere to halal standards, particularly when it comes to food. However, most visitors also consider other services, such as the availability of daily Muslim newspapers and other services that adhere to Islamic laws and cultural customs (Halkias et al., 2014). Halal employers should not offer alcohol, non-halal food, and non-halal beverages. Additionally, a 100% Halal and alcohol-free label must be provided. In addition, halal business owners must respect other people's traditions and beliefs while attempting to be understanding and sensitive to their customer's demands. For instance, service providers must promptly remove alcohol from guests' rooms and tables if they are Muslims (Halkias et al., 2014). Additionally, all food containing pork and alcohol should be removed from the menu; this also applies to other guests (for sensitivity reasons and to avoid common cross-contamination). Swimming pools and other "sensitive areas" (like health centres, ballrooms, and gyms) can be restricted to women only, serve only Halal food and beverages, and activate special services and products within a few days. Other facilities can also be converted to Islam for Muslim visitors (Shnyrkova & Predvoditeleva, 2022).

Businesses that sell halal products ought to use different vendors. As a result, they can sell some of the products that are Halal-certified to their Muslim clients. A specialized team with expertise in halal services should be available to halal business owners. When it is noted that they have Muslim clients, halal service providers can train several specific workers. These experts can be taught Islamic culture, manners, and all other formalities, including learning a few Arabic words for greetings (Jia & Chaozhi, 2020).

Certain services, such as halal requirements and a particular dress code, can also be modified for Muslim clients. Moreover, only female employees served female clients. Halal business owners are urged to employ women dedicated to visiting Muslim women clients (Halkias et al., 2014). Halal business owners should set up their workplace to be Muslim-friendly by, for example, fostering a peaceful environment and avoiding interrupting worshipers. Entrepreneurs who practice halal may provide their products under specific circumstances, such as during Ramadan. Muslim guests can eat before dawn and after sundown during Ramadan, thanks to the interior restaurant's modified opening hours (Arasli et al., 2021).

5 Halal Entrepreneurs' Perspectives Regarding Medical Tourism, Space Tourism, Educational Tourism, and Sports Tourism

"Tourism is defined as a dynamic, evolving, customer-driven force; it is a science and a business, attracting and transporting visitors, accommodating them, and kindly attending to their needs and wants." Islam's influence on travel and tourism is crucial for both Muslim and non-Muslim nations, not just because of the size of the Muslim population but also because travel and tourism are incorporated into many Islamic policies (political, economic, legal, and social), not to mention that, in Islam's worldview, they are significant and an integral part of Addin (a way of life). Islamic teachings encourage Muslims to visit their brothers and sisters, and as a result, tourists travelling to Muslim nations including Egypt, Indonesia, Jordan, Malaysia, Morocco, Tunisia, Turkey, and the United Arab Emirates (UAE) have been influenced. Conflicts and challenges that travellers encounter when travelling to non-Muslim nations add to their predilection for doing so. The issues include a shortage of halal goods and services and challenges for some travellers in getting visas and travel documents (Jia & Chaozhi, 2020).

The notion of a destination image may be used in marketing and management strategies in the travel industry. A person's destination image is made up of their beliefs, thoughts, and perceptions about a location. These constructions are internally accepted and are based on the information periodically presented by various sources. In order to comprehend visitor behaviour better, evaluation and analysis of destination pictures are helpful. From a marketing standpoint, the destination image must create an effective plan for marketers to give what potential travellers anticipate and generate realistic expectations while tying personal motivation to destination decisions.

Meeting visitor demands as best as possible is crucial in marketing tourist locations. For Muslim visitors, destination marketers should highlight Halal tourism goods and services and provide vacation packages and locations created to cater to and suit Muslim demands. Tourists must enjoy the utmost luxuries, including services that are reasonable in price and allow them to fulfil their religious commitments while travelling. When customers stay at a hotel, they should be accommodated and comfortable. Marketing tourism destinations requires a focus on providing the best possible service to visitors. For Muslim travellers, destination marketers should emphasize Halal tourism products and services and provide holiday packages and destinations designed to appeal to and fit Muslim preferences. Travellers must have access to the finest amenities, such as reasonably priced services that enable them to fulfil their religious obligations. Customers should feel welcomed and at ease when staying at a hotel.

Halal travel encompasses a variety of interests, such as sports, education, medicine, and space exploration. Due to several unpleasant school-related incidents, including bullying, halal business owners are exploring educational tourism. The development of academic tourism to educate the public about the halal educational system and reduce bullying trauma is possible. It is used in various nations where Islamic institutions and Madrasas are comparable to public schools. Another kind of education tourism used in many nations is study trips to institutions of higher learning that practice Islam.

Because various sports activities come with Muslim-friendly gear like swimwear, halal business owners have also considered the sports tourism industry. Additionally, each pool often has separate locker rooms for men and women. There is also gender segregation in a few athletic disciplines. It demonstrates that halal businesspeople are becoming interested in the halal sports industry, starting with the facilities and equipment.

While this is happening, halal businesses have not paid much attention to medical or space tourism due to their niche demands and significant dangers. People interested in the health industry, such as physicians and nurses, are the only section included in the medical tourism category. Additionally, medical terrorism has a significant danger of loss of life that cannot be replaced. Similar issues exist with space travel, which costs money and is extremely difficult. Therefore, demand will also be influenced by the availability of finances.

References

Ameraldo, F., Saiful, S., & Husaini, H. (2019). Islamic banking strategies in rural area: developing halal tourism and enhancing the local welfare. *Ikonomika, 4*(1), 109–136.

Aniqoh, N. A. F. A., & Hanastiana, M. R. (2020). Halal food industry: Challenges and opportunities in Europe. *Journal of Digital Marketing and Halal Industry, 2*(1), 43–54.

Arasli, H., Saydam, M. B., Gunay, T., & Jafari, K. (2021). Key attributes of Muslim-friendly hotels' service quality: voices from booking. com. *Journal of Islamic Marketing* (ahead-of-print).

Arcese, G., Valeri, M., Poponi, S., & Elmo, G. C. (2021). Innovative drivers for family business models in tourism. *Journal of Family Business Management, 11*(4), 402–422.

Cetin, G., & Dincer, M. Z. (2016). Muslim friendly tourism (MFT): A discussion. *Journal of Tourismology, 2*(1), 65–67.

Danjuma, I. (2021). An increasing demand for Halal products and services: A call for the enactment of an international convention on Halal industries. In *Contemporary issues in Islamic social finance* (pp. 260–272). Routledge.

Elasrag, H. (2022). *Blockchain for Halal industry*. Hussein Elasrag.

Ganesan, V., & Varkkey, H. M. (2022). State-owned enterprises and environmental decision-making. *Malaysian Journal of Tropical Geography (MJTG), 48*(1), 45–63.

Halkias, D., Pizzurno, E., De Massis, A., & Fragoudakis, M. (2014). Halal products and services in the Italian tourism and hospitality industry: Brief case studies of entrepreneurship and innovation. *Journal of Developmental Entrepreneurship, 19*(2), 1450012.

Hidayat, S. E., Rafiki, A., & Nasution, M. D. T. P. (2022). Halal industry's response to a current and post-COVID-19 landscape and lessons from the past. *Journal of Islamic Marketing, 13*(9), 1843–1857.

Hong, M., Sun, S., Beg, A. R., & Zhou, Z. (2019). Determinants of halal purchasing behaviour: Evidences from China. *Journal of Islamic Marketing, 10*(2), 410–425.

Husnain, M., Rehman, B., Syed, F., & Akhtar, M. W. (2019). Personal and in-store factors influencing impulse buying behavior among generation Y consumers of small cities. *Business Perspectives and Research, 7*(1), 92–107.

Ikram, U., & Ali, R. (2020). Developing a scale for measuring non-financial service performance of Islamic banks in Pakistan. *Review of Applied Management and Social Sciences, 3*(1), 99–112.

Jia, X., & Chaozhi, Z. (2020). "Halal tourism": Is it the same trend in non-Islamic destinations with Islamic destinations? *Asia Pacific Journal of Tourism Research, 25*(2), 189–204.

Kallmuenzer, A. (2018). Exploring drivers of innovation in hospitality family firms. *International Journal of Contemporary Hospitality Management.*

Kotler, P., Kartajaya, H., & Setiawan, I. (2019). *Marketing 3.0: From products to customers to the human spirit*. Springer.

Peters, M., & Kallmuenzer, A. (2018). Entrepreneurial orientation in family firms: The case of the hospitality industry. *Current Issues in Tourism, 21*(1), 21–40.

Rachmawati, D., Shukri, S., Azam, S., & Khatibi, A. (2019). Factors influencing customers' purchase decision of residential property in Selangor, Malaysia. *Management Science Letters, 9*(9), 1341–1348.

Shnyrkova, A., & Predvoditeleva, M. (2022). The needs of Muslim hotel customers: Evidence from Russian guests. *Journal of Islamic Marketing, 13*(1), 133–160.

Utomo, S. B., Sekaryuni, R., Widarjono, A., Tohirin, A., & Sudarsono, H. (2021). Promoting Islamic financial ecosystem to improve halal industry performance in Indonesia: A demand and supply analysis. *Journal of Islamic Marketing, 12*(5), 992–1011.

Reshaping the Mindset of Halal Entrepreneurs Toward Sustainable Business: The Case of Indonesia

Lucky Nugroho

Abstract The purpose of this book chapter is to reshape the mindset of Muslim entrepreneurs toward sustainable business. The method used is a descriptive method that describes how conditions and circumstances related to Muslim entrepreneurs in running their business at this time. Furthermore, to limit the discussion in this book chapter, the problem formulations include: (i) What is the concept of sustainable business activities in Islamic economics; (ii) What is the potential of the Islamic Business Ecosystem that exists in Indonesia today; (iii) How is the strategy to implement sustainable business in the Islamic Business Ecosystem? The result of this book chapter is to provide information and references related to solutions to improve the literacy of Muslim business actors who are also MSMEs related to the concept of sustainability in business and the contribution of the ulama. The implication of this book chapter is to provide information and references for stakeholders who focus on Islamic economics, Islamic finance, and environmental sustainability. The novelty of this book chapter is related to the relationship between sustainable business and the concept of Islamic economics.

1 Introduction

The phenomenon of global environmental degradation is a serious problem facing our planet today. Environmental degradation encompasses all forms of undesirable changes to the environment and can threaten the sustainability of life on Earth. These global environmental problems have made human life in recent decades vulnerable to disasters and tragedies. According to Kurniawan (2022), Robinson (2023), there are several important issues related to environmental problems, which include:

- Global Warming from Fossil Fuel

L. Nugroho (✉)
Universitas Mercu Buana, Jakarta, Indonesia
e-mail: lucky.nugroho@mercubuana.ac.id

L. Raimi et al. (eds.), *Contemporary Discourse of Halal and Islamic Entrepreneurship*,
https://doi.org/10.1007/978-981-99-6427-7_14

Global warming from fossil fuels is the process of global warming caused by greenhouse gas emissions resulting from the combustion of fossil fuels such as coal, oil, and natural gas (Steinberg, 1999). Greenhouse gases, such as carbon dioxide (CO_2), methane (CH_4) and nitrous oxide (N_2O), trap heat in the atmosphere and cause an increase in global temperatures. Therefore, global warming from fossil fuels threatens environmental sustainability and human health, including sea level rise, climate change, increased frequency and intensity of natural disasters, and increased health risks from air pollution (Rahman, 2009). Some examples of global warming are the devastating wildfires in the Americas and Australia; locust pests that have destroyed crops in several countries in Africa, the Middle East and Asia; 13% of deaths in the European Union caused by various forms of pollution, and so on;

- Food Waste

Food waste is organic waste generated from unused or wasted food or ingredients during food preparation, expired or spoiled food disposal, and uneaten food scraps in restaurants, canteens, eateries, or households (Camilleri, 2021; Paužuolienė et al., 2022). Food waste consists of various types of organic waste, such as leftover vegetables, fruits, meat, fish, rice, bread, and so on. Food waste is often thrown away and, if not appropriately managed, can cause environmental impacts such as methane gas emissions from landfills (Dilkes-Hoffman et al., 2018; Thi et al., 2015). One-third of the food intended for human consumption (about 1.3 billion tons) is wasted. Furthermore, this amount is enough to feed 3 billion people. In addition, food waste contributes 4.4 gigatons of greenhouse gas emissions every year. If this amount of food waste were to be likened to a country, it would be the third highest emitter of greenhouse gases, behind China and the U.S.;

- Plastic Waste

Plastic waste is a solid waste of various plastic materials that are difficult to decompose. The plastic itself is made from chemicals in the form of polymers that are durable and difficult to decompose in the environment (Rhodes, 2018). Plastic waste consists of plastic products such as bottles, food packaging, plastic bags, household appliances, children's toys, etc. (Połomka et al., 2020). In 1950, the world produced more than 2 million tons of plastic annually. By 2015, this annual production had swelled to 419 million tons, exacerbating environmental plastic waste. If no action is taken on this increase, plastic waste could reach 600 million tons by 2040.

- Biodiversity Loss

Biodiversity loss is a condition in which the number and diversity of species, habitats, and ecosystems in a region or planet significantly decrease due to human activities such as deforestation, poaching, climate change, pollution, and overuse of chemicals (Alao, 2009). Biodiversity is an essential component of life on planet Earth, as its existence dramatically affects the balance of ecosystems and human survival. For example, a recent WWF report found that population sizes of mammals, fish, birds, reptiles, and amphibians have declined by an average of 68%

between 1970 and 2016 (Roberts, 2020). The report attributes the loss of biodiversity to land use change, particularly the conversion of habitats, such as forests, grasslands and mangroves, to agricultural systems (de Chazal & Rounsevell, 2009).

- Deforestation

  Deforestation is the systematic and destructive process of removing forests to acquire land or timber within the forest (Li et al., 2016). Deforestation can be legal or illegal and is usually carried out by humans to fulfill their needs, such as to expand agricultural land, plantations, and settlements, or for industrial purposes such as road construction, housing, or the timber industry. The current condition is that a forest the size of 20 soccer fields is cut down every minute (Lai, 2022). Therefore, it is estimated that by 2030, the planet may only have 10% of its forests if deforestation is not stopped. Even the existence of forests could be lost in less than 100 years.

- Air Pollution

  Air pollution is when the air around us is polluted by harmful materials that can harm human health and the environment. Air pollution can come from various sources, such as motor vehicles, factories, fossil fuel combustion, agricultural activities, and forest fires (Bernard et al., 2001). One of the most significant environmental problems today is air pollution. Research from the World Health Organization (WHO) shows that an estimated 4.2–7 million people die from air pollution worldwide each year and that nine out of 10 people breathe air containing high levels of pollutants (WHO, 2023). Air pollution has caused over 10,000 deaths, 5,000 hospitalizations, and 7,000 children to experience various health problems yearly in Jakarta, at the cost of trillions of rupiah. However, these illnesses, deaths, costs, and long-term impacts on children can be avoided if the government fulfills the demands of citizens who have won lawsuits related to air pollution at the appeal level.

When viewed from the contributors of global warming countries based on greenhouse gas emissions as one of the leading causes of global warming, Indonesia is the eighth-ranked country in the world as a contributor to global warming, as shown in the table below.

Referring to Table 1, China is the most significant contributor to greenhouse emissions globally, with 12,399.6 million metric tons of carbon dioxide equivalent. ($MtCO_2e$). Furthermore, the second and third ranks are the United States and the European Union. At the same time, Indonesia is ranked eighth in the world by contributing 827.9 million MtCO2e. Therefore, based on Table 1, the challenge of all business actors, including Sharia business actors in Indonesia, where Indonesia is also a country with the largest Muslim population in the world, is to reduce the current global warming increase (Nugroho, 2016; Nugroho et al., 2017a, 2017b, 2017c).

Table 1 Top ten countries contributing to global warming in 2020

No	Name of country	$MtCO_2e$ (million)
1	China	12,399.6
2	United States of America	6018.2
3	European Union	3572.6
4	India	3366.1
5	Russia	2545.1
6	Japan	1186.6
7	Brazil	1042.5
8	Indonesia	965.3
9	Iran	827.9
10	Canada	722.8

Source Pusparisa and Bayu (2021), Muniarty et al. (2023)

In addition, the current era of globalization and business dynamics demands competitive business competition. Initially, the business was built with an economic-based paradigm called the single P (Profit), which is the primary goal of the company to generate the highest possible profit without considering the impacts arising from these activities (Gimenez et al., 2012; Hidayah et al., 2021; Nugroho et al., 2020a, 2020b, 2020c, 2020d, 2020e). However, in its development, the company has to consider social and environmental aspects as an impact on the activities of the company so that the existence of the company can be maintained and able to operate sustainably and get support from all relevant stakeholders. Therefore, according to Hussain et al. (2018), Nugroho et al. (2017a, 2017b, 2017c) to maintain the continuity and sustainability of the company's operations, the company must implement the triple P concept, namely profit (financial aspects), people (social aspects) and planet (environmental sustainability aspects).

Therefore, referring to the above phenomenon, the problem of environmental sustainability has threatened human life, so action is needed to prevent environmental damage from getting worse and repair the environmental damage that has occurred (Labetubun et al., 2022; Sandin & Peters, 2018). On the other hand, the majority of business actors in Indonesia are Muslims, and there is an Islamic business ecosystem that can mitigate environmental damage and prevent environmental sustainability. Therefore, Muslim business actors must make a breakthrough by implementing Sustainable Development in their operations. Business entities have begun to think about how their business activities can participate and be responsible for all causes in social and environmental conditions (Hidayah et al., 2019; Nugroho et al., 2020a, 2020b, 2020c, 2020d, 2020e; Nugroho et al., 2017a, 2017b, 2017c). Sustainable Development aims to balance two interests at once, namely economic and environmental development at the same time. Sustainable Development is a development that meets the needs of the present world without neglecting the ability of future generations to meet their needs (Jabareen, 2008; Nugroho et al., 2019a, 2019b; Nugroho et al., 2019a, 2019b).

Following the above phenomenon, the problem formulations in this book chapter are: (i) What is the concept of sustainable business activities in Islamic economics?; (ii) What is the potential of the Islamic Business Ecosystem that exists in Indonesia today?; (iii) How is the strategy to implement sustainable business in the Islamic Business Ecosystem?. Furthermore, based on the formulation of the problem, the objectives of this book chapter are (i) Understanding the concept of sustainable business activities in Islamic economics; (ii) Understanding the potential of the Islamic Business Ecosystem that exists in Indonesia today; (iii) Understanding the strategy of implementing a sustainable business in the Islamic Business Ecosystem. The implication of this book chapter is to provide information and references for stakeholders who focus on Islamic economics, Islamic finance, and environmental sustainability. The novelty of this book chapter is related to the relationship between sustainable business and the concept of Islamic economics.

2 The Concept of Sustainable Business Activities in Islamic Economics

In the initial stage, to understand the extent to which Islamic business entities are concerned about environmental sustainability, it is necessary to understand the concepts and principles of Islamic economics that support environmental sustainability. Furthermore, Islamic business entities are business entities based on the principles of Sharia which, according to Choudhury (2018), Nugraha et al. (2020), Nugroho et al. (2023) Based on the Tawhid String Relationship (TSR) sourced from the Qur'an and Hadith and other sources of Islamic law such as Ijma and Ijtihad. If illustrated, the concept of an Islamic business entity based on the principles of Islamic finance that support environmental sustainability is as follows:

Based on Fig. 1, it can be explained that the concept of an Islamic business entity that is in line with sharia principles is as follows:

- The operational foundation of Islamic business entities is maqasid sharia which has six elements, namely: (i) Maintaining religion; (ii) Maintaining the soul; (iii) Maintaining the mind; (iv) Maintaining offspring; (v) Maintaining property; (vi) Maintaining the environment. Hence, according to Darmaningrum et al. (2023), Imani et al. (2022), and Kamal et al. (2022), Islamic business entities are organizations that care about business sustainability, environmental sustainability, and the existence of the next generation (environmental aspects). Thus, the business activities of Islamic financial institutions must consider the sustainability of both business aspects, social aspects, environmental aspects, and aspects of good corporate governance or professionalism (Diantanti et al., 2021; Fasa et al., 2020; Nugroho, 2021);
- Furthermore, from these six elements, Sharia business entities in operations can be reflected not only in adhering to the principle of the triple bottom line or 3 P'S (Profit-Finance, People-Social, and Planet-Environment) but adhering to the

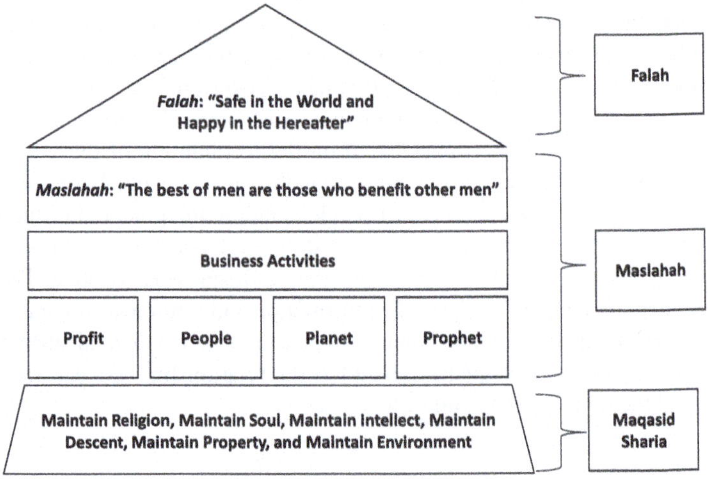

Fig. 1 Concept of Sharia business entity based on Sharia principles. *Source* Nugroho (2022)

quad bottom line or 4 P'S (Profit-Finance, People-Social, Planet-Environment, and Prophet-Spiritual) (Diantanti et al., 2021; Karyanto et al., 2019; Nugroho, 2022; Nugroho et al., 2019a, 2019b; Whittaker, 1999). Further explanation of the 4 P'S is as follows: (i) Profit, this aspect refers to the ability of a business to generate financial returns that can finance long-term growth and development (Nugroho et al., 2018a, 2018b; Triani et al., 2017); (ii) People, this refers to how a business impacts the well-being of communities, workers, and other stakeholders. This includes the business's efforts to promote social justice, improve the quality of life in the community, and establish good relationships with all parties involved in the business (Missimer & Mesquita, 2022; Pavlic et al., 2015); (iii) Planet, this aspect refers to how a business impacts the surrounding natural environment. This includes a business's efforts to reduce its negative impact on the environment, such as pollution, waste, and environmental damage (Moravcikova et al., 2017); (iv) Prophet, this aspect refers to the spiritual aspect where business activities must be in accordance with sharia principles, namely related to halal businesses and also not doing business with those that contain maysir (gambling and speculation), gharar (uncertainty) and riba (interest rate) (Jihad et al., 2022; Nugroho et al., 2022a, 2022b). Furthermore, based on the 4 P'S concept, Islamic business entities aim to achieve benefits where all human economic activities must be based on the aim of providing goodness to other humans (Arafah & Nugroho, 2016; Badawi et al., 2021; Nugroho et al., 2020a, 2020b, 2020c, 2020d, 2020e; Nugroho et al., 2017a, 2017b, 2017c). Thus, the peak or the ultimate goal of humans doing economic activities or muamalah is to get the blessing of Allah. Therefore, the ultimate goal of economic activity is to achieve safety in the world and also happiness in the hereafter or called Falah (Nugroho & Bararah, 2018);

- In addition, because the foundation of the activities of Islamic business entities is based on maqasid sharia, benefit and sourced from the Qur'an, Hadith, and other sources of Islamic law, the existence of Islamic business entities aims to support Muslims to implement their teachings in kafah or totality (Ihwanudin et al., 2020; Nugroho et al., 2020). Therefore, the main purpose of the existence of Islamic business entities is to help muamalah activities, especially in the economic field, to be in accordance with religious teachings so that humanity can achieve safety in the world and happiness in the hereafter-Falah (Afoukane et al., 2021; Nugroho et al., 2018a, 2018b).

3 Islamic Business Ecosystem that Exists in Indonesia Today

Indonesia, as the country with the largest population in the world, has an Islamic business ecosystem and needs to be connected to one another, and also needs to increase literacy on the importance of understanding related to Islamic business entities that are embedded with the principle of business sustainability or 4 P'S. The Islamic business ecosystem that exists in Indonesia consists of eleven categories which include:

- Muslim population ecosystem where the total Muslim population in Indonesia reached 236.53 million in 2021 (Kusnandar, 2021);
- The ecosystem of houses of worship consisting of 295 thousand mosques throughout Indonesia, and 324 thousand musholla throughout Indonesia (Muniarty et al., 2023);
- The ecosystem of Islamic hospitals consisting of 500 Islamic hospitals out of 2900 hospitals throughout Indonesia (Muhyiddin & Murdaningsih, 2020);
- Islamic financial ecosystem consisting of: 4500 baitul mal wa tamwil, 184 Sharia rural banks, 14 sharia commercial banks, 20 Sharia business units (dual banking system), 9 Sharia financial technology, 29 Sharia insurance (Nasfi et al., 2022; Nugroho et al., 2022a, 2022b);
- The ecosystem of Nahdatul Ulama (NU) Islamic organizations consisting of: 90 million membership and one of the largest Islamic social organizations in the world, 217 universities under NU, and 27,342 Islamic boarding schools under NU (Muniarty et al., 2023);
- The ecosystem of the Muhammadiyah Islamic organization consists of 33,334 schools under Muhammadiyah, and there are 186 universities under Muhammadiyah (Muniarty et al., 2023);
- The ecosystem of Islamic educational institutions consisting of 55,191 schools under primary and secondary education and madrasah, 23 State Islamic Universities, and 30 State Islamic Institutes (Muniarty et al., 2023);

- The Hajj and Umrah ecosystem comprises 1,500 Umrah travel organizers and 1,559 Hajj guidance groups and organizers. In addition, there is the potential for 1 million Umrah pilgrims to depart each year and 220 thousand Hajj pilgrims to depart each year (Muniarty et al., 2023);
- The halal industry ecosystem consists of 7,356 products and services that have received halal certification, in addition, there are currently 19,071 products and services that are in the process of halal certification (Mahliza et al., 2020);
- The ecosystem of Islamic boarding schools where the number of Islamic boarding school students, according to the Ministry of Religious Affairs in 2022, reached 3.4 million students with 36,600 Islamic boarding schools (Khoeron, 2022);
- Zakat, Infaq, Sadaqah, and Waqf (ZISWAF) ecosystem consisting of potential Zakat of Rp3327.6 trillion, and potential Waqf of money reaching Rp820 Billion (Kamal et al., 2022).

Referring to the potential of the Islamic business ecosystem in Indonesia, the large number of Muslim business actors in Indonesia has a significant contribution to the national economy. Furthermore, according to Nugroho and Chowdhury (2015), Nugroho and Lubis (2020), the majority of Muslim business actors are micro, small, and medium entrepreneurs (MSMEs), besides that Indonesian MSMEs are also the backbone of the national economy (Widodo et al., 2022).

MSMEs are the backbone of Indonesia because the number reaches 99.9% of the total business actors in Indonesia (Hasan et al., 2022; Labetubun et al., 2021). On the other hand, according to research conducted by Cassells and Lewis (2011) and (Nugroho et al., 2017a, 2017b, 2017c) MSMEs contribute to environmental damage. There are several causes of MSMEs as contributors to environmental damage, including:

- Limited access to information: MSME entrepreneurs often have limited access to information on environmental sustainability and environmentally friendly business practices. This can be due to limited resources and technology that make it difficult for MSMEs to access the necessary information (Allet, 2014; Allet & Hudon, 2015; Ferdousi, 2015);
- Lack of awareness and understanding: Many MSME entrepreneurs do not understand the importance of environmental sustainability and its impact on their business. This lack of awareness and understanding can make them less interested in learning or implementing environmentally friendly business practices (Hillary, 2004);
- Focus on financial gain: Many MSME entrepreneurs prioritize financial returns over environmental sustainability. This can make them less interested in investing time, energy, and resources in developing environmental skills and knowledge (Allet, 2017);
- Lack of government and community support: Lack of government and community support can make MSME entrepreneurs feel less motivated to learn or implement environmentally friendly business practices (Nugroho, 2014).

On the other hand, Islam teaches its followers to pay attention and care for the environment, and maintain a balance between human needs and the preservation of nature. This is stated in the Qur'an and Hadith of the Prophet Muhammad, among others:

- "And do not corrupt the earth after it has been well-ordered by Allah…" (QS. Al-A'raf: 56)
- "Allah loves every good deed; even clearing something from the road is a good deed." (HR. Bukhari)

Thus, referring to the condition that there are still many MSMEs in Indonesia, the majority of whom are Muslims, which contribute to natural damage, this shows that there are still many Muslim entrepreneurs who have not implemented their religious teachings in totality.

4 The Strategy to Implement Sustainable Business in the Islamic Business Ecosystem

The existence of violations in business activities that damage environmental sustainability carried out by MSMEs in their business activities, which in fact they are Muslim entrepreneurs, requires efforts to reshape the mindset of Muslim entrepreneurs toward sustainable business. Furthermore, if illustrated, some solutions that involve various parties, including the role of the ulama in increasing the literacy of Muslim MSME entrepreneurs related to sustainability issues in doing business, can be shown as follows:

In accordance with Fig. 2, there are several ways to improve the literacy of business sustainability from Muslim business actors, which are also MSMEs, as follows:

Training and education: Provide specialized training and education on business sustainability and environmentally friendly business practices for MSMEs. This training can be conducted online or offline and can involve experts or practitioners with experience in the field;

Adopt environmentally friendly business practices: Encourage MSMEs to adopt environmentally friendly business practices, such as reducing the use of single-use packaging, minimizing the use of hazardous chemicals, optimizing the use of energy and natural resources, and paying attention to the environmental impact of the products or services produced. By adopting green business practices, MSMEs can reap financial and social benefits and help sustain their business;

Expanding access to information and networks: MSMEs can expand their information and network by participating in activities and events related to business sustainability, such as exhibitions, seminars, or discussion forums. By expanding networks and access to information, MSMEs can learn from the experiences and business practices of others, as well as obtain new opportunities for cooperation to develop their business;

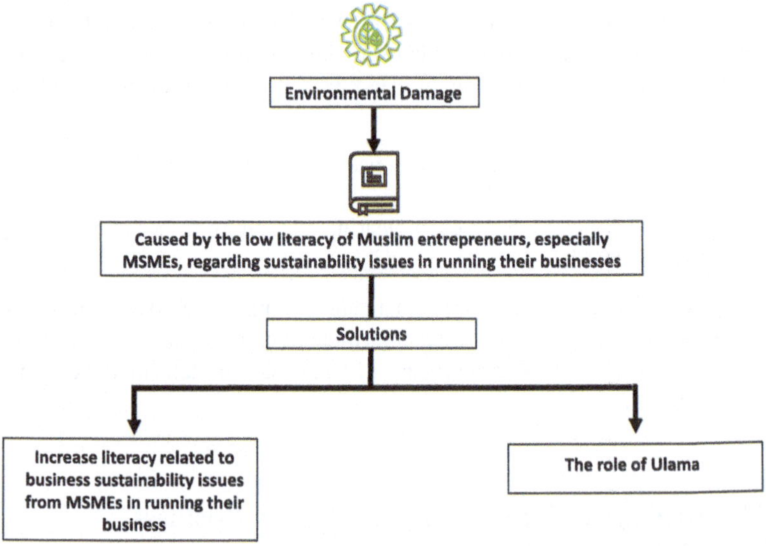

Fig. 2 Solutions in reshaping the mindset of Muslim entrepreneurs toward sustainable business

Establish partnerships with other parties and investors: MSMEs can establish partnerships with other parties, such as companies, organizations, investors, or institutions that share the same vision and mission in terms of business sustainability. These partnerships can provide additional benefits, such as access to resources, technology, and information that can help improve MSME literacy on business sustainability.

In addition to the above efforts, the role of the ulama is very important in increasing the literacy of Muslim businesses regarding the importance of environmental sustainability. As spiritual and social leaders, ulama greatly influences the perspective and behavior of Muslim business actors related to the environment. Some of the roles of ulama in improving the literacy of Muslim business actors related to the importance of maintaining environmental sustainability in carrying out their business activities are as follows:

- Advising and teaching: Ulama can advise and teach Muslim businesses about the importance of environmental sustainability and its impact on human life on Earth. This can be done through mosque speeches, lectures, or discussions;
- Provide educational programs: Ulama can provide educational programs focusing on environmental sustainability in business, such as recitations, courses, or seminars integrating Islamic teachings and principles of environmental sustainability in business. These programs can help improve the literacy of Muslim businesses regarding the importance of environmental sustainability;
- Provide and set a good example: Ulema can apply Islamic teachings and principles of environmental sustainability in daily life, including in business. By setting a

good example, ulama can help Muslim businesses understand and internalize the importance of environmental stewardship in business;

- Providing fatwas and explanations on environment-related issues: Ulama also has an important role in providing fatwas and explanations on environment-related issues, such as environmental laws and the impact of business activities on the environment. This can help Muslim businesses understand the importance of environmental sustainability within the framework of Islamic teachings.

Thus, Ulama also contributes through their role in preserving the environment and are able to adapt the way of teaching and delivering environmental messages in business to the conditions of Muslim businesses and the environment, so that they can be more easily understood and applied in their business.

References

Afoukane, M., Utami, W., & Nugroho, L. (2021). Assessing the adaptability of Islamic microfinance loans to the needs of small enterprises in Indonesia. *Journal of Islamic Economics & Social Science (JIESS), 2*(1), 9–23.

Alao, J. S. (2009). Need for biodiversity conservation in Nasarawa State, Nigeria. *Biological Diversity and Conservation*, *2*(1), 1–20.

Allet, M. (2014). Why do microfinance institutions go green? An exploratory study. *Journal of Business Ethics, 122*(3), 405–424. https://doi.org/10.1007/s10551-013-1767-2

Allet, M. (2017). Mitigating environmental risks in microenterprises: A case study from El Salvador. *Business and Society, 56*(1), 57–91. https://doi.org/10.1177/0007650315574738

Allet, M., & Hudon, M. (2015). Green microfinance: Characteristics of microfinance institutions involved in environmental management. *Journal of Business Ethics, 126*(3), 395–414. https://doi.org/10.1007/s10551-013-1942-5

Arafah, W., & Nugroho, L. (2016). Maqhashid Sharia in Clean Water Financing Business Model at Islamic Bank. *International Journal of Business and Management Invention, 5*(2), 22–32.

Badawi, A., Nugroho, L., & Hidayah, N. (2021). Islamic bank performance: Does low-cost fund and labor cost affect it ? (Empirical cases in Bank Syariah Mandiri-Indonesia). *Business, Economics and Management Research Journal, 4*(2), 81–92.

Bernard, S. M., Samet, J. M., Grambsch, A., Ebi, K. L., & Romieu, I. (2001). The potential impacts of climate variability and change on air pollution-related health effects in the United States Isabelle Romieu Published by: The National Institute of Environmental Health Sciences Stable URL: https://www.jstor.org/stable/3435010 R. *Environmental Health Perspective, 109*(2), 199–209.

Camilleri, M. A. (2021). Sustainable production and consumption of food. Mise-en-place circular economy policies and waste management practices in tourism cities. *Sustainability (Switzerland), 13*(9986), 1–13. https://doi.org/10.3390/su13179986

Cassells, S., & Lewis, K. (2011). SMEs and environmental responsibility: Do actions reflect attitudes? *Corporate Social Responsibility and Environmental Management, 18*(3), 186–199. https://doi.org/10.1002/csr.269

Choudhury, M. A. (2018). The ontological law of Tawhid contra 'Shari'ah-compliance' in Islamic portfolio finance. *International Journal of Law and Management, 60*(2), 413–434. https://doi.org/10.1108/IJLMA-01-2017-0001

Darmaningrum, K., Miftahorrozi, M., Zulfikar, M., Fitriana, Y., Nurzianti, R., Anggraini, R. I., Shiddieqy, H. A., Putra, B. P., Manggabarani, A. S., Miftah, M., Muzayyanah, M., Mubarok, M. K., Muslim, U. B., Nugroho, L., Wijiharta, W., & Lestari, F. P. (2023). Kewirausahaan Syariah. In E. Damayanti (Ed.), *CV Widina Media Utama.* CV Widina Media Utama.

de Chazal, J., & Rounsevell, M. D. A. (2009). Land-use and climate change within assessments of biodiversity change: A review. *Global Environmental Change, 19*(2), 306–315. https://doi.org/10.1016/j.gloenvcha.2008.09.007

Diantanti, N. P., Trimulato, T., Mahriani, E., Nugroho, L., Shaleh, M., Supatminingsih, T., Faujiah, A., Rachmawati, E., Jumiati, E., Isnandar, F. R., Bahri, S., Djuanda, G., Sudarmanto, E., & Saravistha, D. B. (2021). Pengantar Bisnis Islam (Tinjauan Konsep dan Praktis). In *Widina Bhakti Persada Bandung*. Widina Bhakti Persada Bandung.

Dilkes-Hoffman, L. S., Lane, J. L., Grant, T., Pratt, S., Lant, P. A., & Laycock, B. (2018). Environmental impact of biodegradable food packaging when considering food waste. *Journal of Cleaner Production, 180*, 325–334. https://doi.org/10.1016/j.jclepro.2018.01.169

Fasa, I., Febrianty, M., Khoerulloh, A. K., Arisa, A., Utami, W., Santoso, I. R., Arifudin, O., Suganda, A. D., Nugroho, L., & Haerany, A. (2020). *Eksistensi Bisnis Islami Di Era Revolusi Industri 4.0*. Widina Bhakti Persada Bandung. www.penerbitwidina.com

Ferdousi, F. (2015). Impact of microfinance on sustainable entrepreneurship development. *Development Studies Research, 2*(1), 51–63. https://doi.org/10.1080/21665095.2015.1058718

Gimenez, C., Sierra, V., & Rodon, J. (2012). Sustainable operations: Their impact on the triple bottom line. *International Journal of Production Economics, 140*(1), 149–159. https://doi.org/10.1016/j.ijpe.2012.01.035

Hasan, M., Hartoto, H., Abdelina, A., Riyaldi, M. H., Aswanto, A., Akbar, T., Juliansyah, R., Talakua, B. A., Firmansyah, H., Nugroho, H., Ferdinandus, A. Y., Sattar, S., Apriyeni, D., & Nugroho, L. (2022). Ekonomi Pembangunan Sebuah Tinjauan Teori dan Praktis. In R. Septiani (Ed.), *Widina Media Utama*. Widina Media Utama.

Hidayah, N., Badawi, A., & Nugroho, L. (2019). Factors affecting the disclosure of sustainability reporting. In *International Journal of Commerce and Finance* (Vol. 5, Issue 2).

Hidayah, N., Nugroho, L., Prihanto, H., & Prihantini, D. (2021). Company characteristics, disclosure of social responsibility, and its impact on company performance: An empirical study in Indonesia. *Journal of Asian Finance, Economics and Business, 8*(6), 889–895. https://doi.org/10.13106/jafeb.2021.vol8.no6.0889

Hillary, R. (2004). Environmental management systems and the smaller enterprise. *Journal of Cleaner Production, 12*(6), 561–569. https://doi.org/10.1016/j.jclepro.2003.08.006

Hussain, N., Rigoni, U., & Orij, R. P. (2018). Corporate governance and sustainability performance: Analysis of triple bottom line performance. *Journal of Business Ethics, 149*(2), 411–432. https://doi.org/10.1007/s10551-016-3099-5

Ihwanudin, N., Maulida, S., Fatriansyah, A. I. A., Rahayu, S. S., Nugroho, L., Harnovinsah, Widyastuti, S., Rahman, M. R. R., Fachri, S., Rijal, K., Agrosamdhyo, Senjiati, I. H., Isnandar, F. R., & Jiwantara, F. A. (2020). *Pengantar Perbankan Syariah (Konsep, Regulasi & Praktis)*. Widina Bhakti Persada Bandung. https://repository.penerbitwidina.com/publications/323594/pengantar-perbankan-syariah-konsep-regulasi-parktis

Imani, S., Zulfikar, M., Mahmudah, S. N., Nugroho, L., Ardana, Y., Sudarmanto, E., Ernayani, R., & Kinanti, R. A. (2022). *Dasar-Dasar Ekonomi Islam*. Global Eksekutif Teknologi. https://books.google.co.id/books?hl=id&lr=&id=OLaYEAAAQBAJ&oi=fnd&pg=PR1&ots=219Zylj_jx&sig=_pwjpIfx_bDxCq2FyYoEa8MD4s8&redir_esc=y#v=onepage&q&f=false

Jabareen, Y. (2008). A new conceptual framework for sustainable development. *Environment, Development and Sustainability, 10*(2), 179–192. https://doi.org/10.1007/s10668-006-9058-z

Jihad, F. M., Nugroho, L., & Sugiarti, D. (2022). Kajian Pengembangan Bisnis Syariah di Era Digitalisasi. *Jurnal Cakrawala Ilmiah, 2*(3), 1167–1168.

Kamal, S., Zulkifli, Agusti, N., Asmadia, T., Rahmat, F., Firda Zulfa Fahriani Muhammad Iqbal, Monady, H., Octaviani, R., Mubarok, A., Hakim, L., Masruroh, N., Athief, F. H. N., & Nugroho, L. (2022). *ZISWAF (Zakat, Infak, Sedekah & Wakaf)* (M. N. Sayuti & I. Nur (eds.)). Az-Zahra.

Karyanto, B., Aziz, L. H., Yusuf, M., Muzayyanah, Putra, A. R., Darussalam, A. Z., Fauziah, Djuanda, G., Wicaksono, G., Puspita, Y., Kusumaningrum, R., Nugroho, L., & Alfalisyado. (2019). *Pengantar Ekonomi Syariah* (Vol. 1). Widina Bhakti Persada Bandung.

Khoeron, M. (2022). *Pesantren: Dulu, Kini, dan Mendatang*. Kemenag.Go.Id. https://kemenag.go.id/read/pesantren-dulu-kini-dan-mendatang-wkgol

Kurniawan, A. (2022). *Permasalahan Lingkungan Global yang Harus Diperhatikan, Ancaman Serius bagi Kehidupan*. www.Merdeka.Com. https://www.merdeka.com/jabar/permasalahan-lingkungan-global-yang-harus-diperhatikan-ancaman-serius-bagi-kehidupan-kln.html

Kusnandar, V. B. (2021). *Persentase Populasi Muslim Indonesia Posisi 35 Dunia*. Databoks.Katadata.Co.Id. https://databoks.katadata.co.id/datapublish/2021/11/03/persentase-populasi-muslim-indonesia-posisi-35-dunia

Labetubun, M. A. H., Kembauw, E., Hasan, M., Arifudin, O., Yulistiyono, A., Maulina, D., Tanjung, R., Nopralia, S., Hasanuddin, H., Mustamin, S. W., Rachmarwi, W., Hartoto, H., Azizi, M., Siregar, R. T., Solikin, A., & Nugroho, L. (2021). Sistem Ekonomi Indonesia. In *Widina Bhakti Persada Bandung*. Widina Bhakti Persada Bandung.

Labetubun, M. A. H., Nugroho, L., Pinem, D., Mukhtadi, Sinurat, J., Pusporini, Umiyati, H., Hendrayani, Y., Anwar, K., Lahallo, F. F., Rahayu, P. S., Ahmad, D., & Gaol, S. L. (2022). *CSR PERUSAHAAN "Teori Dan Praktis Untuk Manajemen Yang Bertanggung Jawab"* (First). Widina Bhakti Persada Bandung. https://repository.penerbitwidina.com/media/publications/355240-csr-perusahaan-teori-dan-praktis-untuk-m-a900fc8d.pdf

Lai, O. (2022). *10 Deforestation Facts You Should Know About*. Earth.Org. https://earth.org/deforestation-facts/

Li, Y., Zhao, M., Mildrexler, D. J., Motesharrei, S., Mu, Q., Kalnay, E., Zhao, F., Li, S., & Wang, K. (2016). Potential and actual impacts of deforestation and afforestation on land surface temperature. *Journal of Geophysical Research, 121*(24), 14372–14386. https://doi.org/10.1002/2016JD024969

Mahliza, F., Nugroho, L., & Ali, A. J. (2020). Antecedents and consequences of muslim millennials attitude towards halal personal care products. *IKONOMIKA, 5*(2), 249–270. https://doi.org/10.24042/febi.v5i2.7203

Missimer, M., & Mesquita, P. L. (2022). Social sustainability in business organizations: A research agenda. *Sustainability (Switzerland), 14*(5), 1–13. https://doi.org/10.3390/su14052608

Moravcikova, D., Krizanova, A., Kliestikova, J., & Rypakova, M. (2017). Green marketing as the source of the competitive advantage of the business. *Sustainability, 9*(12), 1–13. https://doi.org/10.3390/su9122218

Muhyiddin, & Murdaningsih, D. (2020). *100 RS Ditarget Miliki Sertifikasi Syariah pada 2020*. www.Republika.Co.Id. https://www.republika.co.id/berita/q41yzr368/100-rs-ditarget-miliki-sertifikasi-syariah-pada-2020

Muniarty, P., Muhtadi, R., Aziz, M., Sudarmanto, E., Amriadi, Soehardi, D. V. L., Tomisa, M. E., Jaswita, D. I., Ummah, K. A., Kornitasari, Y., Hamid, A. M., Nurma, F., Nugroho, L., & Mutmaina, L. (2023). *Membangun ekosistem industri halal di Indonesia*. Global Eksekutif Teknologi. https://globaleksekutifteknologi.co.id/membangun-ekosistem-industri-halal-di-indonesia/

Nasfi, N., Solikin, A., Irdiana, S., Nugroho, L., Widyastuti, S., Kembauw, E., Luhukay, J. M., Alfiiana, A., Nuryani, N. N. J., Riyaldi, M. H., & Firmialy, S. D. (2022). Uang Dan Perbankan. In L. Nugroho (Ed.), *CV Widina Media Utama*. CV Widina Media Utama.

Nugraha, E., Nugroho, L., Lindra, C., & Sukiati, W. (2020). Maqashid Sharia Implementation in Indonesia and Bahrain. *Etikonomi, 19*(1), 155–168. https://doi.org/10.15408/etk.v19i1.14655

Nugroho, L. (2014). *Central bank regulation and its impact on green microfinance*. Universite Libre de Bruxelles.

Nugroho, L. (2016). Islamics principles versus green microfinance. *European Journal of Islamic Finance Meaning: 3*(December 2015), 1–9. https://doi.org/10.13135/2421-2172/1046

Nugroho, L. (2021). The role of information for consumers in the digital era (Indonesia Case). *ACU International Journal of Social Sciences, 7*(2), 49–59.

Nugroho, L., Badawi, A., & Hidayah, N. (2019a). Discourses of sustainable finance implementation in Islamic Bank (Cases Studies in Bank Mandiri Syariah 2018). *International Journal of Financial Research, 10*(6). https://doi.org/10.5430/ijfr.v10n6p108

Nugroho, L., Hidayah, N., Badawi, A., & Ali, A. J. (2019b). Socialization of mobile banking and internet banking for mikro and small entrepreneur (gender and business sector perspective-Kemayoran night market community). *ICCD, 2*(1), 419–426.

Nugroho, L., & Bararah, H. N. (2018). Pengaruh good corporate governance dan Biaya Operasional dan Pendapatan Operasional (BOPO) terhadap stabilitas keuangan bank umum syariah di Indonesia Tahun 2012–2017. *Inovbiz: Jurnal Inovasi Bisnis, 6*(2), 160–169.

Nugroho, L., & Chowdhury, S. L. K. (2015). Mobile banking for empowerment muslim women entrepreneur: evidence from Asia (Indonesia and Bangladesh). *Tazkia Islamic Finance and Business Review, 9*(1), 83–100.

Nugroho, L., Ghazali, A., Dadan Suganda, A., Ode Angga, L., Anshary Hamid Labetubun, M., Ihwanudin, N., Haerany, A., Anwar, S., Hartono, R., & Anwar, A. (2020a). *Pengantar Perbankan Syariah* (U. Saripudin (ed.)). Widina Bhakti Persada Bandung. www.penerbitwidina.com

Nugroho, L., Lubis, C., Fitrijanti, T., Sukmadilaga, C., Akuntansi, M., & Padjajaran, U. (2020b). Peluang Pengusaha Mikro dan Kecil (UMK) Menggunakan Layanan Digital Lembaga Keuangan Mikro Syariah. *JURNAL AL-QARDH, 5*(1), 56–68.

Nugroho, L., Meiwanto Doktoralina, C., Indriawati, F., Safira, S., & Yahaya, S. (2020c). Microeconomics and Tawhid String Relation Concept (TSR). *International Journal of Economics and Business Administration (IJEBA), 8*(3), 293–306. https://doi.org/10.35808/ijeba/516

Nugroho, L., Nugraha, E., & Badawi, A. (2020d). Sustainable finance portfolio analysis in Islamic Bank (segment perspective). *International Journal of Commerce and Finance, 6*(2), 226–240.

Nugroho, L., Suganda, A. D., Febrianty, F., Hamid, M. A. L., Ihwanudin, N., Trimulato, T., Haerany, A., Anwar, S., Hartono, R., & Anwar, A. (2020e). *Pengantar Perbankan Syariah*. Widina Bhakti Persada Bandung. www.penerbitwidina.com

Nugroho, L., Husnadi, T. C., Utami, W., & Hidayah, N. (2017a). Maslahah and Strategy to Establish a Single State-Owned Islamic Bank in Indonesia. *Tazkia Islamic Finance and Business Review, 10*(1), 1–17.

Nugroho, L., Utami, W., Akbar, T., & Arafah, W. (2017b). The challenges of microfinance institutions in empowering micro and small entrepreneur to implementating green activity. *International Journal of Energy Economics and Policy, 7*(3), 66–73. www.econjournals.com

Nugroho, L., Utami, W., Doktorlina, C. M., Soeharjoto, S., & Husnadi, T. C. (2017c). Islamic banking capital challenges to increase business expansion (Indonesia cases). *International Journal of Commerce and Finance, 3*(2), 1–10.

Nugroho, L. (2022a). The relationship between Maqasid Sharia and profitability ratio in Islamic Banking industries performance. *Sosyoekonomi, 30*(53), 243–259. https://doi.org/10.17233/sosyoekonomi.2022.03.13

Nugroho, L., Melzatia, S., Indriawati, F., Nurhasanah, & Safira. (2022b). *Lembaga Keuangan Syariah Dari Konsep Ke Praktik*. Widina Bhakti Persada. https://books.google.co.id/books?hl=en&lr=&id=w4uREAAAQBAJ&oi=fnd&pg=PA1&dq=LEMBAGA+KEUANGAN+SYARIAH+DARI+KONSEP+KE+PRAKTIK&ots=dSE4xAIAPW&sig=u3UePO4CgAY1YKBUNt2-L4hLyq0&redir_esc=y#v=onepage&q=LEMBAGAKEUANGANSYARIAHDARIKONSEPKEPRAKTIK&f=false

Nugroho, L., Miglietta, F., & Nugraha, E. (2022). Islamic Bank profitability: Financing micro and small segment, promotion, financing quality, labor aspects (Indonesia Cases). *European Journal of Islamic Finance, 9*(3), 38–46. https://doi.org/10.13135/2421-2172/6714

Nugroho, L., Nurrohmah, S., & Anasta, L. (2018). Faktor-Faktor Yang Mempengaruhi Opini Audit Going Concern. *SIKAP, 2*(2), 96–111. http://jurnal.usbypkp.ac.id/index.php/sikap

Nugroho, L., Utami, W., & Sugiarti, D. (2023). Tawhid string relation and itsar concept of islamic bank in covid-19 pandemic on value creation perspective (Indonesia Evidence). *Bil Turk: Journal of Economics and Related Studies, 5*(1), 1–18. https://doi.org/10.47103/bilturk.1174770.1

Nugroho, L., Villaroel, W., & Utami, W. (2018). The challenges of bad debt monitoring practices in islamic micro banking. *European Journal of Islamic Finance, 11*, 1–11. http://www.ojs.unito.it/index.php/EJIF

Paužuolienė, J., Šimanskienė, L., & Fiore, M. (2022). What about responsible consumption? A survey focused on food waste and consumer habits. *Sustainability (Switzerland), 14*(8509), 1–13. https://doi.org/10.3390/su14148509

Pavlic, I., Portolan, A., & Puh, B. (2015). The social impacts of tourism on local community's quality of life. *Tourism in Southern and Eastern Europe, 3*, 259–272. https://search.proquest.com/central/docview/1702272932/963452106B9646B4PQ/2?accountid=35994

Połomka, J., Jedrczak, A., & Myszograj, S. (2020). Risk and opportunity of using plastics from waste collected in a yellow bag. *Polymers, 12*(8). https://doi.org/10.3390/polym12081815

Pusparisa, Y., & Bayu, D. J. (2021). *10 Negara Penyumbang Emisi Gas Rumah Kaca Terbesar | Databoks*. Katadata.Co.Id. https://databoks.katadata.co.id/datapublish/2021/02/16/10-negara-penyumbang-emisi-gas-rumah-kaca-terbesar

Rahman, H. A. (2009). Global climate change and its effects on human habitat and environment in Malaysia. *Malaysian Journal of Environmental Management, 10*(2), 17–32.

Rhodes, C. J. (2018). Plastic pollution and potential solutions. *Science Progress, 101*(3), 207–260. https://doi.org/10.3184/003685018X15294876706211

Roberts, C. (2020). *68% Decline in Spe*. Earth.Org. https://earth.org/68-decline-in-species-population-sizes/

Robinson, D. (2023). *14 Biggest Environmental Problems of 2023*. Earth.Org. https://earth.org/the-biggest-environmental-problems-of-our-lifetime/

Sandin, G., & Peters, G. M. (2018). Environmental impact of textile reuse and recycling—A review. *Journal of Cleaner Production, 184*, 353–365. https://doi.org/10.1016/j.jclepro.2018.02.266

Steinberg, M. (1999). Fossil fuel decarbonization technology for mitigating global warming. *International Journal of Hydrogen Energy, 24*, 771–777.

Thi, N. B. D., Kumar, G., & Lin, C. Y. (2015). An overview of food waste management in developing countries: Current status and future perspective. *Journal of Environmental Management, 157*, 220–229. https://doi.org/10.1016/j.jenvman.2015.04.022

Triani, N. N. A., Satyawan, M. D., & Yanthi, M. D. (2017). Determining the effectiveness of going concern audit opinion by ISA 570. *Asian Journal of Accounting Research, 2*(2), 29–35. https://doi.org/10.1108/AJAR-2017-02-02-B004

Whittaker, M. (1999). Emerging "triple bottom line" model for industry weighs environmental, economic, and social considerations. *Oil and Gas Journal, 97*(51), 23–26.

WHO. (2023). *Air pollution*. www.Who.Int. https://www.who.int/health-topics/air-pollution#tab=tab_1

Widodo, Z. D., Purwaningrum, J. P., Purbasari, I., Rini, G. P., Putra, A. R., Uran, B. E. K. R., Mulyani, M., Soegoto, A. S., Nugroho, L., Nurzianti, R., Nugroho, H., Sudirman, A., Santosa, S., Novianti, R., Pattiapon, M. L., Pinem, D., & Ridwan, N. H. (2022). Manajemen Koperasi dan UMKM. In E. P. Sari & D. E. Putri (Eds.), *Widina Bhakti Persada*. Widina Bhakti Persada.

The 21st Century Innovative Marketing Strategies for Halal Entrepreneurs in the Various Segments of the Halal Industry

Shukurat M. Bello and Muazu Hassan Muazu

Abstract In today's global marketplace, the halal industry has become a vital player, and innovative marketing strategies are essential for entrepreneurs to succeed. This paper aims to provide insights into twenty-first century innovative marketing strategies for halal entrepreneurs in various segments of the halal industry. The chapter utilizes a qualitative research approach, including a literature review and a discussion of innovative marketing strategies. It discusses the background and importance of Halal industry, reviews relevant literature on innovative marketing strategies for Halal products, and presents a discussion on the effective marketing strategies for Halal entrepreneurs. It was found that digital marketing, social media marketing, and influencer marketing are critical marketing strategies for halal entrepreneurs in the twenty-first century. Other strategies include mobile, programmatic, and video marketing tactics. To succeed, businesses must prepare for innovation and technology, build scalable, digitally enabled business models, and implement marketing strategies that resemble a customer's preferences. Moreover, the chapter recommends halal entrepreneurs to consider local culture and trends when implementing marketing strategies.

1 Introduction

The Halal industry has become an essential component of the global economy, with an estimated worth of over $2.3 trillion (Thomson Reuters, 2018). In recent years, the global Halal market has been growing significantly, with the Halal industry expected to reach a market value of $3.2 trillion by 2024 (Grand View Research, 2019). The Halal industry refers to products and services that are permissible for Muslims to use or consume under Islamic law. The halal industry is rapidly expanding, and halal entrepreneurs are competing for market share in various segments of the

S. M. Bello (✉) · M. H. Muazu
Department of Business Administration and Entrepreneurship, Dangote Business School, Bayero University Kano, Kano, Nigeria
e-mail: smbello.bus@buk.edu.ng

L. Raimi et al. (eds.), *Contemporary Discourse of Halal and Islamic Entrepreneurship*,
https://doi.org/10.1007/978-981-99-6427-7_15

halal industry, including food, cosmetics, finance, and tourism. With the increasing Muslim and non-Muslim population globally and the growth of the Halal industry, there is a need for Halal entrepreneurs to adopt innovative marketing strategies to remain competitive in the market. To succeed in this competitive environment, halal entrepreneurs need to embrace innovative marketing strategies that reflect changing consumer trends and preferences.

Innovation and technology are critical factors in the success of any business in today's fast-paced, digital world. In the context of Halal offerings, products or services, there is a need for businesses to embrace innovative technologies and marketing strategies that resonate with the preferences of their customers.

The growth of the Halal industry has led to an increase in the number of Halal entrepreneurs worldwide. Halal entrepreneurship is becoming an important segment of the global marketplace. This exposure has made Halal entrepreneurs face significant challenges in differentiating their products and services in a crowded market. These entrepreneurs are specifically, faced with the challenge of developing effective marketing strategies to reach their target audience and stand out in the market. Therefore, it is essential to develop innovative marketing strategies that reflect changing consumer trends and preferences to capture the attention of potential customers and achieve business growth. This chapter aims to explore twenty-first century innovative marketing strategies that halal entrepreneurs can adopt to succeed in the halal industry.

In response to the growth in market of Halal products and services, businesses are seeking to capitalize on this market growth by offering Halal products and services. To succeed, businesses must prepare for innovation and technology, build scalable, digitally enabled business models, and implement marketing strategies that resemble a customer's preferences.

This chapter explores various approaches to preparing for innovation and technology, building scalable, digitally enabled business models, and marketing strategies that incorporate digital marketing, social media marketing, influencer and experience marketing, mobile marketing, programmatic marketing, and video marketing to promote Halal offerings, products or services.

2 Preparation for Innovation and Technology

Innovation and technology are essential for businesses to remain competitive and meet the changing demands of consumers. In the context of Halal offerings, products, or services, innovation and technology can help businesses improve their production processes, ensure compliance with Halal standards, and develop new and innovative products.

To prepare for innovation and technology, Halal businesses must be willing to invest in research and development, stay up-to-date with the latest trends and technologies, and be open to experimentation. This process involves identifying areas where technology can improve the customer experience, streamline operations, and enhance business performance.

Also, for preparation for innovation and technology, Halal businesses need to assess their current technology infrastructure and identify areas for improvement. One of the ways to achieve this is by investing in the latest technologies, such as AI, IoT, and blockchain, which can help improve the quality and safety of Halal products. For instance, blockchain technology can be used to track the supply chain of Halal products from the farm to the table, providing customers with greater transparency and assurance.

According to Tahir and Amin (2020), businesses can prepare for innovation and technology by adopting a Halal certification system. The certification system can provide businesses with guidance on Halal requirements and help them comply with the standards. Additionally, businesses can invest in research and development to develop new products and improve their production processes. For instance, technology can be used to automate processes, reduce waste, and improve efficiency.

According to a report by Deloitte, companies should prioritize technology investments in three key areas: digital customer experience, digital operations, and digital innovation. Digital customer experience involves using technology to provide customers with personalized and seamless experiences across multiple channels. Digital operations focus on improving efficiency and reducing costs through automation, data analytics, and machine learning. Digital innovation in the context of Halal business is about exploring new technologies and business models to create new value propositions and revenue streams for Halal offerings.

3 Building Scalable, Digitally Enabled Business Models

Scalable, digitally enabled business models are critical for businesses to grow and succeed in the digital age. In the context of Halal offerings, products, or services, businesses can leverage technology to scale their operations and reach a larger customer base.

Therefore, to build scalable, digitally enabled business models, Halal businesses need to adopt a customer-centric approach, embrace agile methodologies, and use data analytics to inform decision-making. This process involves identifying customer needs, pain points, and preferences, and developing digital solutions that address these issues.

Furthermore, in building a scalable, digitally enabled business models for Halal businesses, there is the need to embrace e-commerce platforms and develop mobile applications that enable customers to order Halal products online. This can help increase customer reach and create a more convenient shopping experience. Moreover, Halal businesses can explore opportunities for international expansion by establishing partnerships with e-commerce platforms, such as Amazon and Alibaba, to sell their products globally.

According to Kamarulzaman Ab Aziz et al. (2023), businesses can build scalable, digitally enabled business models by adopting e-commerce platforms. E-commerce platforms enable businesses to reach a wider audience and offer their products and services online. Additionally, businesses can leverage on social media platforms to engage with their customers and build brand awareness.

A study by McKinsey & Company suggests that businesses should focus on four key capabilities to build scalable, digitally enabled business models: customer insights, digital product development, agile operations, and analytics-driven decision-making. Customer insights involve using data and analytics to gain a deep understanding of customer behaviour and preferences. Digital product development is about designing and developing products that meet customer needs and expectations. Agile operations involve using agile methodologies to improve speed, flexibility, and responsiveness. Analytics-driven decision-making involves using data and analytics to inform decision-making and optimize business performance.

4 Innovative Marketing Strategies

Marketing strategies are essential for businesses to reach their target audience and communicate the value of their products or services. In the context of Halal offerings, products, or services, businesses must develop marketing strategies that resemble their customers' preferences. Consequently, to promote Halal offerings, products or services, businesses need to adopt marketing strategies that resonate with the preferences of their target customers.

To develop marketing strategies that resemble a customer's preferences, Halal businesses need to understand their target audience's demographics, behaviour, and psychographics. They can achieve this by conducting market research and gathering customer feedback. Furthermore, Halal businesses can leverage social media platforms, such as Facebook, Instagram, and Twitter, to reach their target audience and create engaging content that resonates with their preferences.

Some Innovative marketing strategies can include a range of techniques, such as digital marketing, mobile marketing, social media marketing, influencer marketing, and experiential marketing (Ali & HadžiMuhamedović, 2020). Additionally, Mobile marketing, Programmatic, and Video Marketing Tactics are other strategies Halal businesses could explore. They are not mutually exclusive to conventional businesses but also Halal entrepreneurs can explore innovative marketing strategies.

4.1 Digital Marketing Strategy

Digital marketing has become a vital tool for businesses of all kinds, including Halal businesses. The Halal market is growing rapidly worldwide, and digital marketing offers an effective and cost-efficient way to reach potential customers.

Digital marketing has become a critical component of modern marketing strategies. Halal entrepreneurs can leverage digital marketing tools such as search engine optimization (SEO), pay-per-click (PPC) advertising, and social media marketing to reach their target audience.

When it comes to creating a digital marketing strategy for Halal businesses, it's essential to keep in mind the cultural sensitivities and values of the target audience. Here are some key steps to consider:

1. Identify your target audience: Determine who your target audience is and understand their needs, preferences, and behaviours. Consider the age, gender, income level, geographic location, and interests of your target market.
2. Develop a Halal brand identity: Create a brand identity that reflects Halal values and principles. This includes developing a logo, tagline, messaging, and visual design elements that resonate with your target audience.
3. Create a mobile-friendly website: Your website should be mobile-friendly and optimized for search engines. This includes creating relevant content, using keywords that align with Halal values, and optimizing images and videos for fast loading speeds.

   Make a website that provides information about your Halal products or services. Your website should be visually appealing, easy to navigate, and optimized for search engines. Additionally, create social media profiles on platforms like Facebook, Instagram, and Twitter, and regularly update them with engaging content.
4. Leverage social media: social media is an effective tool for engaging with your target audience and building brand awareness. Consider creating a social media strategy that aligns with Halal values and principles, including creating relevant content, leveraging influencers, and engaging in conversations with your audience.
5. Build an email list: Email marketing is an effective way to stay in touch with your target audience and promote your products or services. Consider building an email list and sending regular newsletters with relevant content and promotions.
6. Leverage paid advertising: Consider using paid advertising to increase brand awareness and drive traffic to your website. This includes running targeted ads on social media platforms and search engines.
7. Leverage influencer marketing: Partner with influencers who have a significant following among your target audience. Influencers can help you reach new customers and build brand awareness.
8. Use search engine optimization (SEO): Optimize your website and social media profiles for search engines so that your business appears at the top of search results. Use keywords relevant to your business, and create quality content that answers your customers' questions.
9. Monitor and measure your results: Track your digital marketing efforts and measure your results. This includes monitoring website traffic, social media engagement, email open and click-through rates, and conversion rates.

By following these steps, you can create a digital marketing strategy that resonates with your target audience and reflects Halal values and principles.

4.2 Social Media Marketing

Social media marketing, in particular, is a powerful tool for halal entrepreneurs to engage with customers and promote their products and services. According to Islam (2019), businesses can develop marketing strategies that resemble their customers' preferences by leveraging social media platforms. Social media platforms enable businesses to engage with their customers, build brand awareness, and promote their products and services. Social media marketing is a powerful tool for Halal entrepreneurs to reach their target audience and build brand awareness. .

Social media marketing involves using social media platforms to build brand awareness, engage with customers, and drive sales. It could be said that social media marketing is one of the effective ways for Halal businesses to connect with their customers and build brand awareness today. This is because everyone in the world uses one or more social media handles today—it is either WhatsApp, Instagram, Twitter, Facebook, LinkedIn etc. By leveraging social media platforms, businesses can create engaging content, run targeted ads, and interact with their customers in real-time.

Halal businesses can leverage social media to reach a wider audience and promote their products and services. Here are some social media marketing strategies that Halal businesses can consider:

1. Highlight Halal certification: Halal certification is an essential aspect of Halal businesses, and it can be a significant selling point. Highlighting Halal certification on social media can help build trust and credibility with customers.
2. Share Halal recipes: Sharing Halal recipes and cooking tips on social media can help create engagement and build a community of followers who are interested in Halal cuisine.
3. Partner with Halal influencers: Halal businesses can collaborate with Halal influencers to reach a wider audience. These influencers can help promote Halal products and services to their followers and generate buzz.
4. Use social media ads: Social media ads can be an effective way to target a specific audience and promote Halal products and services. Targeting options can include demographics, interests, and behaviours.
5. Showcase Halal lifestyle: Halal businesses can showcase the Halal lifestyle on social media by sharing content related to Halal fashion, travel, and entertainment. This can help create a connection with customers and build brand loyalty.
6. Encourage user-generated content: Encouraging user-generated content, such as customer reviews and photos, can help build trust and social proof for Halal businesses.

7. Engage with the community: Engaging with the Halal community on social media by responding to comments, sharing relevant content, and participating in discussions can help build a loyal following.

Overall, Halal businesses can use social media to showcase their unique selling points and connect with a wider audience. By using a mix of the above strategies, businesses can create a strong social media presence and generate more leads and sales.

4.3 Influencer Marketing Strategy

Influencer marketing is another essential marketing strategy for halal entrepreneurs. Influencer marketing involves partnering with individuals who have a large following on social media to promote Halal products and services to their audience. Halal entrepreneurs can partner with influencers who share similar values and beliefs to promote their products and services to a wider audience. Influencer marketing involves collaborating with celebrities and sports personalities who have a significant following too.

Influencer marketing can be a powerful tool for promoting halal businesses, as it allows you to tap into the reach and credibility of popular social media personalities who have a strong following in your target market. Here are some tips for creating an effective influencer marketing strategy for your halal business:

1. Identify the right influencers: Look for influencers who have a large following among your target audience and who align with your brand values and messaging. You can use social media monitoring tools to track conversations and engagement in your industry to identify relevant influencers.
2. Build relationships with influencers: Once you've identified potential influencers, start building relationships with them by following them on social media, commenting on their posts, and sharing their content. This will help you establish a rapport with them and show that you're genuinely interested in their work.
3. Create engaging content: Work with influencers to create content that's both informative and engaging for your target audience. This could include product reviews, tutorials, or behind-the-scenes looks at your business. Make sure the content aligns with your brand values and messaging.
4. Leverage social media platforms: Share the content created by influencers on your own social media channels to amplify its reach. You can also use paid social media ads to target specific audiences and increase visibility.
5. Measure and track results: Use analytics tools to measure the success of your influencer marketing campaigns. Look at metrics such as engagement rates, click-through rates, and conversions to determine the effectiveness of your strategy and make adjustments as needed.

By following these tips, you can create a successful influencer marketing strategy for your halal business and reach a wider audience with your message.

4.4 Experiential Marketing Strategy

Experiential marketing involves creating an immersive experience for potential customers to engage with Halal products (Khan, 2019). Experiential marketing is a powerful way to engage customers and create a memorable brand experience. For Halal businesses, there are several strategies that can be employed to effectively reach and connect with potential customers. Here are a few ideas:

1. Host a Halal food festival: One way to introduce your Halal business to the community is to organize a food festival. This event can showcase the variety of Halal cuisine that your business offers, as well as provide an opportunity for attendees to learn more about Halal food and its significance. You can also invite other Halal businesses to participate in the festival to create a larger community event.
2. Create an interactive online experience: With the rise of social media and virtual events, creating an interactive online experience can be a great way to reach a wider audience. For example, you could host a live cooking demonstration or a virtual tour of your Halal facility. This type of experiential marketing can help to build brand awareness and showcase your unique selling proposition.
3. Host a charity event: Aligning your business with a charitable cause can be a powerful way to create a positive association with your brand. Consider partnering with a local charity organization that aligns with your values and hosting a charity event. This can include a fundraising dinner, a charity walk or run, or a community service project.
4. Offer Halal cooking classes: Many people are interested in learning how to cook Halal food, and offering cooking classes can be a great way to engage with potential customers. These classes can be hosted at your restaurant or a local community centre and can provide an opportunity to educate people about the importance of Halal food and its cultural significance.

There are many ways to create an experiential marketing strategy for Halal businesses. By focusing on creating a positive brand experience that engages customers, Halal businesses can build lasting relationships with their target audience and create a strong brand identity in the market.

4.5 Mobile Marketing Strategy

Mobile marketing strategies, such as mobile applications and mobile-optimized websites, enable businesses to reach their customers on their mobile devices. According to M. H.businesses can leverage mobile applications to offer their customers convenient access to their products and services.

Mobile marketing involves using mobile devices to reach and engage with customers through mobile apps, mobile websites, and SMS marketing.

Mobile marketing can help Halal businesses reach their customers through mobile devices, such as smartphones and tablets. For example, Halal businesses can use mobile apps to offer exclusive discounts, promotions, and loyalty programs to their customers.

When it comes to mobile marketing strategies for Halal businesses, there are several key factors to consider. Here are some tips to help you develop an effective mobile marketing plan:

1. Understand Your Audience: The first step in any marketing strategy is to understand your target audience. In the case of Halal businesses, this means understanding the needs and preferences of Muslim consumers. Take the time to research the habits and behaviours of your target audience, including their mobile device usage, social media habits, and preferred modes of communication.
2. Create a Mobile-Friendly Website: Your website is the centrepiece of your mobile marketing strategy. Ensure that your website is mobile-friendly and optimized for mobile devices. This means using responsive design, optimizing images for mobile, and minimizing load times.
3. Leverage Social Media: Social media is an essential tool for mobile marketing. Use platforms like Facebook, Instagram, and Twitter to reach your target audience and engage with them. Consider running paid social media ads to increase visibility and drive traffic to your website.
4. Offer Mobile Coupons and Deals: Offering mobile coupons and deals is an effective way to drive traffic to your business. Consider partnering with mobile coupon platforms like Groupon or offering exclusive deals to customers who opt into your mobile marketing program.
5. Use SMS Marketing: SMS marketing is a highly effective way to reach customers directly on their mobile devices. Use SMS to send targeted messages, reminders, and promotions to your customers.
6. Monitor Your Results: It's essential to track your mobile marketing campaigns to see what's working and what's not. Use analytics tools to monitor traffic, engagement, and conversions. Adjust your strategy as needed based on your results.

By following these tips, you can create an effective mobile marketing strategy that will help you reach and engage with your target audience. Remember to stay up to date with the latest mobile marketing trends and best practices to ensure that your strategy remains effective over time.

4.6 *Programmatic Marketing Strategy*

Programmatic advertising tactics enable businesses to reach their target audience by using artificial intelligence and machine learning algorithms. According to Muhammad Naeem et al. (2019), programmatic advertising tactics can help businesses reach their target audience more effectively and efficiently. Programmatic marketing involves using algorithms and automation to deliver targeted and relevant ads to customers across multiple channels.

Programmatic marketing uses AI and machine learning to deliver personalized ads to customers based on their behaviour, interests, and preferences. Halal businesses can use programmatic marketing to target specific customer segments and deliver relevant messages that resonate with their needs.

Programmatic marketing can be an effective way for Halal businesses to reach their target audience and promote their products or services. Here are some steps to develop a programmatic marketing strategy for Halal businesses:

1. Identify your target audience: Determine who your potential customers are, what they need, and how they behave online. You can use demographic and psychographic data to create audience segments based on factors such as age, gender, income, interests, and behaviours.
2. Develop a creative strategy: Create compelling ad creatives that speak to your target audience and align with your brand messaging. Highlight the Halal aspects of your products or services, and emphasize the quality and benefits of your offerings.
3. Choose programmatic channels: Select the programmatic channels that best suit your marketing goals and target audience. Consider platforms such as Google Ads, Facebook Ads, Instagram Ads, and LinkedIn Ads.
4. Set campaign objectives: Define clear objectives for your programmatic campaigns, such as increasing website traffic, generating leads, or driving conversions. Make sure your objectives align with your overall business goals.
5. Use data to optimize campaigns: Monitor your programmatic campaigns closely and use data to optimize your targeting, creatives, and bidding strategies. Use A/B testing to compare different ad variations and refine your approach.
6. Measure and analyse results: Use analytics tools to measure the success of your programmatic campaigns and identify areas for improvement. Monitor key performance indicators such as click-through rates, conversion rates, and return on ad spend.

By following these steps, Halal businesses can develop an effective programmatic marketing strategy that helps them reach their target audience and achieve their business objectives.

4.7 *Video Marketing Strategy*

Video marketing involves using video content to tell engaging stories, showcase products, and provide valuable information to customers.

Video marketing can help Halal businesses tell their brand story and showcase their products or services in a visually compelling way. Videos can be shared on social media platforms, e-commerce websites, and other digital channels to reach a wider audience and generate more engagement.

Video marketing can be an effective way for Halal businesses to reach their target audience and promote their products or services. Here are some tips to consider when creating a video marketing strategy for your Halal business:

1. Understand your target audience: Before creating any video content, it's important to understand who your target audience is and what their interests and preferences are. This will help you tailor your video content to resonate with your audience and create content that they will find engaging and relevant.
2. Highlight your Halal certification: One of the key selling points for Halal businesses is their Halal certification. Make sure to prominently display your certification in your video content and emphasize how important it is to your business.
3. Showcase your products or services: Use video content to showcase your products or services in action. Show how they are made, highlight their unique features, and demonstrate how they can benefit your customers.
4. Use storytelling: People love stories, so use storytelling techniques to make your video content more engaging and memorable. Tell the story of your business, share customer success stories, or create a video series that takes your audience on a journey.
5. Use social media platforms: Social media platforms like Instagram, Facebook, and YouTube are great places to share your video content and reach a wider audience. Use hashtags and tags to increase your reach and engage with your audience.
6. Collaborate with influencers: Collaborating with influencers in the Halal community can be a great way to reach new customers and build brand awareness. Identify influencers that align with your brand values and collaborate on content that showcases your products or services.
7. Keep it professional: Make sure your video content looks and sounds professional. Poor quality videos can detract from your brand image and turn off potential customers.

By following these tips, Halal businesses can create effective video marketing strategies that help them reach their target audience and grow their business.

5 Discussion

Halal entrepreneurs can adopt various innovative marketing strategies to succeed in the Halal industry. These strategies include creating compelling brand stories, leveraging social media platforms, collaborating with influencers, and creating experiential marketing campaigns (Khan, 2019). It is important to note that Halal entrepreneurs need to consider local culture and trends when developing marketing strategies. Additionally, Halal entrepreneurs should consider the preferences and needs of their target audience, such as product packaging and labelling, to appeal to their customers effectively.

Mobile, programmatic, and video marketing strategies are also essential strategies for businesses to reach their target audience and communicate the value of their products or services.

Halal entrepreneurs should focus on building relationships with customers and engaging with them through social media platforms. Additionally, halal entrepreneurs need to create a unique brand identity that reflects their values and beliefs. By doing so, they can differentiate themselves from their competitors and create a loyal customer base.

6 Conclusion

In conclusion, the Halal industry is rapidly growing, and Halal entrepreneurs must adopt innovative marketing strategies to stay competitive in the market. Halal businesses need to prepare for innovation and technology, build scalable, digitally enabled business models, develop marketing strategies that resemble a customer's preferences, and adopt products or services built on certain strategies to stay competitive in the market.

Innovation and technology are critical factors in the success of businesses offering Halal products or services. To prepare for innovation and technology, businesses must invest in research and development, stay up-to-date with the latest trends and technologies, and be open to experimentation. To build scalable, digitally enabled business models, businesses need to adopt a customer-centric approach, embrace agile methodologies, and use data analytics to inform decision-making. Hence, to promote Halal offerings, products or services, businesses need to adopt marketing strategies that leverage mobile, programmatic, and video marketing to create engaging and personalized customer experiences.

Other effective marketing strategies, such as digital marketing, social media marketing, influencer marketing, and experiential marketing, can help Halal entrepreneurs to increase brand awareness, engage with their target audience, and achieve business growth. By embracing these strategies, Halal businesses can improve their customer reach, increase sales, and build brand loyalty. Additionally, halal entrepreneurs need to consider local culture and trends when developing marketing strategies.

Halal entrepreneurs should prioritize investment in digital marketing, social media marketing, influencer marketing, and experiential marketing to remain competitive in the market. Furthermore, mobile, programmatic, and video marketing tactics are also essential for businesses to reach their target audience and communicate the value of their products or services.

Additionally, they should consider the preferences and needs of their target audience, such as product packaging and labelling, to appeal to their customers effectively. They should also consider partnering with influencers who share similar values and beliefs. Moreover, halal entrepreneurs should create a unique brand identity that reflects their values and beliefs.

References

Ab Aziz, A., & Woods, P.C. (2023). Digital customer experiences: A multiple case study approach of Malaysia financial institutions. *International Journal of Marketing, Communication and New Media, 14*(13).

Ab Rahman, S., & Ibrahim, H. (2019). A conceptual framework of halal tourism destination marketing. *Journal of Islamic Marketing, 10*(4), 1070–1090.

Ali, A., & HadžiMuhamedović, M. (2020). Halal marketing strategies: A review of literature. *Journal of Economics, Business and Management, 8*(1), 34–40.

Hassan, R., & Anuar, A. R. (2020). The role of influencer marketing in promoting halal tourism. *International Journal of Academic Research in Business and Social Sciences, 10*(10), 1917–1928.

Islam, J. U. l., Ahmad R. R., & Hollebeek, L. D. (2019). Tourism-based customer engagement: The construct, antecedents, and consequences. *The Service Industries Journal, 39*(7–8), 519–540.

Khalid, S., & Waqas, A. (2018). The impact of social media marketing on halal tourism industry: The Malaysian perspective. *Journal of Islamic Marketing, 9*(2), 512–532.

Khan, M. A. (2019). Marketing strategies for the Halal industry: A review. *Journal of Islamic Marketing, 10*(4), 1163–1178.

Kusumo, A. R., & Sugiarto, H. (2020). Innovative marketing strategies for halal cosmetic products: A study of muslim millennials in Indonesia. *Journal of Halal Industry and Services, 3*(2), 32–44.

Rahimi, R., & Nawi, N. M. (2019). Developing an experiential marketing framework for Halal tourism. *Journal of Halal Industry and Services, 2*(1), 23–36.

Sabri, M. F., Nordin, N., & Abdullah, S. S. (2019). Exploring the role of social

Tahir, I. M., & Amin, S. H. M. (2020). E-marketing strategies of halal cosmetic entrepreneurs in Malaysia

Thomson Reuters. (2018). State of the Global Islamic Economy Report 2018/19

References

Green Marketing as an Ethical Practice for Halal Entrepreneurs for a Sustainable Ecosystem

Monsuru Adekunle Salisu, Rafiu K. Showole, and Tijani Usman Moyosore

Abstract The negative impacts of human activities on the environment have been generating considerable amounts of concern for several decades. Today, governments all over the world are making efforts to minimize human impacts on the environment. Understanding society's new concerns, businesses have begun to modify their behaviours while integrating environmental issues into organizational activities. This has led to the emergence of green marketing strategy which entails minimizing environmental pollution at all stages involved in the life cycle of products. It is essentially a market branding targeted at capturing the market by appealing to people's desire to choose products and services that are better for the environment. Likewise, the Halal industry is witnessing unprecedented growth across the world and beyond religion barriers due to its pure, sustainable and ethical credentials or basis. The term 'halal' which means permissible or lawful and its compliment 'toyyiban', fundamentally implies production and consumption activities that are wholesome, of quality, healthy, green or environmentally sustainable. This strongly establishes the position that green production and green marketing had ever been inherent and integral parts of the Halal industry. Literatures have established that implementation of green marketing concept in the supply chain of the halal industry influences positive economic, environmental, and social impacts. Hence, this chapter examines the inherent relationship between Halal entrepreneurship and green marketing. It also explores how halal entrepreneurs can adopt best marketing strategies to project their green credential as a unique leverage and competitiveness of halalpreneurship.

M. A. Salisu (✉)
Faculty of Technical and Vocational, Sultan Idris Education University, 35900, Tanjung Malim, Perak, Malaysia
e-mail: salisuadekunle@upsi.edu.my

R. K. Showole
International Institute for Halal Research and Training (INHART), International Islamic University (IIUM), Kuala Lumpur, Malaysia
e-mail: showole.rk@live.iium.edu.my

T. U. Moyosore
Lagos State University, Lagos, Nigeria
e-mail: usman.tijani@lasu.edu.ng

L. Raimi et al. (eds.), *Contemporary Discourse of Halal and Islamic Entrepreneurship*,
https://doi.org/10.1007/978-981-99-6427-7_16

Keywords Green marketing · Halal entrepreneurs · Halalan-toyyiban

1 Introduction

The word "Halal" is an Arabic and Quranic word which is related to the Islamic lifestyle whereas it literally means permissible or lawful. Additionally, meanings and application of the concept of Halal preclude the concept of "Toyyib" as well. This is because, in several places in the Quran (e.g. 2:168, 5:88, 8:69, 16:114), human beings are instructed to consume what is halal and toyyib. The meaning of toyyib can be translated as pure, good, quality, healthy, and sustainable (Mustaffa 2019). Hence, the association of the toyyib aspect broadens the meaning and implication of halal economy. Therefore, halal means not only what is permissible or lawful in Islam but also what is good and sustainable. The opposite of halal is haram which means prohibited. In the Quran, Allah (SWT) has also prescribed what is prohibited and what to avoid in consumption as well as in human conduct of Muslims and the whole ummah. For example, consuming alcohol and pork is prohibited in Islam. Likewise, gambling, pornography, riba (usury), hoarding goods, deceiving customers, etc. are also prohibited. Hence, in defining Halalpreneurship all three concepts namely halal, tayyib, and haram must be considered. "Halalpreneurship" are Halal businesses that didn't negate any of the principles of Islam. They are the businesses that are in line with Quran and Sunnah of the Prophet Muhammad (S.A.W). They are not haram businesses i.e. typical businesses that are prohibited by the Quran and Sunnah of the Prophet) such as those involved pork, alcohol, gambling, interests (usury) and their derivatives.

Halal production, services and consumptions implicitly apply to every conduct of human life such as social, personal, economic, cultural, or political matters. From an economic perspective, the term has been used to denote the Islamic economy driven by the Halal industry. For instance, the Malaysian Standard (MS) for regulations of Halal certifications, products and services provides an elaborated definition with all the requirements for Halal products and services across nine industries or sectors. Also, Halal industry has been witnessing unprecedented growth and acceptance amongst consumers across the globe irrespective of religion or race. This is not unconnected with its pure, sustainability and green appeals to consumers. Also, it is uncontestable that green production and green marketing have been inherent and integral parts of Halal production since centuries ago. Hence, Halal products have gained credibility worldwide as wholesome, of higher quality, and linked to environmentally friendly practices, fair trade, and animal welfare (Islamic Services of America, ISA, 2021). This explains why many consumers in North America, Europe and Malaysia (regardless of their religion) patronize Halal products.

Section one of this chapter will review relevant literature and discuss sub-topics that are related to Halal and green marketing. Sections 2.1–2.7 will examine: Islam and business ethics; Islam and environment; Sustainable Development Goals (SDGs), entrepreneurship and sustainable environmental practices; supply chain management in Halal business and green practices; sustainable Halal green marketing; consumers' concerns about green products; and discussion of what matters arising between profit, sustainability and green marketing. Conclusion of this chapter will be presented in Sect. 3.

2 Literature Review

2.1 *Islam and Business Ethics*

Religious beliefs and practices of a group of people do have a great influence on all their social and economic behaviours and approaches to issues. People do have heritage, culture and religious beliefs which dictate how they carry out their day-to-day activities or transactions. Ethics refer to standards of behaviour which indicate how individuals ought to behave in the society or group that they find themselves. This point has been argued by Josephson (1989) who defined the concept of ethics as a "system or code of conduct based on universal moral duties and obligations which indicate how one should behave; it deals with the ability to distinguish good from evil, right from wrong and propriety from impropriety" (p. 2). Belt (2002) notes that the term Islam itself is a word that means submission to God—Allah, with its roots in the Arabic word "salam" which means peace. Islam is a religion of peace that professes Allah as the only God to be worshipped. According to the Muslim faith, submission to God implies that all actions undertaken by Muslims are acts of worship and hence should be guided by the Islamic ethics, values, and principles which are dictated by Islamic jurisprudence (Shariah). Thus eating, drinking, socializing, buying, selling, promoting, manufacturing, education and so on have to comply with God's rules (Alhersan 2011, p. 5).

In business, there are different people to be responded to such as customers, shareholders, clients, suppliers and government amongst others. Business ethics refers to the moral rules and regulations governing the business world. In other words, they are the moral values that guide the way corporations or other business makes decisions. Therefore, Islam and business ethics have a direct relationship with each other because they both deal with what guide the behaviour of people in society and what shows the people what is good and bad. Though ethics is not only about religion, and of course not the same as morality, there appear to be interlinkages and relationships between these concepts.

2.2 *Islam and Environment*

It has been identified by scholars that a good understanding of the interaction between human and ecological or environmental systems requires a better knowledge of the religious dimensions involved (Jenkins & Chapple, 2011). Likewise, it has often been observed that Islam cannot ordinarily be described as a mere religion because it prescribes a way of life that goes beyond the performance of rituals. Islam views the protection of the environment and natural ecosystem as a fundamental part of faith because they are the perfect creation of Allah—the sole Creator and Sustainer of the universe (Aung, 2016). In different parts of the Qur'an Allah calls the attention of mankind to the significance of the environment and their responsibilities towards the ecosystem:

> "… He has created everything, ordaining it precisely.". (Qur'an 25:2)

> "Surely in the creation of the heavens and the earth are signs for the believers. And in your own creation, and whatever living beings He dispersed, are signs for people of sure faith. And in the alternation of the day and the night, the provision sent down from the skies by Allah—reviving the earth after its death—and the shifting of the winds, are signs for people of understanding." (Quran 45:3–5).

> "It is He who made the sun a shining light and the moon a derived light and determined for it phases—that you may know the number of years and account [of time]. Allāh has not created this except in truth. He details the signs for a people who know." (Quran 10:5).

Also, as vicegerents or trustees of Allah on earth, it is a major responsibility of human beings to protect and preserve the environment. This Islamic worldview is predicated on Maqaasid Shariah—the goals and objectives of Islamic law which are: protection of faith; protection and preservation of life; protection of intellects; protection of lineage (offspring) and protection of prosperity (Aung, 2016). The essence of Shariah is for both individual and communal benefits (Maslaha) hence its laws are designed to protect and facilitate the improvement and perfection of the conditions of human life on earth (Kamali, 2019).

In general term environment is defined as the immediate surroundings of people while business environment are the uncontrollable factors that affect an organization either internally or externally. Business internal environment constituted by players such as employees, machineries, and board of directors affects the organization internally while its external environment cannot be controlled directly by the organization as it affects all businesses in general. External environments can be classified further into micro and macro environments. Micro environment involves customers, suppliers and competitors while macro environments are the political, socio-cultural, economic and ecological environment. Religion environment is one of the factors that affect an organization externally.

2.3 *Sustainable Development Goals (SDGs), Entrepreneurship and Sustainable Environmental Practices*

The United Nations adopted 17 Sustainable Development Goals (SDGs) in 2015 as a universal call to action to end poverty, protect the planet, and ensure that by

2030 all people enjoy peace and prosperity. The global goals are: no poverty; zero hunger; good health and well-being; quality education; gender equality; clean water and sanitation; affordable and clean energy; decent work and economic growth; industry, innovation and infrastructure; reduced inequalities; sustainable cities and communities; responsible consumption and production; climate action; life below water; life on land; peace, justice, and strong institutions; and partnership for the goals. These integrated global goals are premised on the consensus that action in one area will affect outcomes in others, and that development must balance social, economic and environmental sustainability.

Though environmental sustainability is a value-laden concept in which the importance of its different aspects is perceived differently, the concept generally has three components namely environmental, social and economic (Velenturf & Purnell, 2021). Environmental sustainability can be defined as a balance condition where the needs of human society are satisfied without diminishing biological diversity or exceeding the capacity of supporting ecosystems to continue to sustain itself and the human society (Morelli 2011). It entails achieving current development without compromising the ability of future generations to meet their own needs (Barkemeyer et al. 2014). Some view sustainable development as a "process of change in which resource exploitation, technology development, investment, and institutional change are consistent with future and present needs" (Velenturf & Purnell, 2021).

Achieving sustainable development is crucial, especially at this challenging time when every economy of the world is struggling to recover from COVID-19 pandemic economic shocks. The world is faced with challenges of maintaining a balance between reducing the adverse impacts of high production of fossil fuel on the depletion of the environment and achieving economic growth and development. Continuous environmental degradation like floods, depletion of ozone layers, air pollution, destruction of marine lives due to water pollution etc. have been largely attributed to entrepreneurial activities. Also, it has been realized that it is no longer viable to continue with the same environmentally unsustainable patterns of production, energy and goods consumption. Hence, a paradigm shift from the prevailing systems to ones that will bring inclusive, environmentally friendly, long-term sustainable development is imperatively required.

Hence, green marketing fosters green industry where in their supply chain priority is given to efficiency in the use of resources such as non-fossil electrical energy, efficient use of water, raw materials and use of environmentally friendly substitutes. According to Chen and Chen (2020), It is a broad range of marketing activities (planning, process, production, promotion and people) directed to all consumers and demonstrating the firm's goal of minimizing the environmental impact of its products and services (Martins, 2022). Green marketing indicates that a manufacturer's products are safe, in compliance with environmental protection standards, and energy efficient and its packaging materials are recyclable, reusable, and decomposable (Chen & Chen 2020). Products that are harmful to living organism or linked to immoral experiments with animal or humans and consumes a lot of renewable energy are avoided by green customers (Nekmahmud & Fekete-Farkas, 2020). Also, the resulting waste must be processed further while air and noise pollution also need to be minimized to prevent damage to the green ecosystem. Plant and animal habitations in industrial areas will also be preserved while human populations in residential areas close to industries are not disturbed.

Likewise, environmental impact is a crucial consideration in all stages involved in the production of Halal goods. Efficient use of resources, waste management, animal non-cruelty methods etc. in raw materials processing, logistics and distribution or from farm to fork are important halal requirements and standards. This a reflection of both Halal and toyyiban with the latter largely representing green or environmentally friendly production and consumption. These green and wholesome credentials are major catalysts of growth in the Halal industry across countries and breaking religion barriers. Consumers across the globe view Halal products as pure, of higher quality, linked to environmentally friendly practices, fair trade, and animal welfare (Islamic Services of America, ISA, 2021).

However, the impact of entrepreneurship on environmental sustainability is undoubtedly significant to economic and social development. The global slow economic growth and development, social inequality and environmental degradation are still creating unprecedented challenges for the international community. As earlier established, Halal entrepreneurship is fundamentally based on protection and preservations of life and environments while satisfying human needs and consumptions. Thus, a well-integrated green marketing and Halal entrepreneurship will promote sustainable production and responsible consumption. These will facilitate speedy achievement of the SDGs goals given that most of the goals are directly or indirectly related to the impacts of economic production on the environment and sustainable development.

2.4 Supply Chain Management in Halal Business and Green Practices

Researchers' interest in the symbiotic link between green practices (GPs) and supply chain performance has grown recently (Rao et al. 2005). According to Mentzer et al. (2001), the ability of supply chain participants to use their available resources, skills, and knowledge to apply green practices is substantially connected with the power of those participants to achieve sustainable business performance while satisfying customer needs. Additionally, supply chain management (SCM) is a key element in evaluating the performance of the company (Kirchoff et al. 2016). Additionally, it is emphasised that the degree of cooperation between supply chain partners directly correlates with the success of SCM (Talib et al. 2015). These eco-friendly business practices are crucial for a company's consistently producing high-quality goods as mandated by Islamic law (Shariah).

Companies have adopted Halal-compliant business practices in response to the rising demand for Halal-certified products (Abdul Rahman et al. 2013). The profitable global Halal market also allows businesses to enter a booming market sector

(Muhamed et al. 2020). The value of the worldwide Halal market is projected to be USD 1.292 billion in 2016 and USD 2.537 billion by 2019 (Zailani et al. 2017). However, it is emphasised that the majority of Halal businesses are small and medium-sized enterprises (SMEs), which lack resources such as money, expertise, and knowledge to enhance supply chain performance (Ali & Suleiman 2016; Muhamed et al. 2020; Kirchoff et al. 2016). Halal SMEs must follow GP's strategic practice to ensure their competitiveness in the emerging Halal market. A Halal business must employ this strategy to focus on its core competencies and readily available resources. As a result, GP is one of the potential methods that could aid a company in adhering to environmental and Shariah requirements. To make the entire Halal food SC more environmentally friendly and to preserve a competitive edge, GP must be integrated (Ortas et al. 2014; Salim et al. 2020). To maintain the product's quality and Halalness, Rejeb et al. (2021) emphasised the importance of incorporating environmental factors into SCM, such as Halal SCM, including product design, material sourcing and selection, manufacturing processes, and delivery of the final product. Azevedo et al. (2011) assert that all food SC activities, including procurement, manufacturing, and logistics, should fall under the purview of GP. The literature describes several operational green practices, including green Halal production and green halal suppliers (Ali et al. 2017; Ali & Suleiman 2016).

Green Halal logistics is another practice mentioned in the study (Haleem et al. 2021). Any activity taken across the Halal SC (into the focus firm and incorporating relationships with partners upstream and downstream) to remove or mitigate any adverse environmental impact while preserving the product's Halal certification is referred to in this document as a "green practice." As a result, the GP can be recognised at the strategic, tactical, or operational level and may be connected to the method used to provide food, the product itself, the distribution method, or cutting-edge, inventive actions. To make the entire Halal food SC more environmentally friendly and to preserve a competitive edge, GP must be integrated (Ortas et al. 2014; Salim et al. 2020). To maintain the product's quality and Halalness, Rejeb et al. (2021) emphasised the importance of incorporating environmental factors into SCM, such as Halal SCM, including product design, material sourcing and selection, manufacturing processes, and delivery of the final product Azevedo et al. (2011) assert that all food SC activities, including procurement, manufacturing, and logistics, should fall under the purview of GP. The literature describes several operational green practices, including green Halal production and suppliers (Ali et al. 2017; Ali & Suleiman 2016). Moreover, the principle of "Akhirah," or the afterlife, can be applied to green practices by promoting products and practices that are sustainable and environmentally friendly in the long term. Businesses can promote sustainable practices that will benefit future generations, such as reducing waste and promoting renewable energy sources. The combination of Islamic Marketing Ethics and green marketing can promote ethical and sustainable practices in marketing strategies. By promoting Halal, Tawheed, Adl, and Akhirah principles, businesses can ensure that their products and practices are environmentally friendly, socially just, and sustainable in the long term Chahal and Sharma (2018).

2.5 Sustainable Halal Green Marketing

Achievement of sustainable green marketing in the Halal industry beyond concepts and ideas has become more critical. This is given the significant attention that green marketing has been receiving due to the increase in green consumerism (Mukonza et al., 2021). The monumental need to keep the consumers in the fold as well as our natural environment safe has been a challenge in the modern era of globalization (Sarkar, 2012). Also, green awareness has created a highly competitive business environment by transforming consumers, increasing pressures on companies as well as other business stakeholders to be more sensitive to products' carbon footprints, environmental protections and sustainability (Ali et al., 2021; Nekmahmud & Fekete-Farkas, 2020; Siba Borah & Korankye, 2022; Yusiana et al., 2020). Moreover, Halal businesses can't afford to be passive or inactive in sustainable green marketing leadership because this constitutes their core concept, fundamental domains and business niches. This becomes more essential because the Halal sector serves the largely untapped and fastest-growing faith-based consumer group in the world (Izberk-bilgin & Nakata, 2016).

According to Manzaneque-Lizano et al. (2019), sustainability performance of a business refers to the capability of an organization to generate sustainable wealth over time and continue its activities indefinitely. It is the ability to meet the needs and expectations of the organisation's customers and other stakeholders in the long term, balanced by an effective and quality management systems (Stanciu et al., 2014). The role of stakeholders in a firm sustainability performance is very crucial (Manzaneque-Lizano et al., 2019). Hence, it can be concluded that sustainable green marketing as a business performance metric is the capability of a business to achieve long-term needs, expectations and goals of the customers, the business and other stakeholders while maintaining its green marketing strategy.

Sustainable green marketing in Halal production can be achieved through integration of Halal marketing mix with well-established marketing strategy perspectives such as segmentation, targeting and positioning (STP) and the 4Ps of the marketing mix. Two fundamental principles of halal marketing activity are: abiding by injunctions and ethics stipulated by Allah SWT; and a considerate concern for Allah's creatures which includes everything in the environment (Zainuddin, 2021). Islam captivates all the 4Ps of marketing mix: Product, Price, Place and Promotion in addition to 3Ps of halal marketing mix namely process, physical environment and people (Abdullah et al., 2022). As the basis of all marketing strategies STP process is one of the most important frameworks used in the marketing strategy (Lynn, 2012; Shah et al., 2020). It is based on the identification of viable consumer segments (Segmentation) so as to engage them in mutually beneficial ways by directing marketing activities at the segment (Targeting) and positioning the offerings (Positioning) (El-bassiouny, 2014; Shah et al., 2020).

It has been established that religion is one of the factors that shape consumers' decision and these are explored in adopting marketing strategy (Shah et al., 2020). Three variables of consumers' market segmentation namely, background customer characteristics, customer attitudes and customer behaviour (Shah et al., 2020) distinguish Muslim consumers market. Muslim population is currently the second-largest religious group in the world with an increase of 12.9% of total trade between 2019 and 2021 by Organisation of Islamic Cooperation (OIC) countries (ICDT-OIC, 2022). According to Shah et al. (2020), there is a rising visibility of Muslims as a consumer segment which is closely linked to their purchasing power. This is supported by the rise of middle-class Muslims who share common interests despite their diverse geographical spread (Shah et al., 2020). Appealing to the Muslim consumer sector has become the target of foresighted and dynamic multinational consumer companies in their marketing strategies (Izberk-bilgin & Nakata, 2016). These factors make Muslim consumer markets fulfilling measurability and substantiality which are two important conditions of segmentation hence making it economically viable (Shah et al., 2020). As a segmentation strategy, it is also required that Halal green market be separated from the rest of the market to enable firm to target them with a different market offering (Shah et al., 2020).

Positioning refers to capturing a place in the minds of consumers ahead of the competitors by emphasising attributes of a chosen product to differentiate their products from competitors (Shah et al., 2020). Halal firms need to embark on vigorous marketing strategies that constantly remind Muslims that: keeping the environment green and safe is a religious duty; and entrench in the minds of non-Muslims the image of the halal product as a global symbol of wholesomeness, quality assurance, healthy consumption and green production (Okdinawati et al., 2021; Shah et al., 2020). While product positioning is important, foremost is the credibility positioning of halal entrepreneurs through transparency, integrity and honesty as exemplified by the Prophet (S.A.W) as a successful entrepreneur of all time (Abdullah et al., 2022; Zainuddin, 2021). Also, the Prophet (S.A.W) adopted the following method of product differentiation: declared the weak points of products and disliked the practice of hiding them; and he instructed traders not to mix different qualities of the same product but separate them (Abdullah et al., 2022; Zainuddin, 2021). Halal marketing requires that product marketing must be carried out ethically, with fairness to other competitors and without falsification (Abdullah et al., 2022).

2.6 *Consumer's Concerns About Green Products*

Understanding consumer behaviour is vital in marketing while prioritising personal and psychological characteristics of customers is essential for entrepreneurs (Abdullah et al., 2022). Equipped with knowledge of how earth resources are gradually depleting, some consumers are giving close attention to products that do not harm the environment and mitigate its effects on health (Nekmahmud & Fekete-Farkas, 2020; Siba Borah & Korankye, 2022). This vital emerging force behind green marketing is called green consumers (Nekmahmud & Fekete-Farkas, 2020) and their behaviour undoubtedly plays an important role in achieving a greener marketplace (Brouwer, 2016).

However, this group of consumers despite their keen interest in green products are not without their concerns which have led to some scepticism, criticism and confusion (Bonini & Oppenheim, 2008; Brouwer, 2016; Urbański & Ul Haque, 2020). Major concerns of green consumers are greenwashing vs green quality and green pricing of green products (Nekmahmud & Fekete-Farkas, 2020; Urbański & Ul Haque, 2020). Empirical findings reveal that these concerns have strong influences on consumers' green purchase decisions (Nekmahmud & Fekete-Farkas, 2020).

I. **Greenwashing and Green quality**

Due to increased attention to global warming and its environmental effects, businesses need to adopt procedures and strategies that demonstrate their green philosophies (Urbański & Ul Haque, 2020). According to the authors, successfully proven green strategies such as labelling products as recyclable or environmentally friendly, physical green packaging and green advertisements are being used to attract customers. However, not all the environmental claims are real but some are misleading strategies known as greenwashing. Examples are some inherently non-environmentally friendly claims such as nonhybrid cars, plastic bottles, and airline flights. According to Lee et al. (2018), consumers often use the intrinsic green attributes of a product to conclude on its quality but may be motivated by their perception of its price to scrutinize further. If it is perceived that the quality of the product has been compromised or only a fraction of the attributes are green whereby the whole are promoted as green products (i.e. greenwashed products), the consumers' willingness to buy a green product decreases (Lee et al., 2018).

II. **Green pricing**

According to Nekmahmud and Fekete-Farkas (2020), green pricing means setting green product prices that balance consumers' price sensitivity and their interest in paying more for environmental safety. Studies have shown that price is a strategic hindrance to consumers from purchasing green products hence they are not ready to pay a premium without scrutinizing their cost–benefit compared to alternatives (Ansu-Mensah, 2021; Lee et al., 2018; Nekmahmud & Fekete-Farkas, 2020). Thus, if consumers conclude that green products are usually priced too high this may constitute a barrier to environmental buying (Hasan et al., 2018).

The perception that green products are significantly expensive may give some insights into the demographic nature or economic status of an average green consumer. According to Witek and Ku (2021), some studies show that high income earners show greater concerns for the environment and buy more green products than low-income earners. However, he pointed out that others argue that income impacts only on the quantity of green products bought, and not on overall readiness to purchase. Also, the effect of price on consumers' buying decisions may vary and be dictated by their perceptions of the product's value rather than the actual price of the products (Nya et al., 2019).

2.7 Between Profit, Sustainability and Green Marketing

Profitability as one of the key metrics of the financial performance of a firm as well as its business sustainable performance also serves as a balance between the firm objectives and environmental concerns (Martins, 2022). While some studies have found positive relationships others have reported insignificant or mixed results between firms' green efforts and their financial performance. Also, it has been argued that due to the difficulty in measuring green practice and the different measures used, determining the direct relationship between green practice and profit will likely come with biases according to Martins (2022). Furthermore, green production is beneficial to both financial and non-financial performance (Ali et al., 2021; Martins, 2022; Wong et al., 2020).

However, from Halal entrepreneurship perspective primary motive of engaging in Halal business is not limited to financial rewards but extends to other non-financial and vital motivations. According to Abdullah et al. (2022) applying the concept of halal, green marketing should be considered for the following reasons:

I. It is an opportunity from Allah to act as His vicegerent on earth
II. a desire to actualise one's idea and fulfil professional or career ambition
III. Motivation to earn Allah's blessings (Barakah) and success (Al-Falah)
IV. service to the ummah (Muslim community) and humanity in general
V. financial gains and success
VI. A desire to be independent

Some of the benefits of green marketing accrued to a firm include: image improvement before stakeholders through their positive social performance impacts; sustainable long-term growth; improved and positive firm sustainability performance through adoption of manufacturing practices that reduce carbon dioxide emissions, wastes, and pollutants and energy consumption; operational benefits of cost reduction, improved production flexibility, accelerated product delivery, and improved product quality (Ali et al., 2021; Nekmahmud & Fekete-Farkas, 2020).

3 Conclusion

Sustainable green marketing requires Halal firms to maintain their inherently green tradition and niche over the long term while meeting the needs, expectations and goals of consumers and other stakeholders. To achieve this, Halal businesses have to fully explore the potentials of the fast-growing Muslim consumer markets through the integration of the Halal marketing mix with the strategic market concepts of segmentation, targeting and positioning (STP) and the popular 4Ps marketing mix. This will establish the credibility of halal marketing and the inextricable links between halal products and green marketing. Therefore, the image of halal green products will be well positioned in the minds of consumers, their patronages will increase and consequently, sustainable green marketing in halal production will be achieved.

References

Abdullah, M. A., Elgharbawy, A. A. M., & Azam, M. S. E. (2022). *Halal entrepreneurship* (First Edit). International Intitute of Islamic Thought East & Southeast Asia Office, IIUM Malaysia.

Ali, H., Chen, T., & Hao, Y. (2021). Sustainable manufacturing practices, competitive capabilities, and sustainable performance: moderating role of environmental regulations. *Sustainability (Switzerland), 13*(18). https://doi.org/10.3390/su131810051.

Ansu-Mensah, P. (2021). Green product awareness effect on green purchase intentions of university students': An emerging market's perspective. *Future Business Journal, 7*(1), 1–13. https://doi.org/10.1186/s43093-021-00094-5

Aung, T. S. (2016). Islam and environmental protection: The awareness of the Malaysian muslim community. *Al-Shajarah, 21*(2), 225–244.

Bonini, S., & Oppenheim, J. (2008). Cultivating the green consumer. *Stanford Social Innovation Review, 6*(4), 56–61. http://search.ebscohost.com/login.aspx?direct=true&db=bth&AN=34705924&site=ehost-live.

Brouwer, A. (2016). *Revealing greenwashing: A consumers ' perspective* (pp. 245–252).

El-bassiouny, N. (2014). The one-billion-plus marginalization: Toward a scholarly understanding of Islamic consumers ☆. *Journal of Business Research, 67*(2), 42–49. https://doi.org/10.1016/j.jbusres.2013.03.010

Hasan, A., Irfan, R., Shaari, Z. H., & Sharif, A. M. (2018). *Consumers ' perception o f barriers effecting green purchase behavior: Instrument assessment. 02008.*

ICDT-OIC. (2022). *Annual report on trade among The OIC member states* (Vol. 3, Issue 1). www.icdt-oic.org, https://doi.org/10.47575/jpkm.v3i1.297.

Islamic Service of America. (2021, April). Pure and good. The Halal and green consumer. Islamic Services of America. https://www.isahalal.com/news-events/blog/pure-and-good-halal-and-green-consumer

Izberk-bilgin, E., & Nakata, C. C. (2016). A new look at faith-based marketing: The global halal market. *Business Horizons*. https://doi.org/10.1016/j.bushor.2016.01.005

Jenkins, W., & Chapple, C. K. (2011). Religion and environment. *Annual Review of Environment and Resources, 36*, 441–463. https://doi.org/10.1146/annurev-environ-042610-103728

Kamali, M. H. (2019). Maqāṣid Al-Sharīᶜah made simple. *Maqasid Al-Shariah Made Simple*, 1–24. https://doi.org/10.2307/j.ctvkc67vz.4.

Lee, J., Bhatt, S., & Suri, R. (2018). When consumers penalize not so green products. *Psychology and Marketing, 35*(1), 36–46. https://doi.org/10.1002/mar.21069

Lynn, M. (2012). *Segmenting and targeting your markets: Strategies and limitations.*

Manzaneque-Lizano, M., Alfaro-Cortés, E., & de la Cruz, A. M. P. (2019). Stakeholders and long-term sustainability of SMEs. Who really matters in crisis contexts, and when. *Sustainability (Switzerland), 11*(23), 1–27. https://doi.org/10.3390/su11236551.

Martins, A. (2022). Green marketing and perceived SME profitability: The meditating effect of green purchase behaviour. *Management of Environmental Quality: An International Journal, 33*(2), 281–299. https://doi.org/10.1108/MEQ-04-2021-0074

Mukonza, C., Hinson, R. E., Adeola, O., Adisa, I., Mogaji, E., & Kirgiz, A. C. (2021). *Green Marketing: An Introduction* (pp. 3–14). https://doi.org/10.1007/978-3-030-74065-8_1.

Nekmahmud, M., & Fekete-Farkas, M. (2020). Why not green marketing? Determinates of consumers' intention to green purchase decision in a new developing nation. *Sustainability (switzerland), 12*(19), 1–31. https://doi.org/10.3390/su12197880

Nya, C., Tan, L., Ojo, A. O., & Thurasamy, R. (2019). Determinants of green product buying decision among young consumers in Malaysia. *Young Consumers Insight and Ideas for Responsible Marketers, 20*(2), 121–137. https://doi.org/10.1108/YC-12-2018-0898

Okdinawati, L., Simatupang, T. M., Imran, A., & Lestari, Y. D. (2021). Value co-creation model of halal logistics services. *Jurnal Ilmiah Teknik Industri, 20*(1), 45–60. https://doi.org/10.23917/jiti.v20i1.13028.

Sarkar, A. (2012). *Green marketing and sustainable development-challenges and opportunities*. https://www.researchgate.net/publication/362223391.

Shah, S. A., Azhar, S. M., & Bhutto, N. A. (2020). Halal marketing: A marketing strategy perspective. *Journal of Islamic Marketing, 11*(6), 1641–1655. https://doi.org/10.1108/JIMA-11-2018-0211

Siba Borah, P., & Korankye, B. (2022). An evaluation on the prevalence of green marketing: A business myth or reality. *Future of Business Administration, 1*(2), 15–29. https://doi.org/10.33422/fba.v1i2.332.

Stanciu, A.-C., Constandache, M., & Condrea, E. (2014). Concerns about the sustainable performance of firm in the context of quality management systems implementation. *Procedia—Social and Behavioral Sciences, 131*, 340–344. https://doi.org/10.1016/j.sbspro.2014.04.127

Urbański, M., & Ul Haque, A. (2020). Are you environmentally conscious enough to differentiate between greenwashed and sustainable items? A global consumers perspective. *Sustainability (switzerland), 12*(5), 1–25. https://doi.org/10.3390/su12051786

Velenturf, A. P. M., & Purnell, P. (2021). Principles for a sustainable circular economy. *Sustainable Production and Consumption, 27*, 1437–1457. https://doi.org/10.1016/j.spc.2021.02.018

Witek, L., & Ku, W. (2021). *Green purchase behavior: The effectiveness of sociodemographic variables for explaining green purchases in emerging market* (pp. 1–18).

Wong, C. Y., Wong, C. W. Y., & Boon-itt, S. (2020). Effects of green supply chain integration and green innovation on environmental and cost performance. *International Journal of Production Research, 58*(15), 4589–4609. https://doi.org/10.1080/00207543.2020.1756510

Yusiana, R., Widodo, A., & Hidayat, A. M. (2020). *Green marketing: Perspective of 4P's*.

Zainuddin, M. T. (2021, February). *Utilisation of Islamic marketing mix in resolving rising cost of living: A literature review* (pp. 911–924). https://oarep.usim.edu.my/jspui/handle/123456789/14549, https://oarep.usim.edu.my/jspui/bitstream/123456789/14549/1/29.BI. SAIS2021—Utilisation Of Islamic Marketing Mix In Resolving Rising Cost Of Living_ A Literature Review.pdf.

Halal Entrepreneurship and Its Impact on Sustainable Economy: Opportunities and Challenges

Muazu Hassan Muazu and Effa Ratna Sjahrir

Abstract Halal entrepreneurship is a growing trend in the global economy due to the increasing demand for Halal products and services by Muslim consumers. This chapter examines the impact of Halal entrepreneurship on sustainable economy, by exploring the opportunities and challenges that arise from this emerging sector. The study employs a qualitative research method that analyses the existing literature on halal entrepreneurship, sustainable economic development, and the halal industry. The review focuses on the definition of halal entrepreneurship, the market potential, and the challenges facing entrepreneurs in this field. The chapter highlights the significance of the Halal market and the potential for entrepreneurs to tap into this niche. Additionally, it explores theories of entrepreneurship, global standardization of certificate, political stability and social change as enabling factors for the growth of the sector. The discussion section analyses the opportunities, impact and challenges of Halal entrepreneurship on sustainable economy by examining the economic, social, and environmental benefits of this sector as a transformational driver for the achievement of SDGs 2030. It suggests that Halal entrepreneurship can create sustainable economic development by promoting ethical, socially responsible, and environmentally friendly business practices. The chapter concludes that Halal entrepreneurship can have a positive impact on sustainable economy, but entrepreneurs need to address key challenges to fully realize its potential. The challenges in implementing Halal entrepreneurship are due to regulatory and compliance issues, lack of awareness and education, and inadequate infrastructure. Recommendations were made for policymakers and entrepreneurs to support the development of Halal entrepreneurship and promote sustainable economy.

Keywords Halal entrepreneurship · Sustainability · Regulatory support

JEL classification M13 · M38 · O11 · O31 · P23 · P31

M. H. Muazu (✉)
Department of Business Administration and Entrepreneurship, Dangote Business School, Bayero University Kano, Kano, Nigeria
e-mail: mhmuazu.dbs@buk.edu.ng

E. R. Sjahrir
Exemplar Synergy Consultancy, Kuala Lumpur, Malaysia

L. Raimi et al. (eds.), *Contemporary Discourse of Halal and Islamic Entrepreneurship*,
https://doi.org/10.1007/978-981-99-6427-7_17

1 Introduction

The global halal market is estimated to be worth over $2.3 trillion, with a projected growth rate of 6.3% per year (Ministry of Economy Malaysia, 2021). The demand for halal products and services is driven by the growing Muslim population, increasing consumer awareness of halal requirements, and the desire for ethical and sustainable products. Halal entrepreneurship has the potential to contribute significantly to the sustainable economy by creating job opportunities, promoting ethical business practices, and reducing environmental impacts.

Halal entrepreneurship is an emerging trend that has the potential to contribute to sustainable economy. A sustainable economy refers to economic growth that takes into account social, environmental, and economic factors. The Halal market represents an opportunity for entrepreneurs to create products and services that meet the needs of a rapidly growing global population. This chapter examines the opportunities and challenges of Halal entrepreneurship and its impact on sustainable economy.

The concept of Halal entrepreneurship is gaining popularity worldwide, especially in Muslim-majority countries, due to the growth of the industry. The industry is not only significant for Muslims but also for non-Muslims who seek ethical and sustainable products (Khan et al., 2018). Halal entrepreneurship can promote sustainable economic development by adhering to ethical and socially responsible business practices. The purpose of this chapter is to explore the opportunities and challenges of halal entrepreneurship and its impact on sustainable economic development.

2 Literature Review

The literature on halal entrepreneurship identifies several challenges facing entrepreneurs in this sector, including access to funding, lack of standardization and certification, and limited market information (Farooq & Shah, 2019). Despite these challenges, halal entrepreneurship offers significant opportunities for entrepreneurs to tap into the growing market and contribute to sustainable economy. The market potential for Halal products and services is significant, particularly in emerging markets with large Muslim populations. Furthermore, halal entrepreneurship promotes ethical and socially responsible business practices, which can lead to long-term economic benefits and consumer loyalty.

Earlier Halal entrepreneurship literature highlights the significant potential for entrepreneurs in this market. Research shows that the Halal market is growing rapidly, and there is a need for entrepreneurs to create innovative products and services to meet the demand (Abu Bakar, Hamzah & Mohamad, 2021). However, Naseer and Nor (2019) argued that there are several challenges that entrepreneurs face in this market, such as lack of awareness, limited access to finance, and regulatory barriers. To overcome these challenges, entrepreneurs can adopt strategies such as networking, collaborating with stakeholders, and leveraging technology.

Halal businesses adhere to strict standards of hygiene, quality, and safety, which promote consumer trust and loyalty (Hashim, 2019). Halal entrepreneurship can also provide employment opportunities, promote local industry, and contribute to economic growth.

The literature also highlights the impact of Halal entrepreneurship on the sustainable economy (e.g. Salman & Chelliah, 2021). The study by Salman and Chelliah, (2021) explores the impact of Halal entrepreneurship on various dimensions of sustainability, including economic, social, and environmental aspects. The findings of the review shed light on the positive contributions of Halal entrepreneurship towards building a sustainable economy. Therefore, Halal entrepreneurship has the potential to contribute significantly to sustainable economic development, promoting ethical and sustainable practices, social responsibility, and economic growth. Halal entrepreneurship can also promote the development of small and medium-sized enterprises, job creation, and poverty reduction.

2.1 *Factors that Drive the Growth of Halal Entrepreneurship*

Halal entrepreneurship has the potential to be a transformational driver for sustainable development and achieving the SDGs by promoting economic growth, creating jobs, and reducing poverty (Jalil et al., 2020). The increasing population of ethical consumers segment and the promotion of ethical values can also drive the growth of halal entrepreneurship. The growing demand for Halal products and services, driven by the increasing Muslim population and rising awareness of Halal principles, plays a crucial role in the growth of Halal entrepreneurship (Ali & Abdullah, 2012; Bağdadioğlu & Ay, 2019).

Halal Certification and Compliance: Obtaining Halal certification and ensuring compliance with Halal standards is essential for Halal entrepreneurs to gain consumer trust and access the Halal market (Abdul Rahman & Yusoff, 2015; Sundararajan & Ahmad, 2018).

Networking and Collaboration: Ishaq et al. (2019) are of the view that networking is as important as market demand for Halal entrepreneurship because it provides the opportunity for players in the industry to connect and upgrade knowledge on recent developments in the sector.

Supportive Regulatory Environment: A supportive regulatory environment that promotes and facilitates Halal entrepreneurship can drive its growth. Policies and regulations that address Halal standards, labelling, and marketing can create an enabling ecosystem for Halal entrepreneurs. (Abdullah, 2018; Othman et al., 2017).

Access to Financing: Availability of Sharia-compliant financing options and access to capital are important growth factors for Halal entrepreneurship. Islamic finance institutions and Islamic microfinance initiatives play a vital role in providing financial support to Halal entrepreneurs (Ahmad & Ghazali, 2014; Mehmood & Osman, 2018).

Entrepreneurial Skills and Training: Developing entrepreneurial skills and knowledge specific to the Halal sector can drive the growth of Halal entrepreneurship. Training programs and educational initiatives that focus on Halal entrepreneurship can equip entrepreneurs with the necessary skills for success (Sidique & Omar, 201; Ali, 2017).

2.2 *Theories of Entrepreneurship*

Theories of entrepreneurship can provide insights into the motivations and behaviours of halal entrepreneurs. According to Schumpeter's theory of entrepreneurship, entrepreneurs are the driving force of economic development and create new products and services that disrupt existing markets. Halal entrepreneurs can be seen as disruptors in the Halal industry, creating new products and services that cater to the needs of the Muslim population. According to Kirzner's theory of entrepreneurship, entrepreneurs identify and exploit market opportunities that others have overlooked. Halal entrepreneurs can identify untapped markets in the halal industry and create new businesses that cater to these markets.

Theories of entrepreneurship, such as the opportunity theory, resource-based theory, and social entrepreneurship theory, can be applied to halal entrepreneurship to explain its growth and success. These theories suggest that entrepreneurship is driven by the recognition of opportunities, the availability of resources, and the desire to create social value (Farooq & Shah, 2019). However, the challenge that remained was the lack of global standardization of the halal certificate, which has been a barrier to the growth of the halal industry. It is, therefore, important that efforts should be made to establish a global standard certification process.

Theories of entrepreneurship that are applicable to Halal entrepreneurship include:

1. Opportunity-based theory: This theory suggests that entrepreneurship is driven by the identification of opportunities and the ability to exploit them. In the context of Halal entrepreneurship, this could mean identifying a market gap for halal products and services and creating a business to fulfil that need. It emphasizes the ability to identify and act on opportunities.
2. Social entrepreneurship theory: This theory suggests that entrepreneurship can be a force for social change and impact. In the context of Halal entrepreneurship, this could mean creating a business that not only provides halal products and services but also addresses social issues such as poverty, inequality, and environmental sustainability.
3. Cultural theory: This theory suggests that entrepreneurship is influenced by cultural norms, values, and beliefs (Fayolle & Tornikoski, 2013). In the context of Halal entrepreneurship, this could mean that the principles of Islam and the importance of halal practices shape the way entrepreneurs create and operate their businesses.

4. Resource-based theory: This theory suggests that entrepreneurship is driven by the ability to access and utilize resources effectively. This theory emphasizes the importance of resources in entrepreneurship, and how they interact to influence the performance of entrepreneurial ventures (Maritz et al., 2019). In Halal entrepreneurship, this can be applied by leveraging Halal-certified resources and building a supply chain that caters to the needs of the Halal market. Specifically, in the context of Halal entrepreneurship, this could mean leveraging halal certification and networks to access resources such as capital, suppliers, and customers.
5. Effectuation theory: This theory suggests that entrepreneurship is a process of creating new opportunities rather than just exploiting them. It emphasizes the use of existing resources to create opportunities (Mian & Fayolle, 2016). In the context of Halal entrepreneurship, this could mean creating new halal products and services that do not yet exist and building a market around them. In Halal entrepreneurship, this can be applied by leveraging Islamic values and principles such as honesty, trustworthiness, and social responsibility to create businesses that cater to the Halal market.
6. Social Network Theory: This theory emphasizes the role of social networks in entrepreneurship. In Halal entrepreneurship, this can be applied by building networks within the Muslim community to create businesses that cater to their needs and preferences (Beshir & Hussain, 2019).
7. Islamic Entrepreneurship Theory: This theory emphasizes the importance of Islamic values and principles in entrepreneurship. In Halal entrepreneurship, this can be applied by creating businesses that adhere to the principles of Halal and promote social responsibility and ethical behaviour (El-Gohary, 2017; Ismail, 2018).

Overall, the application of these theories in Halal entrepreneurship can lead to the creation of businesses that not only cater to the needs of the Halal market but also adhere to Islamic values and principles.

2.3 *Global Standardization of the Halal Certificate*

Global standardization of the Halal certificate is another factor that can drive the growth of Halal entrepreneurship. The lack of a global standard for the Halal certificate has been a barrier to the growth of the industry, as it has led to confusion and mistrust among consumers.

Global standardization of halal certificates is essential for the growth and development of the industry. The lack of standardization in Halal certification creates confusion and uncertainty among consumers and businesses. The Organization of Islamic Cooperation (OIC) has developed the OIC/SMIIC Halal Standard, which provides guidelines for Halal certification (Abdullah & Hassan, 2016). However, there is still a need for global standardization of the certification to ensure consistency and transparency in the industry. The International Halal Accreditation Forum

(IHAF) is working towards establishing a global accreditation system that can provide a reliable and transparent certification process (IHAF, 2023).

The global standardization of the Halal certificate is an important issue for the development of the sector. The certificate is a document that certifies that a product or service complies with Islamic dietary laws and other requirements. It is an essential requirement for many Muslim consumers, who rely on these certificates to ensure that the products they buy are Halal.

Currently, there is no global standard for halal certification, and different countries and regions have different standards and requirements. This can create confusion and complexity for businesses and consumers alike, as they navigate different certification processes and criteria.

To address this issue, there have been efforts to develop a global standard for halal certification. In 2010, the Organization of Islamic Cooperation (OIC) established the Halal Standards and Metrology Institute (HSMI) to develop halal standards and promote their implementation worldwide. The HSMI has since developed a number of halal standards, including guidelines for halal certification bodies and guidelines for halal food production (Abdullah & Hassan, 2016).

In addition to the efforts of the HSMI, other organizations have also been working to develop global halal standards. For example, the International Halal Accreditation Forum (IHAF) was established in 2016 to promote the harmonization of halal standards and the recognition of halal certificates globally. IHAF currently has members from more than 30 countries, and its accreditation system aims to ensure the consistency and credibility of halal certification bodies.

The development of a global standard for Halal certification would have several benefits. It would simplify the certification process for businesses and reduce costs associated with complying with different certification requirements. It would also increase consumer confidence in halal products, as they would know that the products have been certified to a consistent and recognized standard.

Furthermore, the development of the Halal sector has significant economic potential, as the global Muslim population continues to grow and demand for halal products and services increases. The global halal market is estimated to be worth trillions of dollars, and the development of a global halal standard could help to unlock this potential and create new business opportunities.

The global standardization of the Halal certificate and the development of the sector are important issues that have the potential to benefit businesses, consumers, and economies around the world.

2.4 *Political Stability*

Political stability is also a crucial factor that can impact the growth of halal entrepreneurship. Political instability can create uncertainty and hinder investment in the halal industry, while political stability can promote economic growth and attract investment (Ministry of Economy Malaysia, 2021). On the other hand, a stable political environment can provide a conducive atmosphere for the growth of Halal entrepreneurship. Stable governments are often more able to provide an enabling business environment, including legal and regulatory frameworks that can facilitate the growth of the Halal industry (Abu Bakar, Hamzah & Mohamad, 2021). This can include, for example, the establishment of Halal certification bodies, favourable tax regimes, and access to finance for Halal businesses.

Moreover, political stability can also positively impact consumer confidence and trust in Halal products and services. Consumers are more likely to trust Halal products that come from countries with stable political environments, which can boost demand and stimulate the growth of Halal entrepreneurship.

2.5 *Social Change and Halal Entrepreneurship Growth*

Social change can play a significant role in the growth of Halal entrepreneurship. Halal entrepreneurship refers to businesses that adhere to Islamic principles and values, particularly in terms of the production and distribution of halal products and services (Hassan, 2017). The growth of Halal entrepreneurship is influenced by various factors, including changes in consumer behaviour, attitudes, and beliefs.

1. One of the key drivers of social change in the context of Halal entrepreneurship is the growing Muslim population around the world. As this population increases, so too does the demand for Halal products and services. In addition, many non-Muslim consumers are also showing an interest in Halal products, as they see them as healthier and more ethical alternatives to conventional products (Jalil et al., 2020). Where social attitudes and behaviours change, there is an increased demand for halal products and services. For example, the growing Muslim population worldwide and their increased purchasing power have led to a higher demand for halal products. The increasing religious awareness and adherence among Muslims is an important factor here, since more Muslims seek to follow Islamic principles in their daily lives, they are more likely to seek out Halal products and services, creating a growing market for Halal entrepreneurs.
2. Social change can also impact the perception of halal products and services. As awareness and education about the halal industry increase, more non-Muslim consumers may be willing to try halal products. This could result in increased market potential and business opportunities for Halal entrepreneurs.
3. Another factor driving social change is the increasing awareness of the environmental and ethical impact of consumer choices. Many consumers are now seeking out products and services that are sustainable, cruelty-free, and ethically sourced. Halal entrepreneurship, with its focus on ethical and sustainable practices, is well-positioned to benefit from this trend.
4. In addition, social change can also affect the regulatory environment for Halal entrepreneurship. Governments and regulatory bodies may need to adapt and change regulations and policies to accommodate the growth of the Halal

industry (Jalil et al., 2020). This can include certification processes, labelling requirements, and other regulations that may impact Halal businesses.

5. The growing emphasis on health and wellness has led to greater demand for natural and organic products, including Halal products. This has created opportunities for Halal entrepreneurs to provide high-quality, healthy products that meet the requirements of Halal certification.
6. The rise of social media and other digital platforms has made it easier for Halal entrepreneurs to connect with customers and build brand awareness. This has helped to create a more supportive ecosystem for Halal entrepreneurship, with customers and investors alike more willing to support these businesses.
7. The increasing globalization and multiculturalism of society. Where people from different cultures and religions interact and become more familiar with each other's practices and beliefs, there is greater acceptance and demand for Halal products and services.

Social change can have a significant impact on the growth of Halal entrepreneurship. As attitudes and behaviours change, Halal entrepreneurs need to be aware of these changes and adapt their business strategies accordingly to take advantage of new opportunities. For example, as more people become aware of the benefits of Halal products and services, entrepreneurs are seizing the opportunity to create new ventures and expand existing ones (Abdullah & Hassan, 2016). With the increasing demand for ethical and sustainable products, Halal entrepreneurship is well-positioned to continue its growth in the years to come.

3 Halal Entrepreneurship Contribution to the Achievement of SDGs 2030

Halal entrepreneurship can contribute to achieving SDGs 2030 in several ways. Firstly, halal entrepreneurship can promote economic development and create job opportunities. According to the State of the Global Islamic Economy Report 2020/21, the global halal economy is worth $2.4 trillion, and halal tourism alone is worth $274 billion. Secondly, Halal entrepreneurship can promote social change by promoting ethical values and healthy lifestyles. Halal entrepreneurs can play a vital role in promoting awareness of halal food and lifestyle choices that align with Islamic principles. Thirdly, halal entrepreneurship can contribute to sustainability by promoting ethical sourcing, responsible production, and environmental conservation.

Halal entrepreneurship can contribute to the achievement of several Sustainable Development Goals (SDGs) by promoting sustainable economic growth, reducing inequalities, and promoting social inclusion. Some of the key ways that Halal entrepreneurship can contribute to the achievement of SDGs 2030 are:

1. Economic Growth: Halal entrepreneurship can drive economic growth by creating new businesses and jobs in the halal sector. This can help to reduce poverty, promote economic inclusion and empower communities. The halal

industry is expected to reach USD 3.2 trillion by 2024, providing ample opportunities for entrepreneurs to create businesses and generate income.

2. Decent Work and Economic Growth: Halal entrepreneurship can also promote decent work and economic growth by creating job opportunities for people from different backgrounds, including those from marginalized communities. Halal entrepreneurship can help to address the challenges of unemployment, underemployment, and poverty.
3. Industry, Innovation and Infrastructure: Halal entrepreneurship can promote innovation and infrastructure development in the halal industry. This can help to improve the quality of halal products and services, enhance supply chain efficiency, and promote sustainable business practices.
4. Reduced Inequalities: Halal entrepreneurship can promote inclusivity and reduce inequalities by providing opportunities for people from diverse backgrounds to participate in the halal economy. This can help to address the challenges of economic exclusion and promote social cohesion.
5. Responsible Consumption and Production: Halal entrepreneurship can promote responsible consumption and production by promoting the use of sustainable and eco-friendly materials and production methods in the halal industry. This can help to reduce environmental degradation, conserve natural resources, and promote sustainable development.

Halal entrepreneurship has the potential to contribute significantly to the achievement of SDGs 2030 by promoting sustainable economic growth, reducing inequalities, and promoting social inclusion. Entrepreneurs in this industry can play a vital role in driving positive social and economic change in their communities and beyond.

4 General Discussion

The discussion highlights the opportunities and challenges of halal entrepreneurship and its impact on sustainable economic development. Halal entrepreneurship has the potential to contribute to a sustainable economy by generating economic, social, and environmental benefits. Economically, halal entrepreneurship can create job opportunities and contribute to economic growth by tapping into the growing halal market. Socially, halal entrepreneurship can promote ethical and socially responsible business practices, which can lead to improved consumer confidence and brand loyalty. Environmentally, halal entrepreneurship can promote sustainable practices, such as reducing waste and conserving resources, which can have positive impacts on the environment and contribute to sustainable development.

The chapter examines the opportunities and challenges of Halal entrepreneurship and its impact on sustainable economy. The Halal market presents significant opportunities for entrepreneurs to create innovative products and services that cater to the growing demand. However, there are several challenges that entrepreneurs face in this market, such as lack of awareness, limited access to finance, inadequate infrastructure, compliance, and regulatory barriers. These challenges can be addressed through networking, collaborating with stakeholders, and leveraging technology. Governments as well, need to provide a supportive regulatory framework, promote education and awareness, and develop adequate infrastructure to promote halal entrepreneurship development.

5 Conclusion

In conclusion, halal entrepreneurship can create sustainable economic development by promoting ethical and socially responsible business practices. Halal entrepreneurship offers significant opportunities for entrepreneurs to tap into the growing halal market and contribute to sustainable economy. It provides significant opportunities for entrepreneurs and investors, especially in Muslim-majority countries. However, halal entrepreneurship faces several challenges, including regulatory and compliance issues, lack of awareness and education, and inadequate infrastructure. These challenges facing entrepreneurs in this sector must be addressed to realize the full potential of halal entrepreneurship. To promote halal entrepreneurship, governments and stakeholders need to work together to develop a supportive regulatory framework, promote education and awareness, and develop adequate infrastructure.

Halal entrepreneurship has the potential to contribute to a sustainable economy, but entrepreneurs need to address key challenges to fully realize its potential. The Halal market represents a significant opportunity for entrepreneurs to create innovative products and services that cater to the growing demand. Therefore, policymakers and entrepreneurs can take steps to support the development of halal entrepreneurship, such as providing access to funding, promoting standardization and certification, and increasing market information. By promoting halal entrepreneurship, we can create a more sustainable and ethical economy that benefits both entrepreneurs and consumers.

Halal entrepreneurship has significant potential as a transformational driver for sustainable development and achieving the SDGs 2030. The increasing population of ethical consumers segment, the promotion of ethical values, and the application of entrepreneurship theories can drive the growth and success of halal entrepreneurship. Theories of entrepreneurship provide insights into the motivations and behaviours of halal entrepreneurs, who can be seen as disruptors and market opportunity exploiters in the Halal industry. The global standardization of halal certificates is crucial for the growth and development of the halal industry, providing consistency and transparency for consumers and businesses. Efforts should be made to establish a global standard for the halal certificate and promote political stability in Muslim countries and the rest of the world to promote investment in the halal industry.

6 Recommendation

Policymakers and entrepreneurs should collaborate to develop a supportive ecosystem for halal entrepreneurship, which includes providing access to funding, promoting standardization and certification, and increasing market information. Policymakers can also provide incentives for halal entrepreneurship, such as tax breaks and regulatory support. Entrepreneurs can take steps to differentiate themselves in the market by promoting their ethical and socially responsible business practices, such as fair labour practices, sustainable sourcing, and responsible waste management. By working together, policymakers and entrepreneurs can promote halal entrepreneurship and contribute to a more sustainable and ethical economy.

To fully realize the potential of Halal entrepreneurship, it is recommended that entrepreneurs focus on developing a strong network of stakeholders and partners, leveraging technology, and adopting innovative financing models. Additionally, policymakers should create an enabling environment that supports Halal entrepreneurship and promotes sustainable economy.

To promote halal entrepreneurship and sustainable economic development, the following recommendations are specifically proposed:

1. Develop a supportive regulatory framework that promotes halal entrepreneurship and ensures compliance with halal standards.
2. Promote education and awareness about halal entrepreneurship and its benefits to the economy and society.
3. Develop adequate infrastructure, including halal certification bodies, halal logistics, and distribution channels.
4. Encourage research and development in the halal industry to promote innovation and sustainability.
5. Foster collaboration between governments, businesses, and stakeholders to promote halal entrepreneurship and sustainable economic development.

References

Abdullah, F., & Hassan, R. (2016). An overview of the global halal industry: Growth, challenges and opportunities.

Abdullah, N. (2018). Islamic marketing: The role of regulation and its impact on entrepreneurial decision-making. *Journal of Islamic Marketing, 9*(4), 891–905.

Abdul Rahman, A. R., & Yusoff, R. Z. (2015). Understanding the halal concept and the importance of halal logistics. *Procedia-Social and Behavioral Sciences, 195*, 1799–1808.

Abu Bakar, I. A., Hamzah, H. A., & Mohamad, M. S. (2021). Halal entrepreneurship: A systematic review and synthesis of research. *Journal of Business Research, 137*, 624–637.

Ahmad, N., & Ghazali, Z. (2014). Access to finance and performance of small and medium enterprises: Evidence from Islamic and conventional finance. *Journal of Small Business and Enterprise Development, 21*(3), 416–434.

Ali, A., & Abdullah, M. F. (2012). Halal food and products: The global industry development. In The Economics of the Islamic Finance and Securitization (pp. 63–82). Palgrave Macmillan, London.
Ali, S. A. (2017). Factors influencing Halal entrepreneurship among students of higher education institutions in Malaysia. *International Journal of Academic Research in Business and Social Sciences, 7*(8), 296–309.
Bağdadioğlu, N., & Ay, N. (2019). Factors affecting the growth of Halal tourism sector. *Journal of International Trade, Logistics, and Law, 5*(2), 60–68.
Beshir, H. M., & Hussain, M. (2019). Social network theory and Halal entrepreneurship: An exploratory study. *Journal of Global Entrepreneurship Research, 9*(1), 8. https://doi.org/10.1186/s40497-019-0140-3
El-Gohary, H. (2017). Islamic entrepreneurship: A review of empirical literature and directions for future research. *Journal of Small Business and Enterprise Development, 24*(3), 471–493.
Farooq, O., & Shah, N. (2019). Halal entrepreneurship: Challenges and opportunities. *Journal of Islamic Business and Management, 9*(2), 13–28.
Fayolle, A., & Tornikoski, E. T. (2013). Discourse and cultural perspectives on entrepreneurship. *Entrepreneurship & Regional Development, 25*(7–8), 611–626.
Mian, S. A., & Fayolle, A. (Eds.). (2016). Effectuation, aspirations, and risk: A research Agenda for entrepreneurship. Edward Elgar Publishing.
Hashim, N. H. (2019). Halal entrepreneurship: Understanding the concept and exploring the literature. *Journal of Islamic Marketing, 10*(3), 739–750.
Hassan, R. (2017). Halal entrepreneurship: From micro to small and medium enterprises (SMEs) in Malaysia. *Journal of Small Business and Enterprise Development, 24*(2), 363–378.
International Halal Accreditation Forum. (n.d.). About IHAF. Retrieved 12 July, 2023, from https://ihaf.org.ae/about-ihaf/.
Ishaq, M. I., Abdul Rasheed, S., & Rafay, A. (2019). Networking, collaboration and the growth of Halal industry: A review and proposed framework. *Global Business Review, 20*(6), 1502–1517.
Ismail, A. G. (2018). Islamic entrepreneurship: A framework for innovation and sustainable development. *Journal of Entrepreneurship and Business Innovation, 5*(1), 33–48.
Jalil, R. A., Razak, D. A., & Che Munaaim, M. A. (2020). Halal entrepreneurship: A review of the literature and research agenda. *Journal of Islamic Marketing, 11*(1), 113–130.
Khan, M. S., Ali, S., & Malik, S. (2018). Halal entrepreneurship: Opportunities, challenges, and prospects. *Journal of Islamic Marketing, 9*(1), 144–162.
Khan, M. S., & Ali, S. (2020). Halal entrepreneurship: A review of literature and future research agenda. *Journal of Small Business Management, 58*(1), 67–84.
Maritz, A., Brown, I., & Hugo, W. (2019). Resource-based theory and entrepreneurial orientation: Towards a comprehensive model. *South African Journal of Business Management, 50*(1), a1738.
Mehmood, R., & Osman, A. (2018). Access to finance and performance of Halal SMEs in Malaysia. *Journal of Islamic Accounting and Business Research, 9*(3), 357–375.
Ministry of Economy Malaysia. (2021). Halal Industry Master Plan 2.0. Retrieved from https://www.miti.gov.my/miti/resources/HIMP_2.0.pdf.
Naseer, S., & Nor, M. M. (2019). Challenges and opportunities for halal food entrepreneurs: A systematic literature review. *British Food Journal, 121*(10), 2405–2421.
Othman, J., Mohd Ghazali, N., & Ali, A. (2017). Halal certification and SMEs performance in Malaysia: Government support as moderator. *Global Business and Management Research, 9*(3), 222–234.
Pew Research Center. (2017). The future of world religions: Population growth projections, 2010–2050. Retrieved from https://www.pewforum.org/2015/04/02/religious-projections-2010-2050/.
Salman, A., & Chelliah, S. (2021). The role of Halal entrepreneurship in promoting sustainable economy: A systematic literature review. *Journal of Islamic Marketing, 12*(2), 644–669.
Sidique, S. F., & Omar, A. (2015). Halal entrepreneurship: Conceptualization and insights. *Journal of Small Business and Enterprise Development, 22*(3), 593–607.

State of the Global Islamic Economy Report 2020/21. (2020). Retrieved from https://halaldevcom.wpengine.com/wp-content/uploads.

Sundararajan, M., & Ahmad, N. H. (2018). Halal assurance systems in the food service sector: A review. *International Journal of Advanced Research in Engineering and Technology, 9*(3), 283–288.

Thomson Reuters. (2018). State of the Global Islamic Economy Report 2018/19.

SPRINGER NATURE

GPSR Compliance

The European Union's (EU) General Product Safety Regulation (GPSR) is a set of rules that requires consumer products to be safe and our obligations to ensure this.

If you have any concerns about our products, you can contact us on ProductSafety@springernature.com

In case Publisher is established outside the EU, the EU authorized representative is:

Springer Nature Customer Service Center GmbH
Europaplatz 3
69115 Heidelberg, Germany

The manufacturer's authorised representative in the EU is Springer Nature Customer Service Centre GmbH, Europaplatz 3, 69115 Heidelberg, Germany. If you have any concerns regarding our products, please contact ProductSafety@springernature.com

Printed and bound by CPI Group (UK) Ltd, Croydon, CR0 4YY
30/09/2026
02225319-0007